OUR FATHERS
WHO AREN'T IN HEAVEN

The Forgotten Christianity of Jesus, the Jew

**Sir Anthony F. Buzzard, Bt.,
MA (Oxon.), MA Th., A.R.C.M.**

Restoration Fellowship
1999 (2nd edition)

Website: www.mindspring.com/~anthonybuzzard
E-mail: anthonybuzzard@mindspring.com

ISBN 0-9673249-1-2

Acknowledgments

My special thanks go to my daughters for their invaluable proofreading, typing and computer skills; to my wife Barbara for her constant support and encouragement; to members of the Church of God (Abrahamic Faith) who have held high the torch of hope for a better world coming on earth; and most of all to the God of Israel, in whom we live and move and have our being.

"It may be said that the teaching of Jesus concerning the Kingdom of God represents His whole teaching. It is the main determinative subject of all of His discourse. His ethics were ethics of the Kingdom; His theology was theology of the Kingdom; His teaching regarding Himself cannot be understood apart from His interpretation of the Kingdom of God.

"And it may not only be said that all His teaching had relation to the Kingdom, but also His action, everything He did from the days of His baptism...all the events of His life until the final culminating event, the crucifixion, had reference to the coming of the Kingdom. From His baptism on, His whole life was dedicated to the mission of announcing the Kingdom's approach and of calling men to prepare for entering it upon the conditions which by divine authority He announced" (F.C. Grant, "The Gospel of the Kingdom," *Biblical World*).

"There is only one real problem in Christianity — the problem of the future" (Wolfhart Pannenberg, *Theology of Hope*).

"Many of the greatest of Jesus' sayings are found lying in a corner like explosive shells from which the charges have been removed. No small portion of elemental religious power needed to be drawn off from His sayings to prevent them from conflicting with our system of religious world-experience. We have made Jesus hold another language with our time from that which He really held" (Albert Schweitzer, *The Quest of the Historical Jesus*).

"John Wesley observed of the idea entertained by many, that the soul at death departs immediately to glory and the presence of Christ, that 'this opinion has no foundation in the Scriptures'" (Daniel Taylor, *The Reign of Christ on Earth*).

"The scepter of the wicked will not remain over the land allotted to the righteous" (Psalm 125:3, NIV).

Table of Contents

Author's Preface

I am sure that my attitude to the Bible was typical of many British public school boys. "R.E." (religious education) was the one subject few of us rated on a par with our "real" academic studies. Few of us can remember the sermon topics of the hundreds of addresses we must have listened to Sunday by Sunday in chapel at boarding school and at home during the holidays in the local village Church of England. (I do, however, remember the visit of an American pastor whose name was Rev. O'Hec. His sermon was to do with Samson and an ice cream machine with a complicated set of cogs and wheels. The point of the sermon I have forgotten.)

The stimulus for this book was my initial shock at reading the Bible seriously for the first time during university days. I found in the pages of the New Testament a Jesus who seemed in so many ways foreign to the Christ presented in church. There was nothing of the ecclesiastical, stained-glass figure about the towering personality portrayed in the Gospels. Impressionable as one is in one's twenties, I was riveted by the question as to how that apparent difference between the Jesus of the Bible and the Jesus of the Church had come to be. As churchgoers, we all said we believed in the Bible, though none of us knew much of what was in it. We certainly never quoted it or discussed it.

Forty-five years later, having had the opportunity to search widely for answers, and having seen religion both from the lay and "professional" angle, I am convinced that there are clear reasons for the contrast between the Jesus of much popular piety and the historical Messiah.

A close study of the fascinating set of documents we call the Bible reveals an extraordinary unity which can be reasonably explained only on the basis of a divine guiding hand responsible for the astonishing drama unfolded in the sacred pages. The "good book," however, will remain closed unless we grasp the fact that Jesus was a Jew whose whole mission must be understood in its original Hebrew context. This, I suggest, means disentangling the Messiah from the layers of matted tradition by which the Church has often made Him respectable, compatible with ourselves, and above all politically innocuous. Building its monumental tradition, the Church has created a largely unmessianic Messiah. Political irrelevance is the one characteristic which can never be true of the Messiah of Israel, who was put on a cross mainly because claiming to be the Messiah was a threat to the Roman government. This is not to overlook the other factor in Jesus' early death: He challenged the Jewish religious establishment which had so tragically misinterpreted its own Scriptures that it was unable to recognize the Messiah when he appeared.

It seems to me that much traditional theology, despite its industry and the refinement of its learning, makes it extraordinarily difficult for the public to have the faith as Jesus taught it. While Jesus obviously treated the Hebrew Bible as a divine revelation from the Creator, many of the Church's scholars view Scripture in an entirely different light. While Jesus claimed to be the Messiah of Israel and announced as his Gospel the Good News about the coming Kingdom of God, theology admits that it has had little interest in the Kingdom for most of the Church's history — or at least not in a sense which Jesus could possibly have attached to His favorite term "Kingdom of God."

It is, in fact, not difficult to document the Church's uncertainty about what Jesus meant by the Kingdom. This is a confession of failure to know what the Gospel is. Yet churches continue to function year after year, unconcerned that the Christianity they offer the public may have dispensed with key elements in the religion of the Jesus of history.

All this seems to me most problematic. There is something of the "fair play" instinct in me, inculcated in school days, which rebels against the notion that Christianity can be the real thing if it does not derive from the teaching of Christ. It is the same question which prompts a Yale scholar to write a book entitled *Jesus and the Future: Unresolved Questions for Understanding the Faith* in which he says "the eschatological Jesus [i.e., one who looks forward to the dramatic, apocalyptic arrival of the Kingdom of God] depicted in the historical tradition is not the Jesus of any modern church or school of theology."[1] The problem surfaces again when a Cambridge professor admits that the Jesus preached from pulpits is not the Jesus of the Bible: "Most preachers talk as if the Christ they preach is identical with the Jesus of history. Theologians know that this is not so…The theories devised in the attempt to connect the modern Christ with the original Jesus have become far-fetched and obscure."[2]

The following chapters represent an attempt to resolve the unsettling problem of the difference between the Jew Jesus and the Jesus of much popular devotion. In a world which seems to thrive on investigative journalism, one might expect the question of integrity in the presentation of Jesus to be a burning issue. I am not convinced that most churchgoers are even aware of any discrepancy. There has been an alarming stifling of the critical faculty.

The Jewish Jesus, bearer of an apocalyptic, Messianic and political Message of Hope about the future of the world, continues to offer Himself as the only answer to our deepest spiritual needs and our desire for immortality. He is likely to make a comeback (even before His promised return in power and glory) when churchgoers commit themselves to a personal study of the Bible, laying their foundation in the Books of Daniel and Matthew, Mark and Luke, which provide a core of Messianic information about the career and teaching of the Christ of history.

I see much more clearly now reasons for the sharp contrast between the Jesus of the Church and the magnetic and disturbing personality who inspired such heroism in His disciples. My failure to delight in the biblical documents was simply that I was reading the Book through spectacles clouded by a conventional perspective of Jesus which tones down His vivid Messianic colors. Only an "all or nothing" acceptance of all His teaching meets the demands He makes on His followers. In subtle ways, however, churches have been hiding that Jewish Jesus.

---

[1] Richard Hiers, *Jesus and the Future*, Atlanta: John Knox Press, 1981, p. ix.
[2] Don Cupitt, *The Debate about Christ*, London: SCM Press, 1979, p. 133.

How different the churches might be if they ceased trying to fit Jesus into a traditional, Greek philosophically-influenced straitjacket and presented Him as the Jewish Messiah and Savior of the world, offering His followers something far beyond promises of "heaven" — as a disembodied soul!

This book represents my own journey of discovery. I have been helped along the way by countless biblical experts, many of whom I have kept in the background, in the interests of not overcrowding the text. In the investigation which follows, I have mingled biblical theology with the history of ideas in order to present a central conviction: The Bible, if read as a Messianic document, tells a thrilling story of the gracious Creator's intention to rescue our planet and restore permanent peace and security for all nations.

Introduction

Would Jesus recognize in our modern churches the faith which He labored to preach and teach nearly two thousand years ago? Would Paul, the commissioned agent of Jesus Christ, be welcome in contemporary congregations?

For the occasional churchgoer (in my own country of origin, Britain, this is especially true) Christianity has become little more than an acquaintance with a crib in Bethlehem and a babe in a manger, a helpless infant whose birth story evokes a seasonal emotional response. For others allegiance to official Christianity is important, though it is seldom informed by serious study of the Bible. For many Jesus' adult ministry remains largely irrelevant to current problems. Nominal Christianity in its various forms can hardly be reckoned as a deep involvement with the one who demanded uncompromising devotion from His disciples and who died for His faith, as well as for the world's failure to know the true God.

Millions across the world claim to be following the Jesus revealed in the Bible. But what sense can we make of a Church represented by hundreds of differing groups, all professing to hold the faith of Jesus and the Apostles? We are confronted with a state of ecclesiastical confusion so perplexing that we might expect a widespread alarm at such obvious departure from the New Testament ideal for the body of Christ. Yet churches seem to conduct their business as usual, with little awareness of the self-contradiction implied by the denominational factions which rend their unity.

A divided Church continues to be the most powerful barrier against effective evangelism — defined in the New Testament as the spreading of the Good News about the Kingdom of God and the name of Jesus (Acts 8:12). A leading New Testament scholar put the point forcefully when he said:

> Disunity is disobedience to the commandment of love, and is the same thing as unbelief (I John 5:1-3). Church unity is not a "desirable feature" in the life of the Church; it is a condition of the Church's existence, a test of whether the Church is the Church. A divided Church is a contradiction of its own nature as Church; it is witnessing to a falsehood. Its evangelism cannot be effective. Jesus prayed "that they all may be one, even as you, Father, are in unity with me and I with you, that they also may be in unity with us: that the world may know that you sent me" (John 17:21; cp. 17:23). If we took the New Testament point of view seriously, we should expect to find that the single most serious obstacle to the evangelization of the world is the disunity of "the churches."[1]

Presumably Christians do want to take the New Testament seriously. The problem posed by the scandal of a permanently divided Church ought indeed to engage their earnest attention. How can the one faith be proclaimed when it obviously is not one faith? Nor can it be argued that the differences between the groups concern the finer points of theological definition only. There are fundamental and long-standing issues at stake, as is proved by the persistent failure of the denominations to settle their differences. It is a pleasant illusion to suppose that all these separated Christian groupings are really one in spirit and truth.

A supermarket issuing a single procedures manual for use in its four hundred branches would be astonished to find that its instructions were being implemented in hundreds of different ways. The problem would suggest either a lack of clarity in the manual or a lack of understanding in those attempting to follow it. A troubleshooter would be dispatched to see where things had gone wrong. A close comparison between the manual and the practices of the employees would reveal how so many divergent procedures had arisen from a single blueprint.

Christians are supplied with an account of the apostolic faith as it was transmitted by eyewitnesses to the ministry of Jesus and His resurrection. A close investigation of the information recorded in

---

[1] Alan Richardson, *An Introduction to the Theology of the New Testament*, London: SCM Press, 1958, p. 287.

these unique documents ought to teach believers where they have gone wrong. Details of the original faith have been carefully compiled for us in the works of Luke, the physician, John, the disciple whom Jesus specially admired, and Paul, the intrepid convert who shook the Roman world with his proclamation of a resurrected Savior destined to rule the world. Can it really be that the best efforts of those intelligent witnesses to convey to us the teaching of their Lord must founder in the chaos of hundreds of versions of the faith?

Paul's assessment of the contemporary religious scene can be measured by his horror at three conflicting parties within the church of Corinth. He made no attempt to conceal his intolerance of the disunity which threatened to destroy Christian witness:

> I entreat you, my brothers, by the name of our Lord Jesus Christ, all to speak the same thing. I desire that there be no divisions among you, that you show perfect harmony of mind and judgment...There is one body and one spirit...one hope...one Lord, one faith, and one baptism, one God and Father of us all (I Cor. 1:10; Eph. 4:4, 5).

His statement brings before us the simple ideal from which the churches have fallen. Has Christianity failed then? Has its original purity been lost? How much of the real, historical Jesus and His Message is known in the churches which bear the name of Christ?

It cannot be denied that from the one "faith once delivered to the saints" (Jude 3) many "faiths" have sprung. We cannot believe that the Christian Scriptures are responsible for a fragmented Church. The problem must lie elsewhere. In order to detect it, we must look closely at the original Christian documents. We must hold up contemporary versions of the faith against the light of apostolic teaching. As we read the Bible, we must strenuously try to rid ourselves of denominational bias and traditional presupposition. We must above all read the documents in their historical setting, "hearing" them as they would have been heard in their own unique and very Jewish context. We must be constantly on guard against tradition unexamined and uncritically accepted as true to the Bible.

We shall contend that subtle influences have worked to blur our vision of the original faith and that in the ensuing confusion the divided churches have lost sight of the central Christian Message, that "glue" which bonds the entire scriptural revelation into a coherent whole and points so certainly to a guiding hand in history. We do not believe the Message to be irretrievably lost; merely buried under a rubble of traditional misconceptions and awaiting rediscovery by those whose desire is to seek and find the Truth. To that task, inviting the reader's critical evaluation, we dedicate the following chapters.

1. The Message in Outline

The Background: Our Human Predicament

The writers of the Old Testament — the Hebrew Bible — were in no doubt that God had spoken. Not only had He brought into being the heavens and the earth by His divine fiat, His incredibly powerful Word, but He continued to speak through certain chosen agents, the prophets. In this way God's people were not left in the dark about the Plan and purpose which the Almighty, who had made everything alone (Isa. 44:24; Job 9:8), was executing for the benefit of His creation. The character of the God of creation was summed up in His divine Name which revealed Him as "compassionate and gracious, slow to anger and abundantly kind and faithful."[1]

The role of the prophet, as God's representative, was to make clear the direction in which men were to go in order to align themselves with the divine program. Their compliance with God's instructions would be in their best interest, for to resist God was in the long run to court disaster. Men might appear to "get away with it" for a time, but ultimate retribution would be swift, sure and terrible. "It is a fearful thing," says the New Testament writer to the Hebrews, "to fall into the hands of the Living God" (Heb. 10:31). The compassion of the One God of Israel was in no way inconsistent with the reality of His displeasure at wrongdoing. The judgment which the evildoer brings upon himself is a constant feature of the biblical Message.

The diagnosis of the human corruption which in all ages was evident on every hand had been declared in the earliest documents of

---

[1] Exod. 34:6; Num. 14:18; Deut. 4:31; Neh. 9:17; Ps. 86:15; 103:8; 108:4; 145:8; Joel 2:13; Rom. 2:4. The latter text appeals to the gracious character of God as a reason for our repentance in order to seek mercy.

the Hebrew religion. A mysterious being, known as "the Serpent" (the definite article suggests that he was a well-known figure, Gen. 3:1) had questioned the truth of the Creator's Word and lured the first woman into disobedience, using a subtle, sophisticated appeal to her desire for wisdom (Gen. 3:1-6). The Serpent's propaganda was worthy of the most modern techniques of manipulation of fact. God's Word was first questioned and then contradicted. Thus tricked into disobedience, though they had been fully instructed in the Creator's will, the first pair were made to understand the gravity of their error by suffering the curse of banishment from the Paradise Garden of Eden (Gen. 3:23, 24). The supreme tragedy was that their potential for immortality, the reason for which God had created them in the first place, was lost (Gen. 3:19). For God will not grant endless life to any who have not proved by their conscientious obedience that they will serve Him alone. Adam and Eve had clearly failed the test. Placed on the earth to exercise dominion over it (Gen. 2:28), the parents of the human race surrendered to the alien authority of the Devil. Man forfeited his right to be king as God's vice-regent on earth. He voted for the lies of the Devil thus making him "god of this age" (II Cor. 4:4).

The situation seemed hopeless but for one redeeming fact. A promise was announced by the Creator that in later generations (just how much later was not revealed at this stage of the Plan) a descendant of the woman Eve would arise to undo the catastrophic work of the Serpent and make possible the recovery of man's potential for endless life (Gen. 3:15). Apart from the appearance of that promised Deliverer, however, man must consider himself subject to inevitable death, the cessation of conscious existence,[2] the just punishment for his disobedience to his Maker.

Against this background there arises in the Hebrew Scriptures (what we rather unfortunately call the Old Testament — "Original Testament" would be a better term) the fundamentally important notion of the Word or Message,[3] a body of inspired information about the divine program for rescuing mankind from the consequences of

---

[2] Ecc. 9:5; Ps. 6:5; 104:29; 146:4; John 11:11, 14.

[3] Cp. Alan Richardson's observation that "the whole biblical theology is a theology of the word: God speaks His word, man must hear and obey" (*An Introduction to the Theology of the New Testament*, p. 29).

his rebellion and subsequent slavery to evil powers. In Adam and Eve the human race had become guilty of the ultimate crime. They had yielded to the instructions of the Serpent, whose clever lie[4] had been more attractive than the Creator's truth. Their conduct showed a careless disregard for the divine will. Failure to discern between truth and lie was a poor recommendation indeed for candidates for immortality. A universe peopled by immortals unable to distinguish right from wrong and truth from error would be unthinkable.

The way out of the impasse in which fallen man now found himself, and the way back to the tree of life, is the subject of the divine Message revealed progressively throughout the sacred writings. It is the single concern of the whole Bible. The Message revealed the solution to the terrible predicament now facing the human race. Like a beacon in a dark world, it held forth the hope of rescue from death, the attainment of immortality, the restoration of Paradise on earth, justice for all, and harmony throughout the universe. This Master Plan provides a source of unshakable optimism for every human person conscious of his or her mortality and the desperate condition of our world. The Plan is God's own story — a drama full of suspense, an epic involving "kingship lost and kingship regained," forever.

Man's Continued Rebellion

The immediate descendants of Adam and Eve proved themselves incapable of avoiding the traps which had been the downfall of their first parents. Having broken loose from the protective relationship offered them by their Creator, they became victims of the evil powers who sought to destroy them. According to Genesis 6 a ghastly disruption of human affairs occurred when evil angelic beings interfered with the human biological chain by uniting sexually with chosen women (Gen. 6:4). The result was the production of a race of terrifying giants (Gen. 6:5) who dominated the earth and became the legendary heroes remembered in Greek mythology.

Displeased with the wanton disobedience of His creatures, God determined to punish the world with a Flood as the divine response to

---

[4] Cp. Jesus' statement that the Devil was "a murderer from the beginning, and does not stand in the truth, because there is no truth in him. Whenever he speaks a lie he speaks from his own nature; for he is a liar, and the father of the lie" (John 8:44).

the rampant evil which prevailed on earth (Gen. 6:7). God was actually sorry that He had created man at all (Gen. 6:6). His children continued to listen to the beguiling voice of Satan, transferring their loyalty from the Creator to a created being. Violence filled the earth (Gen. 6:11-13). The Almighty resolved to wipe out every living thing, mankind and animals alike, sparing a single family, Noah and his wife and their three sons and their wives. A large boat was constructed to house the favored few during the days of the deluge which destroyed on a massive scale. According to the records eight human beings only survived that ravaging judgment (Gen. 7:13, 22, 23; I Pet. 3:20).

The human race continued to fall short of the destiny for which God had granted it existence.[5] The erection of the tower of Babel, designed to reach up to heaven itself, represented mankind's first attempt at one-world government. Its failure to impress the Deity is obvious when the Genesis narrator reminds us that God had to come down from heaven to inspect the feeble project under way at Babylon (Gen. 11:1-9).

A New Start: Abraham, the Father of the Faithful

Millennia had passed since the fatal disobedience of Adam and Eve. Their rejection of the Creator in favor of His enemy the Devil had meant nothing less than the transfer of government into the hands of the Serpent. The story of the recovery of divine supremacy over mankind is the story of the whole Bible. It is a drama still in process, as the human family, still largely in the grip of Satan,[6] fails to recognize what God is doing in history.[7] Insight into the divine purpose now in progress can be gained by a careful examination of God's dealings with Abraham, who was privileged to receive the Christian Gospel in advance (Gal. 3:8).

Ten generations after the Flood, the Lord God laid the basis for a new creation by selecting a single family, residents of Ur of the Chaldees in Babylon. Genesis 12:1-4 records the summons to Abram

---

[5] Nimrod, according to the LXX of Gen. 10:8, 9, was a "giant" and a "giant hunter" before the Lord. His kingdom was the prototype of man's government in rebellion against God.

[6] John 16:11; II Cor. 4:4; I John 5:19; Rev. 12:9.

[7] I Cor. 2:8: If the rulers had understood they would not have killed the Lord of glory (i.e., the Kingdom).

to leave what lay closest to his heart — his native land and his kinsfolk — and to set out for a new land which God would show him. The divine declaration to Abraham contains the ingredients of the Christian Gospel and thus of the entire biblical drama:

> Now the Lord said to Abram, "Go forth from your country, and from your relatives and from your father's house, to the land which I will show you; and I will make you a great nation, and I will bless you, and make your name great. And so you shall be a blessing; and I will bless those who bless you and the one who curses you I will curse. And in you all the families of the earth will be blessed." So Abram went forth as the Lord had spoken to him.

Believing obedience to the divine Word, response to the very same test which Adam and Eve had failed, would result in incredible blessing for Abraham, his descendants and all who modeled their relationship with God on his. In the words of Genesis, "In association with [Abram] all the families of the earth will be blessed" (Gen. 12:3). The promise made to Abram (later called Abraham) provides the bedrock foundation for God's subsequent dealings with mankind. The Christian faith is incomprehensible when divorced from the divine oath of promise which formed the basis of God's covenant or contract with Abraham (Gen. 15:18), justly called "the father of the faithful" (Rom. 4:1, 11, 12, 16). As Paul the Apostle remarked, the Christian Good News (or Gospel) of salvation had been preached in advance to Abraham (Gal. 3:8). God's dealings with Abraham forge a link between the patriarchs and the Christian faith as taught by Jesus, uniting the story of the Bible in a coherent whole.[8]

Divine Communication to Abraham

The great process of recovery and restoration began with the communication of the divine Message to Abraham. His very name nominates him a founding father. Even the opening letters of his name suggest primacy and foundation, like the beginning of the alphabet. "Ab" is the Hebrew for father and Abraham means "father of a multitude" (Gen. 17:4, 5). Abraham demonstrated an exemplary faith in God, an unquestioning obedience, by responding to the divine call

---

[8] Ps. 105:8-15 celebrates the covenant made with the patriarchs and calls them messiahs and prophets (v. 15).

to leave his native country and to journey to a land unknown which God would show him. Twenty-four years later, by a solemn confirmation of the divine covenant, the land of Canaan was promised both *to him* and to his descendants, and in a special sense, to his Descendant, in the singular: "And I will give *to you* and to your seed after you the land of your sojournings, all the land of Canaan, for an everlasting possession" (Gen. 17:8). Paul's comment illuminates the promise: "Now the promises were spoken to Abraham and to his seed. He does not say 'and to seeds,' as referring to many, but rather to one, 'and to your seed,' that is Christ" (Gal. 3:16).

The terms of this covenant with Abraham require close scrutiny, since they form the foundation of the entire biblical story of redemption and have momentous implications for the future of the world. The Abrahamic covenant, which Jesus came to reconfirm (Rom. 15:8), provides an indispensable guide to the meaning of New Testament Christianity, a blueprint for the ongoing Plan of God. It would be no exaggeration to say that failure to grasp the terms of God's arrangements with Abraham is the root of the massive confusion now existing in the minds of churchgoers in regard to the whole purpose of the Christian faith. The solemn words of God to Abraham were repeated on several occasions. The promise runs like a golden thread through the Genesis narrative:

> Now lift up your eyes and look from the place where you are, northward and southward and eastward and westward; for all the land which you see I will give to you and to your descendants forever...Arise, walk about the land through its length and breadth; for I will give it to you (Gen. 13:14-17).

> On that day the Lord made a covenant with Abraham, saying, "To your descendants I have given this land" (Gen. 15:18).

> And I will establish my covenant between Me and you and your descendants after you throughout their generation for an everlasting covenant, to be God to you and to your descendants after you. And I will give to you and to your descendants after you the land of your sojournings, all the land of Canaan, for an everlasting possession; and I will be their God (Gen. 17:7, 8).

A primary lesson in Bible study, perhaps the key to a grasp of Scripture, is to recognize that these divine promises still, to this day, remain unfulfilled. In the past, it is true, they have been partially realized in the history of Israel. As promises of things yet to come, they are the basis of Christian hope and account for the eager expectation of early Christians who faced martyrdom rather than abandon their vision of an endless blissful inheritance based on the promise to Abraham confirmed in Christ.

The early Christians were keen to point out that Abraham had never yet received the promised land:

> God gave him [Abraham] no inheritance in the land, not even a foot of ground, and yet even when he had no child He promised that He would give it to him as a possession and to his offspring after him (Acts 7:5).

> All these [heroes of the faith, including Abraham] died without receiving the promises, but having seen them and having welcomed them from a distance, and having confessed that they were strangers and exiles in the land...And all these, having gained approval through their faith, *did not receive* what was promised (Heb. 11:13, 39).

Jesus was a committed adherent to belief in the destiny of the faithful to gain possession of the land as originally promised to Abraham: "Blessed are the meek for they will receive the land [or earth] as their inheritance" (Matt. 5:5).

The essence of the divine drama being worked out on earth is stated by the writer to the Hebrews, commending Abraham for his faith in the Plan:

> By faith Abraham, when he was called, obeyed by going out to a place which he was to receive for an inheritance and he went out not knowing where he was going. By faith he lived in the land of the promise as in a foreign land, dwelling in tents with Isaac and Jacob, fellow heirs of the same promise (Heb. 11:8, 9).

It is from the extraordinary tension created by the non-fulfillment of this divine promise that the New Testament derives its infectious excitement, as it strains towards the grand dénouement of the divine Plan. Abraham lived in the promised land but never gained possession of it. Therein lies the fascination of the Bible and the challenge of faith. Excitement is maintained as each day brings us a step closer to the reappearance of those heroes of faith (and all subsequent believers) to attain, *by resurrection from the dead*, their prize (Heb. 11:35). As the writer to the Hebrews observed, the patriarchs had "*all died without receiving the promises*" (Heb. 11:13, 39). The New Testament teaches that our hope is their hope and their land ours also. The land belongs to Jesus, and he will share it with his followers who are co-heirs of the land-promise (Gal 3:19; Rom. 8:17; II Tim. 2:12).

The important references in Genesis to Abraham's offspring, his "seed" (Gen. 13:15; 15:18; 17:8), recall the "seed" promised to Eve (Gen. 3:15). In Him the disaster caused by the Serpent would be reversed. As we have seen, Paul recognized that the great Descendant was none other than the Messiah Himself ("to your seed, that is Christ," Gal. 3:16), the long-awaited deliverer of Israel and of the whole world (John 1:49; 4:42). To Jesus was assigned the task of undoing the chaos wrought by Satan. Through Jesus man's divine status as God's representative on earth would be restored. By Him the evil powers would be defeated forever (Col. 2:15). John the Apostle described the Messiah's role succinctly: "The Son of God appeared for this reason: to undo the works of the Devil" (I John 3:8). Jesus defined how that work would be accomplished when He stated the purpose for His mission: "I must proclaim the Gospel about the Kingdom to the other cities also. *That is the reason for which I was commissioned*" (Luke 4:43). This remains the purpose of the Church until the return of Christ to take over the reins of world government (Matt. 24:14).

The Message which came to Abraham contains all the essential elements of the divine Plan and therefore of the whole Bible. The promises made to the "father of the faithful" provide the indispensable basis for a right understanding of apostolic Christianity. They are at the root of all that Jesus taught. Instilled in the thinking of Jesus, from His profound meditation on the Hebrew Bible, was the following conception of God's purpose for the world: A Descendant promised to Eve, later designated the Messiah or Anointed King (Christ), will arise from the family of Abraham, and He will gain possession of the land of Palestine and the world forever. Abraham, as the prototypical believer, will also enjoy this promised inheritance, though during his lifetime he had inherited nothing. The permanence of the divine blessing destined for Abraham at once raises the question of immortality. For what is the point of an endless inheritance for

Abraham unless his life can be prolonged indefinitely to enjoy it? Abraham died and slept with his fathers. An everlasting inheritance can make sense, therefore, only if Abraham can be brought to life again. We confront here the absolute necessity for the *resurrection of the dead* in the divine scheme.

Generations pass and the descendants of Abraham, Isaac and Jacob grow into the nation of Israel (Exod. 1:1-7). Emerging from their terrible slavery in Egypt (Exod. 14; 15), the people wander in the wilderness, guided by Moses (Exod. 16-40), and enter the promised land under Joshua (Josh. 1-24). Can this be the fulfillment at last of the promise to Abraham? Clearly not in its ultimate form, for Abraham, to whom the gift of the land was granted, has long since been buried and the promised Descendant, the great Deliverer, has not yet appeared. The Message persists throughout the centuries as the guiding light of the nation of Israel. Far from becoming obscure as time goes on, it gains remarkable clarity in the life of the beloved king of Israel, David, son of Jesse. As God worked in the career of this celebrated Psalmist, prophet and monarch the Message received a new impetus, projecting the hopes of the faithful towards the birth of Messiah Jesus and far beyond to the promised Kingdom of peace.

David, a "Sketch" of the Future Messiah

The unimportant eighth son of a sheep farmer, a mere shepherd boy with beautiful eyes (I Sam. 16:12), David becomes (next to Abraham and Moses) the most significant figure in the history of Israel and the development of the divine Plan. Despite obvious lapses he is distinguished by his wholehearted devotion to God, and he is equipped for his high office by the gift of the divine Spirit which marks him out as God's anointed king (i.e., a messiah) (I Sam. 16:1-3, 12, 13). He is truly a man after God's own heart and Spirit, sensitive to the unfolding divine Plan (I Sam. 13:14; 16:7; Acts 13:22). Through Nathan the prophet the ancient Message is confirmed to David. Once again there is the promise of the notable Descendant, who will one day establish forever the Kingdom granted to David as his promised inheritance (II Sam. 7:12-17). The link with the earlier oath-bound promise to Abraham is obvious. The grant of land automatically requires a government to go with it. A perpetual dynasty and kingdom is covenanted to David. In this *Message about the*

Kingdom, the seed of the Gospel of the Kingdom as Jesus later preached it (Matt. 13:19), David sees "a set of instructions, an oracle by which the destiny of mankind will be directed."[9] The Message has become universal in its scope. The future of all of humanity is bound up with the promise of the Greater Son of David, *the* Messiah, whose Kingdom, the land of promise, will provide the ultimate solution to all the world's ills, as well as the final answer to the "Jewish problem." Built upon the earlier land contract with Abraham, the Davidic promises contained the following assurances: "I will also appoint a place for My people Israel and will plant them, that they may live in their own place and not be disturbed again, nor will the wicked afflict them any more as formerly" (II Sam. 7:10).

On these mighty themes of permanent security, monarchy and territory, the whole structure of the biblical story rests. The Message, it should be carefully noted, is never merely "religious." It is both national and universal — and related to the future of the earth.

Exile and Return to the Land

The division of the kingdom of David into the northern Israel and the southern Judah occurred soon after the death of Solomon, David's illustrious but very fallible successor. With some notable exceptions in the house of Judah, the descendants of David who ruled in Israel and Judah failed to exemplify the high ideals of David. Progressive evil made divine judgment inevitable. Israel in the north succumbed to the invasions of the Assyrian empire and was deported in the late eighth century BC (II Kings 17). The ten tribes were lost to history. The southern kingdom of Judah survived until the end of the sixth century. The wickedness of the Jewish kings attracted a divine visitation in the person of the Babylonian king Nebuchadnezzar who removed Zedekiah, king of Israel, and many of the Jews to Babylon (II Kings 24; 25). The throne of Israel ceased to exist. The Persian king Cyrus granted the Jews a return to the land under Ezra and Nehemiah (II Chron. 36:20-23; Ezra; Nehemiah), but the promised Kingdom of God on earth did not appear. The Messiah, the Deliverer, had not yet been born. During much of the four hundred "silent years" between the end of the Old Testament canon and the birth of Jesus the people

---

[9] W.J. Dumbrell, "The Davidic Covenant," *The Reformed Theological Review* (39), May-Aug. 1980.

struggled under the domination of the Greek Seleucid kingdom. Despite all their disappointments, the faithful never abandoned hope in God's covenants with Abraham and David, guaranteeing a final restoration and liberation under the reign of the promised Prince Messiah.

The Birth of the Deliverer

Words are inadequate to describe the feelings of the two women selected to bear the children in whom the age-old promises would come to fruition. Luke's account of the birth of John the Baptist, forerunner to the Messiah, and of his far greater and unique successor Jesus, is alive with the thrill of Messianic expectation. Since the dawn of history the faithful had awaited the coming of the one who was to be empowered to reverse the tragedy which had befallen Adam and Eve and the human race as a whole. This was the King Messiah, God's legal agent, imbued with the divine Spirit, who would triumph over the spiritual powers of darkness that had enslaved mankind's first parents and their descendants ever since. The Serpent's devastating work was apparent everywhere in suffering humanity,[10] but the Spirit of God in Jesus was stronger by far. The New Testament accounts of His ministry describe a dramatic conquest of evil by means of the extraordinary divine Spirit with which He was gifted. Using Jesus as His human agent, the Second Adam, God was beginning to reassert His authority and recover rebel province earth from the clutches of the Devil. In the words of the beloved Apostle, Jesus was commissioned to "unravel the work of the Devil" (I John 3:8). Peter captured the essence of the work of Jesus the Messiah with these words: "You know of Jesus of Nazareth, how God anointed Him with the Holy Spirit and with power, and how He went about doing good, and healing all who were oppressed by the Devil, for God was with Him" (Acts 10:38).

The ministry of Jesus, as we shall see, consisted of the proclamation of the Good News of the approach of the Kingdom of God, that turning point in the history of the world longed for by every

---

[10] A leading nutritionist states that America is "epidemically sick" (Ruth Swope, *Green Leaves of Barley*, National Preventive Health Services, 1987, p. 13). The strong parallel between physical and spiritual health (as well as between the practice of medicine and theology) suggests that we may also be spiritually diseased.

pious Israelite. The Gospel Message of Jesus renewed hope for the fulfillment of all that the prophets, as exponents of the Abrahamic and Davidic covenants, had foreseen. The substance of Jesus' preaching was both promise and warning: The Kingdom of God is coming; turn in repentance to God. Believe the Gospel Message. Prepare for the great day of destiny. Prepare for the great sifting of mankind into the two categories of good and evil, believers and unbelievers, wheat and chaff (Matt. 3:12). The Message announced by Jesus is to be the Church's Message until the arrival of the Kingdom for which we pray (Matt. 24:14; 28:19, 20).

Despite the majesty of His career in Palestine, a handful of people only responded to Jesus' Message. His rejection is described by John in these memorable words: "He came to His own land but His people did not receive Him" (John 1:11).[11] It was the exponents of traditional religion, blinded by their manmade theology yet claiming allegiance to the same sacred writings as He (Matt. 23:13ff; 15:7-9; 22:29), who joined the Roman authorities in consigning Him to the ignominious death of a criminal on the cross. And there, but for the supreme miracle of the resurrection, the story would have ended. Yet, in reality, it had just begun. The return of Jesus to life by resurrection (Acts 1:3; 10:41) marked a crucial stage in the grand scheme for the rescue of mankind. It was the initiation of a new creation of immortal human beings, the restoration of the ideal which God had envisaged from the beginning. Mankind makes another new start in Jesus. With the resurrection of the one man, Jesus, to endless life, the prospect of the same destiny is open to all who follow in Jesus' steps.

The failure of the divided Church is that it has ceased to bear the Message of deliverance onwards to its great climax. Uncertain about where it is going, it cannot speak to the world with conviction. Something has happened to cast a smoke screen across the path which leads to the goal. A fragmented Church is symptomatic of that devastating loss of vision. Fortunately we do not need to remain in doubt or darkness. The early Christians have bequeathed to us a fair warning about where the danger of blindness lies. The difficulty is

---

[11] Cp. the comment of E.C. Hoskyns (*The Fourth Gospel*, London: Faber and Faber, 1947, p. 146): "He came to his own property or home." The land of Palestine belonged to the Messiah as His inheritance. His rejection at His first coming does not cancel God's Plan to give Him the land at His Second Coming.

that twentieth-century man, in his wisdom, has scorned those warnings and does his utmost to explain them away as superstition. The amazing advances of "science," which is really only the discovery of how God's universe works, have lured many into the delusion that we should believe only in what can be measured in a test tube or seen with the physical eye. This philosophy immediately casts a shadow over the truth of the divine Plan in the Bible. Once again the Serpent reappears to question the Word of God (II Cor. 11:3, 4). The Devil's propaganda insists that the Bible's miracles do not fit with the modern scientific world view. The resurrection of Jesus was not observed by science. Thus the hand of God in history is rejected, and His purpose to grant immortality to those who recognize Him as the active architect of a Plan to rescue us from our growing plight, including our universal slavery to death, is treated with disdain. This is the great human tragedy. Despite our show of religion, many largely close their eyes to God's purpose for the earth. Many churchgoers would be hard pressed to give an account of the Abrahamic and Davidic covenants and their vital importance for the Christian Gospel. Most are perplexed when asked to the define the Kingdom of God in the teaching of Jesus. The observation of the well-known translator, J.B. Phillips, points to a disturbing ignorance of the Christian faith in the sophisticated western world. He has been shocked by the hundreds of conversations he has had with men of the highest intellectual caliber

> who quite obviously had no idea of what Christianity was about. I was in no way trying to catch them out; I was simply and gently trying to find out what they knew about the New Testament. My conclusion was that they knew virtually nothing. This I find pathetic and somewhat horrifying. It means that the most important event in history is politely and quietly bypassed. For it is not as though the evidence has been examined and found unconvincing; it has simply never been examined.[12]

> It is one of the curious phenomena of modern times that it is considered perfectly respectable to be abysmally ignorant of the Christian faith. Men and women who would be deeply ashamed of having their ignorance exposed in matters of poetry, music, ballet or painting, for example are not in the least perturbed to be found

---

[12] *The Ring of Truth*, Hodder and Stoughton, 1967, p. 11.

ignorant of the New Testament…Very rarely does a man or woman give honest intelligent adult attention to the writings of the New Testament and then decide that Jesus was merely a misguided man…The plain fact is not that men have given the New Testament their serious attention and found it spurious, but that they have never given it their serious attention at all.[13]

It is the function of the united Church to be custodian of the divine information which alone gives meaning to the universe in which man finds himself. To her has been committed the Message, the Master Plan, by which the destinies of the human race are to be directed. The voice of God is heard in her proclamation. These are no empty theological platitudes. They represent the heart of the biblical heritage on which the Church must be founded, if indeed she is to be the Church. The presence of many conflicting churches points only to the urgency of the need to restate the Message clearly, to regroup the fragmented Church around it, and offer it for the comfort and hope of the whole world.

---

[13] *The Young Church in Action,* London: Geoffrey Bles, 1955, pp. ix, x.

2. Unmasking the Villain

A large proportion of those who claim to be followers of the Christian revelation have long since ceased to take seriously the reality of one of the principal figures in the biblical record. His name is Satan, the Adversary. The New Testament and the earliest post-apostolic writings identify him with the Serpent who disrupted the tranquillity of the Garden of Eden.[1] His Hebrew name is linked in the Hebrew Bible (what we call the Old Testament) with the word seraph,[2] suggesting his connection with the world of angelic beings in whose company he is found in the book of Job (Job 1:6; 2:1). The New Testament Christians are very much aware of him. He is permitted to exercise an extensive influence over the affairs of mankind (I John 5:19; Rev. 12:9) and is entitled to be called the "god of the present age" (II Cor. 4:4), that is, the whole period of human history until the return of Christ to inaugurate the new age of the Kingdom of God on earth.[3]

Satan is also the original liar (John 8:44). He is the arch-deceiver (II Cor. 11:3, 4, 13-15). Bent on the destruction of as many of the human race as possible, his work is aimed at obstructing and obscuring the truth of the divine Message which illuminates the path

---

[1] II Cor. 11:3, 14 where the Serpent is parallel with the Devil. Rev. 12:9 and 20:2 identify them.

[2] In Num. 21:6, 8 *nachash* (serpent, Gen. 3:1) and *saraph* (fiery serpent) are closely connected. *Seraphim* (the plural) appear as heavenly beings in Isa. 6:2, 6.

[3] Paul refers to the whole period of human history leading up to the future establishment of the Kingdom as the "present evil age" (Gal. 1:4).

to immortality.[4] His methods are subtle and treacherous. They would be the envy of any contemporary con-artist. As the enemy of God and mankind Satan would prefer to remain hidden. His work is more easily accomplished when men are convinced that he does not exist!

It was the common belief of the New Testament Church, including Jesus, that Satan is a fallen angel. Paul describes him as wearing the mask of an angel of light, implying that he is in fact an angel of darkness in camouflage (II Cor. 11:14). He has the power to fascinate, as he masquerades as a messenger of light. His human agents, Paul revealed, conceal their real identity behind a facade of goodness (II Cor. 11:13, 15). Evidently the Satanic administration is a redoubtable enemy worthy of close scrutiny by Christians desiring to avoid falling for its trickery. John, the Apostle, states that Satan has the entire world in the grip of his deception (I John 5:19; Rev. 12:9). His program of relentless anti-biblical propaganda aims at getting men to believe his lies. His method is the presentation of half-truth, the cleverest form of falsehood. Paul sees him as extremely active, an ever-present threat to the Christians whom the Apostle counsels not to be unaware of his devices (II Cor. 2:11). Paul makes no bones about labeling preachers of fake Christianity as the Devil's servants (II Cor. 11:13, 15). The only antidote to being duped is a thorough knowledge of and passion for Truth (II Thess. 2:10-13).

The New Testament makes it more than clear that Satan operates extensively in the field of religion. The Scribes and Pharisees, the representatives of the religious establishment in Jesus' day, were seen by Jesus as Satan's principal exponents (Matt. 23:33).[5] They had become servants of the Devil, and Jesus was uncompromising in His condemnation of them. They were the target of His righteous indignation because their religious traditions were in conflict with the

---

[4] In I Thess. 2:18 Paul's missionary activity is obstructed by the Devil. When the Gospel about the Kingdom is preached the Devil is on hand to swallow up the Message before it can take root in the human mind (Matt. 13:19; Luke 8:12). His purpose is to destroy the people of the Kingdom. Hence Herod's attempt to eliminate the Messiah (Matt. 2:3-18) and the Devil's threat to the Messianic community headed by Jesus (Rev. 12:4, 13-18). Peter speaks of Satan as "your opponent prowling about like a roaring lion seeking someone to devour" (I Pet. 5:8).

[5] He threatened them with destruction in Gehenna, a fate prepared for the Devil himself and his angelic cohorts (Matt. 25:41).

divine Message and effectively kept the people in darkness. Though these spurious leaders of religion were zealous to make even a single convert, they turned their disciples into "children destined for hellfire" (Matt. 23:15).

It is naive to think that established religion could be the enemy of the truth only in first-century Palestine. Both Jesus and the Apostles saw degenerate religion as a permanent, if not increasingly prevalent, feature of man's failure to know God (Matt. 24:4, 5, 24; I Tim. 4:1-3; II Tim. 3:13). In searching for the causes of the divisions which beset our contemporary churches, we must take full account of the way in which tradition, uncritically handed down from one generation to another, can make unbiased reading of the New Testament documents almost impossible. A leading spokesman for evangelicals in England alerts us to this danger:

> People who adhere to "Sola Scriptura" ["we follow the Bible only"] (as they believe) often adhere in fact to a traditional school of interpretation of "Sola Scriptura." Evangelical Protestants can be as much slaves of tradition as Roman Catholics or Greek Orthodox Christians; only they don't realize it is tradition.[6]

It is rare indeed to find anyone who is willing to examine his beliefs in the light of the blueprint which he professes to follow. It is hard to believe that churchgoers actually study the Bible to check up on what their church is teaching them.[7] Most simply assume that their creed is based on what Jesus and the Apostles taught.

One of the most baffling examples of tradition versus the Christian documents is found amongst a small group of believers known as the Christadelphians. Their founder[8] had come near to death in a disaster at sea and had vowed that if ever he reached land safely, he would thoroughly investigate the Christian religion. He then set himself the noble task of scrutinizing the Bible in an effort to recover the original teachings of Jesus. He became convinced that much of what went by the name of Christianity was based on traditions which

---

[6] F.F. Bruce, in correspondence, June 13, 1981.

[7] The classic example of the benefits of personal, firsthand investigation of the Scriptures is recorded in Acts 17:11. The Bereans studied the Bible daily to see if what Paul was saying was true. The result was that many became believers.

[8] John Thomas (1805-1871).

had begun to infiltrate the Church some 100 years after the death of Jesus. In his zeal to oppose popular error, which pictured Satan as a horned monster stoking the fires of hell, he maintained that the term Satan in the Scriptures denoted nothing more than the evil inherent in human nature.[9] While it is true that many churchgoers may think of Satan in impersonal terms, unlike the early Christians, it is astonishing to find that the Christadelphians, with their passionate devotion to a plain reading of the Bible, can continue to see in the encounter between the Adversary and Jesus in the wilderness an account of Jesus having a conversation with Himself, indeed with His own evil human nature! (Matt. 4:1-11; Mark 1:12, 13; Luke 4:1-13).

It is one of the clearest teachings of the Bible that Satan is a personality external to man. The term "Satan" is never in the Hebrew Bible a word describing the internal evil of the human heart. "Satan," in the Bible on which Jesus was reared, always meant an enemy, human or superhuman, *external* to man.[10] It is therefore a serious mistake to assign the meaning "human nature" to the word "Satan" when it appears in the New Testament. A great deal of space is taken up by the New Testament writers to show that there is a world of unseen evil spirits as real as the holy angels (Eph. 6:10-17). The conquest of these evil powers by Jesus was proof to the disciples that the cosmic forces lying behind the visible evil on earth were being defeated (Luke 10:17-20). It was the superior energy of the Spirit of God invested in Jesus which enabled Him to accomplish the extraordinary miracles of exorcism and healing reported in all four accounts of His ministry (Acts 10:38). To deny the reality of Satan and the demons when the Christian writers labor to demonstrate their existence is proof indeed of the viselike grip which tradition can exercise upon the mind even of those whose devotion to the service of their faith is amply demonstrated by their exemplary lives. The denial of the world of supernatural evil is part and parcel of the "scientific" rationalism which has overtaken even some believers in divine revelation.

---

[9] His arguments may be examined in *Elpis Israel,* pp. 88-91.

[10] See I Kings 11:14; I Sam. 29:4; Job 1:6; 2:1; Zech. 3:1, where "Satan" is an external opponent. For a discussion of the personality of the Devil, see the author's "Satan, the Personal Devil," Restoration Fellowship, 1981.

Satan scored a notable victory when he succeeded in relegating belief in his existence to a former "non-scientific" age — not least because Jesus and the Apostles were made to appear far less intelligent than sophisticated modern man. When Luke penned (what we call) the fourth chapter of his treatise on Christianity he described an encounter between the Devil and Jesus. The account is placed squarely in history. The scene was the wilderness of Judea and the episode lasted for a period of some six weeks. When Satan had completed his attempts to seduce the Messiah from His loyalty to God, he left Him (Luke 4:13) whereupon angels arrived to minister to Him (Matt. 4:11) — not a moment too early, since Jesus had eaten nothing for forty days. Satan's approach to Jesus — he came up to Him and spoke (Matt. 4:3) — was no less a solid fact of history than the approach of the disciples or the Pharisees (Matt. 24:1; 19:3). We misread the accounts badly if we think otherwise. We also overlook the remarkable parallel between the temptation records in Genesis and the Gospels. In the former, the external tempter, the "Serpent," approaches the first woman (Gen. 3:1). In the latter, the external adversary, Satan, makes his appearance to tempt the head of the new human race. In Genesis the account concludes with the arrival of angels to guard the way to the Tree of Life (Gen. 3:24). In the Gospels also, angels approach to minister to the triumphant Second Adam, the Messiah Jesus (Matt. 4:11), who is Himself the way to Life (John 14:6). Mark also lets us know that Jesus was with the wild beasts,[11] a token of the fact that even nature will one day return to the harmony of Paradise when the Messiah comes back to rule in His Kingdom (Hos. 2:18; Isa. 11:6-9).

In the Bible the reality of a person is not judged by his being visible. A fashionable school of contemporary theology would have us believe that the supernatural dimension in the New Testament should be "reinterpreted" (in fact erased from the record) so that Christianity may be made palatable to twentieth-century secular man. This daring theory would, however, leave secular man as secular as ever. It would do nothing to involve him in the real world of the Spirit, where alone the solution to all his ills can be found.

---

[11] Mark 1:13. As Son of Man, "the true human being," Jesus was the one who would overcome the "beasts" of Daniel 7, thus fulfilling the role intended for man as Adam, who was to dominate nature (Gen. 1:26).

Thanks to the careful work of the biblical writers we are not left in the dark as to Satan's methods. He clearly understands human nature. He also knows his Bible. He is not above quoting it if it serves his purpose, and he is skilled at altering words here and there for effect (Matt. 4:6). As the Serpent in Genesis he was persuasive enough to lure Eve into fatal disobedience in two short statements, amounting to just twenty-six words (Gen. 3:1, 4, 5). His technique included questioning what God had said, misquotation, an assertion which was true, followed by a flat contradiction. The performance created a sufficient confusion to prevent Eve from thinking clearly (Gen. 3:6). Satan has long proved himself master of the half-truth. Ignorance of the Bible allows his work easy progress (cp. Hos. 4:6).

The history of mankind, and especially of religion, bears the marks of Satan's unceasing interference — never, however, outside the limits prescribed for him by the One who created all things for a very good purpose. Next to the persons of God, the Father, and His Son Jesus, the Messiah, Satan is the most significant figure in the spiritual drama described by the New Testament. He is treated as a constant threat, especially to the progress of the Good News or Gospel — the divine Message which contains the secret of immortality (Matt. 13:19; Luke 8:12; I Thess. 2:18). His design is to prevent the Christian from achieving his goal, which is to attain to the gift of life forever (Rom. 2:7). The reality of Satan should, however, be no source of terror to the properly instructed believer. The latter is more than conqueror through the infinitely superior power of the God who sustains him, provided, that is, he diligently seeks the truth as opposed to Satan's lies, checking and rechecking what he has learned against the divine standard of truth contained in Scripture. The activity of Satan is centered on a campaign to frustrate the progress of Christians, principally by confusing the divine instructions revealing the way to endless life (I Thess. 2:18; II Cor. 11:3, 4, 13-15).

Satan has been quick to see that the Bible contains divinely revealed information by which the Christian venture may be undertaken with success. It is his intention to make those "secrets" unintelligible. A variety of avenues are open to him in this respect. One is to cast doubt upon the reliability of the documents which record the divinely authorized original faith. A large segment of the Christian world is no longer at all certain that it is possible to recover what Jesus actually taught. An army of scholars have busied themselves with debating whether the words attributed to Jesus in the Bible actually originated with Him.[12] If we do not have access to the words of Jesus, however, we have no basis for calling ourselves Christians. One of the marvels of the contemporary Church is its capacity to maintain the name of Christ while feeling free to teach almost anything thought to be suitable as religion for modern man.[13] The "Christ" of faith often has only a tenuous link with the Jesus of history. Jesus may be imagined by the fertile religious mind of man in a bewildering variety of ways which have little or nothing to do with Jesus as a historical figure.

Another Satanic ploy is to accuse the original writers of being deluded about the actual facts of the life of Jesus. Their belief in the resurrection, he maintains, is explicable as wishful thinking, or perhaps hallucination. The effectiveness of these techniques is borne out by the widespread doubts among churchgoers, stemming from the doubts held by preachers and university theologians, about the resurrection of Jesus as a historical fact. By New Testament standards such disciples are relegated to the ranks of unbelievers. Their position is sad indeed, since no one is likely to hold out much hope for his own resurrection if he doesn't believe in Christ's! A "Christianity" without belief in the resurrection as a solid historical fact, both Jesus' resurrection in the past and the believer's in the future, is not the same faith as the faith of the Bible. Paul put it succinctly: "If Christ has not been raised from death, we have nothing to preach and you have nothing to believe" (I Cor. 15:14, GNB).

Not all, however, can be easily shaken from their faith in the Christian documents. For those who maintain a firm belief in the reliability of the Scriptures, a more subtle form of deception is required. They must be led to think that they have grasped what Jesus taught, while they are presented with a distorted or reduced version of His Message. Over a long period of time this will effectively induce a

---

[12] In recent years the Jesus Seminar has astonished the public with its arbitrary decisions about which of the words attributed to Jesus really go back to Jesus Himself. They conclude that Jesus said only about 20% of what is attributed to Him.

[13] The approval of sexual practices condemned by the Bible provides a striking example.

false sense of security from which they will be very unwilling to be shaken.

The point must be emphasized. Unexamined tradition is Satan's great weapon. He knows that if men are brought up to accept a particular creed, a statement of faith assumed to be based upon the original teachings of the Apostles or having the support of the "great names" of church history, very few will ever trouble to verify its truth against the New Testament standard. They will leave it to their leaders to do this for them, and they will not be much perturbed by the fact that leaders of conflicting groups, also claiming to be Christian and reading the same Bible, have come to quite different conclusions about the faith. In this way they will insulate themselves against the uncomfortable realities of a divided Christendom. Through tradition, tenaciously held, divided Christianity may be perpetuated *ad infinitum.*

Christianity without a well-developed sense of the reality of Satan and the Christian's daily spiritual conflict with him, has lost touch with its founding fathers, and has also lost the battle against the Devil. It will inevitably adopt an uncritical attitude to what is taught as the truth, resting in the belief that all versions of Christianity are valid in their way, since all are honestly held by sincere believers. The next step will be to adopt the conviction that all the world religions lead to salvation, since all promote the worship of the same God. It will not have occurred to those holding a "generous" view of the divided churches to ask whether the Devil has not been extremely active in preaching a version or versions of "Christianity" which hide some of the essential elements of the divine Plan for rescue.

In calling for a return to the Christian blueprint, the apostolic faith once and for all delivered to the saints (Jude 3), we must insist that Christians follow Jesus by recovering a belief in the reality of Satan and the demons and their continuous campaign of deception. They must reckon with them as the forces orchestrating the theological chaos represented by so many Christian groupings. In so doing believers will be enabled to enter the world of the early Church, rather than the world as presented to us by scientific humanism. It is the failure to understand the real enemy which alienates much of Christianity from Paul's classic statements that as Christians we are not wrestling against "flesh and blood" but against the unseen "world rulers, the spirits of evil in heavenly places" (Eph. 6:12), led by "the Prince of the power of the air" (Eph. 2:2), "the god of the present era" (II Cor. 4:4). It would be helpful if Paul's terminology were reinstated amongst believers. Paul sees the Christian struggle as warfare against the "cosmocrats" (Eph. 6:12),[14] astral deities with enormous power. For Paul there is a major spiritual super-criminal at large working tirelessly to destroy human beings by whatever means he can, deception being his primary tool (Rev. 12:9).[15]

The identification of the biblical enemy does not exempt us from responsibility for our own errors. We are responsible for resisting the Devil (James 4:7). Divine revelation is provided for our constant study (Ps. 1:1-2; 119; Josh. 2:8), a source, as Paul said, of the "wisdom that leads to salvation" (II Tim. 3:15), which is victory over Satan through Jesus. The antidote to deception in any field is proper instruction. If the Church does not "go to school" with Christ and the Apostles (Acts 2:42), it has lost the battle against the "disinformation" of the Devil. The tools for overcoming the power of Satan are at hand, if we will only reach out and grasp them, immersing ourselves in the words of Jesus and the Apostles summarized as the Gospel of the Kingdom of God.

The Good News is that the King Messiah has already defeated Satan, even though the effects of His victory are not yet fully apparent (John 16:11; Col. 3:15). The Bible does not hold out hope for a complete reversal of the human tragedy this side of the Second Coming of Jesus.[16] Until then, in Paul's words, "evil men will wax worse and worse, deceiving and being deceived" (II Tim. 3:13). The final victory must await the future installment as king of the hero of the biblical drama, Jesus, the Messiah, the appointed ruler of Israel and the world; and "of his government on the [restored] throne of David there shall be no end" (Isa. 9:7).

---

[14] Paul's word is *kosmokratores*.

[15] Correct teaching is essential if God is to be worshipped in spirit and truth (John 4:24). Hosea laments the loss of proper instruction: "My people are destroyed for lack of knowledge" (Hos. 4:6).

[16] Satan is bound "so that he can no longer deceive the nations" only at the return of Christ to rule (Rev. 20:3).

3. The Messiah-King, His Kingdom and the Neglect of His Message

A learned American theologian of the last century was intrigued by the extraordinary capacity of the religious to read the Bible with the conviction that its Message must be wrapped in obscurity. Words which under normal circumstances allow no room for misunderstanding seem in a biblical context to provoke complex problems of interpretation:

> One of the strangest things in the world is the manner in which some people read the Bible. It would almost seem as if they turned it upside down and read it backwards. "Eyes they have, but they see not." They praise it and hold it in holy regard, and insist that everyone ought to have it; yet they look into it only as some recondite volume, which is a good textbook for preachers, but is quite beyond the reach of their understanding…Many seem to view it as a sublime riddle-book, full of mystic poetry and unsearchable wisdom rather than as a plain piece of information and advice given by a Father to his inexperienced and exposed children. Many who sit down to write commentaries on it seem to be continually haunted with the idea that there is something recondite in every word, or that the real mind of the spirit is not to be found in the plain import of the letter, but in some abstruse or mystic analogy which it is their business to dig after.

> I hold that the Bible is a book for everybody, in which God speaks for the purpose of being understood by everybody; that its language is conformed to the ordinary uses of speech; and that it is to be interpreted in the same common-sense way in which we would interpret the will of a deceased father, or ascertain the meaning of a

business letter. Its design is to instruct, and in the most familiar way to express to men the mind and will of God. When Christ speaks of the Son of Man He means the Son of Man and not the Roman armies. When He speaks of His Coming in the clouds of heaven, He means His Coming in the clouds of heaven, and not the sailing of warships on the Mediterranean, or the marching of soldiers over the earth…Christ knew what He wished to say and how to say what He meant; and I feel myself bound to understand Him to mean just what He says.[1]

There is much wisdom in the learned Doctor's approach to the Scriptures. Though the Bible story is set in a culture far removed from ours, it is written to convey plain information about God's intention for the whole world. Popular notions about the meaning of Christianity would undergo a radical change, if biblical statements were treated as language designed to be understood. If someone were to state that a British prince will one day assume the throne of his mother, Queen Elizabeth, and reign as king of England, no one would misunderstand. When a divine emissary announces to Mary that her son Jesus is to inherit the throne of His ancestor David and reign over the people of Israel (Luke 1:32, 33), the proposition is apparently fraught with difficulty. The need is felt for an army of learned expositors to assist with an interpretation.

Royal Language about Jesus Means What It Says

A large measure of Christian unity could be achieved overnight if Christians would read the divine messenger's words as plain statements of fact and accept them as true. To do so would be the essence of good Abrahamic faith — believing what God has said is going to happen, taking Him at His Word. Firstly, it would be understood that Jesus was born for royal office, and secondly that David's throne must sometime be reestablished, so that Jesus can inherit it and become King of Israel. This He has plainly never done. If, then, the account of Jesus' life in Palestine were studied, it would be found that, far from becoming king, He died as a common criminal at the hands of the Romans and His own people, the Jews (Acts 2:23).

---

[1] J.A. Seiss, *The Last Times and the Great Commission*, Philadelphia: Smith, English and Co., 1863, p. 26.

Now Luke knew all this, for it had become history by the time he wrote his report of the angel's message to Mary (having gathered his information in all probability by talking to Mary herself). Luke, however, saw nothing at all problematic in Jesus having died without becoming king. It was clear to him that the first part of Gabriel's message, given in advance of the conception of Jesus, had been amply fulfilled in the Savior's birth at Bethlehem. There was therefore not the slightest reason to doubt that Jesus would also become king over Israel. That part of the announcement had simply not yet come to pass. That it would was not in doubt. The New Testament, echoing the Old, promises the accession of Jesus to the restored throne of David in Jerusalem at His future return to the earth.[2] In this way He will also inherit the land promise of which He is the rightful heir according to the oath sworn to Abraham (Gal. 3:19).

An extraordinary confusion comes over the minds of some when confronted with the proposition that Jesus is to reign over the house of Israel. The ordinary churchgoer has no difficulty with the historical narrative stating that Jesus was born in Bethlehem in the days of Herod the king (Matt. 2:1), but seems baffled by the prospect of His reign over Israel in the future. Non-acceptance of clear statements amounts to unbelief. Would this indicate that Christians have not yet fully become believers in the full range of blessings contained in the Gospel? The reception of Luke's simple piece of information about the future career of Jesus would at once dramatically unite churchgoers under the banner of a brand new tenet — or rather, one discovered afresh after years of neglect. It would bestow upon them a single hope and make them bearers of astonishingly Good News to a perplexed world. They would be enabled to proclaim with absolute certainty something of stupendous significance for the future of mankind. They would once again be in possession of Jesus' own Gospel Message — the Message about the coming Kingdom of God, of which He is the ruler designate (Mark 1:14, 15).

By comparison with the tremendous implications of Jesus' forthcoming reign on the throne of David, arguments about

---

[2] Acts 1:6; 3:21; Acts 26:6, 7; Rev. 11:15-17. Note that the Messiah "begins to reign" (v.17) at His return, the time of the resurrection of the dead (Rev. 11:18). Matt. 25:31 similarly makes the beginning of the reign of Christ the time when He "comes in His glory."

episcopacy, communion, women priests, or the mode of baptism would rapidly pale into insignificance. The denominational barriers would come crashing down. Such a dramatic revolution would in fact mean only that the churches had come to accept Jesus as *Messiah*, as the one destined to rule the world from Jerusalem. Little do they seem to realize that their traditional creeds leave almost no room for real conviction about His Messiahship. Ecclesiastical tradition has robbed Him of His throne and His land. It is one of those great ironies of history that Jesus' own people did not want Him in the land which belonged to Him as Messiah.[3] But do twentieth-century Christians want to see Him back in the land of Israel — the land which is His birthright according to the land grant covenanted with Abraham and his "seed"?

What has happened to render the simplest piece of information about Jesus obscure? How did the promise of His future Kingship over Israel fade from the creed? Why do the classic creeds contain no word about the destiny of Jesus as ruler of the world in Jerusalem?[4] As things stand, the great majority of churchgoers do not subscribe to the basic fact about Jesus which the angel Gabriel communicated to Mary, and which the whole New Testament embraces as the central tenet of the faith — that Jesus is destined for royal office as heir to David's throne (Luke 1:32, 33). Can the popular Jesus really be the Jesus of the Bible when the biblical description of Him is so widely rejected? Would belief in a royal prince who has no hope of becoming king of England be belief in the prince who is heir apparent?

No doubt some will protest that Jesus has already assumed His kingship on David's throne in heaven at His ascension. The suggestion would not be accepted by the New Testament Church. For though they recognized that Jesus had been exalted after His resurrection to His Father's throne in heaven (Acts 2:33), nothing would have appeared more problematic than that David's throne had

---

[3] John 1:11 states that Jesus came to His own domain (NASV margin) and His own people did not receive Him.

[4] The creeds in fact say very little about the historical life of Jesus except to mention His birth. They speak vaguely about what He is going to do in the future. The Nicene Creed comes closest to the language of the Bible when it speaks of "the resurrection of the dead and the life of the world to come." The latter phrase, however, should read "the life of the *age* to come."

been permanently relocated in a realm beyond the skies. David's throne never had been and never would be anywhere else but in Jerusalem. Countless prophecies had taught them to look forward to Israel's national restoration under the Messiah, and to a world renewed and reordered under His government (Jer. 3:17; 23:5, 6; 33:15, etc.).

It is clear beyond a shadow of a doubt that Jesus and the disciples, even after the resurrection, fully expected the Kingdom to be reestablished *in Israel*. This is only to say that they believed in the Hebrew Bible which their teacher had said He came *not* to destroy (Matt. 5:17). After the Apostles had spent six weeks with their risen master, discussing the Kingdom of God, they were eager to know if the time was then ripe for the expected national restoration of the Messianic throne in Israel. They asked: "Lord, is this the time for the restoration of the Kingdom to Israel?" (Acts 1:6). There was no hint that the Message of all the prophets and the hopes of generations of pious Israelites had failed. Jesus did nothing at all to dash their hopes or correct their Messianism. He merely stated that the time for the future restoration of the Kingdom could not be known (Acts 1:7).[5] As Luke later makes clear, Jesus, as Messiah Designate, must be temporarily retained in heaven until the time comes for the national and universal restoration on which the entire biblical heritage was founded. The point received the highest apostolic confirmation when Peter, clarifying the divine Plan, announced: "Heaven must retain the Messiah until the time comes for the restoration of all things, about which the prophets spoke" (Acts 3:21). With these words Peter summarized the whole sweep of God's Plan for the world, projecting it into the Messianic era which Jesus would introduce at His return. Peter's audience would recall at once, among many other passages, the stirring words of the prophet Isaiah: "Then I will restore Jerusalem's administrators as at the first and your counselors as at the beginning. After that you will be called a city of righteousness, a faithful city" (Isa. 1:26; cp. Ezek. 39:25, 26).

Acts 3:21 is one of the great definitive statements of the New Testament revelation — a text which one might expect would receive

---

[5] The ascension of Jesus was the guarantee of His future reign on earth. The coming of the Spirit "not many days hence" was definitely *not* the coming of the Kingdom, at a time undisclosed.

equal time with John 3:16. We may say therefore, with all confidence, that unless the throne of David is reestablished under the Messiah, all the seers and prophets of the Old and New Testament will have turned out to be frauds and their Message an empty fantasy. The Apostles will be exposed as naive dreamers trading on a religious illusion. Jesus Himself will have been revealed as an impostor. Christianity must yet triumph in a renovated earth, and with the returned Messiah as universal king, or fail. There is no third alternative.

The Neglect of the Message

If there is one element of biblical faith which churches often seem to avoid and theologians have obscured, it is the matter of the meaning to be attached to Jesus' favorite term, "the Kingdom of God," which is a thoroughly Hebrew Messianic concept. To interpret any document intelligently one must enter the thought world of those whom one is attempting to understand. If one blunders in the interpretation of key terms and expressions, a disastrous misunderstanding will result. That such a breakdown in the transmission of the original faith, due to a failure to reckon with the Jewishness of Jesus and His Message about the Kingdom, has occurred was noted by an astute scholar of the Church of England. Critical of trends which developed in the Church from the second to the fourth century, he wrote: "The Church as a whole failed to understand the Old Testament and the Greek and Roman mind in turn came to dominate the Church's outlook: From that disaster the Church has never recovered either in doctrine or in practice."[6]

The root of the problem was similarly diagnosed by a Jewish historian, a translator of the New Testament and sympathetic to Christianity:

> Christians would gravely delude themselves if they were to imagine that Jews on any major scale could subscribe to the tenets of the Christian religion, which owe so much to the legacy of polytheism. Because Christians have not become Israelites, but have remained essentially Gentiles, their spiritual inclinations are towards

---

[6] H.L. Goudge, "The Calling of the Jews," *Essays on Judaism and Christianity*, cited by H.J. Schonfield, *The Politics of God*, Hutchinson, 1970, p. 98.

doctrines for which they have been prepared by inheritance from the pagan past.[7]

This tragic departure of the Church from the biblical Message was noted also by an Archbishop of the Anglican Church. He expressed his astonishment that the central, fundamental concept of Jesus' Gospel Message — the Kingdom — had been neglected for most of church history:

> Every generation finds something in the Gospel which is of special importance to itself and seems to have been overlooked in the previous age or (sometimes) in all previous ages of the Church. The great discovery of the age in which we live is the immense prominence given in the Gospel to the Kingdom of God. *To us it is quite extraordinary that it figures so little in the theology and religious writings of almost the entire period of Christian history.* Certainly in the Synoptic Gospels [Matthew, Mark and Luke] it has a prominence that could hardly be increased.[8]

It is almost impossible to exaggerate the significance of this observation of the Archbishop. A glance at the Gospel accounts of Jesus' ministry will reveal to every reader the simple fact that Jesus, the original herald of the Christian Gospel, was a preacher of the Kingdom of God. There can be absolutely no doubt about this: Can anyone question F.C. Grant's assessment of Jesus' purpose?

> It may be said that the teaching of Jesus concerning the Kingdom of God represents His whole teaching. It is the main determinative subject of all His discourse. His ethics were ethics of the Kingdom; His theology was theology of the Kingdom; His teaching regarding Himself cannot be understood apart from His interpretation of the Kingdom of God.[9]

It is equally clear that Jesus intended His own Kingdom Message, the Gospel or Good News, to be the chief concern of those who claimed to represent Him for the whole period of history until His promised return. Giving his marching orders to the Church, Jesus commanded His followers to teach *everything He had taught* to those

---

[7] H.J. Schonfield, *The Politics of God*, p. 98.

[8] William Temple, *Personal Religion and the Life of Fellowship*, Longmans, Green and Co. Ltd., 1926, p. 69, emphasis added.

[9] "The Gospel of the Kingdom," *Biblical World* 50 (1917), pp. 121-191.

whom they discipled and initiated into the faith by baptism (Matt. 28:19, 20). The task of the faithful, as Jesus saw it, would be to preach "*this* Gospel about the Kingdom in all the world" (Matt. 24:14).

A sure sign of the continuing presence of the living Christ in His Church must be a clarion-call proclamation of the Kingdom of God, just as Jesus preached it. To say, as Archbishop Temple does, that the Kingdom of God "has figured so little in the theology and religious writings of almost the entire period of Christian history" is to admit only that the Church has not done what Jesus told it to do. The Church has been sailing under false colors. While it claims the name of Christ, it has not been busy faithfully relaying His saving Gospel Message about the Kingdom to the world. How can it, when it admits to uncertainty about what the Kingdom means?[10] A reappraisal of the Church's task, including the frank admission that its Gospel has lacked an essential Messianic element, seems to be in order.

It is a very simple matter to document the absence of the Gospel of the Kingdom of God from the Church's preaching. Listen, for example, to the call of evangelists today to potential converts. Is the phrase "Gospel of the Kingdom" the main subject of the appeal for men and women to become Christians? Do pulpits the length and breadth of the land resound with clear expositions of what Jesus meant by the Kingdom?

Apparently this is not the case. In his book *Church Growth and the Whole Gospel* the noted American church planter, Peter Wagner, agrees with G.E. Ladd that "modern scholarship is quite unanimous in the opinion that the Kingdom of God was the central message of Jesus." Wagner then reflects:

> If this is true, and I know of no reason to dispute it, I cannot help wondering out loud why I haven't heard more about the Kingdom of God in the thirty years I have been a Christian. I certainly have read about it enough in the Bible. Matthew mentions the Kingdom 52 times, Mark 19 times, Luke 44 times and John 4. But I honestly cannot remember any pastor whose ministry I have been under actually preaching a sermon on the Kingdom of God. As I rummage

---

[10] For example, Robert Morgan wrote, "It is time someone called the bluff of those who think they know what exactly Jesus meant by the Kingdom of God" (*Theology*, Nov. 1979, p. 458).

through my own sermon barrel, I now realize that I myself have never preached a sermon on it. Where has the Kingdom been?[11]

In an article entitled "Preaching the Kingdom of God" the British expositor, Dr. I. Howard Marshall of the University of Aberdeen, says:

> During the past sixteen years I can recollect only two occasions on which I have heard sermons specifically devoted to the theme of the Kingdom of God...I find this silence rather surprising because it is universally agreed by New Testament scholars that the central theme of the teaching of Jesus was the Kingdom of God...Clearly, then, one would expect the modern preacher who is trying to bring the message of Jesus to his congregation would have much to say about this subject. In fact my experience has been the opposite, and I have rarely heard about it.[12]

From a Roman Catholic writer comes the extraordinary admission that what he had learned in seminary did not include an explanation of Jesus' Message about the Kingdom:

> As a teacher of New Testament literature..., it early became obvious to me that the central theme of the preaching of the historical Jesus of Nazareth was the near approach of the Kingdom of God. Yet, to my amazement, this theme played hardly any role in the systematic theology I been taught in the seminary. Upon further investigation I realized that this theme had in many ways been largely ignored in the theology and spirituality and liturgy of the Church in the past two thousand years, and when not ignored, often distorted beyond recognition. How could this be?[13]

A further striking example reinforces our contention that for modern preachers the Gospel of the Kingdom of God does not have anything like the comprehensive significance it had for Jesus and the whole New Testament Church. While Jesus concentrated single-mindedly on the propagation of a Gospel about the Kingdom, modern preachers seem to steer clear of the phrase "Gospel of the Kingdom." In an editorial in the journal *Missiology* Arthur F. Glasser writes:

---

[11] *Church Growth and the Whole Gospel: A Biblical Mandate*, San Francisco: Harper & Row, 1981, p. 2.

[12] *The Expository Times* (89), Oct. 1977, p. 13.

[13] B.T. Viviano, *The Kingdom of God in History*, Michael Glazier, 1988, p. 9.

Let me ask: When is the last time you heard a sermon on the Kingdom of God? Frankly, I'd be hard put to recall ever having heard a solid exposition of this theme. How do we square this silence with the widely accepted fact that the Kingdom of God dominated our Lord's thought and ministry? My experience is not uncommon. I've checked this out with my colleagues. Of course, they readily agree they've often heard sermons on bits and pieces of Jesus' parables. But as for a solid sermon on the nature of the Kingdom of God as Jesus taught it — upon reflection, they too began to express surprise that it is the rare pastor who tackles the subject.[14]

One needs no special theological training to conclude that something is drastically askew, when leading exponents of the faith in our day confess that Jesus' Message is unfamiliar to them. At the level of popular evangelism it is evident that the critical Kingdom element is missing from presentations of the saving Message. Billy Graham defines the Gospel by dividing it into two main components. The first element is the death of Jesus, which is half the Gospel. The other half, he says, is the resurrection of Jesus.[15] But this definition omits the basis of the Gospel Message. Jesus announced the Kingdom of God as the heart of the Gospel long before He said a word about His death and resurrection. Luke reports that the disciples went out proclaiming the Gospel *even before they had any knowledge of the death and resurrection of Jesus* (Luke 18:31-34). *It follows, therefore, that there is more to the Gospel than the death and resurrection of Christ, essential as these things are.*

Michael Green, an expert on evangelism, poses the question raised by the obvious difference between what we call evangelism and how Jesus defined it. At the Lausanne International Conference on World Evangelism in 1974, he asked: "How much have you heard here about the Kingdom of God? Not much. It is not our language. But it was Jesus' prime concern."[16] How can it be that our language as 20th-century Christians is not the language of Jesus Himself? The situation demands an explanation. It should alert us to the fact that all is not

---

[14] April 1980, p. 13.

[15] Roy Gustafson, "What is the Gospel?" Billy Graham Association.

[16] Cited by Tom Sine, *The Mustard Seed Conspiracy*, Waco: Word Books, 1981, pp. 102, 103.

well with our version of the Christian faith. We are not preaching the Gospel as Jesus and His Apostles preached it, as long as we omit mention of the substance of His entire Message, the Good News of the Kingdom.

Other scholars warn us that the all-embracing expression Kingdom of God, which is the axis around which everything Jesus taught revolves, is strange to churchgoers. Noting that Jesus opened His ministry by alerting the public to the approaching advent of the Kingdom without an explanatory comment about the meaning of the Kingdom, Hugh Anderson observes:

> For Jesus' first hearers, as presumably for Mark's readers, [Kingdom of God] was not the empty or nebulous term it often is today. The concept had a long history and an extensive background in the Old Testament, extra-canonical works of the intertestamental period, and in the rabbinical literature.[17]

Jesus' audience knew what He meant by the Kingdom of God for the simple reason that they knew the Hebrew Bible, which was replete with glorious promises of peace and prosperity on earth to be enjoyed by those counted worthy to find a place in the Kingdom of the Messiah. To Jesus' contemporaries the Kingdom of God was about as well known as the Statue of Liberty, the Declaration of Independence or the Tower of London. One can imagine how confusing things would be if Americans and Englishmen today were unable to define clearly what is meant by these terms. What if the Second World War was a nebulous idea in the minds of historians or Buckingham Palace a strange term to Londoners? When an idea is deeply rooted in the national identity of a people, it does not have to be defined every time it is mentioned. Such was the case with the Kingdom of God. God's Kingdom meant a new era of world government on earth destined to appear with the arrival in power of the promised King of the line of David, the Messiah, or Anointed Agent of the One God.

A perceptive theologian, conscious of the need to define basic Christian ideas within the framework provided by their original

---

[17] *The New Century Bible Commentary, Gospel of Mark*, Eerdmans, 1984, p. 84. Anderson notes that "the Kingdom of God was without doubt at the heart of Jesus' historic message" (*ibid.*, p. 83).

environment, has this to say about the Kingdom of God in Jesus' teaching:

> The Kingdom of God was basically a political idea — but political in the ancient religious sense, according to which "politics" was part of religion and expressed practically the doctrine of God's rule in the world…It meant the world empire of God…It was this idea which Jesus made His own, the vehicle of all his teaching…which he identified with the purpose of God in his own time, and adopted as the clue to his own prophetic or messianic mission: He was — or was to be — God's agent in the final establishment (or reestablishment) of the divine Reign in this world…The Kingdom of God, in the New Testament period, was still the old prophetic dream of the complete and perfect realization, here upon earth, of the sole sovereignty of the one and only God.[18]

The Kingdom of God: The Key to Unlock the Bible

It is impossible to explain the Christian religion without clarifying the meaning of the term Kingdom of God. With that concept Jesus opened His preaching ministry, making it the foundation of all He taught. The Kingdom of God was the master idea summing up the essence of all that the nation of Israel aspired to. It contained the two major elements of Israel's prophetic tradition: the burning desire for occupation of the land promised to Abraham and his descendants together with the expectation that a divinely ordained ruler would ascend the restored throne of David.

The first thing said about Jesus in Luke's account of the faith concerned the Kingdom of God. God is going "to give Him the throne of His ancestor David and He will rule over the house of Jacob forever" (Luke 1:32, 33). Intelligent discipleship requires a grasp of that fundamental fact. It means also that we recognize that Jesus was a Jew whose whole teaching was deeply embedded in the Hebrew Scriptures to which He always appealed as a repository of divine truth. If we hope to understand Jesus' Gospel we shall have to immerse ourselves in the Jewish environment which provides the background of our New Testament documents. Otherwise we run the

---

[18] F.C. Grant, *Ancient Judaism and the New Testament*, New York: Macmillan, 1959, pp. 114-119.

risk of creating "another Jesus," the projection of our own ideas and ideals.

Jesus Himself began by summoning the people to repentance and belief in the Gospel about the Kingdom (Mark 1:14, 15; Matt. 4:23). At the Last Supper He expressed His earnest longing to be reunited with the Apostles in the future Kingdom (Matt. 26:29; Mark 14:25; Luke 22:16, 18). Following His resurrection Jesus immediately resumed His teaching by speaking of the Kingdom of God for some six weeks (Acts 1:3). The last question posed to Him by the disciples before His ascension focused on the restoration of the Kingdom (Acts 1:6). As a true disciple of the Messiah, Paul labored to proclaim the Kingdom. We find him constantly at work "speaking out boldly...reasoning and persuading them about the Kingdom of God" (Acts 19:8). Just as Jesus had declared the preaching of the Kingdom to be the reason for His mission (Luke 4:43), Paul summarized his entire ministry to Jew and Gentile as a "proclamation of the Kingdom of God" (Acts 20:25). Luke ends his account in Acts where he began by speaking of the Kingdom. He gives us a final glimpse of Paul, a prisoner in Rome, as he preached "the Kingdom of God and the name of Jesus unhindered" for two years (Acts 28:30, 31). The Gospel of the Kingdom of God is virtually a synonym for the Christian religion. It is obvious that Paul was no less a preacher of the Kingdom than Jesus. The fact is that "preaching about the Kingdom of God sums up the ministry of Jesus, the Apostles, disciples and Paul."[19] But can this be said of contemporary disciples?

Jesus the Heir to the Throne of David

The ministry of Jesus was informed by the Hebrew Scriptures in which He had been schooled from early childhood. As a believer in the God of Israel and His divine revelation through the prophets, He shared the yearning of the Jewish people for the great day of liberation from foreign powers and the return of the Israelites to the promised land. It is a fatal mistake of interpretation to divorce New Testament Kingdom language from its roots in the Old Testament and the history of Israel. The glory of David's and Solomon's rule provided the model for a much greater Israelite empire of the future. Since Jesus

---

[19] Robert O'Toole, in *The Kingdom of God in 20th-Century Interpretation*, ed. Wendell Willis, Hendrickson, 1987, p. 153.

was believed to be the distinguished heir to that Davidic throne (Luke 1:32, 33), the following Old Testament texts, containing a direct or implied reference to the throne of David, build a bridge between Jesus' royal heritage and the Christian hope:

> To David and his descendants and his house may there be peace from the Lord forever (I Kings 2:23).

> The Lord has sworn to David...to transfer the kingdom from the house of Saul, and to establish the throne of David over Israel and Judah, from Dan to Beersheba (II Sam. 3:9, 10).

> And Solomon sat on the throne of David his father and his kingdom was firmly established (I Kings 2:12).

> The throne of David shall be established before the Lord forever. Thus the Kingdom was established in the hands of Solomon (I Kings 2:45, 46).

> The Lord lives, who has established me and set me on the throne of David my father (I Kings 2:24).

The throne of David naturally means the ruling seat of the dynasty of David in Jerusalem. Of critical importance is the fact that the same throne may also be called the throne of the *Kingdom of the Lord*, the latter phrase being equivalent to the Kingdom of God. This means that the king of Israel, ruling in Jerusalem, is God's chosen ambassador on earth. He presides over the Kingdom of God while administering the Davidic Kingdom in Palestine. Thus it was that Israel looked forward to the expected Messiah, the ideal king of the line of David, who perfectly represents the One God. David's Kingdom, *which is also God's Kingdom*, is on earth, and it is ultimately to be administered by God's commissioned agent, the ultimate sovereign of the royal house of David ruling from Jerusalem. The term Kingdom of God is rooted in the divine covenant made with David. The crucial link between the Kingdom of Israel and the Kingdom of God is found in a number of key Old Testament passages:

> Then Solomon sat on the *throne of the Lord* as king instead of David his father; and he prospered and all Israel obeyed him (I Chron. 29:23).

> God has chosen my son Solomon to sit on the throne of *the kingdom of the Lord* over Israel (I Chron. 28:5).

> You are resisting *the kingdom of the Lord* in the hands of the sons of David (II Chron. 13:8).

> But I [God] will settle him [Solomon] in My house and *My kingdom* forever and his throne shall be established forever (I Chron. 17:14).

The kings of Israel were keenly aware of their position as God's rulers. In I Kings 2:24 Solomon understands his reign to be by divine appointment: "The Lord lives, who has established me and set me on the throne of David my father."

When the Queen of Sheba visited the magnificent kingdom of Solomon she also understood the meaning of the term Kingdom of God. In her excitement over the exalted position of Solomon and the destiny of Israel in the divine Plan, she declared: "Blessed be the Lord your God who delighted in you, setting you on *His throne* as *king for the Lord your God;* because the Lord loved Israel, establishing them forever; therefore He made you king over them, to do justice and righteousness" (II Chron. 9:8).

The same statement, as recorded in the parallel verse in Kings (I Kings 10:9), speaks of the *throne of Israel*, confirming once again that the Kingdom of Israel is also the Kingdom of God. The same verse states also the ideal function of the king. It is "to do justice and righteousness" — exactly the ideal set before all followers of Christ, whose aim is to succeed where Adam failed and regain the kingship lost by him.

The Kingdom of God, then, is an empire ruled by the king of Israel enthroned in Jerusalem. This definition will throw a flood of light on what Jesus meant by the Good News about the Kingdom of God. The Hebrew term "Kingdom of the Lord" reappears in Revelation 11:15, where, at the seventh trumpet blast, the power of present political states is to be transferred to the "Kingdom of our Lord and of His Christ."

An examination of the work of Israel's prophets reveals their unshakable faith in a coming era of justice and peace for all mankind. The prophet Isaiah expressed God's vision and intention for Israel and the world when he spoke of the Message of one "who announces peace and brings good news of happiness, who announces salvation, and says to Zion [Jerusalem], 'Your God reigns!'" (Isa. 52:7).[20] Amidst scenes of tribulation and judgment the Kingdom of God would appear, and the reign of the Lord would be established on earth in the person of the coming King of Israel, the Messiah. Such is the supreme hope of the prophets of Israel whose Message Jesus made His own as He summoned His countrymen to repentance in view of the great day. The gist of Jesus' Gospel was that the threshold of the great future had been reached. The promises made to Israel's founding fathers were to be realized at last.

Our task is now to become acquainted in greater detail with the divine arrangements which Israel claimed as her unique heritage and on which Jesus built His saving Message about the Kingdom. The Christian Gospel cannot be understood apart from its mooring in the Hebrew Bible (see Gal. 3:8; Rom. 1:1, 2; 15:8; 16:25, 26).

---

[20] The Jewish paraphrase is: "The Kingdom of God will be revealed." Isa. 40:10 describes the event as God coming in might with His arm ruling for Him and His reward with Him. The New Testament interprets this Kingdom activity as the task of the supreme representative of the One God, i.e., Jesus the Messiah. The coming Kingdom of God was predicted in a number of key verses, i.e., Exod. 15:18; Isa. 24:23; 31:4; 40:9; 52:7; Ezek. 7:7, 10; Obad. 21; Micah 4:7, 8. The interpretative comment in the Jewish Targum is in every case "The Kingdom of God will be revealed."

4. The Christian Hope: Life in the Land of the Promise Made to Abraham

In one of the most solemn declarations of all time the Almighty God promised to give Abraham an entire country. On a mountaintop somewhere between Bethel and Ai, in the land of Canaan, God commanded the "father of the faithful" (Rom. 4:16) to "look from the place where you are, northward, southward, eastward and westward: For the entire land you are looking at I will give to you and your descendants forever" (Gen. 13:14, 15). As an additional assurance of God's gift to him, God then instructed Abraham to "arise, walk through the length and breadth of the land, for I will give it to you" (Gen. 13:17).

Abraham's conception of the ultimate reward of faith was firmly linked to the earth. As he looked northward Abraham would have seen the hills marking the border with Samaria. Towards the south the view extended to Hebron where later the patriarchs were to be buried in the only piece of land ever owned by Abraham (Gen. 23:17-20). To the east lay the mountains of Moab and to the west the Mediterranean Sea. The divine oath guaranteed to Abraham perpetual ownership of a large portion of the earth. Later the promise was repeated and made the basis of a solemn covenant, to be cherished by subsequent Israelites as the foundation of hope for Israel and mankind.

> And I will establish My covenant between Me and you and your descendants after you in their generations as an everlasting covenant...and I will give to you and your descendants after you the land in which you now reside as a foreigner — all the land of Canaan — as an everlasting possession (Gen. 17:7, 8).

It would not seem possible that the terms of God's promise could be misunderstood. And yet, by a miracle of misinterpretation, traditional Christian theology has handled these innocent passages in a way which deprives Abraham of his inheritance and makes God an unreliable witness. Christian preachers over the centuries have had almost no interest in the land as the inheritance promised to Abraham and the faithful. This can be seen by inspecting the indexes of standard systematic theologies, Bible dictionaries and commentaries, or indeed by listening to sermons in which, strangely, much is said about the prospect of "heaven" and almost nothing of the land in which Abraham hoped to reside permanently.

As Gerhard von Rad says, in the first six books of the Bible "there is probably no more important idea than that expressed in terms of the land promised and later granted by Yahweh."[1] The promise is unique. "Among all the traditions of the world this is the only one that tells of a promise of land to a people."[2] Because the land is promised on oath another scholar suggests that it might more properly be called "the sworn Land."[3] So compelling was the promise of land to Abraham that it became a "living power in the life of Israel."[4] "The promise to Abraham becomes a ground for ultimate hope...There is a Gospel for Israel in the Abrahamic covenant."[5] This fact was recognized by Paul. He spoke of the (Christian) Gospel as having been "preached in advance to Abraham" (Gal. 3:8), an apostolic statement which throws a flood of light on the content of the New Testament Good News and shows that biblical Christianity is embedded in the Hebrew Bible.

W.D. Davies points out that large sections of the Old Testament make "the divine promise to Abraham the bedrock on which all the subsequent history rests."[6] Von Rad maintains that "the whole of the Hexateuch [Genesis to Joshua] in all its vast complexity was governed by the theme of the fulfillment of the promise to Abraham in the

---

[1] *The Problem of the Hexateuch and Other Essays*, 1966, p. 79, cited in W.D. Davies, *The Gospel and the Land,* University of California Press, 1974, p. 19.

[2] M. Buber, *Israel and Palestine*, London, East and West Library, 1952, p. 19.

[3] *The Gospel and the Land*, p. 15.

[4] *Ibid.*, p. 18.

[5] *Ibid.,* p. 21.

[6] *Ibid.*

settlement of Canaan."[7] It is the thesis of this book that the Abrahamic promise permeates the whole Bible. This would be self-evident to all Bible readers had not the Church in the early centuries abandoned the roots of the faith in the Hebrew Bible and attached itself to the alien thought patterns of the Greek world.

That the patriarchs expected to inherit a portion of this planet is obvious not only from the divine promises made to them but also from their zeal to be buried in the land of Israel (Gen. 50:5). Knowing that God had promised to give them permanent residence in the land, they also understood that by being resurrected from death they would stand once again on the soil of the Holy Land.

The land promise to Abraham and his offspring runs like a golden thread through the book of Genesis. The key words in the following passages help us to catch the atmosphere of the Bible's principal theme:

> Go to *the land* I will show you (Gen. 12:1). All the land which you see I will give to you and your *offspring* forever (Gen. 13:15). A son from your own body will be your heir (Gen. 15:4). I am the Lord who brought you out of Ur of the Chaldees to give you this land to *take possession* of it (Gen. 15:7). On that day the Lord made a *covenant* with Abram and said, "To your descendants I give this land (Gen. 15:18). I will make nations of you and *kings* will come from you. I will establish my covenant as an *everlasting covenant* between Me and you and your descendants after you...The whole land of Canaan where you are now an alien, I will give as an everlasting possession to you and your descendants after you and I will be their God (Gen. 17:6-8). Abraham will surely become a great and powerful nation, and all the nations on earth will be blessed through him. For I have selected him (Gen. 18:18, 19). Your descendants will take possession of the cities of their enemies (Gen. 22:17). God promised me on oath, saying, "To your offspring I will give this land" (Gen. 24:7). [Abraham] is a prophet (Gen. 20:7).

Isaac

> I will establish My covenant with him as an everlasting covenant for his descendants after him...My covenant I will establish with Isaac (Gen. 17:19, 21). Through Isaac your offspring will be

---

[7] *Ibid.*, p. 23.

reckoned (Gen. 21:12). To you and your descendants I will give all these lands and will confirm the oath which I swore to your father Abraham (Gen. 26:3).

Jacob

May God give you and your descendants the blessing given to Abraham, so that you may take possession of the land where you now live as an alien, the land God gave to Abraham (Gen. 28:4). I will give you the land on which you are lying...I will bring you back to this land (Gen. 28:13, 15). The land I gave to Abraham and Isaac I also will give to you, and I will give this land to your descendants after you (Gen. 35:12).

The Twelve Tribes

God will surely come to your aid and take you up out of this land to the land which He promised on oath to Abraham and Isaac and Jacob (Gen. 50:24).

The promise to the nation of Israel received a primary fulfillment under Joshua's leadership (Josh. 21:45). Many commentators would have us believe that the land promise to Israel was no longer relevant once the children of Israel conquered Palestine. Both the Law and the writings of the prophets, however, express the conviction that Israel's settlement of the land under Joshua was only an incomplete fulfillment of the covenant. Everyone knew that Abraham, Isaac and Jacob had never been able to call the land their own. They had been aliens living in temporary dwellings. It was obvious, then, that a further and final event was to be expected by which the patriarchs could actually take charge of their inheritance.

The point is a simple one with momentous implications for New Testament Christians who saw themselves as heirs to the Abrahamic covenant with Jesus. Von Rad points out that "promises which have been fulfilled in history are not thereby exhausted of their content, but remain as promises on a different level."[8] Davies agrees: "The tradition, however changed, continued to contain *the hope of life in the land*. Deuteronomy makes it clear that there is still a future to look

---

[8] *The Problem of the Hexateuch*, p. 92ff.

forward to: the land has to achieve rest and peace...The land looks forward to a future blessing."[9]

Naturally, then, in the Old Testament the hope of an ultimate and permanent settlement in the land, accompanied by peace, remains in view.

It is appropriate at this point to gather a number of passages, mostly from the prophets and Psalms, to illustrate the ongoing importance of a great future for the Promised Land and those counted worthy to inherit it:

> My people shall live in peaceful dwelling places, in secure homes, in undisturbed places of rest (Isa. 32:18).[10]

> Descendants from Jacob and Judah...will possess My mountains [i.e., the land]; My chosen people will be righteous and they will inherit the land forever (Isa. 65:9).

> Then all your people will be righteous and they will inherit the land forever (Isa. 60:21).

> Israel will possess a double portion in their land; everlasting joy will be theirs (Isa. 61:7).

> Thus they will inherit the land *a second time* and everlasting joy will be upon their heads (Isa. 61:7, LXX).

> But the man who makes Me his refuge will inherit the land and possess My holy mountain (Isa. 57:13).

> The righteous shall never be removed: but the wicked will not inherit the land (Prov. 10:30).

> Dwell in the land and enjoy safe pasture...The meek will inherit the land and enjoy great peace...The inheritance of the blameless will endure forever...Those the Lord blesses will inherit the land...Turn from evil and do good, then you will dwell in the land forever...The righteous will inherit the land and dwell in it forever...God will

---

[9] *The Gospel and the Land*, p. 36, emphasis added.

[10] Cp. Heb. 4:1 which speaks of the future "rest" as the objective of the faithful.

> exalt you to inherit that land; when the wicked are cut off you will
> see it...There is a future for the man of peace (Ps. 37:3-37).

> The days are coming, declares the Lord, when I will bring My
> people Israel and Judah back from captivity and restore them to the
> land I gave their forefathers to possess (Jer. 30:3).

The integrity of divine revelation is at stake in this question of the future of the Promised Land. The entire Plan for rescuing mankind depends on the covenanted land promise to Abraham, to be fulfilled in Jesus, who "came to confirm the promises made to the fathers" (Rom. 15:8). Certainly Abraham had not received what had been promised. Moses was not allowed to enter the Promised Land, and Israel was eventually expelled from her homeland. Jesus, as heir to the promises, was also rejected in the country that belonged to Him: "He came to His own land and His own people did not accept Him" (John 1:11).

Despite centuries of disappointment the faithful in Israel clung with passionate tenacity to the expectation that the land of Israel would indeed become the scene of ultimate salvation. That hope remained as the beacon light not only of the prophets but also of the original Christian faith as preached by Jesus and the Apostles. It was extinguished by the intrusion of a non-territorial hope of "heaven when you die." A contradictory idea that the patriarchs have already "gone to heaven" destroyed the Bible's passionate sense of yearning for a successful outcome of human history on earth, when the faithful of all ages would reappear *by resurrection,* to participate in the glories of the new Messianic era *on earth.*

A non-biblical view of the future, divorced from the land and the earth, was promoted by Gentiles who dominated the post-biblical Church and were unsympathetic with the heritage of Israel, for whom the expectation to be "next year in Jerusalem" was their deepest aspiration. The effects of the loss of the land promise in Christianity have been devastating. A major disruption occurred when the faith was severed from its roots in the Abrahamic covenant which guaranteed a restored Eden. To lose sight of God's promise to Abraham is to strike at the heart of biblical faith and the divine Plan. It was like canceling the American Constitution or abolishing the British monarchy.

In direct contradiction to Jesus, gentilized Christianity has to this day substituted "heaven" for dying souls for the biblical promise of life in the land on a renewed earth. The message of Jesus' famous beatitude, "Blessed are the meek, for they are going to have the land [or earth] as their inheritance" (Matt. 5:5), faces constant opposition in sermon and funeral service announcing that the dead have "gone to heaven." Gentile antipathy to the covenant made by the One God with Abraham has rendered large parts of the Bible meaningless to churchgoers. The whole framework of Jesus' teaching is dismantled, since it relies for its basic terms of reference on the divine promises made to the fathers of Israel. All the major doctrines of the faith are adversely affected by this wholesale departure from the roots of Christianity, which was the religion of a Jew and Christian, Jesus, the rightful claimant to Messiahship as defined by the text of Scripture.

The "murder of the [Old Testament biblical] text"[11] by critical scholarship has been equally responsible for the suppression of the covenant-hope of "life in the land." Fragmenting the Hebrew Bible in the interests of a theory of composition, scholarship lost sight of what James Dunn has called the Pauline presupposition about the authority of Scripture, "that a single mind and purpose [God's] inspired the several writings [the Bible]."[12] After nearly two thousand years of uncomprehending Gentile opposition, the promise to Abraham of progeny, blessing, greatness, and land must be reinstated in the churches' teaching as the coherent and unifying theme of biblical faith in God and Christ and the essential core of the Christian Gospel about the Kingdom of God. There could be no greater rallying point for fragmented Christendom. No other theme than that which ties together all of divine revelation can provide the churches with the unified Message they so desperately need.

The Gospel as Jesus and the Apostles proclaimed it rests on the oath-bound covenant with Abraham that in association with Christ all the faithful of all the nations will be gathered together at the resurrection to possess the land forever. In the words of Jesus: "Many will come from the north, south, east and west and sit down with Abraham, Isaac, Jacob and all the prophets at the banquet table in the

[11] *The Gospel and the Land*, p. 48. Cp. Jesus' observation that apostate Israel had murdered the prophets (Matt. 23:31).

[12] *Romans, Word Biblical Commentary*, Dallas: Word Books, 1988, p. 202.

Kingdom of God" (Matt. 8:11; Luke 13:28, 29). Together as members of the Messianic community drawn from all colors and races they will "rule as kings *upon the earth*" (Rev. 5:10), which is what Jesus meant by "inheriting the earth." In so speaking Jesus was simply echoing the ancient promise to the faithful that God would "exalt them to inherit the land" (Ps. 37:34). Jesus is clearly a prophet of restoration, seeing Himself as the agent of God commissioned to head up the divine operation for the rescue of man from the tyranny and deception of the Devil.

The writer to the Hebrews spoke of attaining the "future inhabited earth" (Heb. 2:5). This goal set before Christians was the "greatness" or "importance" of salvation which at all costs should not be neglected: "How shall we escape if we disregard so great a salvation...For God did not put the coming society on earth under the authority of angels" but the Son of Man (Heb. 2:3, 5).[13] The Son of Man was a title not only for Jesus but for the saints corporately (Dan. 7:14; cp. vv. 18, 22, 27). The New Testament thus expects the prophecies of Daniel to come true. The time is coming when "the saints possess the Kingdom" and "all nations serve and obey them" (Dan. 7:22, 27). Such is the logical outworking of the promise made to Abraham, the key to the secret of God's activity in human history.

Resistance to the Covenant

The results of traditional theology's attempts to avoid the uncomfortable political element in salvation can be illustrated by the remarks of the *Pulpit Commentary* on Genesis 13:14-17. The problem for the commentator, who sees no relevance in the land promises for Christians, is to reconcile God's declaration, "I will give the land to you [Abraham]" with the assertion made by Stephen that God

> did not give Abraham any inheritance [in the land of Palestine] — not even a square foot of land, but He promised to give it to him as a possession [*kataschesis*; cp. LXX Gen. 17:8, "everlasting possession"] and to his descendants with him (Acts 7:5).

How is the apparent contradiction to be resolved? The *Pulpit Commentary* makes two attempts to solve the difficulty. Firstly, a

---

[13] A most unfortunate paragraph break between vv. 4 and 5 in many Bibles destroys the connection between salvation and supervising the future world order.

retranslation so that the promise in Genesis 13:15 reads: "To you I will give the land, that is to say, to your descendants." In this way the failure of Abraham ever to receive the land personally will be explained: God promised it only to his descendants, Israel, and they received it under Joshua. But this is no answer to the problem. Throughout God's dealings with Abraham the promise of land to the Patriarch himself is made repeatedly. Genesis 13:17 reads: "Walk through the length and breadth of the land; to you I will give it." Abraham would have every right to complain if this were to mean that he personally should not expect to inherit the promised land!

The commentary offers a second way round the difficulty. It maintains that the land did in fact become Abraham's possession during his lifetime. "The land was really given to Abram as a nomadic chief, in the sense that he peacefully lived for many years, grew old, and died within its borders." This, however, is to contradict the emphatic biblical assertions that Abraham definitely did not possess the land, certainly not forever:

> And I will establish My covenant between Me and you and your descendants after you in their generations to be their God to you and your seed after you. And I will give to you and to your seed after you the land in which you are a stranger — all the land of Canaan for an everlasting possession (Gen. 17:7, 8).

These, then, are the biblical premises: Abraham is to gain possession of the land forever. He lived out his life as a stranger owning none of the land except for a small piece of property bought from the Hittites as a burial site for Sarah (Gen. 23:3-20). Abraham himself confessed to the Hittite inhabitants of Canaan: "I am an alien and a stranger among you" (Gen. 23:4). Stephen's observation was correct: "God gave Abraham no inheritance here [in Palestine], not even a foot of ground. But God promised him that he and his descendants after him would possess the land" (Acts 7:5).

How then is the covenant grant of land to Abraham, Isaac and Jacob to be realized? The answer provides a key to the Christian faith. There is only one way in which the covenant promises can become historical reality — by the future return to life of Abraham and the faithful by resurrection from the dead. The restoring of the patriarchs to life will bring them their cherished desire and reward, to join the Messiah and His followers in the renewed land of Palestine, thus becoming executives with Jesus of the Kingdom of God. All this is implied in Jesus' announcement of the Gospel.

To the Land of Promise Via Resurrection

The absolute necessity for resurrection in the divine Plan was the point of Jesus' important exchange with the religious teachers of his day. (One might expect He would have much to say to theologians on the same topic in the twentieth century.) The Sadducees did not believe in any resurrection and thus denied the covenant hope of life in the land for the faithful. Jesus' response to their defective understanding of the divine Plan involved a stern rebuke that they had departed from God's revelation:

> You are in error because you do not know the Scripture or the power of God. At the resurrection people will neither marry nor be given in marriage; they will be like the angels in heaven. But about the resurrection of the dead, have you not read what God said to you: "I am the God of Abraham, the God of Isaac and the God of Jacob?" He is not the God of the dead but of the living (Matt. 22:29-32).

The logic of Jesus' argument was simply that since Abraham, Isaac and Jacob had long been dead, there must be a future resurrection to restore them to life, so that their relationship with the living God could be resumed and they could receive what the covenant had guaranteed them. On no account is Jesus' answer to be used as a justification for believing that the patriarchs were *already* alive. The issue between Jesus and His opponents was whether there would be a future resurrection. Jesus argued that the covenant would fail if the patriarchs were left in their graves. For God to be God of the living, the patriarchs must rise to life again in the future resurrection (Dan 12:2).

The book of Hebrews pursues exactly the same line of argument as it expounds the drama of Abraham's faith in the great promises of God. The mystery of Abraham's failure to attain his place in the land forever can be solved only by a decisive intervention in the future by which he would be restored to life. In the course of his discussion, the writer makes statements flatly contradictory to traditional ideas about an afterlife in "heaven." "By faith Abraham, when called to go to *a place* which he would later receive as *his inheritance*..." (Heb. 8:11).

So the story begins. Abraham's inheritance, we observe, is to be the place to which he was invited to go, i.e., the geographical Canaan. This is exactly what the Genesis account describes. That very land, according to the New Testament Christian writer, Abraham was destined to receive "later," but how much later we are not yet told. The writer continues: "By faith Abraham *made his home in the land of the promise* like a stranger in a foreign country; he lived in tents as did Isaac and Jacob who were heirs with him of the same promise" (Heb. 11:9). Abraham, Isaac and Jacob and other heroes of faith "died in faith not having received the things promised; they only saw them and welcomed them from a distance and admitted that they were aliens and strangers *in the land*" (Heb. 11:13). A wrong impression is given by our versions when they translate "in the land" as "on the earth."[14] This might suggest that the patriarchs shared the traditional notion of "heaven" as their destiny. The point, however, is that people who say that they are aliens in the land "show that they are looking for a country of their own" (Heb. 11:14), namely the same land renewed under the promised government of the Messiah, the Kingdom of God.

The much overlooked truth about the land promise for Christians has been rescued by George Wesley Buchanan:

> This promise-rest-inheritance was inextricably tied to the land of Canaan, which is the place where the Patriarchs wandered as sojourners (11:13). It was called the land of the promise (11:9) and the heavenly country (11:16)...This does not mean that it is not on earth any more than the sharers in the heavenly calling (3:1) who had tasted the heavenly gift (6:4) were not those who lived on earth. Indeed, it was the very land on which the patriarchs dwelt as "strangers and wanderers" (11:13). ["Heavenly"] means that it is a divine land which God himself has promised.[15]

"Heaven" Will Be on Earth

Traditional explanations of these verses attempt to evade the implications of Hebrews 11:8, 9. "Heaven" as the reward of the faithful will not fit with this plain biblical statement that Abraham

---

[14] See the remarks of G.W. Buchanan, *Anchor Bible, To the Hebrews*, Doubleday and Co., 1972, pp. 193, 194.

[15] *Ibid.*, pp. 192, 194.

was expecting to inherit the very land he had lived in. Abraham was obviously resident in a geographical location on earth, and he anticipated returning to that land and possessing it. "He made his home in the land of the promise" (Heb. 11:9). The Promised Land for the faithful is to be on this planet — our own earth renewed and restored. It will not do to argue that Canaan was a "type" of heaven as a place for departed souls at death. Such an idea has invaded Christianity from the world of Greek philosophy and obstructs belief in the Bible's promise of an inheritance in the land of life, Palestine as the center of the future Messianic world order. Resurrection in the future at the return of Jesus is the only path by which the patriarchs can achieve their goal and possess the land which they have never owned. Indeed, as Hebrews emphasizes, none of the distinguished faithful ever "received what had been promised" — the inheritance of the Promised Land (Heb. 11:13, 39). They died in faith, a virtue closely linked to hope, fully confident of the resurrection which would bring them into possession of the land with the Messiah. This is a very far cry from the idea, which so many have accepted under the pressure of post-biblical Gentile tradition, that the patriarchs and subsequent believers have already gained a reward in heaven.

Paul and Abraham

Paul treats the story of Abraham as the model of Christian faith with no hint that Abraham's inheritance is different from that of every Christian believer. In fact, the very opposite is true: Abraham is "the father of all who believe" (Rom. 4:11). Abraham demonstrated the essence of Christian faith by being willing to believe God's Plan to grant him land, progeny and blessing forever. Faith for Abraham was an eager response to the divine initiative expressed in words. It is precisely that kind of faith which Jesus demands with His summons to "repent and believe in the Gospel of the Kingdom" (Mark 1:14, 15). Jesus is thus the exponent *par excellence* of Abrahamic Faith. He gives up everything, including His life, for the cause of God's grand design for the rescue of fallen mankind, and He calls on His supporters to do the same. Following the example of Abraham, who was willing to give up even family for the divine cause (Gen. 12:1), Jesus invited His followers to recognize the prior claims of the family of faith. His real relatives were not His blood brothers and sisters but "those who hear the Word of God [the Gospel of the Kingdom, Matt. 13:19] and do it" (Matt. 12:46-50). Loyalty to Jesus and the Gospel supersedes the claims of family and country (Luke 14:26, 27, 33; Cp. Gen. 12:1).

Justification — coming into a right relationship with God — includes an intelligent grasp of God's Plan, believing like Abraham in what God has promised to do (Rom. 4:3, 13). The scope of the Gospel Message is wider than just an acceptance of the death and resurrection of Christ. Apostolic faith invites participation in the ongoing divine Plan in history which we might call "Operation Kingdom." It involves grasping the divinely revealed *future* as the goal of the Christian venture. Grasping what God is doing in world history enables a man to attune his life to God within the teaching of Jesus as both the prophet and the king of the Kingdom. A Christian according to Paul is one who "follows in the footsteps of the faith of our father Abraham" (Rom. 3:12). The link with the patriarchal covenant could not be clearer. Abraham's faith "was characterized by (or based on) a hope which was determined solely by the promise of God...Abraham's faith was firm confidence in God as the one who determines the future according to what he has promised."[16] So Jesus and the Apostles invite us, with the Message of the Kingdom,[17] to preparation for the great event which is nothing less than the final outcome of the covenant made with Abraham and his (spiritual) offspring. Paul defines that promise and specifies the Christian objective. He reminds us that Abraham was to be "heir of the world" (Rom. 4:13), which is simply to repeat the promise of Jesus that "the meek are to inherit the land [or earth]" (Matt. 5:5; cp. Gen. 17:8).

As James Dunn says:

> The idea of "inheritance" was a fundamental part of Jewish understanding of their covenant relationship with God, above all, indeed almost exclusively, in connection *with the land* — the land of Canaan theirs by right of inheritance as promised to Abraham...[This] is one of the most emotive themes in Jewish national self-identity...Central to Jewish self-understanding was the conviction that Israel was the Lord's inheritance...Integral to the national faith was the conviction that God had given Israel the

---

[16] *Commentary on Romans*, p. 219.
[17] Mark 1:14, 15; Acts 8:12; 19:8; 28:23, 31.

inheritance of Palestine, the promised land. It is this axiom which Paul evokes and *refers to the new Christian movement as a whole, Gentiles as well as Jews.* They are heirs of God. Israel's special relationship with God has been extended to all in Christ. And the promise of the land has been transformed into the promise of the Kingdom...That inheritance of the Kingdom, full citizenship under the rule of God alone, is something still awaited by believers.[18]

It is easy to see how devastating to New Testament Christianity any severing of the link between Christ and the Abrahamic covenant will be. While Jesus and the Apostles labored to proclaim the Gospel of the Kingdom as the essence of the unfolding covenant guarantees given to Israel and now extended to all believers, traditional Christianity has interfered with this principal biblical thesis. It has promoted a goal in "heaven" which makes impossible or pointless the fulfillment of the land promise confirmed by Jesus (Matt. 5:5; Rev. 5:10). Our fathers are not in heaven and never expected to be. They looked forward, as did New Testament Christians, to entering and inheriting the land of promise, the Kingdom of God on earth, by resurrection from the dead. This reentry into the land of Canaan renewed would mean the recovery of divine rule on earth, the reversal of the disaster which had overcome mankind from the beginning. For this "joy which lay before Him" the Messiah had died at the hands of His own unbelieving people (Heb. 12:2). For this inheritance, granting the right to rule in the Kingdom, the early Christians suffered as part of their preparation for kingship. Having embraced the Message of the Kingdom they strove to be "worthy of God who calls us into His Kingdom and glory" (I Thess. 2:12). The path to glory was not easy. "It is through much tribulation that we must enter the Kingdom" (Acts 14:22), that is, attain to kingship with Jesus in the coming new government.

Again we must insist on the direct link between early Christianity and the covenant with Abraham. As Dunn says:

The degree to which Paul's argument is determined by the current self-understanding of his own people is clearly indicated by his careful wording which picks up four key elements in that self-understanding: the covenant promise to Abraham and his seed, the

---

[18] *Romans, Word Biblical Commentary*, pp. 213, 463, emphasis added.

inheritance of the land as its central element...It had become almost a commonplace of Jewish teaching that the covenant promised that Abraham's seed would inherit the earth...The promise thus interpreted was fundamental to Israel's self-consciousness as God's covenant people: It was the reason why God had chosen them in the first place from among all the nations of the earth, the justification for holding themselves distinct from other nations, and the comforting hope that made their current national humiliation endurable...

Paul's case reveals the strong continuity he saw between his faith and the fundamental promise of his people's Scriptures...Paul had no doubt that the Gospel he proclaimed was a continuation and fulfillment of God's promise to Abraham. But he was equally clear that the heirs of Abraham's promise were no longer to be identified in terms of the law. For Genesis 15:6 showed with sufficient clarity that the promise was given and accepted through faith, quite apart from the law in whole or in part.[19]

The point to be grasped is that Paul does not question the content of the promise. How could he without overthrowing the whole revelation given by the Bible? The territorial promise was clearly and repeatedly spelled out in the Genesis account and was his people's most cherished national treasure. To faithful Israel, represented first by Abraham, God had given assurance that they would inherit the land as a restored paradise. The glory of Paul's ministry is to introduce a revolutionary new fact — that this grand prospect is open to all who believe in the Messiah as the seed of Abraham and the one who would head up the new administration of the Kingdom. It was obviously to Messiah that the promises were made as the distinguished descendant of Abraham. But Gentile Christians, upon accepting the claims of Jesus as the Christ of Israel, may acquire a full share in the same promised inheritance. Paul reaches a triumphant moment in his argument when he declares to his Gentile readers that "if you are a Christian you count as Abraham's descendants and are heirs [of the world, Rom. 4:13] according to the promise [made to Abraham]" (Gal. 3:29).

---

[19] *Ibid.*, pp. 233, 234.

The promises are sure, however, only, as Paul says, to "those who are of the faith of Abraham" (Rom. 4:16), i.e., those whose faith is of the same type as his, resting on the same divine arrangements. Hence Paul speaks of the need for Christians to become "sons of Abraham" (Gal. 3:7), "seed of Abraham" (Gal. 3:2; Rom. 4:16), and to reckon Abraham as their spiritual father (Rom. 4:11), to walk in his steps (Rom. 4:12), and consider him a model of Christian faith (Gal. 3:9), because the Gospel had been preached to him in advance (Gal. 3:8). But how much do we hear today about the Christian Gospel having its basis in the covenant promises made to Abraham? Paul speaks to the Galatian church about the "blessing of Abraham" now made available to all in Christ. This phrase is quoted from Genesis 28:4 where it is defined. It means "to take possession of the land where you now live as aliens, the land God gave to Abraham." Once again an illuminating link is made between the Hebrew Bible and New Testament Christianity providing a wonderful basis for restructuring the present fragmented Church on a biblical foundation.

Never for a moment did Paul abandon the roots of the faith revealed in God's dealings with Abraham. Since the Promised Land of Canaan would one day be the center of the Messianic government it was obvious that inheritance of the land implied inheritance of the world. The promise remains geographical and territorial, related to the earth of the coming age, and corresponding exactly with Jesus' affirmation of His Jewish heritage when He promised the meek (again quoting the Hebrew Bible) the inheritance of the earth/land (Matt. 5:5, citing Ps. 37:11). Jesus believed that Jerusalem would yet be worthy of the title City of the Great King (Matt. 5:35) and that believers would supervise a new world order with Him.[20] In short the promise of the land is repeated in the New Testament as the promise of the Kingdom of God, which is the basis of the Christian Gospel. The Kingdom is offered to believers as their destiny. It is the renewed "inhabited earth of the future" (Heb. 2:5), which is not to be subject to angels but to the Messiah and the saints, the "Israel of God" (Gal. 6:16), "the true circumcision" (Phil. 3:3). Much of the excitement of New Testament Christians lies in the high privilege extended to them as the people of God in Christ. Their hope corresponds exactly with

---

[20] Matt. 19:28; Luke 22:28-30; Rev. 2:26; 3:21; 5:10; 20:1-6.

the hope of the prophets of Israel. J. Skinner observes that "the main point [of Jeremiah's hope for the future] is that in some sense a restoration of the Israelite nationality was the form in which he conceived the Kingdom of God."[21] Jesus, who also considered Himself to be a prophet (Luke 13:33), would have agreed.

Paul's application of the Abrahamic covenant to Christians, both Jews and Gentiles, does not lead him to think that unconverted Israel will remain forever outside the divine blessing in Christ. In Romans 11:25, 26 he looked forward, as an important element in the future development of the Kingdom, to a collective conversion of a remnant of the nation of Israel at the Second Coming.[22] The Jew/Gentile Church, however, in Paul's thinking, would be leaders in the Messianic Kingdom (I Cor. 6:2; II Tim. 2:12; I Cor. 4:8). In this way the Abrahamic covenant guarantees a part in the Messiah's rule for all those who now believe the Gospel, and it assures us that there will, in addition, be a further wave of conversion when national Israel finally accepts her Messiah. To that event the Apostles rightly looked forward when, in a final conversation with the departing Jesus, they asked: "Has the time now arrived for the restoration of the Kingdom to Israel?" (Acts 1:6). For those who have not had the benefit of a Calvinist training this question will present no problem. After all, if you have been told by Jesus that you are going to administer the twelve tribes (Luke 22:28-30), you would anticipate with some eagerness the restoration of those tribes in the Kingdom. Mention of the Holy Spirit (Acts 1:5), which was the endowment of royalty and priests, very naturally prompted the Apostles' keen interest in the dénouement of the Plan of salvation. But note carefully: the coming of the Spirit was not the coming of the Kingdom (Acts 1:5-7)

Worldwide Inheritance

It was common to Jewish thinking and to Paul, as well as to the whole New Testament, that the whole world was to benefit from the Messianic promise made to Abraham that he would "inherit the world" (Rom. 4:13) by inheriting the promised land. This fact can be seen from both biblical and extra-biblical texts. A celebrated

---

[21] *Prophecy and Religion*, Cambridge University Press, 1922, p. 308.
[22] Micah 2:12 envisages the restoration of "all of Jacob" as "the remnant of Israel."

Messianic Psalm, which Jesus in His Revelation interprets as a Christian prophecy for Himself and the Church (Rev. 1:1), is demonstrably a political Psalm outlining the career of the Messiah:

> I have installed My King on Zion...Ask of Me [God] and I will make the nations Your [Messiah's] inheritance and the ends of the earth Your possession. You will rule them with an iron scepter; you will dash them to pieces like pottery.[23]

> May [God] strengthen you, and may you inherit all the earth (Jub. 22:14).

> And there will be kings from you [Jacob]. They will rule everywhere that the tracks of mankind have been trod. And I will give your seed all the land under heaven [cp. Dan. 7:27: "the kingdom under the whole heaven"], and they will rule in all nations as they have desired (Jub. 32:19).

> But to the elect there shall be light, joy, and peace, and they shall inherit the earth (I Enoch 5:7).

> The righteous...are confident of the world which You have promised to them with an expectation full of joy (II Bar. 14:12, 13).

> The righteous will receive the world that is promised to them (II Bar. 51:3).

> If the world has indeed been created for us, why do we not possess our world as an inheritance? How long will this be so? (IV Ezra 6:59).

The poignant New Testament answer to this Jewish question is that the people of the covenant have not, as a whole, accepted the one claiming to be their Messiah. (How much a distorted traditional Gentile Christianity may be to blame for this is a matter for serious consideration.) Paul is hopeful that many of his compatriots will finally recognize the returning Jesus. Meanwhile he continues to propagate the Message of the Messiah by which first Jew and then Gentile is invited into the Messianic community preparing to rule in

---

[23] Ps. 2:6, applied to Jesus in Rev. 12:5 and the Church in Rev. 2:26, 27.

the Kingdom. Pauline theology is born of the conviction that Abraham was designated "heir of the world" (Rom. 4:13), an idea which fits naturally into the texts just cited. Henry Alford comments on the connection between Paul's aspirations and Jewish hopes:

> The rabbis already had seen, and Paul who had been brought up in their learning, held fast to the truth, that much more was intended in the words "in thee or in thy seed shall all families of the earth be blessed," than the mere possession of Canaan. They distinctly trace the gift of the world to this promise [Gen. 12:3]. The inheritance of the world...is that ultimate lordship over the whole world which Abraham, as the father of the faithful in all peoples, and Christ, as the Seed of the promise, shall possess...[24]

A distinguished German commentator notes that to be "seed of Abraham" meant that one was destined to have "dominion over the world," based on Genesis 22:17: "Your descendants shall gain possession of the gates [i.e., towns] of their enemies."[25] With this promise in mind, Jesus envisages the faithful assuming authority over urban populations: "Well done, loyal servant, assume responsibility for ten cities" (Luke 19:17).

The *International Critical Commentary* on Romans 4:13 catches the flavor of Old Testament anticipation of the Messianic Kingdom. It speaks of the promise that Abraham's seed (in Christ) should "enjoy worldwide dominion," "the right to universal dominion which will belong to the Messiah and His people," and "the promise made to Abraham and his descendants of worldwide Messianic rule."[26] Something of the fervor of Israel for the land may be seen in the 14th and 18th Benedictions repeated in the synagogue since AD 70:

> Be merciful, O Lord our God, in Thy great mercy towards Israel Thy people and towards Jerusalem, and towards Zion the abiding place of Thy glory, and towards Thy temple and Thy habitation, and towards the Kingdom of the house of David, the builder of Jerusalem Thy city. Bestow Thy peace upon Israel, Thy people and

---

[24] *Greek New Testament*, London: Rivingtons and Deighton, Bell & Co., 1861, Vol. II, p. 350.

[25] H.A.W. Meyer, *Commentary on John*, Funk and Wagnalls, 1884, p. 277.

[26] W. Sanday and A.C. Headlam, *Epistle to the Romans*, T & T Clark, 1905, pp. 109, 111.

upon Thy city and upon Thine inheritance, and bless us, all of us together. Blessed art Thou, O Lord, who makest peace.

Even when the land is not mentioned directly, it is implied in the city and the temple which became the quintessence of the hope of salvation. Exactly the same hope is reflected in the New Testament, binding early Christianity to its Abrahamic/Davidic origins in the Hebrew Bible:

> The Lord God will give [Jesus] the throne of His father David, and He will reign over the house of Jacob forever; and His Kingdom will never end (Luke 1:32, 33).

> [God] has helped His servant Israel, remembering to be merciful to Abraham and his descendants forever, even as He said to our fathers (Luke 1:55).

> [God] has raised up a horn [political dominion] in the house of His servant David…to show mercy to our fathers and to remember His holy covenant, the oath which He swore to our father Abraham (Luke 1:69, 72, 73).

> [Simeon] was waiting for the consolation of Israel (Luke 2:25).

> [Anna] gave thanks to God and spoke about the child to all who were looking forward to redemption in Jerusalem (Luke 2:38).

> Blessed is the coming Kingdom of our father David (Mark 11:10).

> Joseph of Arimathea [a disciple of Jesus, i.e., a Christian, Matt. 27:57], a prominent member of the Council…, was himself waiting for the Kingdom of God (Mark 15:43).

> We [disciples of Jesus, i.e., Christians] had hoped that [Jesus] was the one who was going to redeem Israel (Luke 24:21).

> The Apostles asked: "Is this the time that you are going to restore the Kingdom to Israel?" (Acts 1:6).

> It is because of my hope in what God promised our fathers that I am on trial today. This is the promise our twelve tribes are hoping to

see fulfilled as they earnestly serve God day and night (Acts 26:6, 7).

The evidence is overwhelming that New Testament Christianity has not abandoned the territorial hopes of the prophets. The disciples' question about the restoration of Israel arises out of a forty-day period of instruction on the Kingdom of God (Acts 1:3, 6). On trial for his faith, Paul publicly defined Christianity as hope for the fulfillment of the patriarchal promise. He expressly identifies this Christian objective as the promise "to which our twelve tribes hope to attain" (Acts 26:7). The nature of this expectation is defined by a rabbinical saying of the third century, reflecting the ancient prospect of life in the land: "Why did the patriarchs long for burial in the land of Israel? Because the dead of the land of Israel will be the first to be resurrected in the days of the Messiah and to enjoy the years of the Messiah."[27]

Heaven as the Storehouse of a Future Reward

References to "heaven" in the New Testament are limited to contexts in which the future reward of believers is said to be preserved now as treasure with God in heaven (Matt. 5:12).[28] "Heaven" as a place removed from the earth is, however, never in Scripture the destination of the believer — neither at death nor at the resurrection. Christians must now grasp what is promised to them. They must store up treasure with God and expect to receive their reward when Jesus brings it to the earth at His Second Coming. A man may save his money for retirement in a bank. He does not, however, retire in the bank.

When Paul speaks of the "Jerusalem above which is our mother" (Gal. 4:26), he does not mean that Christians go to "heaven" at death. He is quoting a Messianic Psalm which describes Zion (Jerusalem) as "the mother of us all" (Ps. 87:5, LXX). As often in Jewish thinking, the good things of the future are said to be stored with God now in preparation for their revelation on the day of the Messiah's appearance in power and glory. Christians are those whose names are

---

[27] *Gen. Rabbah*, 96:5.

[28] The text reads "your reward is great in heaven." The Christian reward is preserved in heaven and it will come from heaven with Jesus at His return. "In heaven" is equivalent to "with God."

inscribed in the roll of those who will be given "life in Jerusalem" (Isa. 4:3).

Paul speaks of "the faith and love which spring from the hope that is *stored up for you in heaven* and that you have already heard about in the word of truth, the Gospel" (Col. 1:5). Peter sees in the new birth produced by the Gospel a "living hope through the resurrection of Jesus Christ from the dead [leading to] an inheritance [i.e., of the Kingdom] that can never perish, spoil or fade, *kept in heaven for you*, who through faith are shielded by God's power until the coming of salvation that is ready to be revealed in the last time" (I Pet. 1:3-5). The New Testament is consistent with its underlying theme, the Gospel of the Kingdom "promised to those who love God" (James 2:5). Belief in the Gospel in apostolic times was not confined to belief in the death and resurrection of Jesus only, but included the invitation to prepare for a place in the Messiah's worldwide dominion to be introduced at His return to the earth. The situation is very different in contemporary preaching when little or nothing is preached about inheriting the earth with Jesus. There is an urgent need for churches to heed Paul's warning not to be "moved away from the hope held out in the Gospel" (Col. 1:23). The loss of New Testament hope can be traced to the loss of the Gospel of the Kingdom which in turn is symptomatic of the loss of the roots of Christianity in the Hebrew Bible.

Faith in God's World Plan

Nonsense is made of the New Testament scheme, and God's unfolding Plan for world history, when it is proposed that the Christian destiny is to be enjoyed in a location removed from the earth. This destroys at a blow the promises given to Abraham and the faithful that they are to inherit the land and the world. There is no resolution of the original failure of man to carry out the divine mandate to rule the world if, in fact, the world never experiences the restoration of divine rule. The Christian faith is permanently frustrated when hope for the restoration of peace on earth is denied. The substitution of "heaven" at death for the reward of inheriting the earth undermines the revelation of God's Plan for mankind. The repeated offer of "heaven" in popular preaching perpetuates a notion which confuses Bible readers and renders meaningless the whole hope of the prophets (based on the covenant) that the world is going to enjoy an unparalleled era of blessing and international peace under the just rule of the Messiah and the resurrected faithful — those who believe in "the Kingdom of God and the name [i.e., the Messiahship and all that this entails] of Jesus," and are baptized in response to that early creed in Acts 8:12: "When they believed Philip as he proclaimed the Gospel about the Kingdom of God and the name of Jesus Christ, they were being baptized, both men and women."

The text remains a model for evangelism and calls the contemporary Church back to its roots in the covenants of promise made with the "father of the faithful," which can be enjoyed only in Messiah Jesus. For the fulfillment of the divine Plan for rescue, we are to pray "Thy Kingdom come," and strive to conduct ourselves "worthy of God who is calling us into His Kingdom and glory" (I Thess. 2:12). The truth about our Christian destiny will be reinstated when we return to biblical language about "entering the Kingdom," "inheriting the Kingdom," "inheriting the earth" (Matt. 5:5), "reigning as kings on the earth" (Rev. 5:10), "reigning with the Messiah for a thousand years" (Rev. 20:1-6). The Gentile mind, which displays an anti-Semitic dislike for things Messianic, has prevailed for so long that only a revolutionary return to the text of Scripture will break our bad habits. The abandonment of language about "heaven" will set us in the right direction and teach us to love the words of Jesus. The way will then be opened for us to understand that Christianity is God's answer to the initial failure of man in Adam; that the Gospel is a call to kingship and that a saint is one appointed to rule with the Messiah on earth in the coming Kingdom (Dan. 7:18, 22, 27). The tragedy of man is of kingship lost. The goal of man is kingship regained in association with the great King Messiah who has pioneered the way to victory over the world. Henry Alford's comment is a much-needed corrective, summoning us to return to biblical Hebrew Christianity: "The general tenor of prophecy and the analogy of the divine dealings point unmistakably to this earth purified and renewed, and *not to the heavens* in any ordinary sense of the term, as the eternal habitation of the blessed."[29]

---

[29] *Greek New Testament*, Vol. I, pp. 35, 36, emphasis added.

Alford's keen insight reinstates the hope for the future of mankind when the blessings granted to Abraham find their fulfillment in the Kingdom. Jacob and Paul shared the same cheering outlook: "May God give you *the blessing of Abraham* my father, to you and to your seed with you — the inheritance of the land in which you now reside as a foreigner, the land which God gave to Abraham" (Gen. 28:4). "*The blessing of Abraham* [will come] to the Gentiles in Christ" (Gal. 3:14).

Hope for mankind based on God's gracious dealings with Abraham was the dominant theme of all the prophets of Israel. In order to follow Jesus, the greatest of all the prophets (Deut. 18:15, 18; Acts 3:22; 7:37), Son of God, Christ, and the Apostle of our faith (Heb. 3:1), we must now turn our attention to their vision.

5. The Gospel of the Kingdom in the Prophets: The Unfulfilled Dream of Messianic Government

A large portion of the message of the prophets is devoted to descriptions of the coming Kingdom of God. There is not the slightest doubt as to the meaning of these glowing accounts of the Messiah's future worldwide empire:

> For to us a child is born, to us a Son is given; and the government will be upon His shoulder...Of the increase of His government and of peace there will be no end, upon the throne of David, and over His Kingdom, to establish it, and to uphold it with justice and with righteousness from this time forth and forevermore (Isa. 9:6, 7, RSV).

> He [the Messiah] will speak to the nations; and His dominion will be from sea to sea and from the River [Euphrates] to the ends of the earth (Zech. 9:10, NASV).

The appointed ruler will be characterized by "the spirit of wisdom and understanding, the spirit of counsel and strength, the spirit of knowledge and the fear of the Lord. And His delight shall be in the fear of the Lord" (Isa. 11:2, 3, RSV). With Him, "princes will rule in justice" (Isa. 32:1, RSV), a prediction which provides the framework of the whole New Testament idea that Christians are kings in training.[1] The Messiah's perfect government will bring about a new

---

[1] II Tim. 2:12; I Cor. 6:2; Rev. 1:6; 5:10. Cp. Exod. 19:6.

era of freedom from bodily disease. It will produce a joyous humanity with blessings extending even to the inanimate creation.

> The wilderness and the dry land shall be glad, the desert shall rejoice and blossom; like the crocus it shall blossom abundantly, and rejoice with joy and singing. The glory of Lebanon shall be given to it, the majesty of Carmel and Sharon. They shall see the glory of the Lord, the majesty of our God...Then the eyes of the blind shall be opened, and the ears of the deaf unstopped; then shall the lame man leap like a hart, and the tongue of the dumb sing for joy. For waters shall break forth in the wilderness, and streams in the desert; the burning sand shall become a pool, and the thirsty ground springs of water...And the ransomed of the Lord shall return, and come to Zion with singing, with everlasting joy upon their heads; they shall obtain joy and gladness, and sorrow and sighing shall flee away (Isa. 35:1, 2, 5-7, 10, RSV).

Isaiah 40:9 foresees a time in the future when "the Lord God will come with might, with His arm ruling for Him." The executive of this great work of restoration will be a human king, descended from David. His extraordinary gifts will equip Him to rule with perfect justice:

> A shoot will spring from the stock of Jesse, a new shoot will grow from his roots. On Him will rest the spirit of Yahweh, the spirit of wisdom and insight, the spirit of counsel and power, the spirit of knowledge and fear of Yahweh: His inspiration will lie in fearing Yahweh. His judgment will not be by appearances, His verdict not given on hearsay. He will judge the weak with integrity and give fair sentence for the humble in the land. He will strike the country with the rod of His mouth and with the breath of His lips bring death to the wicked.[2] Uprightness will be the belt around His waist, and constancy the belt about His hips (Isa. 11:1-5, New Jerusalem Bible).

Under the just rule of the future King even the nature of animals will be transformed:

> The wolf lives with the lamb, the panther lies down with the kid, calf and cub feed together with a little boy to lead them. The cow

---

[2] Isa. 11:4 (LXX) has "the wicked one," and Paul applies this to a single Antichrist (II Thess. 2:8. Cp. I John 2:18).

and the bear make friends, their young lie down together. The lion eats straw like an ox. The infant plays over the cobra's hole; into the viper's lair the young child puts his hand. They do no hurt, no harm, on all my holy mountain, for the country is filled with knowledge of Yahweh as the waters swell the sea (Isa. 11:6-9, Jerusalem Bible).

The peaceful Kingdom will be established on the ruins of former evil governments:

Once the oppression is over, and the destroyer is no more, and those now trampling the country under foot have gone away, the throne will be made secure in gentleness, and on it there will sit in all fidelity, within the tent of David, a judge careful for justice and eager for integrity (Isa. 16:4, 5, Jerusalem Bible).

The triumph of the Kingdom will mean the banishment of all hostile forces: "That Day, Yahweh will punish above, the armies of the sky, below, the kings of the earth; they will be herded together, shut up in a dungeon, confined in a prison and, after long years, punished" (Isa. 24:21, 22, Jerusalem Bible). Whereupon the glorious Kingdom will appear: "The moon will hide her face, the sun be ashamed, for Yahweh Sabaoth [the Lord of the armies of heaven] will be king on Mount Zion, in Jerusalem" (Isa. 16:23, Jerusalem Bible).

The time will come for God to reassert His sovereignty on earth in the person of His chosen king: "Behold, a king will reign righteously, and princes will rule justly. And each will be like a refuge from the wind, and a shelter from the storm, like streams of water in a dry country, like the shade of a huge rock in a parched land" (Isa. 32:1-2, NASV).

The Old Testament (which more appropriately we should know as the Hebrew Scriptures) speaks often of a great crisis in human history. By a stupendous divine intervention the God of creation will bring to a dramatic close the present era of human misrule and initiate a new government on earth. A number of master texts summarize the hope presented by the prophets of Israel as they pointed to a brand new world epoch:

The God of heaven will set up a Kingdom which will never be destroyed...It will shatter and absorb all the previous kingdoms, and itself last forever (Dan. 2:44, Jerusalem Bible).

A throne will even be established in lovingkindness and a judge will sit on it in faithfulness in the tent of David; moreover He [the Messiah] will seek justice and be prompt in righteousness (Isa. 16:5, NASV).

At that time they shall call Jerusalem "the throne of the Lord" and all the nations will be gathered to it, to Jerusalem, for the name of the Lord; nor shall they walk anymore after the stubbornness of their evil heart (Jer. 3:17, NASV).

And the kingdom and the dominion and the greatness of the kingdoms under the whole heaven shall be given to the people of the saints of the Most High; their Kingdom shall be an everlasting Kingdom and all dominions shall serve and obey them (Dan. 7:27, RSV).[3]

Jesus' Intensified Messianic Hope

The announcement that the Kingdom of God was "at hand" (Mark 1:14, 15; Matt. 3:2; 4:17, etc.) and that men should respond by believing the Good News about the Kingdom (Mark 1:15) challenged Jesus' audiences to understand that their national hopes were to be realized. Jesus did not say when the Kingdom of God would arrive. The announcement that it was "at hand" meant, as it had meant in the same words used by the prophets centuries earlier,[4] that men should prepare for its arrival with the greatest urgency. Jesus' concept of the Kingdom of God was drawn from its rich history in the recorded messages of the prophets of Israel, whose work Jesus expressly said He came not to destroy (Matt. 5:17). His proclamation of the

---

[3] The Kingdom in this verse belongs to the saints as the Messianic community in Christ. The translation "their Kingdom..." is found in the RSV, GNB, the translation by the Jewish Publication Society and the *International Critical Commentary.*

[4] The prophets had announced the "Day of the Lord" (Joel 2:11; Isa. 13:6, 9; Zeph. 1:14), referring to it often as "that day." It is the battle-day of God when He goes forth to reestablish the Kingdom. The New Testament calls the future advent of Jesus the Day of the Lord (II Thess. 2:2; cp. 1:10). The prophets describe the Day of the Lord as "near at hand and coming very quickly" (Zeph. 1:14), though it has not yet come. The prophet is projected forward into the future and sees the end as near. Both Testaments recognize the Day as the time when God punishes the evil of the world. "He arises to shake terribly the earth" (see Isa. 2:10-22).

Kingdom would call attention to the certain fulfillment of those predictions in the future: The establishment on earth of a Divine Government presided over by the ideal King of Israel, the Messiah.

That Israel was looking forward to an era of world peace under the government of the Messiah cannot reasonably be doubted. The fact is documented in hundreds of standard works on the Bible and the history of the Jewish religion. An authority on the literature of the prophets states what is clear to any who have read their writings:

> For many centuries the Jews had believed that some day in the not distant future their God, the Creator of the Universe, would manifest Himself and glorify His Name and His people Israel in the sight of all mankind. This is the essential substance of the Messianic Hope.[5]

In view of this hope the attitude of the early Christians can be stated as follows:

> Their minds were always filled with a sense of expectancy, a sense of an impending change of tremendous import in which Jesus would occupy a central and conspicuous position in the capacity of Messiah, and they, as His chosen disciples, would share in His glory.[6]

Another Old Testament scholar notes that the prophet Daniel "equates the coming kingdom with the golden age and envisages it as being established here *on earth* as the final phase of history."[7] The Kingdom would mean a restructuring of human society under a divine government operating in a renewed earth.

The Good Time Coming

One has only to glance at the subject headings given by the translators of the Jerusalem Bible to catch the flavor of the Old Testament background to Jesus' proclamation of the Kingdom of God. In the writings of the great prophet Isaiah we learn of an era of "Everlasting Peace" (Isa. 2:1-5), "The Future Restoration" (Isa. 4:4-6),

---

[5] H.D. Hamilton, *The People of God*, Oxford University Press, 1912, Vol. II, p. 19.

[6] *Ibid.*, p. 20.

[7] D.S. Russell, *Apocalyptic, Ancient and Modern*, Philadelphia: Fortress Press, 1988, p. 26.

"The Coming of the Virtuous King" (Isa. 11:1-9), "The Liberation of Israel" (Isa. 43:1-7), and "The Glorious Resurrection of Jerusalem" (Isa. 60). In Jeremiah we read of "Zion in the Messianic Age" (Jer. 3:14-18), "The Conversion of the Nations" (Jer. 16:19-21), "The Future King" (Jer. 23:1-8), "Promise of the Recovery of the Northern Kingdom of Israel" (Jer. 30), "Promise of Restoration for Judah" (Jer. 31:23-26), "Jerusalem Magnificently Rebuilt" (Jer. 31:38-40) and "The Institutions of the Future" (Jer. 33:14-26).

Ezekiel gives us a description of "Judah and Israel in One Kingdom" (Ezek. 37:15-28). Hosea speaks of "The Repentance and Reconciliation of Israel: A Promise of Future Happiness" (Hos. 14:2-10); Joel foresees "The Glorious Future of Israel" (Joel 4:18-21); Amos writes warmly about "Prospects of Restoration and Idyllic Prosperity" (Amos 9:11-15); Obadiah describes the political triumph of the Kingdom of God (Obad. 21; cp. Micah 4:1-5); finally, Zechariah provides a vivid picture of "Messianic Salvation" (Zech. 8:1-17), "The Messiah," (Zech. 9:9-10), and "The Restoration of Israel" (Zech. 9:11-17). Zechariah concludes with a description of "The Splendor of Jerusalem" (Zech. 14:1-21).

No one who has pondered this stirring vision of the future can possibly miss its point. With one accord the prophets of Israel proclaimed that there is coming on earth an era of peace and permanent security for all nations under the supervision of God's chosen agent, the promised Son of David. What Irving Zeitlin writes of Isaiah summarizes the Jewish hope of God's Kingdom on earth:

> The prophet looks forward to the end of this era and to ushering in the new, wherein arrogance, oppression, war and idolatry will all vanish together. Only after Israel has been cleansed of her haughtiness will she truly become God's people, and carry his word to the other nations. "For out of Zion shall go forth the law, and the word of the Lord from Jerusalem."[8]

We must here register our protest against the extraordinary idea that this vision of the future was fulfilled during the historical ministry of Jesus, or at any time since. It must be obvious to all that the nations have not beaten their swords into farm instruments (even professing Christians have killed each other in international wars) and that Jesus

---

[8] *Ancient Judaism*, Cambridge: Polity Press, 1988, p. 228.

as King-Messiah has not yet visibly taken up His position as ruler of the nations on the restored throne of David.[9]

Daniel's Vision of the Kingdom

The importance of the book of Daniel for Jesus' thinking needs special emphasis:

> I think there can be no doubt where Jesus Christ found and nourished His doctrine of the Kingdom. He found it in the book of Daniel, and especially in Daniel 7. There are many evidences that the book of Daniel was one of the favorite books of Jesus Christ, one of the books which He diligently and deeply studied during the years of peaceful obscurity in Nazareth before His stormy public ministry began. He makes several references to Daniel, and when the book of Daniel is once understood, it throws quite a flood of light upon the numerous parables in which our Lord described the Kingdom...He declared again and again that the Kingdom was the first object of His life to establish, and, He asserted, it ought to be the first object of our lives to promote. He summed up all our duties in the ever-memorable command to "seek first the Kingdom of God and His righteousness" (Matt. 6:33).[10]

Taking our cue from the book of Daniel, we may easily establish the fact that the Kingdom of God (or Kingdom of Heaven) is a real, external empire. Not only this, it is to be a government which will seize power suddenly and dramatically. Its administration will be in the hands of "the Son of Man" (Dan. 7:13, 14) and "the saints" (Dan. 7:27). On no account, from the evidence of Daniel, could it be an invisible reign established only in the hearts of believers. Its political dimension as well as its location on earth is unmistakably clear. It is equally obvious that the Kingdom of God described by Daniel has not yet appeared.

> And in the days of those kings, the God of heaven will establish a Kingdom [in the New Testament, the Kingdom of God or Kingdom of Heaven] which will never be destroyed, and that Kingdom will not be left for another people; it will crush and put an end to all these kingdoms, but it will itself endure forever (Dan. 2:44, NASV).

---

[9] Luke 1:32, 33; Luke 24:21; Acts 1:6; 3:21; Luke 22:28-30; Matt. 19:28; Rev. 11:15-18; 20:1-6.

In the next verse the impact of the Kingdom is likened to a stone crushing the "iron, the bronze, the clay, the silver and the gold" of former world empires. According to the prophet, whose message we are challenged to believe, "the great God has made known to the king [Nebuchadnezzar] what will take place in the future [in Hebrew, '*be acharit hayamim*,' i.e., in future Messianic times]; so the dream is true and its interpretation trustworthy" (Dan. 2:45, NASV). The Son of Man is to be appointed monarch of the divine Kingdom, sharing rulership with the saints:

> To Him [the Son of Man — Jesus' favorite self title] was given dominion, glory and a kingdom, that all the peoples, nations, and men of every language might serve Him. His dominion is an everlasting dominion, which shall not pass away; and His Kingdom is one which shall not be destroyed...And the kingdom and the dominion and the greatness of the kingdoms under the whole heaven shall be given to the people of the saints of the Most High. Their Kingdom will be an everlasting Kingdom and all dominions shall serve and obey them (Dan. 7:14, 27, RSV).

The Kingdom of God is evidently an empire, exercising sway over all nations. It will come to power on the earth ("under the whole heaven, " Dan. 7:27) and its establishment will be by a catastrophe, an international upheaval resulting in a complete political reorganization. Before its irresistible power the nations of the world will have to bow. A recurring theme of the New Testament (but infrequently preached) is that Jesus and His followers will be the executives of the new World Government — the Kingdom of God.[11] To be a saint in the New Testament is to be one appointed to rule in the coming Kingdom. As Alan Richardson says:

> *To enter the Kingdom means much more than to become a subject of God's Kingdom, it means to receive a share in God's kingship, to be one of those appointed to reign.* Jesus speaks of the poor in spirit, i.e., the Christian "hasidim" [saints] as those to whom the heavenly kingship belongs; they are the meek who, according to the prophecy of Psalm 37:11 shall inherit the earth (Matt. 5:5). As the

---

[10] H.P. Hughes, *Essential Christianity*, Isbister and Co., 1894, p. 59.
[11] Matt. 19:28; Luke 22:28-30; I Cor. 6:2; II Tim. 2:12; Rev. 2:26; 3:21; 5:10; 20:4.

old Israel obtained the inheritance of the promised land so the new Israel shall possess the earth as its inheritance...After the death of the Antichrist in Daniel 7 "judgment was given to the saints of the Most High and the time came that the saints possessed the Kingdom (malchut)."[12]

The Kingdom of God was destined to replace hostile world empires pictured by the great image of Daniel, chapter 2. The seventh chapter of Daniel provides an indispensable blueprint for the later mission of Jesus who saw His own destiny and that of the Church in the great visions granted to the prophet, who himself, foreshadowing the career of believers, both suffered at the hands of the Babylonians and later attained high office in government.

Isaiah's Hope for World Peace

The bright future is nowhere more vividly depicted than in the words of the prophet Isaiah. His vision is of

> days to come [when] the mountain of the Temple of Yahweh shall tower above the mountains and be lifted higher than the hills. All the nations will stream to it; people without number will come to it; and they will say: "Come, let us go up to the mountain of Yahweh, to the Temple of the God of Jacob that He may teach us His ways so that we may walk in His paths; since the law will go out from Zion, and the oracle of Yahweh from Jerusalem." He will wield authority over the nations and adjudicate between many peoples; these will hammer their swords into ploughshares, their spears into sickles. Nation will not lift sword against nation, there will be no more training for war. O house of Jacob, come let us walk in the light of Yahweh (Isa. 2:1-5, Jerusalem Bible).

When that new age dawns, "those who are left of Zion and remain of Jerusalem shall be called holy and those left in Jerusalem, noted down for survival" (Isa. 4:3, Jerusalem Bible). Following the cleansing of the Temple area, when

> the Lord has washed away the filth of the daughter of Zion and cleansed Jerusalem of the blood shed in her, Yahweh will come and rest on the whole stretch of Mount Zion and on those who are

---

[12] Alan Richardson, *An Introduction to the Theology of the New Testament*, pp. 86-87, emphasis added.

gathered there, a cloud by day, and smoke, and by night the brightness of a flaring fire. For, over all, the glory of Yahweh will be a canopy and a tent to give shade by day from the heat, refuge and shelter from the storm and the rain (Isa. 4:4-6, Jerusalem Bible).

The miraculous nature of the predicted Kingdom is matched by the supernatural conception of the Messiah: "The maiden will be with child and will give birth to a son whom she shall call Immanuel" (Isa. 7:14). Matthew sees in the miraculous conception of Jesus the fulfillment of the oracle delivered by Isaiah 700 years earlier. Of Mary's miraculous pregnancy he reports simply that "all this took place to fulfill the words spoken by the Lord through the prophet" (Matt. 1:22, Jerusalem Bible).

Inseparable from the greatness of the future Kingdom is the majesty of the promised King:

> For there is a child born to us, a son given to us and dominion is laid on His shoulders; and this is the name they give Him: Wonderful Counselor, Mighty God ["Mighty God," according to the Hebrew Lexicon, means "Divine Hero"[13]], Father of the Coming Age [so the Greek version of the Hebrew text], Prince of Peace. Wide is His dominion in a peace that has no end, for the throne of David and for His royal power, which He establishes and makes secure in justice and integrity, from this time onward and forever. The jealous love of Yahweh Sabaoth [the Lord of the armies of heaven] will do this (Isa. 9:6, 7).

Later the prophet speaks of one "evangelizing Zion and bringing the Gospel to Jerusalem" (Isa. 40:9). The association of the two ideas of "Gospel" and "God ruling"[14] leads naturally to the concept of the New Testament "Gospel of the Kingdom of God." Whenever the biblical text speaks of God becoming King, the Jewish commentators translate the Hebrew verb "rule" by a noun: "The Kingdom of God will be revealed" (Jewish Targum, i.e., paraphrase of Isaiah 40:10). So also in Exodus 15:18, "the Lord shall reign forever and ever" means that "the Kingdom of the Lord endures forever and ever."

---

[13] *Hebrew and English Lexicon of the Old Testament*, Brown, Driver and Briggs, Oxford: Clarendon Press, 1961, p. 42.

[14] Isa. 40:10; v. 5 speaks of glory and Isa. 52:7 of the reign of God.

Exactly the same connection between the Gospel and the Kingdom is found in Isa. 52:7: "How beautiful on the mountains are the feet of him who brings good tidings, who publishes peace, who brings good tidings of good, who publishes salvation, who says to Zion, 'Your God reigns.'" The context speaks of a public manifestation of the Lord: "The Lord has bared His holy arm before the eyes of all the nations; and all the ends of the earth shall see the salvation of our God" (Isa. 52:10).

These critically important passages, along with the description of the Kingdom of God replacing the empires of the world in Daniel 2:44, convey a clear picture of the Kingdom as a coming reign of God on earth, to be introduced by a supernatural intervention. It is belief in the impending arrival of a new era of history which Jesus demands with His summons to "Repent and believe the Gospel [of the Kingdom of God]" (Mark 1:14, 15).

Isaiah's vision of the bright future epitomizes the hope of the Kingdom:

> For behold, I create new heavens and a new earth; and the former things shall not be remembered or come into mind. But be glad and rejoice forever in that which I create; for behold, I create Jerusalem a rejoicing, and her people a joy. I will rejoice in Jerusalem, and be glad in My people; no more shall be heard in it the sound of weeping and the cry of distress. No more shall there be in it an infant that lives but a few days, or an old man who does not fill out his days, for the child shall die a hundred years old, and the sinner a hundred years old shall be accursed. They shall build houses and inhabit them; they shall plant vineyards and eat their fruit. They shall not build and another inhabit; they shall not plant and another eat; for like the days of a tree shall the days of my people be, and my chosen shall long enjoy the work of their hands. They shall not labor in vain, or bear children for calamity; for they shall be the offspring of the blessed of the Lord, and their children with them. Before they call I will answer, while they are yet speaking I will hear. The wolf and the lamb shall feed together, the lion shall eat straw like the ox; and dust shall be the serpent's food. They shall not hurt or destroy in all My holy mountain, says the Lord (Isa. 65:17-25, RSV).

The Minor Prophets' Vision of the Glorious Future for Israel

The so-called minor prophets repeat the divine assurances of an abundant future for the land when the people of God return to the Lord with all their hearts. The ancient curse imposed because of disobedience to the covenant will be removed and a "milk and honey" condition will prevail in fulfillment of the divine promises of restoration:

> Israel, come back to Yahweh your God; your iniquity was the cause of your downfall...Provide yourself with words and come back to Yahweh. Say to Him, "Take all iniquity away so that we may have happiness again and offer You our words of praise. Assyria cannot save us, we will not ride horses any more, or say 'our God' to what our own hands have made, for You are the one in whom orphans find compassion."

> I will heal their disloyalty. I will love them with all My heart, for My anger has turned from them. I will fall like dew on Israel. He shall bloom like the lily, and thrust out roots like the poplar, his shoots will spread far; he will have the beauty of the olive and the fragrance of Lebanon. They will come back to live in My shade; they will grow corn that flourishes, they will cultivate vines as renowned as the wine of Helbon. What has Ephraim to do with idols any more when it is I who hear his prayer and care for him? I am like a cypress ever green. All your faithfulness comes from me. Let the wise man understand these words. Let the intelligent man grasp their meaning. For the ways of Yahweh are straight, and virtuous men walk in them, but sinners stumble (Hos. 14:2-10, Jerusalem Bible).

"When that day comes," says the prophet Joel:

> the mountains will run with new wine and the hills flow with milk, and all the river beds of Judah will run with water. A fountain will spring from the house of Yahweh to water the wadi of Acacias. Egypt will become a desolation, Edom a desert waste on account of the violence done to the sons of Judah whose innocent blood they shed in their country. But Judah will be inhabited forever, Jerusalem from age to age. I [Yahweh] will avenge their blood and let none go unpunished, and Yahweh will make His home in Zion (Joel 3:18-21, Jerusalem Bible).

These promises will find fulfillment after the great Day of the Lord described in the previous verses (Joel 3:15-17). Amos pictures the future in the same terms. There will be a purging as well as a restoration of Israel:

> Yet I am not going to destroy the house of Jacob [Israel] completely — it is Yahweh who speaks. For now I will issue orders and shake the house of Israel among the nations, as you shake a sieve so that not one pebble can fall to the ground. All the sinners of my people are going to perish by the sword, all those who say, "No misfortune will ever touch us or even come anywhere near us." That day [following the Day of the Lord] I will re-erect the tottering hut of David, make good the gaps in it, restore its ruins and rebuild it as it was in the days of old, so that they can conquer the remnant of Edom and all the nations that belonged to Me. It is Yahweh who speaks, and He will carry this out. The days are coming now — it is Yahweh who speaks — when harvest will follow directly after ploughing, the treading of grapes soon after sowing, when the mountains will run with new wine and the hills all flow with it. I mean to restore the fortunes of my people Israel; they will rebuild the ruined cities and live in them, plant vineyards and drink their wine, dig gardens and eat their produce. I will plant them in their own country, never to be rooted up again out of the land I have given them, says Yahweh your God (Amos 9:8-15, Jerusalem Bible).

The Challenge to Believe in Hebrew Prophecy

> It was the beautiful dream of Hebrew prophecy that in the latter days the Kingdom of God or the Kingdom of the Messiah, should overlap the bounds of human empires, and ultimately cover the whole earth...Prophecy was never weary of telling of the Golden Age she saw in the far future, when the shadows would lift and the new Dawn would steal over the whole world...It is not unlikely that the term Kingdom of God was one of the current phrases of the times, a golden casket holding within it the dream of a restored Hebraism.[15]

The prophets' forecast of a future golden age is essential to our understanding of the Christian Gospel. When Jesus commanded

---

[15] Henry Burton, *Expositor's Bible, St. Luke*, A.C. Armstrong, 1896, p. 251.

repentance and belief in the Good News about the Kingdom of God (Mark 1:14, 15), His Message contained far more than the promise of forgiveness of sins. He demanded belief in the God of history and intelligent faith in His Plan destined to find its climax in the establishment of the Kingdom of God on earth. We are commanded to "repent," i.e., change our entire outlook, and "believe the Good News of the Kingdom" — believe in the Plan that God is working out for the benefit of the world through Jesus. Our commitment to this Plan will ensure that we make every effort to gain a place in the Kingdom. Compliance with the divine program for the rescue of mankind enables us to come under divine protection. Acceptance of the Gospel shields us against the future wrath of God. As Paul put it, "We shall be saved from His wrath" (Rom. 5:9). Salvation in the New Testament is frequently thought of as future: "Salvation is now nearer than when we first believed" (Rom. 13:11).

An obedient response to the Good News about the Kingdom obviously entails an understanding of the meaning of the word "Kingdom." One cannot believe Good News about something which one does not understand! What, then, is this Good News? A number of fundamental texts from the Hebrew Bible lie behind Jesus' use of the term "Kingdom of God." On these the expectation of the Kingdom of God is built. We must insist that the Good News embraced information about a coming world government, with Jesus as its chief executive, and how we must respond by preparing ourselves for its arrival. Though terms like "government" and "executive" may have negative connotations for us who have witnessed the misuse of authority, nevertheless the biblical promise is of justice and peace on earth under the benign rule of the Messiah. And who does not yearn for peace and justice in the affairs of man?

Psalms of Solomon

That the hope of a new political order on earth was very much alive when Jesus began to preach is clear. In the light of the mass of other Messianic material in the Hebrew Bible it is in no way surprising that first-century Jews eagerly expected an era of national glory, to be realized in the Kingdom of the promised Messiah. The following excerpts from the "Psalms of Solomon," dating from about 50 years before the birth of Jesus, depict the Messianic empire of the future. These Psalms are not themselves part of the official canon of Scripture. They draw their inspiration, however, directly from numerous Messianic passages in the Old Testament Psalms and the prophets, and particularly from II Samuel 7, Psalms 72, 89, and 132:

> Lord, you chose David to be king over Israel and swore to him about his descendant forever, that his kingdom should not fail before you...See, Lord, and raise up for them their king, the Son of David, to rule over your servant Israel, in the time known to you, O God. Undergird him with strength to destroy the unrighteous rulers, to purge Jerusalem from Gentiles who trample her to destruction; in wisdom and righteousness to drive out the sinners from the inheritance; to smash the arrogance of sinners like a potter's jar; to shatter all their substance like an iron rod; to destroy the unlawful nations with the word of his mouth; at his warning the nations will flee from his presence; and he will condemn sinners by the thought of their heart. He will gather a holy people whom he will lead in righteousness and he will judge the tribes of the people that have been made holy by the Lord their God. He will not tolerate unrighteousness to pause among them, and any person who knows wickedness shall not live with them. For he shall know them that they are all children of their God. He will distribute them upon the land according to their tribes...and he will have Gentile nations serving under his yoke and he will glorify the Lord in a place prominent above the whole earth. And he will purge Jerusalem and make it holy as it was even from the beginning, for nations to come from the ends of the earth to see his glory, to bring as gifts her children who had been driven out, and to see the glory of the Lord with which God has glorified her.

> There will be no unrighteous among them in his [Messiah's] days, for all shall be holy, and their King shall be the Lord Messiah. For he will not rely on horse and rider and bow, nor will he collect gold and silver for war. Nor will he build up hope in a multitude for a day of war. The Lord himself is his king, the hope of the one who has a strong hope in God...

> O Lord, your mercy is upon the works of your hands forever. You show your goodness to Israel with a rich gift. Your eyes are watching over them and none of them will be in need. Your ears listen to the hopeful prayer of the poor, your compassionate judgments are over the whole world, and your love is for the

> descendants of Abraham, an Israelite. Your discipline for us is as for a firstborn son, an only child, to divert the perceptive person from unintentional sins. May God cleanse Israel for the day of mercy in blessing, for the appointed day when his Messiah will reign. Blessed are those who are born in those days, to see the good things of the Lord which he will do for the coming generation; which will be under the rod of discipline of the Lord Messiah, in the fear of his God, in wisdom of spirit, and of righteousness and of strength, to direct people in righteous acts, in the fear of God, to set them all in the fear of the Lord, a good generation living in the fear of God, in the days of mercy (Pss. of Solomon 17:4, 21-18, 31-34; 18:1-9).

These Psalms capture the essence of the Messianic hope presented by the Old Testament and current at the time when Jesus began to announce the Kingdom of God. They show a striking affinity also with passages in Luke's Gospel (1:32, 33; 2:11), the book of Revelation (11:15-18; 19:15-16), and many other New Testament texts. They delight in the prospect of a world freed from tyrannical government, sharing the vision of Isaiah:

> Once the oppression is over, and the destroyer is no more, and those now trampling the country under foot have gone away, the throne will be made secure in gentleness, and on it there will sit, in all fidelity, within the tent of David, a judge careful for justice and eager for integrity (Isa. 16:4, 5, Jerusalem Bible).

Abraham, the Land and the Kingdom

A sense of the coherence of the biblical story is gained when we recall once again the basic themes on which Israel had been nourished. A number of key texts had established the land promise as an inviolable undertaking on the part of the God of Abraham to secure lasting peace in the Land of Promise, to be administered by those chosen to be sons of God:

> God said to Abraham..."Look all around you from where you are toward the north and the south, toward the east and the west. All the land within sight I will give to you and your descendants forever...Come travel through the length and breadth of the land, for I mean to give it to you" (Gen. 13:14-17).

God said to Abraham, "Here now is my covenant with you: you shall become the father of a multitude of nations. You shall no longer be called Abram, your name shall be Abraham...I will make you into nations, and your issue shall be *kings*. I will establish My covenant between Myself and you, and your descendants after you, generation after generation, a covenant in perpetuity, to be your God and the God of your descendants after you. I will give to you and your descendants after you the land you are living in, the whole land of Canaan, to own in perpetuity, and I will be your God" (Gen. 17:3-8).

And the Scripture, foreseeing that God would justify the Gentiles by faith, preached the Gospel beforehand to Abraham, saying, "all the nations shall be blessed in you" (Gal. 3:8, RSV).

If you [Israel] obey My voice and hold fast to My covenant, you of all the nations will be My very own, for all the earth is Mine. I will count you a kingdom of priests, a consecrated nation (Exod. 19:5, 6, Jerusalem Bible).

Kingship and possession of the land of Palestine formed the basis of God's covenant between Himself and the chosen people, represented initially by Abraham. The royal function of Israel depended, however, on their obedience. How far they succeeded in living up to the high ideal demanded of them is documented in the Old Testament history of the Israelites. It was often a story of failure to meet God's standard, David being an exceptional example of rulership exercised in cooperation with God.[16]

As we have seen, Israel's national hope, kept burning even in times of oppression by their enemies, was that the ultimate ideal King, the Messiah, would eventually bring about the golden age of world peace so vividly predicted by the prophets. With the dawning of that great day, the Kingdom of God would come. We know that prayers for the advent of the Kingdom were being offered continuously in the synagogue at the time when Jesus began to preach. It is impossible not to notice the close affinity of this prayer with "the Lord's prayer":

Magnified and sanctified be His great name in the world which He has created according to His will. May He establish His Kingdom in

---

[16] Asa, Jehoshaphat, Hezekiah and Josiah were also outstanding kings.

your lifetime and in your days and in the lifetime of all the house of Israel, even speedily and at a near time.[17]

As a distinguished German theologian pointed out,[18] "the true background to Jesus' teaching is to be found in...Jewish thought concerning God as ruler, and upon his Kingdom as the manifestation of his kingly activity."

> Weiss claims that this is the dominant emphasis in the Old Testament, and he shows that such an emphasis carries with it the thought of conflict with a worldly or human kingship. The conception is that God will demonstrate his kingship by an act of judgment against the worldly kingship. Against this background we can see that it was natural for the prophets...when they proclaimed the great crisis that was to come, to do this in the form of a proclamation of the coming of a mighty act of God as king. The hope expressed in [the prophets] is for the coming of a mighty kingly activity of God whereby his people would be redeemed, his enemies and theirs destroyed, and the present evil state of things [cp. Galatians 1:4, "this present evil age"] totally and for ever reversed...*It is this hope which lies behind Jesus' usage of the term Kingdom of God.*[19]

Jesus as the Hero of God's Plan for Worldwide Peace

We are only echoing the words of many expert students of Scripture when we assert as our basic thesis: The Old Testament roots of the Kingdom of God must be taken into account when we confront the Kingdom in the Gospel Message of Jesus. Uprooted from its Hebrew background the Kingdom is indeed a vague term in the minds of many Bible readers. There is a grave risk of placing a meaning on Jesus' central Gospel term which will not be the meaning attached to it by Jesus and the Apostles. The result will inevitably be a loss of vital, saving information and the presentation of a Jesus who bears little resemblance to the Jew Jesus whose teachings possess eternal significance.

---

[17] *Kaddish* prayer recited in the synagogue.

[18] Johannes Weiss, *Jesus' Proclamation of the Kingdom of God*, ed. and trans. Hiers and Holland, Philadelphia: Fortress Press, 1971.

[19] Norman Perrin, *The Kingdom of God in the Teaching of Jesus*, SCM Press, 1963, p. 19, discussing the work of Johannes Weiss, emphasis added.

We do not have to read far into our New Testament before we encounter a definitive statement about God's intention for Jesus, in which Davidic throne language reappears. "The Lord God will give Him the throne of His father David and He shall rule over the house of Jacob forever. And His Kingdom will have no end" (Luke 1:32, 33, NASV). This alerts us immediately to the fact that we are now to expect the reappearance of David's royal empire. As Solomon once "sat on the throne of David his father," so Jesus is to occupy the same royal position. The stage is set for the great objective placed before the Messiah. Since, as every Jew knew, the throne of David had ceased to exist since the time of the captivity in Babylon, Gabriel's prediction required the restoration of the Davidic Kingdom. Evidently the great promises given by the divine covenant to the house of David are finally to be realized in Jesus.

In Luke's great opening statement about the career of Mary's son we have a virtual definition of the purpose of Christianity. The role of Jesus is described with precision. He is no vague religious figure. He is strictly linked to the national hopes of Israel, and His function is to become their king, ruling for God in the Kingdom of God. What Luke introduces us to through the communication of Gabriel is the purest Messianism, which can only be understood within its very Jewish environment. The angel's definitive description of Jesus' role in the divine Plan would remind readers acquainted with the Scriptures of an important prophecy about the Kingdom of God found in the little book of Obadiah. What Israel expected was declared by the prophet at the conclusion of the revelation given to him. At a time when the "Day of the Lord draws near on all the nations," the house of Jacob "will possess their possessions" and "deliverers will ascend Mount Zion to govern the mountain of Esau and *the Kingdom will be the Lord's*" (Obad. 15, 17, 21).

Such was the burning hope for liberation fostered by centuries of meditation on the Hebrew prophets, who yearned for a revival of the glory of Israel when David's great descendant would become king. The Bible gives us no authority for supposing the throne of David to be anything other than the seat of the king of Israel in Jerusalem. There is no justification for a sudden alteration of the meaning of "throne of David," to describe an invisible rule in the heavens. The promised king, the Messiah, must rule in the Kingdom of God, which is the Kingdom of David restored. The revelation granted by Gabriel to Mary, reported by Luke as a primary Christian doctrine, requires a fulfillment at the (still future) appearance of Jesus on earth to take up the position assured Him by the divine Word announced at His birth. As the *Pulpit Commentary* on Luke 1:32 notes in a tantalizingly brief remark, "The words of the angel are as yet unfulfilled. They clearly speak of a restoration of Israel, still as far as we can see, very distant...The eventful hour still tarries."[20]

The learned commentator could have added that the promise of royal office for Jesus is the heart of the Gospel of the Kingdom, the Christian Gospel. To that event the entire New Testament looks forward. This is hardly surprising since the same hope had been instilled by the Hebrew prophets when they predicted a permanent Davidic ruler in Jerusalem. Isaiah 9:7 is the key Messianic passage in this regard. Both the Jewish Targum and Christian expositors recognize a reference to the Messiah "in whose days," as the Targum reads, "peace will be great over us": "There will be no end to the increase of His government of peace on the throne of David and over His kingdom to establish it and to uphold it with justice and righteousness from then on and forevermore."

When this magnificent Messianic prophecy (which was certainly not realized in the reign of the eighth-century BC King Hezekiah!) is read at the Christmas season or sung in performances of Handel's *Messiah*, the false impression is gained, in the absence of clear information, that the prophecy has somehow already been fulfilled. In its biblical setting, however, it refers to the future and belongs with the petition "Thy Kingdom come" of the Lord's prayer. It is a companion prophecy to the prediction of Jeremiah:

> Behold the days are coming, declares the Lord, when I shall raise up for David a righteous Branch. And He will reign as king and act wisely and do justice and righteousness in the land. In His days Judah will be saved and Israel dwell securely (Jer. 23:5, 6).

While no Davidic king rules in Jerusalem, the main burden of Messianic prophecy remains to be fulfilled — and in "concrete" terms, as a stupendous political event which will introduce the first divine world government. Such is the staggering proposition of

---

[20] *Commentary on Luke*, p. 8.

biblical Christianity about which the churches have fallen strangely silent.

Unbiblical Definitions of the Kingdom of God

The plain language of the prophets will not yield to a "religious" explanation as an interior "kingdom of the heart" beloved by so many. The vision of the Kingdom does not mean a gradual amelioration of present governments. The earlier kingdoms of Daniel 2 are defined as actual political empires, starting with Babylon. It is on the ruins of these former world empires that the Messianic Kingdom will be set up. It will happen by a sudden divine intervention, causing the destruction of opposing kingdoms. The Kingdom of God in the Bible derives its meaning from these classic passages in Daniel, as well as those we have cited from Chronicles. The Kingdom of God (or Kingdom of Heaven which is a synonym) has as its primary definition, especially in Matthew, Mark and Luke, a world empire, centered in Jerusalem, administered by the Messiah and the saints. It is the goal of the entire divine purpose and the objective placed before every Christian believer. The outcome of history is the restoration of Eden under a new divine rule. The Kingdom of God has nothing to do with present movements designed to reform society, however well intentioned. Much less is it to be a Kingdom *in* heaven as a place for departed souls at death. Nor should the Kingdom of God be reduced to a synonym for the Church.[21] The equation of the Kingdom with the Church has caused untold confusion.

Jesus as the Executive of the Kingdom

The whole thrust of the New Testament is to present Jesus as the promised King of Israel, the Messiah and King of the Kingdom of God. The word "Christ," which is the equivalent of the Hebrew word Messiah, is a title reserved for special human agents of God — prophets, priests and particularly the king. The name "Jesus Christ" does not present us with a Jesus who is the son of "Mary and Joseph Christ," as a child at Sunday School thought. "Christ" is not part of a

---

[21] It is true that the New Testament expects that the Church will become the Kingdom, but only after its present period of suffering. Hence it may be said that Christians have been made into a Kingdom (Rev. 1:6). They are preparing to rule (Rev. 5:10).

proper name. "Jesus Christ" is equivalent to Jesus the Christ, i.e., Jesus the King of Israel. His full title is the "Lord Jesus Christ," "lord" being the royal Messianic title given to kings of Israel and other human superiors. Jesus is therefore, as Luke tells us, the "Lord Messiah" or "King Messiah" (Luke 2:11),[22] according to the title conferred on Him by the Lord God, His Father, in the immensely important prophetic oracle in Psalm 110:1. Luke also calls Jesus the "Lord's Anointed" (or Christ, Luke 2:26),[23] once again linking Him with Israel's kings. It is a noteworthy fact that the later letters of Paul more frequently refer to the Savior as *Christ* Jesus, in that order, as a safeguard against any watering down of the rich implications of the royal word "Christ." It may well be that Paul realized how fragile the Messianic concept could be in the hands of Gentiles unsympathetic to the heritage of Israel. Hence his insistence that Jesus is the Messiah. On that conviction Jesus had based His whole operation:

> "Simon Peter answered, 'You are the Christ, the Son of the living God.' And Jesus replied, 'Blessed are you, Simon Barjona, because flesh and blood did not reveal this to you, but My Father who is in heaven. And I also say to you that you are Peter, and upon this rock I will build My Church'" (Matt. 16:16-18, RSV).

Meaning and understanding are conveyed by words. Any alteration of the meaning of key words in a document will result in a breakdown of communication between the writer and the audience. "Jesus Christ" is the one name we cannot afford to distort, if the New Testament writers are to communicate to us effectively. The very substance of Christianity depends on a correct grasp of Christianity's central figure. The hero of our faith was and is a Jew whose recorded words speak to us at a distance of 2000 years. It does not take much imagination to see that the transmission of ideas over that length of

---

[22] "The Lord Christ" was a recognized Jewish Messianic expression; cp. Lam. 4:20; Pss. Sol. 17:32; 18 (title); 18:7. On no account should "Lord Christ" be confused with "Lord God." Ps. 110:1 had provided an important source for the distinction between two Lords, one of whom was Yahweh, the other the Lord Messiah. The 'my lord' of this Psalm translates *adoni*, which in all of its 195 occurrences never refers to God who is distinguished 449 times as *adonai*. The difference in the Hebrew vowels was deliberate and critical for preserving the uniqueness of the One God as distinct from the Messiah.

[23] This title refers in the Hebrew Bible to kings of Israel.

time is fraught with the peril of misunderstanding. This is particularly true in the sphere of religion which deals with controversial and abstract concepts. The human mind is all too prone to construct a "Jesus" of its own invention in keeping with its own ideals and agendas.

Consider, for example, the possibility of misinterpretation when an American and Englishman converse. Both speak the same language — or so they think. What meaning does an American derive from his colleague across the Atlantic when the latter states that he is "mad about his flat," that "Tom and Jane have just broken up," or that he intends to "open the bonnet and adjust the engine with his spanner"? An Englishman asking for "plasters" or "rawl plugs" in an American store may need an interpreter familiar with both versions of English. Without such help he is unlikely to obtain the desired Band-Aids and anchors.

A parallel situation in the matter of reading the Bible is obvious. One may either investigate the New Testament oneself, paying careful attention to the meaning of leading terms in their first-century context, or one may rely on the Church to tell him what the New Testament means, assuming that one's denominational tradition accurately reflects the Scriptures. The latter course involves a considerable act of faith — faith in the Church. Many Protestants are happy to repose their trust in their chosen denomination. Rather illogically, however, Protestants claim that it is the Roman Catholics who rely on the Church, while Protestants pride themselves on the fact that the Bible — sola scriptura — is the source of their religion. But do most Protestant churchgoers really *study* the Bible?

A useful self-test may be considered by everyone seeking to know and understand the Jesus of the Bible. What is meant by the term "Christ"? As we have seen, the word is equivalent to the king of Israel and in the case of Jesus it designates the ultimate king, heir of the promises made millennia before to Abraham and David. This is exactly what Matthew has in mind when he opens his book with the definitive statement that Jesus Christ is "the son of David and the son of Abraham" (Matt. 1:1, NASV). At once the readers know that the ancestry of Jesus is to be traced to the key figures in the history of Israel and her covenants, specifically to the royal line of David. The regal meaning of "Christ" is emphasized when Matthew speaks of

"Mary from whom was born Jesus, who is called the Christ [Messiah]" (Matt. 1:16, NASV). In his next episode Matthew further defines Jesus as the one "born in Bethlehem," and "born *King of the Jews*" (Matt. 2:1, 2, NASV). There follows an inquiry on the part of the chief priests and theologians (scribes) as to "where *the Christ* was to be born" (Matt. 2:4). An authoritative answer is provided by an inspired statement of the eighth-century prophet Micah that "out of [Bethlehem] shall come forth a ruler who will shepherd [i.e. be king] of my people Israel" (Matt. 2:6, NASV; cp. Mic. 5:2).

The clear political implications of the birth of the rival ruler, the Christ, pose an immediate threat to the current king of Judea, Herod. He orders the destruction of all under two years old in Bethlehem, not knowing that the Messiah's parents have fled with their baby to Egypt. The safe return of Jesus to the land of Israel after Herod's death is marked by the fulfillment of another Old Testament saying: "Out of Egypt I have called My Son" (Hos. 11:1; cp. Matt. 2:15). The same personage who is entitled to be called Christ, King of the Jews and ruler of Israel, is now designated as the Son of God. Matthew's quotation is taken from a verse in the prophet Hosea in which the nation of Israel is called "Son of God." The application of this title to Jesus is right to the point. Jesus is the Son of God in a sense parallel to the status of Israel, the chosen nation. Jesus is the chosen king of the nation, a model for every pious Israelite who also aspired to be worthy of the name "Son of God."

From start to finish the leading player in the New Testament drama is given the technical legal title fit for the great descendant of the house of David. Luke introduces Jesus as the heir to the throne of Israel and later contrasts Him with Caesar, head of the Roman Empire. The crowds, whose theology was often in advance of the religious establishment, hail Jesus as "Son of David," the Messianic title par excellence, associating him with "the coming Kingdom of our father David." John reports that Nathaniel, the Israelite without guile, recognizes Jesus as "the Son of God, the King of Israel" (John 1:49). Philip adds his contribution to the portrait of Jesus by describing Him as "Him of whom Moses and also the prophets wrote." The reference to Moses recalled the famous words recorded in Deuteronomy 18:15, 18: "The Lord God will raise up a prophet like me [Moses] from among you, from among your countrymen. You shall listen to him…And I shall put My words in His mouth, and He shall speak to them all that I command Him." At His baptism Jesus receives a divine anointing as "Son of God," the New Testament synonym for the Messiah, reminiscent of the consecration of King David, to mark Him out as the chosen vehicle of God's activity through His Spirit. Andrew expresses his excitement at having found "the Messiah (which translated means the Christ)" (John 1:41).

The Messianic Claims of Jesus

On a number of occasions Jesus deliberately acts as a king, without, however, attempting to take over rulership of Israel. In Matthew 21:4 Jesus makes His triumphal entry into Jerusalem, attracting attention as at least a potentially political figure. Once again a prophecy is fulfilled. Matthew points to the words of Zechariah calling on Israel to: "Rejoice heart and soul, daughter of Zion! Shout with gladness, daughter of Jerusalem! See now, your king comes to you; He is victorious, He is triumphant, humble and riding on a donkey" (Zech 9:9, Jerusalem Bible; cp. Matt. 21:5).

Jesus here made a deliberate claim to kingship as the expected Messiah. His acceptance of the people's enthusiastic accolades was proof to those who had eyes to see that He considered Himself to be in every sense the rightful claimant to the throne of David. The point was not lost on the crowds, although the officials of established religion, ever conscious of the need to maintain the status quo, as well as friendly relations with Caesar, reacted disapprovingly. For Jesus, however, the episode was alive with Messianic thrill. Even inanimate rocks would have burst forth in an ecstasy of praise if the disciples had remained quiet (Luke 19:40). No more joyful prospect could be imagined than the arrival of "the coming Kingdom of our father David" (Mark 11:10). Jesus did nothing at all to discourage such Messianic fervor.[24]

At His trial the question of the Messiahship of Jesus is the point of contention between the authorities and Jesus. The High Priest introduces the interrogation by using the familiar equation of "Christ"

---

[24] In both Testaments those who recognize God's chosen kings are singled out as examples of faith. In I Sam. 25 Abigail acknowledges the "Messiahship" of David and actually becomes his wife (see especially vv. 23, 27-33, 42). This is a "type" of the marriage of the church to Christ.

and "Son of God." Jesus affirms that He is indeed the Messiah and that they will "see the Son of Man," which Jesus uses as an equivalent Messianic title, "sitting at the right hand of Power and coming on the clouds of heaven" (Matt. 26:64). This was an explicit claim to be the one described by Daniel as the conquering ruler of the Kingdom of God destined to replace the empires of the world at a time when the Kingdom of Heaven would "crush all these other [empires]."

The picture provided by the New Testament is a perfect portrait of the Messiah promised in the Hebrew Scriptures: A descendant of the royal house of David, invested with charismatic power through the Spirit of God and appointed eventually to overthrow the yoke of foreign domination in Israel and to bring about the restoration of the Kingdom covenanted forever to David and faithful Israel. The Messiah's entourage, believers in Jesus as the Christ, would also include Gentiles who could become full members of the Messianic community as the true "Israel of God."

If there is any uncertainty about the claims of Jesus among churchgoers, it is because tradition has conferred upon them a conception of Messiahship, much of which Jesus would not have recognized. The Church in general has been most unwilling to accept the political implications of Jesus' claim to Messiahship. Many are not even aware of these implications, because the impression they have gained from the Church is that Jesus was interested in what has been called a "spiritual" kingdom. Contemporary use of the epithet "spiritual" is responsible for a great deal of mischief. Besides being vague enough not to convey any definite meaning, it drives a wedge between the two concepts "spiritual" and "political" which are then thought to be incompatible. The fact is, however, that in the language and thinking of the Bible, a spiritual kingdom can at the same time be a kingdom based on a "concrete" rule by an individual located in a particular geographical place on earth.

To contest the political claims of Jesus is tantamount to resisting Him as Messiah. Into this trap tradition has lead many well-meaning students of Scripture, who have wanted to accept a "spiritual" Messiah but are far less enthusiastic about Him as the appointed ruler of Israel in Jerusalem. A Jesus who never inherits the throne of His father David, however, is scarcely the Jesus of Nazareth of our New Testament. To reject the political elements in the teaching of Jesus is to read the New Testament in disregard of its Jewish first-century context. It runs the risk of closing one's eyes to historical fact and recreating Jesus in the image of a personal ideal. As the writers of *The Messianic Legacy* point out:

> To accept Jesus as a Messiah while denying his regal and political role is simply to ignore the facts — to ignore the historical context, to ignore what the word "Messiah" meant and implied. Christians have regarded the Messiah as a non-political, wholly spiritual figure who posed no challenge to temporal authority, who had no secular or political aspirations himself...Biblical scholarship during the last two centuries, however, has rendered such an interpretation increasingly untenable...To the extent that [the Messiah's] religious function included freeing his people from bondage, his spiritual role was also political.[25]

Christ and the Kingdom: The Coherent Center of the New Testament Gospel

Christians must awake to the fact that division over Jesus' identity and Message means division over the Christian Gospel. The Kingdom of God cannot remain a "nebulous term" if we hope to share the mind of Christ. Radical reformation is required if the Bible is to be expounded with clarity and the Gospel successfully proclaimed.

The cry for reform is nothing new. The nineteenth-century theologian Richard Rothe complained that received methods of explaining the Bible were inadequate:

> Our key does not open — the right key is lost and until we are put in possession of it again our exposition will never succeed. The system of biblical ideas is not that of our schools and as long as we attempt exegesis without it, the Bible will remain a half-closed book. We must enter upon it with other conceptions than those we have been accustomed to think the only possible ones.[26]

---

[25] Michael Baigent, Richard Leigh, Henry Lincoln, *The Messianic Legacy,* Jonathan Cape, 1986, p. 25.

[26] Richard Rothe, cited by G.N.H. Peters in *The Theocratic Kingdom*, Grand Rapids, reprinted by Kregel, 1952, Vol. I, p. 21. Peters' three-volume work on the Kingdom of God is one of the most remarkable expositions of this major biblical theme ever written.

Explaining the Christianity of Jesus apart from its roots in the Abrahamic and Davidic covenants and the prophets is like trying to give an account of the history of the United States without reference to the Revolutionary War. God's contracts with Abraham and David are the great landmarks in the history of Israel. They are the definitive moments in the biblical story, revealing the divine Plan in its progressive stages and pointing forward to a marvelous outcome in world history. The Christianity of Christ and the New Testament grows out of those two momentous episodes in the life of Israel. Both form the substratum of Jesus' announcement of the coming Kingdom of God, which is the essence of His commission as Messiah of that Kingdom. When Jesus, and later the Apostles, preached, they assumed an understanding that the career of Jesus (thus far His birth, ministry, death, resurrection and ascension) brings these covenants forward towards their yet future ultimate fulfillment. New Testament writers take for granted that the content of the promises made to the patriarchs (the true Church Fathers) is common knowledge: namely that God has guaranteed a permanent possession of the land to Abraham and those who share his faith, and an endless future for the royal house of David when Jesus is installed as king in Jerusalem. As long as these promises remain, as they obviously are, unfulfilled, they stand forth as the great objects of Christian faith and hope. A longing for their realization on earth, in accordance with the Lord's prayer, "Thy Kingdom come!" should be the inspiration of every Christian as well as the substance of all Gospel preaching.

6. A Charter for Mankind

To make sense of the ministry of Jesus and His unchanging Message, we must enter the thought world of first-century Judaism and acquaint ourselves with Israel's Bible, the Hebrew Scriptures to which Jesus was devoted. In these precious documents are to be found the principal ideas which molded the young Jesus' thinking. Knowing Himself to be the heir to the throne of David, He would be drawn to that section of the Hebrew Bible which contained the core of Israel's national hope. It had been communicated to Israel's beloved king David by an extraordinary revelation given to him through Nathan the prophet (found in II Samuel 7, with its parallel in I Chronicles 17). These passages of Scripture record for posterity the divine arrangements made with the royal house of David. From the point of view of many historians and some theologians the Kingdom of Judah amounts to a minor Middle Eastern empire. In Scripture, however, its significance for world history and the destiny of the human race cannot be exaggerated.

One might expect that in the Christian West the terms of the covenant made with the house of David would be required reading of all students of history. The scriptural documents laying out God's intentions for the world through the royal line of David, representing the house of Judah, are vastly more significant than the Magna Carta or the Declaration of Independence. The contract established with David and his descendants is backed by no less a power than the Creator Himself. Underwritten by a divine promise, it guarantees the ultimate future of the human race under a beneficent government in the hands of the Greater Son of David, whom we believe to be Jesus of Nazareth. As the rightful heir to the throne of David, He is now temporarily removed from the earth. He will remain absent until a dramatic turning point in world history is marked by His arrival to take up power over the nations in accordance with the Plan revealed to David through the prophet Nathan and later announced again by Jesus in the Christian Gospel.

The Davidic covenant is thoroughly political. It deals, we might say, in divine politics. It is expressive of the Creator's intention to restore harmony to a distracted earth, whose present political arrangements have in their various ways failed to realize the ideal for which man was created. God's purpose for man was that he should reflect divinity on earth. That is what it means to be a "son of God," to mirror the character of the Father. Adam was put in charge of the world and instructed to rule it. Sustained by a continuing fellowship with their creator, the first pair could have carried out their mandate "to subdue the earth." But this was not to be. A fatal disruption of God's intention occurred when Adam and Eve yielded to the blandishments of a rival power. They were overwhelmed by the lies of Satan. Falling for the counter-propaganda of the Devil, they abandoned the Word of God which expressed His will for the conduct of affairs on earth.

To a large extent the pattern of disregard for the divine Word, set by the original couple, has been characteristic of the whole course of human history. Israel herself, as custodians of the divine revelation which she preserved with meticulous care, failed to recognize her own Messiah, who was supremely the vehicle of the Word and words of God. With notable exceptions — the family of Noah, Abraham, Moses, David, the prophets, as well as outstanding heroes of faith from every nation in every age — the course of history is marked by violence and disharmony at the level of the family and the nation. God's will has not been followed, nor His laws observed. The Apostle closest to Jesus defined the condition of the world as "lying in the hands of the evil one" (I John 5:19). Jesus believed that His Kingdom had an origin quite different from present societies and that Satan was now "prince of the world" (John 14:30). The Bible sees the earth as at present a rebel province which has rejected its Maker. One has only to turn on the nightly news, announcing yet another murder, to understand that the purpose of God for our race continues to be frustrated.

In the face of such obvious unhappiness and injustice, and what appears often to be purposeless suffering, many despair of finding any meaning for existence. The Bible responds to the tendency to abandon hope by assuring us that the world is in fact going somewhere. It is moving inexorably towards the goal for which it was created. But let no one think that human progress will lead us gently to a safe haven of peace and prosperity. It is the heart of the Bible's Message that only a dramatic reversal of present trends will produce the world which theoretically we say we desire.

The Bible's prognosis for mankind is grim. But there is light at the end of the tunnel. The prophets of Israel say two things. Firstly, things are bad and they are not going to improve — at least not to the point of achieving a genuine and lasting peace on earth. Secondly, when God takes a hand in human affairs and removes the wicked and replaces them with the righteous, things are going to be transformed. It is only by an exchange of political systems that lasting improvement is going to come. More specifically, it is only when God's chosen and trained agents take over the reins of government that order will be restored worldwide. This is the essence of "God's Gospel," the announcement of the Kingdom.

Unfortunately this kind of analysis of our problem is not popular, and many reject out of hand the biblical solution. The idea that we are not going to "make it" without a divine intervention deals a blow to our sense of independence. Many who claim to be Christians pick from the Bible what is comforting and reject the massive amount of biblical material dealing with future judgment, an event described in both Testaments as the Day of the Lord. The Day of the Lord is simply the future moment in history when God decides to intervene to change the course of world affairs dramatically, cataclysmically and forever. The Day of the Lord of the Hebrew Bible is equated in the New Testament with the future arrival of Jesus to rule in His Kingdom. This proves once again that New Testament Christians have not discarded the Old Testament. They assume that their readers will know what the Old Testament is about. They do not feel the need to restate what had already been declared by the prophets. They expect us to understand that what the Old Testament reveals about God's Plan will make sense in the light of the continuing revelation in Jesus Christ.

It is most unfair to claim allegiance to Christ if one decides to water down or otherwise explain away unwanted teaching dealing with the coming Day of the Lord, which is also the coming of the Kingdom of God. Jesus was no benign Galilean peasant reassuring the world that everything is all right. He is first and foremost a prophet and spokesman for God, expressing both a tender compassion for human suffering and a fiery denunciation of the folly and wickedness of the world's ways. Above all Jesus is the bearer of Good News — of a bright future for the whole world when the Messiah comes to reign.

The mission of Jesus was driven by His overwhelming desire to carry out the will of His Father, the One God of Israel. Jesus summed up the reason for His ministry as "heralding the Kingdom of God." That was "the reason for which [He] was appointed" (Luke 4:43). It must follow that a grasp of the Kingdom of God will provide us with the key to knowing the mind of Jesus.

Divine Arrangements with David

Little progress is possible in our quest for understanding Jesus' agenda until we subject to careful investigation the vastly important role of the Davidic covenant, which He treated as a blueprint for the unfolding Plan of God for the world. Jesus, as is well known, believed Himself to be the central figure in the world's drama, the appointed legal agent of the One God, heir to David's throne and ordained to take His place as sovereign in the Kingdom of God.

The terms of God's covenant with the celebrated monarch of Israel, King David, appear in II Samuel 7 and I Chronicles 17. From this central declaration of God's purpose Israel derived its inextinguishable hope for a brilliant future. The text from the Samuel version is as follows:

> Once the king had settled into his palace and Yahweh had granted him rest from all the enemies surrounding him, the king said to the prophet Nathan, "Look, I am living in a cedar-wood palace, while the ark of God is under awnings." Nathan said to the king, "Go and do whatever you have in mind, for Yahweh is with you." But that very night, the word of Yahweh came to Nathan: "Go and tell My servant David, Yahweh says this: Are you to build Me a temple to live in? I have never lived in a house from the day I brought the Israelites out of Egypt until today, but have kept traveling with a tent for shelter. In all My travels with all the Israelites, did I say to

any of the judges of Israel: 'Why do you not build me a cedar-wood temple?' This is what you must say to my servant David. 'Yahweh Sabaoth says this: I took you from the pasture, from following the sheep, to be leader of my people Israel; I have been with you wherever you went; I have got rid of all your enemies for you. I am going to make your fame as great as the fame of the greatest on earth. I am going to provide a place for My people Israel; I shall plant them there, and there they will live and never be disturbed again; nor will they be oppressed by the wicked any more, as they were in former times ever since I instituted judges to govern My people Israel; and I shall grant you rest from all your enemies. Yahweh furthermore tells you that He will make you a dynasty. And when your days are over and you fall asleep with your ancestors, I shall appoint your heir, your own son, to succeed you (and I shall make his sovereignty secure. He will build a temple for my name) and I shall make his royal throne secure forever. I shall be a father to him and he a son to Me; if he does wrong, I shall punish him with a rod such as men use, with blows such as mankind gives. But My faithful love will never be withdrawn from him as I withdrew it from Saul, whom I removed from before you. Your dynasty and your sovereignty will ever stand firm before you and your throne be forever secure.'" Nathan related all these words and this whole revelation to David (II Sam. 7:1-17).

The terms of God's Plan for David and Israel are clear. David will not be the one to build the temple. Instead, God will build a dynasty for David. There is a blessing for the nation also. A place of permanent security will be provided for Israel. Associated with that promise is the guarantee of a king who will rule as David's successor forever. The parallel account in I Chronicles 17 omits the reference to a chastisement appropriate for the immediate descendant of David, Solomon. The later version of the covenant thus places a greater emphasis on the ultimate object of the promise — the Messiah. Of Him it is said: "I shall set Him over *My temple and Kingdom* forever and His throne will be forever secure" (I Chron. 17:14). The New Testament, quoting a verse from II Samuel 7, recognizes both Jesus *and the Christians* as Messianic sons and daughters of God to whom the covenant promises apply: "Therefore come out from their midst and be separate, says the Lord, and do not touch what is unclean; and I will welcome you. And I will be a father to you, and you shall be sons and daughters to Me, says the Lord Almighty" (II Cor. 6:17, 18, citing II Sam. 7:14).[1]

The covenant's concluding guarantee — a throne forever — summarized the national hope of Israel and provided the basis of the Christian Gospel about the Kingdom as proclaimed by Jesus. Most appropriately the term "Messiah" or "Anointed King" became the title for the expected king of the line of David who would preside over the temple and the Kingdom of God. It is the essence of Christian belief that the historical Jesus, born in Bethlehem, is the person about whom the inspired documents had spoken.

It is important not to miss the Bible's own definition of the Kingdom. It means the reign on a permanently secure throne of the ultimate ruler, representing God in the Davidic Kingdom as the sovereign of the Kingdom of God on earth. The Messiah or Son of God is to be ruler in "My," i.e. God's, Kingdom (I Chron. 17:14). We must emphasize that the divine Plan has to do with "a place for Israel" (II Sam. 7:10), a throne and a Kingdom. None of these terms must be allowed to slip away from our grasp. These are words with normal, natural meanings. They have to do with an empire on earth and a king ruling in Jerusalem. They are exactly the terms taken up by Gabriel in Luke 1:32, 33 which picks up the threads of the divine drama by pointing back to the Davidic covenant and forward to the arrival of the Davidic empire — a new world order which will supersede our present world system forever.

The birth of Jesus, as the key figure in the divine scheme, was indeed proof that God, His Father, was at work in the world according to the promises made with the chosen people. Gabriel speaks to Mary and to the world in words strongly reminiscent of II Samuel 7:

II Samuel 7:12-14	**Luke 1:32, 33**
"I shall make your own [David's] son succeed you...I shall make His royal throne secure forever. I shall be a father to Him and He a son to Me."	"[Jesus] will be great and He will be called the Son of the Most High. The Lord God will give Him the throne of His father David and He will rule over the

---

[1] Christians are said to be "anointed," i.e., members of the Messianic community, in II Cor. 1:21. As saints, Christians are those appointed to rule (Dan. 7:27).

> house of Jacob forever, and His
> Kingdom will have no end."

The book of Chronicles recognizes the royal covenant as the substance of God's dealings with His people. A king of Judah appeals to the separated northern kingdom of Israel: "Do you not know that the Lord God of Israel gave the rule over Israel to David and his sons by a covenant of salt?...So now you intend to resist the kingdom of the Lord in the hands of the sons of David" (II Chron. 13:5, 8). It is important to be reminded that David's rule over Israel is called the Kingdom of God. The Kingdom, it should be noted, is not a kingdom in the hearts of David's sons. It is in their hands, under their control, as they govern as Yahweh's vice-regents. Looking back at the revelation he had received through Nathan, David reflected on the covenant with these words:

> God has chosen my son Solomon to sit on the throne of the Kingdom of the Lord over Israel. And He said to me, "Your son Solomon is the one who shall build My house and My courts, for I have chosen him to be a son to Me and I will be a father to him" (I Chron. 28:5, 6).

The success of Solomon depended on his faithful obedience. As is well known, he failed the test as did many of his descendants of the royal line. The ultimate permanence of the throne, however, was assured by the divine oath sworn to David:

> For the sake of David Your servant
> Do not turn away the face of Your anointed.
> The Lord has sworn to David
> A truth from which He will not turn back;
> Of the fruit of your body I will set [a descendant] on your throne.
> If your sons will keep My covenant,
> And My testimony which I will teach them,
> Their sons will also sit upon your throne forever.
> For the Lord has chosen Zion;
> He has desired it for His habitation.
> This is My resting place forever;
> Here I will dwell for I have desired it.
> I will abundantly bless her provision;

> I will satisfy her needy with bread.
> Her priests also I will clothe with salvation;
> and her saints will sing aloud for joy.
> There [in Zion] I will cause the horn of David to spring forth;
> I have prepared a lamp for My anointed [Messiah].
> His enemies I will clothe with shame;
> But upon Himself His crown will shine (Ps. 132:10-18).

So impressed was King David by God's provision for the future of His royal family and the hope this provided for the world that he dedicated his last words to a celebration of the Messiah and His worldwide rule. We cite the version of these inspired words suggested by Keil and Delitzsch in their commentary on II Samuel 23:1-6:

> The divine saying of David the son of Jesse, the divine saying of the man, the one highly exalted, of the anointed of the God of Jacob, and the sweet psalmist of Israel. The Spirit of Yahweh speaks through me and His word is upon my tongue. The God of Israel says, the rock of Israel speaks to me, "There will arise a ruler over the human race, a just ruler, and He will exercise His dominion in the Spirit of the fear of God. In the time of this Messiah it will be like the light of the morning when the sun arises, as a morning without clouds. From the shining after rain comes fresh green out of the earth." Does not my house stand in such a relation to God that the righteous ruler will spring from it? For He has made an everlasting covenant with me, established by every assurance. All God's good pleasure and all my salvation will spring forth from this covenant. But the worthless are as rejected thorns...[2]

On these themes Jesus built His conception of the Messianic Kingdom.

The ultimate triumph of the Davidic kingdom was foreseen also by the other prophets of Israel. Isaiah wrote in the eighth century of the "Prince of Peace" and of His "government of peace on the throne of David and over His Kingdom" (Isa. 9:6, 7). The promise of the covenant pointed to an ultimate fulfillment. Prophecy announced that the coming Messiah would "establish and uphold [the Kingdom] with justice and righteousness from then on [i.e., the Messianic future] and

---

[2] Keil and Delitzsch, *Commentary on the Old Testament,* Hendrickson, 1989, Vol. II, pp. 484-490.

forevermore" (Isa. 9:7). The entire project was bound to have a successful outcome. It was underwritten by the Lord God Himself whose zeal would accomplish it.

The Plan of God for Israel laid out in the covenant had dealt with "the distant future" (II Sam. 7:19). A complete fulfillment in the reign of Solomon is therefore impossible. A little-noticed phrase from David's response to the information provided through Nathan deserves comment. From the words of an Australian theologian writing about the Davidic covenant we select this important excerpt:

> The tenor of David's prayer in II Samuel 7:18-29 indicates that David well understood the covenantal significance in the widest terms of the divine promises and their effect upon humanity as a whole...Puzzling in verse 19 is the Hebrew phrase *wezot torat ha'adam* (literally "and this is the law of man" — it needs to be understood that *torah* is a word with a wide meaning range, basically having a sense of "guidance," "direction" rather than that it has full legal overtones like our word "law")...W.C. Kaiser has shown clearly that verse 19b is to be taken as a statement, and that the Hebrew phrase concerned serves to introduce or to summarize (as here) a set of divine instructions. Under the "this," the promises of the first half of the chapter are being referred to, while under the "law of man" their implications for the future, as far as David understood them, are contained. The curious Hebrew expression, "law of man," has been shown to have parallels in the similar Akkadian phrase *terit nishe*, which carries a meaning of a "fateful oracle for man." What is conveyed by the Akkadian term is the notion of an utterance by which the destiny of mankind is controlled or provided for. Such a concept fits the Samuel context admirably and with more than some probability Kaiser suggests that the sense to be given to II Samuel 7:19b is "this is the charter by which humanity will be directed." That is to say, in the oracle delivered to him, David rightly sees the future and destiny of the human race is involved. The promises to David have built upon the broad history of covenant concepts as, from creation onwards, they have covered divine intent for human development, and David has seen the full covenantal connections which Nathan's oracle has offered.[3]

---

[3] W.J. Dumbrell, "The Davidic Covenant," *The Reformed Theological Review* (39), May-Aug. 1980, p. 46.

The implications of this extraordinary divine communication granted to David are far-reaching. They provide a vista view of the outcome of human history. The future of humanity is bound up with the future of the royal house of David. From that family there will emerge a statesman-Messiah competent to solve the world's intractable problems. The covenant granted to David is nothing less than a divine charter authorizing the Messiah and His associates to rule the world. History is marching to that inevitable goal. Ignored by historians, philosophers and anthropologists and neglected by theologians, this precious information illuminates the later story of Jesus and the early Christians. It helps to account for the passionate zeal with which they spread the Good News. They saw themselves as participants in the greatest venture ever conceived by man — or rather conceived by God. Convinced of the claims of Jesus, Christians aligned themselves with the Messiah and His Message. Knowing that Jesus was divinely appointed to govern the world *and that He was inviting them to share that authority with Him,* they saw themselves as a kind of fifth column in a hostile world system. Their true status was unrecognized, as they worked in the service of an absent king, anticipating the overthrow of present governments at the reappearance of the Messiah.

A partial parallel is provided by behind-the-scenes conspiratorial movements in our day, which are reported to have involved plans for a world takeover. It is important to add at once that Jesus was not a clandestine campaigner with dark motives. His methods were entirely peaceful and His Message public. Above all He was the chosen channel of blessing for all who believed in Him. The majority of those who heard His agenda, however, did not accept His claims. It was inevitable, therefore, that Jesus gathered around Him a small number of intimate disciples who became increasingly conversant with the Messianic program for the world unfolding through God's elect servant. This cadre of believers formed an advance guard of the Kingdom of God which would one day be manifested in Jerusalem, according to the covenant-hope of the restoration of the Kingdom. Because so few accepted Jesus and His Messianic agenda ("narrow is the way leading to life [in the Kingdom] and few find it," Matt. 7:14), those who did are said in the New Testament to be in possession of a precious divine secret, an invaluable treasure, for which no sacrifice is too great (Matt. 13:44-46). The secret was their understanding of God's Kingdom Plan, and their goal was to qualify for life in the coming age of the Kingdom and an appointment as co-regent with the Messiah. And even if the hostile world were to put them to death, they would reappear immortalized in the resurrection. The gates of Hades even would not prevail against them.

The Roman authorities viewed Jesus as a potential political threat. They were not unaware of the implications of Messianism. Their worst fears, however, were not justified. Jesus organized no revolution and made no political move. When His less well-instructed followers attempted to make Him king there and then, Jesus promptly removed Himself alone to a mountain (John 6:15). The time had not arrived for Him to accede to the throne. Nevertheless He was God's candidate for royal office. Jesus knew as well as His supporters that the role of the Messiah was to liberate Israel from foreign oppression (Luke 24:21).[4] He also knew that the path to victory was via crucifixion, resurrection, ascension and a period of absence at the right hand of the Father. The time for an overt assumption of world power was not yet ripe.

The Non-Fulfillment of the Covenant

The failure of Jesus, as Messiah, to effect a world revolution or even a change of government in His own country has presented Bible readers with a problem. In what sense can Jesus be the Messiah if He never inherited the throne of David in Jerusalem? How can the Davidic covenant have been realized as long as the Messiah is not in possession of the throne of the royal house of Judah? A traditional solution espoused by churches is to say that Jesus has in fact been exalted to the status promised to Him, by being taken to the right hand of the Father. His position at present satisfies the conditions of the ancient promises. This theory is most problematic. Such an explanation entails giving the Messianic idea an entirely new meaning, divorced, as we think, from the ideas which clustered around the Messianic hope in its historical setting. These ideas the New Testament never abandoned. Jewish commentators faced with the same facts argue, on the other hand, that the failure of Jesus to

---

[4] Josephus refers to the common belief of Jews of the first century that "a man from their country would become ruler of the world" (*Jewish War* 6. 312).

accomplish what the Messiah was destined to do — rule as King in Israel — merely goes to show that Jesus was not the Messiah. He obviously never became Messiah in the sense demanded by the prophets and the covenants.

The tension caused by this enigma is at the root of much of the division amongst those calling themselves Christians as well as between Christians and Jews. Our purpose in these chapters is an attempt to demonstrate that neither the Jew nor traditional Christian holds a position justified by divine revelation. We believe with the Jews that any claimant to Messiahship is a fraud if He never accedes to a restored throne of David. Without such promotion to royal office, inheritance of the land, accompanied by the liberation of His people and world rulership, He simply cannot be the biblical Messiah. The truth of the whole revelation given to Abraham and David is at stake on this point. We believe with the historic Church that Jesus of Nazareth was indeed the Messiah and that He was brought back from death by resurrection, but we strongly object to the distorted notions which the Church has attached to Messiahship. The "received" opinion of many Bible readers that Jesus does not need to ascend the throne of David in Israel in order to justify His claim to be the Messiah seems to us to be clearly mistaken. It leaves the whole Messianic drama unresolved. It calls in question the divine covenants. The churches have spent much energy trying to explain away the obvious import of the role destined for the Messiah. They have had to do this because they want on the one hand to affirm that Jesus is the Messiah and, on the other, to deny that He is going to reappear again on earth in order to reestablish a Davidic empire with power to rule the world. The great difference between traditional Christianity and the faith of the New Testament believers has to do with *the future*. It appears to us that churches constantly attempt an exposition of the Christian documents without taking account of the great climax to which the Bible everywhere looks forward. They are trying to read the biblical story — which from start to finish is colored by its dynamic Messianic hope for the future — with the final chapter, to which the entire narrative looks forward, torn from the book. This anti-Messianic tendency afflicts Bible readers both in the professional "theological" camp as well as those seeking a more "devotional" relationship with God.

The debate is critical for the future of the Church. It is a debate about the meaning of the term Kingdom of God, which it was the concern of Jesus to preach and teach. We are dealing, therefore, with fundamental questions about the nature of the Christian faith and the Christian Gospel. The problem presents itself in this way: If we grant that the covenants made with Abraham and David express the divine intention for the world, we must either abandon our faith in Jesus as the object of the promises, because He has not fulfilled them, or maintain that much yet needs to happen for the Messianic story to reach its goal. It is the latter alternative which we adopt, believing that this is the view of the Apostles and of Jesus who taught them. The resolution of the difficulty presented by the non-fulfillment of the Plan (the world has obviously not returned to paradise under a restored Messianic Kingdom) is possible only when the future coming of Jesus to rule the world with His followers is restored to the prominence it everywhere enjoys both in the Hebrew prophets and in the New Testament.

The Davidic Covenant in Psalms Two and Seventy-Two

A considerable body of literature preserved in the Bible concentrates on the bright future to be expected when the Davidic covenant bears fruit with the appearance of God's world deliverer. A brand new administration is to arise when the Messiah takes up His office as sovereign of a new and peaceful order on earth.

"The sweet singer of Israel" (II Sam. 23:1) had other purposes in writing Psalms than merely the expression of daily thanksgiving and praise, important as these topics are. David and the other writers of Psalms were prophets, driven by the Holy Spirit to foresee and forecast the future. It is one of the amazing features of much contemporary biblical commentary that the predictive element in Scripture is so severely played down. The New Testament, however, treats Messianic passages in the Psalms and prophets as direct predictions of events. Some of these have already been realized in the sufferings of Jesus; others in His birth, resurrection and ascension. A vast amount of prophecy relates to the future establishment of the Messiah's reign on earth.

Psalm 2 stands at the head of the first of the five collections of Psalms in our Hebrew Bible (Psalm 1 is considered introductory). Its topic is world government and the revolution which is going to bring this about. One would expect it to be the focus of much international discussion, since it deals with a major political event destined to effect the course of history and impacting the Middle East. Psalm 2 represents the purest Messianism, confirming the triumph of the rule of the Messiah in Jerusalem and the subjection of nation-states to His dominion. Conscious of the covenant which God made with his family, David tuned his harp to celebrate the coming victory of the Kingdom of God on earth. Those who later heard Jesus proclaim the impending arrival of the Kingdom would have brought to their understanding of Jesus' Message a knowledge of these verses which epitomized the hope of Israel, which is equally the Christian hope. In Paul's words:

> I serve the God of our fathers, believing everything that is in accordance with the Law and that is written in the prophets...And now I am standing trial for the hope of the promise made to the God of our fathers; the promise to which our twelve tribes hope to attain as they earnestly serve God day and night. And for this hope, O King, I am being accused by Jews... (Acts 24:14; 26:6, 7).

The language of Psalm 2, which sustained the Jewish Messianic hope shared by Christians, is quite inappropriate as a description of any historical king or kingdom. It presents a picture of a single ruler, the Messiah of Jewish expectation, installed in Jerusalem as Yahweh's vice-regent for the control of the world. It speaks of a time when the Messiah will take possession of His inheritance as governor of all nations. The scope of the Kingdom is both national and international. Its center is definitely Jewish, but its power extends to "the uttermost parts of the earth" (Ps. 2:8). Psalm 2 speaks of a world rebellion in opposition to Messianic government. In the words of a modern paraphrase, a summit conference is convened to consider how the restraints of the new world power can be resisted. God is unimpressed by the show of human stupidity. Yahweh will have placed His royal representative in Zion in the person of the Messiah/Son of God (the equation of the two titles is critical for New Testament Christology), whom the nations are advised to accept as the legitimate channel of divine authority for the blessing of the whole world. Clearly the change from one world system to the new will not be a smooth transition. This is a measure of the extent of human alienation from God at the time when He intervenes to replace current world leaders with the Messiah and the saints. The mood of the hostile world will express the sentiment of Jewish opposition to Jesus: "We will not have this man to rule over us" (Luke 19:14).

The comments of a leading authority on Hebrew Messianic expectations confirm our impression of the message of Psalm 2:

> The King addressed in Psalm 2 is to exercise absolutely unlimited sway over the world…The simplest view will always continue to be that the poet [prophet!] is transported in spirit to the birthpangs of the Messianic era, and from this standpoint describes the course of things. [5]

Other vivid pictures of the new world order under the reign of the Christ appear in Psalm 72. This Psalm points to a time when initial resistance has been overcome and the benefits of divine rule are becoming apparent. A Jewish-Christian theocracy is hardly what the world expects or desires. Present world systems, as we have seen from Psalm 2, will not yield without a fight to the new regime. We should bear in mind that the Kingdom of God is to be administered not by Jews who have not accepted Jesus as Messiah but by men and women of all nations who by conversion have become engrafted into the true Israel of God headed by the Messiah. These members of the Messianic community, Jews and Gentiles in one body, are seen by Paul the Apostle as "the true circumcision" (Phil. 3:3), that is, those who by an infusion of the Spirit of Christ are the genuine heirs of the Messianic promises. The royal house of David, in the New Testament, is not restricted to the national Jews. It consists of all those, of whatever nation, who have absorbed the Spirit of Jesus and thus gained a right to be part of the theocracy of Messiah. This is the implication of Jesus' promise that believers are constituted Messianic sons of God (John 1:12). Under their benign rule with Jesus the blessings outlined in Psalm 72 will spread across the earth.

The Psalm is probably the work of Solomon who had inherited the Messianic ideal from his father David. It opens with a prayer that God would administer peace on earth through His chosen king: "Give the king Your judgments, O God, and Your righteousness to the king's son" (Ps. 72:1). The gift of divine judgment is to be conferred on the

---

[5] *Hastings Dictionary of the Bible*, Extra Vol., p. 727.

ruler of the Kingdom. Jesus sees Himself as the recipient of that office: "The Father gave [the Son of Man] authority to execute judgment" (John 5:27). Jewish tradition considered the ideal king to be the Messiah. So the Targum reads: "O God, give the knowledge of Your judgments to the King Messiah, and Your justice to the son of King David." The *Midrash Tehillim* says of the sovereign addressed, "This is the King Messiah." A portrait of the Messianic King, functioning as God's instrument to restore peace to the earth, is provided by Isaiah 11:1-5:

> A shoot will spring from the stock of Jesse [David's father]; a new shoot will grow from his roots. On Him will rest the spirit of Yahweh, the spirit of wisdom and insight, the spirit of counsel and power, the spirit of knowledge and the fear of Yahweh: His inspiration will lie in fearing Yahweh, His judgment will not be given by appearances, His verdict not given on hearsay. He will judge the weak with integrity and give fair sentence for the humbles in the land. He will strike the country with the rod of His mouth and with the breath of His lips bring death to the wicked. Uprightness will be the belt around His waist and constancy the belt about His hips.

Christians, following the inspired leadership of Paul, recognize in this passage a portrait of the Messiah Jesus. Paul believed that the Messiah would establish His Kingdom by defeating "the evil one" foreseen by Isaiah. Quoting the ancient prophet, Paul predicted that "the Lord [Jesus] will destroy him [the Antichrist] with the breath of His mouth and will annihilate him with His glorious appearance at His coming" (II Thess. 2:8, citing Isa. 11:4).[6] The Hebrew Bible provided a fund of essential information about events surrounding the future arrival of Jesus to fulfill His Messianic role of ridding the world of evil rulership. Following the violent overthrow of Satanic government represented by the final Antichrist a new and harmonious world would emerge.

---

[6] Paul is interested in the Assyrian seen by Isaiah as a final instrument of divine punishment for Israel (cp. Ps. 83; Micah 5:5).

Psalm 89

The promise of future greatness for David's descendant, declared in the covenant, sustained the faithful during the nation's darkest hours. Psalm 89 celebrates an indomitable trust in God's purpose that the course of history is being guided by the lodestar of divine peace to come under Messiah's reign. Thus the Psalmist rehearses the Almighty's pledge:

> I have made a covenant with My chosen One, sworn an oath to My servant David: I have made your dynasty firm forever, built your throne stable age after age...Once You spoke in a vision, to Your faithful You said, I have given strength to a warrior, I have raised up a man chosen from My people. I have found David My servant, and anointed him [made him a Messiah] with My holy oil. My hand will always be with him, My arm will make him strong. No enemy will be able to outwit him, no wicked man overcome him; I shall crush his enemies before him, strike his opponents dead. My constancy and faithful love will be with him, in My name his strength will be triumphant. I shall establish his power over the sea, his dominion over the rivers. He will cry to Me, "You are my father, my God, the rock of my salvation!" So I shall make him My firstborn, the highest of earthly kings. I shall maintain My faithful love for him always, My covenant with him will stay firm. I have established his dynasty forever, his throne to be as lasting as the heavens...I shall not violate My covenant, I shall not withdraw the word once spoken. I have sworn by My holiness, once and for all, never will I break faith with David. His dynasty shall endure forever, his throne like the sun before Me, as the moon is established forever, a faithful witness in the skies (Ps. 89:3-37).

Once again, we have the authority of the Apostle for applying these words to Jesus. In pursuit of the Messianic ideal God the Father has begun to rescue believers from the Devil's oppressive regime:

> He has rescued us from the ruling force of darkness and transferred us to the kingdom of the Son that He loves...He is the image of the invisible God, the firstborn of all creation...He is the firstborn from the dead [by resurrection], so that He should be supreme in every way (Col. 1:13, 15, 18).

The sublime national hope of Israel, which Jesus, as a Jew, would have shared and which Paul as a model of apostolic Christianity specifically said he endorsed, looked forward to the appearance of the divinely authorized world statesman of this Psalm and the world peace described in outline by Psalm 72. The seventy-second Psalm is not quoted directly in the New Testament, but the function of the king described in the Psalm is exactly that claimed by Jesus. The idyllic portrait of a harmonious world goes far beyond anything ever realized under Solomon. The extent of the Kingdom is worldwide and its duration forever. It can apply only to a time beyond the turning point in history when, in the words of the New Testament Apocalypse, "the kingdoms of this world become the Kingdom of our God and of His Messiah" (Rev. 11:15). The throne of the ideal ruler will be founded on spiritual principles of justice, the only sound basis of government, as many would concur. The seed of righteousness bears fruit when all oppression comes to an end and when refreshment comes to the earth under the influence of a new culture instituted by the Messiah. Eventually all nations will see the benefits of God's rule through His Son.[7]

It was for this happy condition on earth that Jesus, whose heart was moved by the suffering He saw everywhere, urged us to pray "Thy Kingdom come…on earth" (Matt. 6:10). To take part in that Kingdom was to be the supreme desire of believers: "Seek first the Kingdom of God" (Matt. 6:33). The so-called Messianic Psalms are some of the many cheering passages of Scripture assuring the world of a marvelous outcome beyond the day of judgment, when the Messiah will take the faithful to assist Him in the supervision of the new world. The element of judgment and tragedy must not be overlooked. Those who oppose the Christ will be refused entry into the Kingdom. A certain standard of conduct is required of those who hope to enter the Kingdom when it comes: "Unless your righteousness exceeds that of the scribes and Pharisees you will not be able to enter the Kingdom" (Matt. 5:20). Disqualification because of certain unrepented, unethical practices threatened even members of the church community. Paul, like Jesus, insists on Christian standards for salvation:

---

[7] See, for example, Isa.19:16-25.

Do you not understand that the unrighteous will not inherit the Kingdom of God? Do not be deceived; neither fornicators, nor idolaters, nor adulterers, nor effeminate, nor homosexuals, nor thieves, nor the covetous, nor drunkards, nor revilers, nor swindlers will inherit the Kingdom of God (I Cor. 6:9, 10).

Psalm 110

Of all Old Testament passages this Psalm provides the favorite quotation for New Testament writers — not surprisingly since it encapsulates so beautifully the Messiah's progress towards world rule. Psalm 110:1 is cited or alluded to in the New Testament some twenty-five times. It is introduced as a divine oracle: "The utterance of Yahweh to my lord [*adoni*, the king]," and has close affinities with the Davidic covenant. Both the rabbis and Jesus saw in David's "lord" the promised Messiah-King (Mark 12:35-37). The Psalm contains all the elements of the New Testament revelation. Some have suggested that the New Testament is really a discussion and expansion of this Psalm. The book of Hebrews is virtually a commentary on its first verse.

The two principal players in the divine drama are Yahweh and His Messiah, who is the lord, and, paradoxically, also the son of David. Fulfillment of part of this Psalm came with the ascension of Jesus to the right hand of the Father. Peter makes this the concluding point of his revolutionary sermon announcing to dismayed Jews that they have recently crucified their Messiah (Acts 2:34-36). To clarify a perplexing situation Peter brings in the evidence of the prophetic oracle of Psalm 110. According to the Plan, the resurrection of Jesus from the dead introduced the session of the Messiah at the place of honor at God's right hand. Jesus is installed as Lord and Christ, only, however, until God later "makes His enemies His footstool." Thereupon, according to the information supplied by the Psalm, Yahweh will "stretch forth Your strong scepter from Zion," enabling the Messiah to "rule in the midst of [His] enemies" (Ps. 110:2). Evidently the figure described is a warrior, a military commander endowed with both priestly and regal office. Aided by the power of God (*adonai*), He is destined to "shatter kings in the day of [God's] wrath" (Ps. 110:5). Accompanying the conquering Messiah is a people in full support, dressed in shining garments and emerging at the dawn of the New Day (Ps. 110:3). It is not hard to see here a poetic description of resurrected believers assisting the Messiah, at His coming, in the establishment (by force at this stage) of His Kingdom. The Psalm complements the description of the world takeover planned for the Davidic king seen in Psalm 2.

Even the most ingenious exegetical theories cannot get rid of this material as the basis for the Bible's explicit Messianism. There is not a shred of evidence that Jesus or New Testament Christians were embarrassed at the military role outlined for the Messiah. What Psalm 2 describes is not the activity of some Maccabean prince. The figure who acts for God in the restoration of divine government on earth is the Messiah Himself, not, however, the Messiah as much church piety has presented Him. This raises at once the question as to how far the Messiah Jesus of the Bible has been accurately portrayed to those who sit in pews. A theologian at Cambridge suggests that there is cause for concern when he endorses the observation of a colleague that

> most preachers talk as if the Jesus they preach is identical with the Jesus of history. Theologians know that this is not so, but the theories devised in the attempt to connect the modern Christ with the original Jesus have become so far-fetched and obscure as to carry no conviction outside a very small circle.[8]

The professor notes "how very different Christianity has been at different periods."[9] The burning question is whether the royal Christ of the Gospels is really the Jesus presented to potential converts in the 20th century. Professor Cupitt sounds the alarm when he observes that

> developed Gentile Christianity of the sort which was beginning to take shape towards the end of the first century has very little to do with Jesus or the faith of the first generation. It is a new religion developed to *replace the original faith.*[10]

That early substitution of one faith for another would seem to require an urgent investigation, involving, as it must, a confusion about Jesus and His teaching of which most churchgoers are quite unaware. All too often the problem is silently ignored.

---

[8] Don Cupitt, *The Debate About Christ*, p. 133.
[9] *Ibid.*, p. 43.
[10] *Ibid.*, p. 69.

The Jesus of history and faith may be expected to make a comeback when Bible readers begin to imbibe the Messianic atmosphere in which Jesus operated, an atmosphere bequeathed to Him by the Hebrew prophets believed to be the spokesmen of the Creator Himself. At stake in our discussion is the nature of the Kingdom which Jesus came to announce. Crucial to our investigation is a recognition of the supreme authority of the Davidic covenant as the "charter for mankind," the "United Nations Charter," in the truest sense.

When in the course of time the Messiah arrived on the scene, a watchword in which the genius of the divine Plan was concentrated was available to describe the essence of the Christian faith. It was a term with a familiar ring to Jewish ears. It evoked hopes of a future for Israel and the world, promising the triumph of God on the spiritual, material, social and political planes. It was also a thoroughly apocalyptic idea announcing a judgment to come upon all forms of godlessness and, by a spectacular intervention, the appointment of a new government over human affairs. Our New Testament is devoted to the preparation of those who seek to obtain a place in that New Age of the Kingdom of God on earth.

7. The Faith of Jesus

In every system of knowledge there is a fundamental idea to be grasped, a core concept around which all other data must be organized. This central, dominating idea will determine the character of the subject as a whole and give meaning to every part of it. The core concept, the basic thesis, becomes the criterion by which all subsidiary ideas are evaluated. The Christian faith comes to us in the Bible as a body of information challenging us to response and action. The source of that information is ultimately God Himself transmitting His Message through prophets and teachers and supremely through His principal representative, Jesus the Messiah.

What, then, is the central core concept of the teaching of Jesus? What forms the heart of His Message? What one single idea underlies all His preaching and teaching? What primary idea must be grasped and believed by any who want to follow Jesus?

The answer to this question can be discovered by anyone with an ordinary ability to read, any version of the Bible, and an earnest desire to find out what Jesus taught. The importance of Christianity's key idea — the heart of the Gospel — so impressed the writers of the New Testament that they emphasized it over and over again.

It is a testimony to the extraordinary way in which fundamental concepts can be lost that Jesus' master idea is very seldom, if ever, presented to the public in late twentieth-century preaching. Equally amazing is the fact that leaders of organized Christianity admit that they are not proclaiming what Jesus proclaimed as the Gospel.

A number of master texts, spanning the period of time from the opening of Jesus' ministry in Galilee until the death of Paul, demonstrate a refreshingly simple concept: The Bible knows of *one*

Gospel only for Jew and Gentile alike. It is the Gospel about the Kingdom of God:

> Jesus came into Galilee proclaiming God's Gospel [Good News] and saying: "The time has come and the *Kingdom of God* is approaching: Repent and believe *the Gospel*" (Mark 1:14, 15).

> When they believed Philip as he proclaimed *the Gospel about the Kingdom of God* and the name of Jesus Christ, they were being baptized, both men and women (Acts 8:12).

> Paul put his case to them, testifying to *the Kingdom of God* and trying to persuade them about Jesus, arguing from the Law of Moses and the prophets. This went on from early morning until evening, and some were convinced by what he said, while the rest were skeptical (Acts 28:23, 24).

> I solemnly testify, in the presence of God and of Christ Jesus, who is to judge the living and the dead, both to His appearing and *His Kingdom*. Herald *the Message...* (II Tim. 4:1, 2).

Christianity's Central Idea

Three primary witnesses to Jesus' ministry, Matthew, Mark and Luke, unanimously declare Jesus to be an evangelist, the bearer of God's Gospel about the Kingdom of God. Without any possible fear of contradiction we can assert with complete confidence that the axis around which all Jesus' teaching revolves is the Kingdom of God.

Mark provides us with a resume of Jesus' entire career. His public ministry is launched with His announcement of the Gospel about the Kingdom of God. He came into Galilee and summoned His compatriots to a complete change of mind — repentance — and to belief in and commitment to the Good News, or Gospel about the Kingdom of God (Mark 1:14, 15). In so doing they would be aligning themselves with God's great design for the rescue of the human race.

Luke emphasizes the fundamental importance of the Gospel about the Kingdom. The first piece of information about Jesus given us by Luke, when the birth of the Messiah is announced, concerns the Kingdom of God: "The Lord God will give Him the throne of His Father David and He shall reign over the house of Jacob forever" (Luke 1:32, 33).

As any Jew knew well this was a statement about Jesus' kingship in the coming Kingdom of God. Jesus Himself gave a clear definition of the underlying purpose of His ministry with these words: "I must proclaim *the Good News about the Kingdom of God* to the other cities also: That is the reason for which I was sent" (Luke 4:43). This text opens up the mind of Jesus for us and provides the key to the whole Christian religion, which must be based on His teaching.

Luke immediately goes on to tell us that Jesus was preaching "the Message," or "the Word" (Luke 5:1). This is Luke's (and the New Testament's) shorthand term for the Christian Message or Gospel of salvation. A definition of the content of the Message is provided by Matthew when he reports that Jesus was a preacher of the "Message about the Kingdom" (Matt. 13:19). Again Luke calls it "the Word of God" (Luke 8:11) and Mark simply "the Word" (Mark 4:14).

In His celebrated comparison of the sower to the evangelist who meets with varying responses, Jesus describes the Gospel as vital information needing to take deep root within the human heart. A grasp of this Message enables the convert to embark on the Christian journey towards the Kingdom. Nothing could be more crucial for our spiritual welfare than to gain an understanding of this Message. It is one message and one message only — the Good News about the Kingdom of God. Luke 4:43 and 5:1 equate the Message about the Kingdom with "the Message of God." "The Message," "the Word," "the Gospel," and "the testimony" are all interchangeable terms. All subsequent references to "the Word" and "the Gospel" throughout the New Testament should be traced back to and clarified by the more comprehensive "parent text," "*the Gospel about the Kingdom of God.*" This will impart harmony and continuity to the entire New Testament, as well as linking it to the earlier revelation in the Hebrew Bible. As John Bright wrote:

> The concept of the Kingdom of God involves, in a real sense, the total message of the Bible. Not only does it loom large in the teachings of Jesus, it is to be found, in one form or another, through the length and breadth of the Bible...To grasp what is meant by the Kingdom of God is to come very close to the heart of the Bible's gospel of salvation.[1]

---

[1] *The Kingdom of God*, New York: Abingdon Press, 1953, p. 7.

The spreading of the Gospel Message was of paramount importance to Jesus and the disciples He chose to assist Him: "He went round the whole of Galilee teaching in their synagogues, proclaiming the Good News of the Kingdom of God..." (Matt. 4:23; 9:35). "He sent them to proclaim the Kingdom of God" (Luke 9:2). He charged His followers with the responsibility of spreading the news about the Kingdom: "Allow the dead to bury their dead; but as for you, go and proclaim everywhere the Kingdom of God" (Luke 9:60).

Jesus defined the ultimate purpose of life for His followers. It was the quest for the Kingdom of God: "Seek first the Kingdom of God..." (Matt. 6:33). The Kingdom was to be the supreme treasure for which no sacrifice would be too great (Matt. 13:44-46). The Kingdom was also the object of their fervent prayer, "Thy Kingdom come" (Matt. 6:10). An understanding of God's Kingdom Plan required a gift of illumination granted to those who wholeheartedly followed Jesus and His teaching, but withheld from the superficial disciple (Matt. 13:13-16).

The same subject of the Kingdom dominated the conversation between Jesus and the disciples after His death and resurrection. When the Lord reappeared to His chosen representatives, for almost six weeks "He spoke to them about the Kingdom of God" (Acts 1:3). In a final conversation with Jesus before He departed from the earth, the disciples asked whether the moment for the restoration of the Kingdom had now arrived (Acts 1:6).

Information Vital for the Potential Believer

Luke informs us about the facts put to potential converts before they could be baptized into the Christian faith. His statement reads like an early creed, providing an ideal model, in summary form, of the essence of evangelism: *"When they believed Philip as he proclaimed the Gospel about the Kingdom of God and the name of Jesus Christ, they were being baptized, both men and women"* (Acts 8:12).

Philip was faithfully following the example of Jesus' own evangelism: Jesus had made belief in the Kingdom of God the basis of salvation: "When anyone hears the Message of the Kingdom and does not understand it, the Devil comes and snatches away the Word which has been sown in his heart [mind] so that he cannot believe and be saved." Salvation was related to the Messiah's promise of a supreme reward to His disciples. They were to assist in the rulership of the New World or New Age of the coming Kingdom: "I assign to you a Kingdom as my Father has assigned a Kingdom to Me, and you shall sit on thrones to govern the twelve tribes of Israel" (see Matt. 19:28; Luke 22:28-30). Earlier Jesus had promised: "Fear not, little flock, your Father has gladly chosen to give you the Kingdom" (Luke 12:32). An invitation to kingship in the Kingdom was evidently the basis of Jesus' appeal to His audiences.

No wonder, then, that Paul, faithfully imitating Jesus, could sum up his whole ministry by calling it a preaching of *the Gospel of the Kingdom* (Acts 20:25). Luke wishes us never to forget what the Apostles always proclaimed as the Gospel. He goes on to inform us that Paul preached the Kingdom of God for three months in Corinth (Acts 19:8). In order to leave no room for doubt or misunderstanding he ends his second treatise, the book of Acts, by describing Paul's activity in Rome: For two years he preached "the Good News about the Kingdom of God and taught concerning the Lord Jesus Christ" (Acts 28:31). This was the Gospel Message of salvation he addressed both to Jews and Gentiles alike (Acts 28:23, 28, 31).

The same Gospel of the Kingdom is to be heralded throughout the whole world as essential preparation for the Kingdom's final arrival at the Day of the Lord, the return of Jesus in power to rule on earth. In Jesus' own words: "This Gospel about the Kingdom will be preached in the whole world…and then the end shall come" (Matt. 24:14).

With this evidence before us — and there is much more — we may say that no one honestly in search of biblical truth can miss recognizing the principal idea behind the Christian Message of salvation. The Kingdom of God is undoubtedly the heart and core of Jesus' and the Apostles' Gospel preaching, the basic idea around which true Christianity revolves.

The Scholarly Consensus on the Mission of Jesus

There is no room for disagreement that the Kingdom of God was the subject of Jesus' entire Message and mission. "On one central point there is a strong consensus of opinion…The consensus can be summarized thus: The central theme in the preaching and life of Jesus was the Kingdom of God."[2] This author points out, however, the extraordinary fact that in the message preached by the Church since those apostolic times "the Kingdom of God has not occupied a central place."[3]

Further distinguished names will confirm the absolute centrality of the Message about the Kingdom in the teaching of Jesus: "This term [Kingdom of God] is at the center of His proclamation."[4] Jon Sobrino writes:

> The most certain historical datum about Jesus' life is that the concept which dominated His preaching, the reality which gave meaningfulness to all His activity, was "the Kingdom of God." This fact and its implications are of fundamental importance. It provides us with two essential keys to understanding Jesus. First, Jesus is not the central focus of His own teaching; this fact is commonly admitted. As Karl Rahner put it, "Jesus preached the Kingdom of God, not Himself."[5]

While it is true that Jesus also made exclusive claims for Himself, His Message nevertheless centered on the Kingdom. Other prominent witnesses corroborate our thesis: "The whole message of Jesus focuses upon the Kingdom of God."[6] "It is generally admitted that the focal point of Jesus' message was the inbreaking of the Kingdom of God."[7]

At the turn of the century, the British scholar Archibald Robertson, delivering the Bampton Lectures on the Kingdom of God, had asserted: "There can be no question that in our Lord's teaching the Kingdom of God is the representative and all-embracing summary of his distinctive mission...Throughout, his message is the good news of the Kingdom."[8]

---

[2] Thomas Groome, *Christian Religious Education*, San Francisco: Harper and Row, 1980, p. 39.

[3] *Ibid.,* p. 42.

[4] Hans Küng, *On Being a Christian*, New York: Doubleday, 1976, p. 214.

[5] *Christology at the Crossroads*, Orbis Books, 1978, p. 41.

[6] Norman Perrin, *Language of the Kingdom*, Philadelphia: Fortress Press, 1976, p. 1.

[7] Reginald Fuller, "The Double Commandment of Love," in *Essays on the Love Commandment*, ed. Schottroff, Philadelphia: Fortress Press, 1978, p. 51.

[8] *Regnum Dei*, New York: The Macmillan Co., 1901, pp. 8, 9.

A chorus of distinguished writers on the Bible proclaims the fact that Christianity is a religion whose leading idea is the Kingdom of God:

> The Kingdom of God is the central theme of the teaching of Jesus, and it involves his whole understanding of his own person and work.[9]

> The Kingdom of God is, in a certain and important sense, the grand central theme of all Holy Scripture...This reign of God arises out of His own sovereign nature, was reflected in the "dominion" bestowed by God on the first Adam, was forfeited quickly by reason of the sin of man, has been restored judicially in the Last Adam, will be realized on earth in the final age of human history, and reaches out endlessly beyond history where we behold a throne which, as John explains, is "the throne of God and the Lamb" (Rev. 22:3)...In the Biblical doctrine of the Kingdom of God we have the Christian philosophy of history.[10]

> The New Testament is not less theocratically undergirded and no less eschatologically oriented toward the Kingdom of God than the Old Testament.[11]

> The ministry of Jesus revolves around a fascinating term — "the Kingdom of God." Everything else is related to it and radiates from it.[12]

> The Kingdom of God is the central point in Christ's teaching...The fundamental teachings of Jesus naturally group themselves round this central theme.[13]

---

[9] Alan Richardson, *A Theological Word Book of the Bible*, London: SCM Press, 1957, p. 119.

[10] A.J. McClain, *The Greatness of the Kingdom*, Chicago: Moody Press, 1968, pp. 4-5.

[11] T.C. Vriezen, "Theocracy and Soteriology," in *Essays on Old Testament Hermeneutics*, ed. C. Westermann, Atlanta: John Knox, 1979, pp. 217-218.

[12] L. Goppelt, *Theology of the New Testament*, Grand Rapids: Eerdmans, 1981, Vol. 1, p. 43.

[13] *Dictionary of Christ and the Apostles*, Vol. 1, p. 486.

The Kingdom of God gives us a coherent center around which to assemble the diverse parts of Scripture. John Reumann says this:

> Ask any hundred New Testament scholars around the world, Protestant, Catholic, or non-Christian, what the central Message of Jesus of Nazareth was, the vast majority of them — perhaps every single expert — would agree that His message centered in the Kingdom of God...The modern investigators agree: The "good news" which Jesus announced had to do with God and His Kingdom...But today when we hear about Jesus' Message of the Kingdom of God, it sounds strange to our ears and prompts a multitude of questions...There is a tremendous danger for modern men that Jesus' teachings and Message, as they are heard read in little snatches in church on Sundays or are scanned piecemeal by individuals, will seem isolated from each other and atomistic. An item here, a ray of light there, a truth somewhere else, but seldom anything to integrate all of Jesus' teachings into a whole that makes sense as a totality...That is why it is so important to see that Jesus had a central Message, and that it was about God's Kingdom. For it is this theme of the Kingdom which integrates all of Jesus' words and deeds...The Kingdom of God is a unifying emphasis around which all that Jesus said and did can be arranged. Mark's Gospel opens, after its brief prologue, with a terse statement of good news, intended to set the tone for the entire book.[14]

An Australian theologian notes the centrality of the Kingdom for evangelism:

> Naive views which separate the Gospel from the Kingdom are impossible if we follow biblical guidelines: In the New Testament (especially the Evangelists) the Gospel is always "the Gospel of the Kingdom..." The nature of the Kingdom is all-important, for it defines the nature of the salvation that Jesus came to bring and the Gospel that we are, therefore, called to preach...Our question is: What Gospel do we preach at two minutes to midnight on the Doomsday scale?...What if we cannot agree on, or are not sure of, the nature of the very Gospel that we are to preach?[15]

---

[14] *Jesus in the Church's Gospels*, Fortress Press, 1968, p. 142ff.

[15] R.A. Cole, "The Gospel and the Kingdom: What Are They?" *Agenda for a Biblical Church*, Sydney, Australia: Anglican Information Office, 1981, pp. 32, 33.

In the light of these facts, it is hard to see how Christ can be preached if His Gospel of the Kingdom is not communicated to potential converts. Uncertainty about the Gospel would seem to be an admission of confusion in the Church. As Paul stated, "faith comes from hearing and hearing from Messiah's Message" (Rom. 10:17). "How," Paul asked, "can they believe in Him *whom they have not heard [preaching]*?" (Rom. 10:14, NASV).[16] His point was that the authentic Gospel preaching of Jesus must be relayed by evangelists representing the Messiah. In Paul's mind the Message which Jesus had delivered must reach the potential convert. To the Ephesians he wrote: "Jesus came and preached peace to you who were far away and peace to those who were near" (Eph. 2:17). "Learning Christ" was a matter of "hearing Him" and being "taught by Him just as the truth is in Jesus" (Eph. 4:20, 21). The Apostles had never heard the modern theory that the historical Jesus' preaching was for Jews only and that the risen Christ had a different Message for Gentiles! Once again we see how critically important it is to believe in the Jesus of history and to anchor our faith in the Gospel as He proclaimed it.

On this point the New Testament shows a wonderful unity. According to the writer to the Hebrews, the Christian Gospel was first preached by Jesus Himself and then passed on to subsequent generations by faithful witnesses of the same Kingdom Message (Heb. 2:3). John warned against the menace of those who do not "bring the teaching of the Messiah" (II John 7-9). Paul insisted on adherence to "sound words, namely the words of the Lord Jesus Christ" (I Tim. 6:3). It is agreed on all sides that Jesus' supreme purpose concerned the Kingdom of God. At the same time those who today claim to be propagating the Gospel as Jesus preached it say almost nothing about the Kingdom! This clearly makes no sense. One obviously cannot have the teacher, Christ, without the teaching, the Message of the Kingdom. It can be very confusing to say that "the Gospel *is* Christ," unless we are thoroughly grounded in the accounts of Matthew, Mark and Luke, which constantly declare that Jesus' Message has an objective reality distinct from Himself as the Gospel of God, His Father: "Whoever loses his life for My sake *and the Gospel's* will save it" (Mark 8:35).

---

[16] For this translation, see W. Sanday and A.C. Headlam, *The International Critical Commentary: Romans,* T & T Clark, 1905, p. 296.

The subject, Christ, is given a clear complement in Scripture. He is not a silent Savior dead on a cross (essential as His death is). He preached the Gospel of the Kingdom. Jesus without His teaching is not Jesus at all! A Jesus divorced from His Hebrew heritage and background in the Hebrew prophets is a Jesus uprooted from history. Without sufficient instruction, would-be believers will imagine Jesus in a thousand different ways. Hence the importance for Christians of being rooted in the Bible and the words of Jesus Himself.

Elizabeth Achtemeier senses the missing element in contemporary presentations of the Christian Message:

> One of the central messages of the New Testament, *which is now rarely heard by the average churchgoer*, is the proclamation of the coming of the Kingdom of God in the person of Jesus Christ. That coming was promised in every major theological complex in the Old Testament...The prophets promised the new age of the kingdom, on the other side of the judgment of the exile, with a new exodus (Isa. 52:11-12) and wilderness wanderings (Isa. 48:20-21) to a renewed promised land (Ezek. 34:25-31), where Israel would dwell in faithfulness and security, in a new covenant relation with her God (Jer. 31:31-34), and would by her light attract all nations into her fellowship (Isa. 60:1-3; 56:6-8). Israel anticipated that coming kingdom and knew a foretaste of it in her worship (Pss. 47, 96-99). Throughout most of the pages of the Old Testament she strains forward toward its arrival.[17]

The point should not be missed that Jesus' Gospel "is now rarely heard by the average churchgoer."

A Summary of the New Testament Facts

We may gain a sense of the massive importance of the Kingdom of God in biblical Christianity by quoting some of the many verses in which Jesus spoke of it (the term "Kingdom of Heaven," used only by Matthew, is the equivalent of "Kingdom of God." They are interchangeable terms. Matthew followed the Jewish practice of avoiding the term "God" and used instead "Heaven"):

---

[17] *Preaching as Theology and Art*, Nashville: Abingdon Press, 1984, pp. 41, 42, emphasis added.

Then Jesus traveled through all Galilee, teaching in their synagogues and proclaiming the Gospel of the Kingdom (Matt. 4:23).

And I tell you that many will come from the east and from the west and will take their seats with Abraham and Isaac and Jacob in the Kingdom of Heaven, while the natural heirs of the Kingdom will be driven out into the darkness outside: there will be weeping and gnashing of teeth (Matt. 8:11, 12).

And Jesus went round all the towns and villages, teaching in their synagogues and proclaiming the Gospel of the Kingdom (Matt. 9:35).

To you [disciples] it is granted to know the secrets of the Kingdom of Heaven, to them it is not (Matt. 13:10).

When a man hears the Message concerning the Kingdom the Devil comes and snatches away the Message from his heart so that he cannot believe and be saved (Matt. 13:19).

Seek first God's Kingdom and righteousness (Matt. 6:33).

The Son of Man will send His angels, and they will gather out of His Kingdom all causes of sin and all who violate His laws; and these they will throw into the fiery furnace (Matt. 13:41).

Then the righteous will shine like the sun in their Father's Kingdom. Listen, everyone who has ears (Matt. 13:43).

In this manner therefore pray, "...May Thy Kingdom come" (Matt. 6:9, 10).

It is easier for a camel to go through the eye of a needle than for a rich man to enter the Kingdom of God (Matt. 19:24).

"Command," she replied, "that these my two sons may sit one at Your right hand and one at Your left in Your Kingdom" (Matt. 20:21).

I tell you I will never again drink the fruit of the vine till the day that I drink the new wine with you in My Father's Kingdom (Matt. 26:29).

And this Gospel of the Kingdom shall be proclaimed throughout the whole world to set the evidence before the nations; and then the end will come (Matt. 24:14).

I must proclaim the Gospel of the Kingdom of God to the other towns also, because for this purpose I was sent (Luke 4:43).

Shortly after this He visited town after town, and village after village, proclaiming the Gospel Message of the Kingdom of God (Luke 8:1).

He sent them out to proclaim the Kingdom of God and to cure the sick (Luke 9:2).

And receiving them kindly He talked to them about the Kingdom of God (Luke 9:11).

"Leave the dead," said Jesus, "to bury their dead; but you go and announce far and wide the Kingdom of God" (Luke 9:60).

Do not be afraid, little flock: it is your Father's good pleasure to give you the Kingdom (Luke 12:32).

So also, when you see these things happening [the events surrounding the return of Jesus to the earth], you may be sure that the Kingdom of God is about to come (Luke 21:31).

You, however, have remained with Me in My trials; and I assign to you, as My Father has assigned to Me, a Kingdom — so that you may eat and drink at My table in My Kingdom, and sit on thrones to govern the twelve tribes of Israel (Luke 22:28-30).[18]

These quotations will suffice to underline the fact that the Kingdom of God is indeed the focus of the ministry and mission of

---

[18] The word "judge" which appears in many versions is properly translated "govern," "administer" or "rule." (Cp. the OT "judge" who was a ruler, and Ps. 2:19, I Macc. 9:73, etc.)

Jesus. The Kingdom is overwhelming in its importance and decisive for the meaning of Christianity, the key which unlocks the teaching of the New Testament.

Jesus inaugurated His ministry in Galilee by calling on the public to "Repent and believe the Good News of the Kingdom of God" (Mark 1:14, 15). With this resounding command the risen Jesus continues to speak to men and women everywhere. The challenge is as urgent today as it was when first issued by Jesus. The challenge of the Bible is this: "Change your minds and your lives and believe in the Good News Message of salvation, the Message about the Kingdom of God which Jesus and the Apostles always proclaimed." Again, in the words of Dr. Robertson, distinguished lecturer of the Church of England: "The Kingdom of God is the Christian answer to the most vital question that man has to solve, the question of the purpose of his being."[19]

The Kingdom Expected by Jesus' Contemporaries

The Kingdom of God eagerly anticipated by Jesus' fellow countrymen was undoubtedly a new world order affecting not just a handful of disciples, but the entire earth. The "Day of the Lord," which was to introduce it, would be a cataclysm like the flood because of its destructive power (Matt. 24:37-39). Yet beyond the awful judgment, a renewed, regenerated earth was to emerge, and sane, peaceful government would ensure a golden age for all permitted to survive into the new Kingdom. Unlike many modern audiences, those who heard Jesus proclaim the Kingdom would have been fully aware of what the prophets had said about the coming great turning point in history:

> The mortal will be humbled, and brought low...Get among the rocks, hide in the dust, at the sight of the terror of Yahweh, at the brilliance of His majesty, when He arises to make the earth quake. Human pride will lower its eyes, the arrogance of men will be humbled, Yahweh alone will be exalted on that day. Yes, that day will be the day of Yahweh Sabaoth [of the armies of heaven] against all pride and arrogance, against all that is great, to bring it down...Human pride will be humbled, the arrogance of men will be brought low. Yahweh alone will be exalted on that day, and all idols

---

[19] A. Robertson, *Regnum Dei*, Bampton Lectures, 1901, p. vii.

thrown down. Go into the hollows and the rocks, into the caverns of the earth, at the sight of the terror of Yahweh, at the brilliance of His majesty, when He arises to make the earth quake. That day man will fling to the moles and the bats the idols of silver and the idols of gold that he made for worship (Isa. 2:9-20, Jerusalem Bible).

The hope of a new era of peace on earth, following the fearful Day of the Lord, is a constant theme of the Hebrew prophets. The expectation about the Kingdom, current when Jesus launched His campaign for repentance and belief in the Good News, has been clearly documented by historian and theologian alike. The facts they present provide an indispensable guide to the meaning of Jesus' favorite phrase, "the Kingdom of God." Unless that term is firmly rooted in its first-century Hebrew environment, it becomes quite impossible to know what Jesus requires of us with His call for "repentance and belief in the Gospel about the Kingdom." Detached from its context, the Kingdom of God has been redefined, with almost total disregard for its biblical meaning, in various different ways acceptable to our own religious ideas and ideals. It is quite wrong, however, to attribute these to Jesus or call them His Gospel. The loss of a proper historical sense for defining the Christian Gospel of the Kingdom lies at the heart of all our theological confusion and division.

One distinguished historian of Christianity describes the historical setting necessary for grasping the impact made by Jesus and John the Baptist's announcement of the Kingdom:

> The expectation of a great deliverance...and of a golden age of righteousness and peace and prosperity, kept alive by the lessons from Scripture which were read and expounded in the synagogues..., gave birth from time to time to prophets, who announced that the great moment was come...[20]

With their proclamation, both Jesus and John were calling upon men and women to prepare for the coming divine intervention, the Day of the Lord, which in the New Testament is the equivalent of the expected arrival of the Kingdom. The teaching of Jesus and the Apostles is dominated throughout by the expectation of the coming

[20] G.F. Moore, *History of Religions*, New York: Charles Scribner's Sons, 1926, p. 107.

judgment and the consequent inauguration of the new world order. Every word of their exhortations is directed towards preparing us for the great event. The whole New Testament is a manual of instruction for those preparing to rule with Jesus in the coming Kingdom.

Apostolic preaching of the Gospel of the Kingdom of God, the Christian Gospel, presupposes an understanding of this Hebrew view of history. Our problem is that audiences are now constantly asked to accept "the Gospel," in ignorance of the Hebrew frame of reference within which Jesus taught. This results in a misunderstanding which can only be corrected when potential converts are taught the basic "vocabulary" of the New Testament. It is no solution to reduce the Gospel to a Message only about the death and resurrection of Jesus. These events, most certainly, guarantee the future establishment of the Kingdom; but the Kingdom remains the Kingdom foreseen by the prophets. We are still to pray for its coming (Matt. 6:10). And it is the heart of the Gospel of salvation (Acts 8:12; 28:23, 31; Matt. 13:19; Luke 8:12).

Man Destined to Be Ruler

The subject of the Christian Gospel, the Kingdom of God, has its roots deep in the Hebrew Scriptures (somewhat unfortunately known to us as "the Old Testament," since many professing Christians think of "old" as practically equivalent to "discarded"). It is well to remember that Paul referred to the Old Testament as the "sacred writings which are able to give you [Christians] the wisdom which leads to salvation through faith which is in Messiah Jesus" (II Tim. 2:15). To be a Christian, therefore, we must acquire the wisdom and understanding found in the sacred revelation of the Hebrew part of our Scriptures.

The very first command given to man was to "rule...over all the earth" (Gen. 1:26). We see here the start of the golden thread of the Kingdom which runs throughout the Bible from Genesis to Revelation. Adam was assigned a position as God's vice-regent. Made in the image and likeness of God, man is a "facsimile" of God, a representation which corresponds to a model (Gen. 1:26). The word "image" means a hewn or carved statue such as an idol, a sculpture. Both "'image' and 'likeness' are expressions which...point back from man to God…God shows himself as the 'prototype' and 'original' of man."[21]

The Psalmist sings of the exalted position conferred upon man by God:

> What is man, that You are mindful of him? And the son of man, that You visit him? For You have made him but little lower than God, and crowned him with glory and honor. You make him to have dominion over the works of Your hands; You have put all things under his feet (Ps. 8:4-6).

Honor and majesty are the attributes of a king ("Clothed with honor and majesty, God is coming to rule the world," Ps. 96:6, 10, 13). Man, therefore, is created to be God's representative ruler on earth. The problem is that "we do not yet see all things subjected to him" (Heb. 2:8).[22]

Kingship over the Promised Land

The promise of the land (Gen. 13:14, 15, etc.) as a possession was made to Abraham on condition that he give up everything in obedience to God (Gen. 12:1-4). Abraham, "the father of the faithful," is a "model Christian," demonstrating his faith in the unseen God. He is commended for his confidence that, despite every evidence to the contrary (Rom. 4:18), he would indeed be the "father" of the promised Messiah. His inheritance included the Kingdom of God which was nothing less than the promised land, extended beyond the boundaries of Palestine to the far corners of the earth: The extension of the land to include the world is the basis of Paul's remark that "the promise to Abraham or to his seed that he would be heir of the world was not through the Law but through the righteousness of faith" (Rom. 4:13).

The paraphrase given by the *International Critical Commentary* on Romans gives the sense exactly: "The promise made to Abraham and his descendants of worldwide Messianic rule, as it was not dependent on circumcision, so also was not dependent on Law, but on a righteousness that was a product of faith. If this worldwide inheritance really depended on any legal system, and if it was limited to those who were under such a system, there would be no place left

---

[21] Friedrich Horst, "Face to Face," *Interpretation*, July 1950, p. 260.

[22] The reference is to Jesus as the representative man.

for Faith or Promise."[23] "The worldwide Messianic rule" is a synonym for the Kingdom of God, which is the principal theme of the Christian Gospel. It must follow that Jesus and the Apostles announced "the worldwide Messianic rule" when they proclaimed the Gospel. It is a rule waiting to be publicly manifested at the Second Coming. All attempts to force it into the present (except in the sense that the Message and the power of the future Kingdom are already active in advance because Jesus now sits at the right hand of the Father) are dislocations of the biblical scheme and account for the confusion which exists on the subject of the Kingdom (and thus about the faith itself). We are to pray "Thy Kingdom come." This means that the Kingdom has not yet come!

The grand central theme of all Scripture is the promise that ideal government will be brought to the earth when Jesus, as Messiah, seed of Abraham and David (Matt. 1:1), returns to rule. Bible readers should be encouraged and humbled to know the meaning of their calling as "children of Abraham," "co-heirs" and prospective "co-rulers" with the Messiah:

> Blessed are the gentle, for they shall inherit the earth (Matt. 5:5).

> Thou has made them to be a Kingdom and priests to our God and they shall reign on the earth (Rev. 5:10).

> They came to life [in resurrection] and ruled as kings with Messiah for a thousand years (Rev. 20:4).

> If we suffer with Him we shall reign as kings with Him (II Tim. 2:12).

> All things belong to you (I Cor. 3:21).

> God has not subjected to angels the inhabited earth of the future, which is our theme, [but He has subjected it to Jesus and His followers] (Heb. 2:5).

> The heavens are the heavens of the Lord, but the earth He has given to the children of men (Ps. 115:16).

---

[23] *International Critical Commentary*, p. 109.

He who overcomes will rule the nations (Rev. 2:26). Take charge of ten cities (Luke 19:17). Rule over many things (Matt. 25:23).

How blessed is the man who fears the Lord...His descendants will be mighty on earth...He has made known to His people the power of His works by giving them the heritage of the nations...He raises the poor from the ash heap to make them sit with princes, with the princes of His people (Ps. 112:2; 111:6; 113:7, 8).

Walk in a manner worthy of God who is calling you into His own Kingdom and glory (I Thess. 2:12).

Once again the voices of distinguished commentators should be heeded, as they complain about a serious absence of understanding on the part of churchgoing Bible readers:

While the majority of Christendom has been in the habit of thinking of "heaven" as the place for which the children of God are destined, Jesus makes the startling statement that the meek are to possess the earth. This accords with the prophetic and apocalyptic traditions almost in their entirety...The Kingdom of God comes from heaven to earth, and earth will be fitted to be the scene of such rule.[24]

How does it come to pass that, with open Bibles before them, men and women should be wrong not so much about certain details with respect to the Gospel, but about the whole thing, about the very essence of the Gospel? It is quite understandable that there should be certain points, certain facets of truth about which people are not clear and about which there may be a division of opinion. This Gospel is many-sided; it has many aspects, so that this is not surprising. But I do suggest that it is indeed very surprising that at the end of the 20th century, men and women should still be all wrong about what the Gospel is; wrong about its foundation, wrong about its central message; wrong about its objective and wrong about the way in which one comes into relationship with it. And yet, that is the very position we are confronted with at this time.[25]

---

[24] G.R. Beasley-Murray, *Jesus and the Kingdom of God*, Grand Rapids: Eerdmans, 1986, p. 163.
[25] Martin Lloyd-Jones, Cassette No. 5356, "The Signs of the Kingdom."

Most people have a wrong view of the kingdom. We will not be floating around on clouds. The kingdom will be a government, which will operate in perfect righteousness. There will be people in positions of authority who were faithful servants of Jesus Christ on earth. Just as a good worker gets a promotion, so Christ's faithful stewards will get promotions in the Kingdom. Some will manage ten cities.[26]

Everything in the Gospels points to the idea that life in the Kingdom of God in the Age to Come will be life on the earth — life transformed by the Kingdom of God when His people enter in their full blessing (Matt. 19:28).[27]

We shall dwell in glorified bodies on the glorified earth. This is one of the great Christian doctrines that has been *almost entirely forgotten and ignored.* Unfortunately the Christian Church — I speak generally — *does not believe this,* and therefore does not teach it. It has lost its hope, and this explains why it spends most of its time in trying to improve life in this world, in preaching politics…But something remarkable is going to be true of us according to the Apostle Paul in 1 Cor. 6:1-3: "Dare any of you having a matter against another, go to law against the unjust and not before the Saints? Do you not know that the Saints shall rule the world?"…*This is Christianity. This is the truth by which the New Testament Church lived.* It was because of this that they were not afraid of their persecutors…This was the secret of their endurance, their patience and their triumphing over everything that was set against them.[28]

The Hope for Just Government on Earth as the Basis of Jesus' Gospel

The tension between the "present evil state of things" (Gal. 1:4) and the hope of the coming Kingdom of God gives a sense of excitement and drama to the whole Bible. A coherent "plot" runs throughout the Scriptures. Adam is created with a divine office. He

---

[26] Tony Evans, *What a Way to Live!* Nashville: Word, 1997, p. 171.

[27] George Ladd, *A Theology of the New Testament*, Eerdmans, 1974, p. 48.

[28] Martin Lloyd-Jones, *Commentary on Romans,* Grand Rapids: Zondervan, 1976, pp. 72, 75, 76, emphasis added.

"sells out" to Satan after being outwitted by the cunning of the Devil (the arch-villain of the drama). The first pair thus "vote for" the evil ruler, and this tendency to submit to Satan is perpetuated in subsequent generations. The accumulating rebellion reaches a crisis in Genesis 6, where evil angelic beings (fallen "Sons of God"[29]) interfere with the human genetic system to produce a race of giants. This terrible condition on earth calls for a world catastrophe at the Flood, in which only eight persons survive the judgment. The descendants of Noah do no better than their predecessors. A second race of tyrants is born of the hybrid angelic-human "marriages" (Gen. 6:4; Num. 13:33; see also Jude 6).

The divine solution for rescuing man from his apparently incorrigible wickedness lies in the promise of the "seed of Abraham" (Christ, Gal. 3:16). The hope for ultimate deliverance from Satanic governments (II Cor. 4:4) will be fulfilled only when the "seed of the woman" (Gen. 3:15) puts an end forever to our present (evil) world systems by crushing the Serpent (Rom. 16:20). This will happen when ownership of the earth passes to its rightful heirs, Christ and His faithful followers. Dominion over the earth was destined for man in Genesis. That rule will become a reality when the Second Adam — man as he was intended to be — takes over the "kingdoms of this world" (Rev. 11:15) and "rules in the midst of His enemies" (Ps. 110:2). With the Messiah at that inauguration of a new world government will be "those who volunteer freely in the day of [Messiah's] power" (Ps. 110:3). His freshly invigorated people, enjoying new life as resurrected, immortal beings, will assist Jesus in His task of establishing the New Society on earth. With this career before them, Christians are the genuine New Age people preparing for the advent of Jesus.

Emphasis should be placed on the fact that it is the "gentle" who are destined for this bright future. Those believers who continue to threaten their enemies and fellow believers in other lands with nuclear extinction should question whether they belong to the category of whom Jesus speaks.

The Sermon on the Mount sets out the qualities of character and behavior required in those who hope to inherit the Kingdom.

---

[29] Ps. 29:1; 89:6; Dan. 3:5; Job 38:7.

Obedience through the Spirit is demanded by Jesus: "Everyone who hears these words of Mine and acts on them will be like a wise man who built his house on a rock" (Matt. 7:24).

The main thrust of Jesus' Message is no less relevant to us in the twentieth century than when He first delivered it in Galilee some two thousand years ago. The Kingdom has not yet come, and its announcement worldwide must precede its arrival (Matt. 24:14). While Christians await the return of the Master they are challenged to develop the character suitable for their future function as members of the royal Messianic administration. All of Jesus' parables of the Kingdom teach lessons about the supreme importance of making the Kingdom the objective of human existence.

The Faith of Jesus

Faith in Jesus has been reduced in many theological systems to believing in His death and resurrection. The Apostles, however, urge us to an imitation of Jesus. We are to have "the faith of Jesus." We are not only to believe in Him but believe what He believed. The faith of the historical Jesus is the model for Christians and should not be relegated to antiquity or "primitive Christianity," as though all that counts now is faith in a risen Christ divorced from the actual Jesus who lived and taught.

A simple retranslation of the phrase "faith in Christ" as "the faith *of* Christ" helps to reattach us to the faith as Jesus practiced it. As many commentators have observed Paul spoke of having "faith like Jesus" in Romans 3:26.[30] Using the same phrase he speaks of "the faith of Abraham" (Rom. 4:16). There is no reason to translate the one phrase as "the faith of Abraham" and the other as "faith *in* Jesus," when the Greek construction is the same. The book of Revelation defines Christians as those who have "the faith of Jesus" (Rev. 14:12).

The faith of Jesus includes also the "faithfulness of Jesus," His trusting obedience to the covenant and His single-minded dedication to the proclamation of the Kingdom. Faith *in* Jesus is in no way diminished when we think also of the faith as He modeled it. The

---

[30] The genitive should be read as subjective, as proposed by G. Howard in "The Faith of Christ," *Expository Times* (85), April 1974, pp. 212-215. See also Ludwig Albrecht, *Das Neue Testament*, Brunnen-Verlag, 1957, pp. 399, 400, notes to his translation of Rom. 3:26.

Gospel of Jesus should not be understood as just a Gospel *about* Him, but the Gospel as He preached it. This will bring us into line with the much neglected testimony of Matthew, Mark and Luke as the basis of Christian faith. It will refocus our attention on the Message of the Messiah which is all too often swallowed up in vague phrases about "preaching Christ," as though He "is" the Gospel. It was with good reason that Jesus spoke of suffering for "His sake and for the sake of the Gospel," equivalent to "Me *and My words*" (Mark 8:35, 38). John's Gospel continually emphasizes the need to believe the "words of Jesus,"[31] a fact which should remind us that John believed with no less intensity than Matthew, Mark and Luke that Jesus' Gospel of the Kingdom is the center of true faith.

Jesus' Expectation of a Dramatic End to Present Governments

A major element in the Gospel of Jesus is His account of events destined to occur in the Middle East prior to His own arrival in the power of the Kingdom. No aspect of New Testament teaching has suffered more at the hands of hostile criticism than those passages which contain a prediction of future events. The notion that Jesus may have been the vehicle of communication about what is going to happen seems to be most unpopular with the scholarly world.

Jesus gave an essentially straightforward outline of what may be expected to occur as a prelude to His arrival. In a long discourse recorded by Matthew, Mark and Luke (Matt. 24; Mark 13; Luke 21), He answered the question posed to Him by His most intimate disciples: "When will these things be [the tearing down of the temple, Matt. 24:2], and what will be the sign of Your coming and the end of the age?" (Matt. 24:3).

Because of a tendency among commentators to ignore the background of Jesus' thinking in the book of Daniel, to which He expressly points us in Matthew 24:15 when He speaks of the "desolating horror"[32] to be expected in the holy place, many have attempted an explanation of the Olivet Discourse divorced from the outline of events already supplied by Daniel. The disciples are

---

[31] John 4:41, 50; 5:24, 34, 38, 47; 6:63, 68; 7:16; 8:31, 37, 38, 43, 47, 52; 12:46-50; 14:23, 24; 15:7; 17:8, 14, 17. Much is said about "receiving Christ" in modern evangelism and very little about "receiving His words" (John 17:8).

[32] The abomination of desolation, referred to in Dan. 8:13; 9:27; 11:31; 12:11.

evidently familiar with Daniel's vision of the future just prior to the inauguration of the Kingdom. Their question about the end of the age, as Mark records it (Mark 13:4), is phrased, in fact, in words drawn from Daniel 12:7 referring to the climax of the distressing events preceding the establishment of the Kingdom, when "all these things will be fulfilled."[33]

Daniel had spoken, in a unified set of prophetic declarations found in chapters 2, 7, 8, 9, 11 and 12, of a final wicked tyrant, the last "king of the North" (Dan. 11:21-45), who would persecute the faithful during a period of extreme trouble, but who would be destroyed just prior to the resurrection of the saints to take part in the Kingdom (Dan. 9:27; 11:31-45; 12:1-3; cp. Matt. 13:38-43). The picture drawn by Daniel describes a final, short outburst of tribulation on the faithful at the hands of the wicked ruler who interferes with the temple by stopping sacrifices for a short period, the last half of the seventieth "heptad" of Daniel 9:27. To this "abomination of desolation *described by Daniel*" (Matt. 24:15) Jesus referred as He gave His inspired vision of end-of-the-age events.

The circumstances of Daniel's "abomination" have a definite "shape." The abomination is set up by a king of the North and for a period of 1290 days just preceding the resurrection. These facts will not fit the history surrounding events in AD 70. The career of Titus is quite unlike the description of Daniel's final ruler and that of Nero comes no closer to fulfilling Daniel's prophecy. Commentators have not paid attention to Jesus' claim to be working from already existing material in the Hebrew Bible. This is symptomatic of a much more general abandonment of the Old Testament.

The account given by Daniel certainly did not find its complete fulfillment in the life of Antiochus Epiphanes IV who persecuted the Jews savagely in the second century BC. Jesus obviously reads Daniel as predicting the coming of a wicked tyrant at a time very close to the end of the age when "the righteous will shine forth in the Kingdom of their Father" (Dan. 12:3; Matt. 13:43).

As long as the framework provided by Daniel is not abandoned, no one will make the mistake of supposing that the events of AD 70

---

[33] See Dan. 12:7, LXX. For a full account of the parallels between Daniel and the Olivet Discourse, see Lars Hartman, *Prophecy Interpreted*, Coniectania Biblica, NT Series 1, Sweden: Gleerup Lund.

and the destruction of the temple at that time satisfy the predictions of Jesus. It is clear that there was no period of seven years, at the time of Jerusalem's invasion by the Romans, during which a cessation of sacrifices occurred for half of the last week of Daniel's seventy "weeks." Daniel described a time of unparalleled distress lasting for 1290 days and ending with the resurrection of the dead.[34] The evil agent portrayed by Daniel as the "king of the North" cannot have been Titus, who anyway did not "come to his end" (Dan. 9:26; 11:45)[35] in Palestine after battling with the "king of the South" (Dan. 11:40-45). By no possible stretch of the imagination can the facts of Daniel's prophecy be made to fit with the events of AD 70. AD 70 was not the "end of the age," a technical expression (also drawn from Daniel) for the time of the manifestation of the Kingdom of God in Jerusalem, when, as Jesus said, the harvest of salvation would come and the righteous would be glorified (Matt. 13:39; 43).

When Jesus responded to the question about the fate of the temple He did not know how much time would elapse before His return. He specifically denied knowledge of the day and the hour of His coming (Mark 13:32) and later told the disciples it was not for them "to know the times and seasons which the Father has set in His own authority" (Acts 1:7). These clear statements of ignorance prove not only that Jesus was not omniscient, but also that His assertion that "this generation would not pass until all these things have happened" does not mean that His arrival in power would happen within forty years. It is impossible for Jesus to have said to the disciples "you are not to have knowledge of times and seasons" and at the same time to have given them earlier a prediction of the end within forty years!

As Jesus and the disciples looked out on the temple complex, both He and the disciples knew the outline of prophecy contained in the writings of Daniel. There would be trouble in the temple and "great tribulation" (Dan. 12:1; Matt. 24:21) in the land just before the coming of the Kingdom (Luke 21:31). The question posed by the disciples assumes this program given by Daniel. They naturally inquire about the destruction of the temple and the Second Coming as closely connected events. Jesus' answer assumes the same connection,

---

[34] Dan. 12:2, 7, 11, referring back to 11:31 when the abomination was set up and the sacrifice stopped.

[35] Nero does not fit the prophecy. He committed suicide in June of AD 68.

since Daniel had described a terrible invasion of the temple just before the resurrection of the dead (which marks the arrival of the Kingdom).

Jesus did not know whether the actual temple they were viewing would in fact be the temple to be invaded by the final Antichrist. What He did know was that any temple constructed in the age prior to His coming again would be destroyed in order to allow for the building of a purified temple in the age of Messiah's reign on earth (Hag. 2:9). Hebrew thinking as we have already noted "grasps a totality." Any temple built at different times on the temple mount may be described as "this temple." Clear evidence of this "synthetic" way of thinking is proved by the words of the prophet Haggai who can speak of "this temple" as different buildings existing at widely separated periods of time. The temple which Haggai's readers viewed in 520 BC is the "same" temple as the one built earlier by Solomon, although a different building: "Who is left among you who saw *this temple* in its former glory?" (Hag. 2:3). Looking to the future, Haggai can report the Lord as saying: "I am going to shake the heavens and the earth [a prediction of the Day of the Lord (Heb. 12:26)] and I will fill *this house* with glory" (Hag. 2:6, 7). "This house" now means a house of the future far superior to the temple of Solomon or that of the sixth century. "The latter glory of *this house* will be greater than the former...and in this place I will give peace" (Hag. 2:9). Any temple built on the one site can be called "this temple."

Misunderstanding this very non-western way of thinking, commentators have struggled to determine what part of Jesus' Olivet Discourse was a prediction of Titus' invasion of the temple in AD 70 and what part a description of His Second Coming. Once it is realized that Jesus is merely elaborating on a scheme of prophecy already given by Daniel, there will be no need to argue that He predicted two events separated by at least 1900 years.[36] As many commentators have

---

[36] Matthew describes the great tribulation (following the pattern in Daniel) as happening "immediately" before the return of Christ (Matt. 24:29). Mark's connection is no less clear (Mark 13:24). Luke likewise has in mind an end-time invasion of Jerusalem immediately preceding the "signs in the sun, moon and stars" (Luke 21:23-25). The final events of Luke 21 are "days of vengeance when *all things which are written may be fulfilled*" (Luke 21:22). This goes far beyond events in AD 70 and causes dismay "among *nations*" (Luke 21:25) and people in "the inhabitable earth" (Luke21:26), not just Israel. The modern theory that AD 70 saw

observed it is simply impossible to divide Jesus' prophetic discourse to make it an account of events in AD 70 and His return (Luke 21:25-31). Jesus is interested in the climax of the age, not in foretelling world history for nearly two millennia (or however much longer it may turn out to be). What He foresaw was a terrible time of distress in Judea triggered by the appearance of an Antichrist in the temple.[37] *Immediately following,* convulsions in the heavens would then announce the impending arrival of the Son of Man in glory to take over the reins of world government (Matt. 24:29-31).

The Loss of Vital Elements in the Gospel

Jesus' elaborate discourse based on Daniel as predictive prophecy has been unpopular in the Church, but this is part and parcel of a Gentile unwillingness to accept the Messianic outlook of Jesus. As a result the Gospel as Jesus taught it has often been reduced to those elements — such as forgiveness and love — thought to be the timelessly valuable "kernel" of the Messiah's teaching as distinct from its disposable, apocalyptic Jewish husk. This appears to us to be a most questionable way to deal with information. Why is it right to "pick and choose" from the Messiah's utterances? The churchgoing public remains largely ignorant of the extraordinarily convoluted theories by which unwanted sections of Jesus' teaching have been set aside.

Jesus and the Apostles made the Kingdom of God the principal theme of all their teaching. The Good News Message of salvation consisted of information concerning the Kingdom of God, and the need to prepare for a position in it, including facts about the death and resurrection of Jesus which advanced the cause of the coming Kingdom. Generally speaking the churches calling themselves Christian admit that they have never said much about the Kingdom. Modern preachers do not preach it. Contemporary evangelists confess that the Kingdom is not part of their evangelistic agenda. This may be easily demonstrated, too, by pointing to the absence of the word "Kingdom" in tracts claiming to promote the Gospel. We conclude, therefore, that there is a startling difference between the Christianity

---

the arrival of Jesus at His Second Coming fails to see that much more is entailed in Jesus' account of the end than the destruction of Israel in the first century.

[37] Mark's use of a masculine participle (13:14) suggests a human person.

of Jesus and the Apostles and what has been called Christianity for some 1900 years — and it affects the heart of the faith.

Throughout the biblical accounts of the preaching of Jesus and the Apostles we find a plain record that the Kingdom of God, to be inaugurated by Jesus as King of that Kingdom, is Christianity's principal concept. Throughout church history there has been a major eclipse of Jesus' central Message. It must follow, we contend, that the Christianity of Jesus and the Apostles and traditional Christianity are substantially different.

To account for that striking difference is our purpose in the chapters which follow.

8. The Message and the Enemy

The promise of rescue for mankind had been handed down through generations spanning many thousands of years. As time progressed the divine information conveyed to Adam and Eve had been expanded to include the promise of both personal, national and world salvation: The covenant of land and distinguished offspring made with Abraham and the covenant of permanent kingship offered to David combined to fill the future with hope:

> The regenerate Kingdom fills the prophets' imagination...Although the realization of the blessed future will be in and for Israel, the whole world will share in it. The regenerate Kingdom will be a channel of blessing to all mankind; even Assyria and Egypt, the two signal representatives of the hostile world empire, will be numbered with Israel as God's people and the work of his hands (Isaiah 33).[1]

The blessings promised to Abraham encompassed all nations (Gen. 12:3). Yet they centered on Christ as the promised seed (Gal. 3:16) in whose company all who chose to respond to the call of the Gospel about the Kingdom could be included in the blessings. The Christ would emerge, according to ancient prophecy, from the tribe of Judah[2] (from which our word Jew is derived) and He would be born in Bethlehem, the city of David (Mic. 5:2; Matt. 2:6). The promised royal personage would be "a rising star" (Num. 24:17), a light to the nations (Isa. 9:2; Matt. 4:16). The political system organized by Moses and his announcement of Israel's divine commission to be "priests and kings" give us yet another strand of Messianic prophecy.

---

[1] A. Robertson, *Regnum Dei*, p. 21.
[2] Gen. 49:10; Matt. 2:6; Rev. 5:5.

Building upon the earlier covenant with Abraham, God said: "Now then if you will indeed obey My voice and keep My covenant, then you will be My own possession among all the peoples, for all the earth is Mine; and you will be to Me a kingdom of priests and a holy nation" (Exod. 19:5, 6). Clearly the function of the nation is intimately related to that of the King Messiah who was also to hold office uniquely as a priest and king (Ps. 110:2-4).

The New Testament transfers this royal status to a multinational group, the Church, who are heirs, in association with Christ, of the promises, and as the Israel of God (Gal. 6:16) take on the role assigned to ancient Israel (Exod. 19:5, 6; cp. I Pet. 2:9; Tit. 2:14). The Church is thus appropriately designated "the true circumcision" (Phil. 3:3, i.e., the true Jews), though composed of both Jews and Gentiles. Though the ancient people of God have suffered a present blindness, and have largely rejected their Messiah, there is hope for them also. It is untrue to the New Testament to say that the Church has permanently superseded Israel. The Church is to become what ideally Israel should have been and what eventually she will again become, but only after "the fullness of the Gentiles has come in" (Rom. 11:25). Prophecy, as expounded by Paul, points to a collective, national conversion of a remnant of the people of Israel[3] consequent upon a terrible time of trouble in the future (Jer. 30:7-9), which will reawaken their desire for Messianic salvation, a last-ditch solution to their troubles. Meanwhile, however, royal office and priesthood are offered to "men from every tribe and people and nation" (I Pet. 2:9; Rev. 5:10) who, in keeping with the now expanded original call to Israel, have been constituted "a kingdom and priests to our God; and *they will reign as kings upon the earth*" (Rev. 5:10).[4] One might expect this sublimely simple encapsulation of the purpose of the Christian faith to ring out from pulpits constantly.

The rich tapestry of Messianic material in the Bible has a single aim. The heart of the Message is the solution to the ultimate problem of man's mortality, the curse of disobedience. Immortality was to be achieved, as the New Testament writers came to understand, when

---

[3] Rom. 11:26, where the salvation of Israel is foreseen. This is obviously not the present "Israel" of the Church since only one verse earlier Paul says that Israel has been temporarily blinded.

[4] See also Rev. 1:6; 2:26; 3:21; 20:6.

frail man received from his maker an imperishable body animated and driven by divine Spirit (I Cor. 15:44). Equipped with an immortal body the Christian would be fit to take up his administrative position with Christ in the Kingdom (Rev. 20:6). This information had by no means been the common property of all Israelites. The divine secret had been entrusted to Abraham, Moses, David and all the prophets, who had labored to share their insights with any who were willing to receive them.

The Bible is most practical in its analysis of the human problem. It recognizes that death is the universal enemy from which we are utterly powerless to rescue ourselves. In God's mercy a divine Plan for dealing with the problem of inevitable death has been provided. The Plan of salvation makes no unreasonable demands on man. It calls upon him first to believe in the one God as Creator of all things and secondly in His agent the Messiah, Jesus, for it is He who has been chosen to pioneer the way of escape from death (Heb. 2:10). Having Himself gained immortality (Col. 1:18), it is His task now to assist others struggling for the same goal (Heb. 2:17, 18). As the key figure in the divine scheme He has been selected to head up the entire divine operation (Eph. 1:10), and this involves not only His present high priesthood over the Church but also His appointment as King of Israel and His future reign, with His followers, over the entire world. This is to be a reign without end (Luke 1:32, 33). It forms the subject matter of the Christian Good News or Gospel of the Kingdom of God.

The Christian records never for one moment suggest that Jesus actually became King of Israel and the Kingdom of God during His ministry in Palestine, though He certainly sought to capture others to the recognition that He was the Messiah, the one destined to be king. On one occasion an attempt was made to make Him king (John 6:15), but Jesus firmly rejected it. On another the crowds were convinced that the reign of Messiah was about to begin. In the atmosphere of Messianic expectation which belief in Jesus as Messiah had generated, the slightest hint could be taken as a sign of His impending enthronement. On the occasion in question Jesus had remarked that the repentant Zaccheus had "this day" come to a knowledge of salvation (Luke 19:9). Salvation had always been associated with the establishment of the Kingdom and mention of it was always likely to trigger an upsurge of Messianic fervor. The fact that Jesus was also approaching Jerusalem (Luke 19:11) made it practically certain that this must be the great moment for reestablishment of the throne of David in the Holy City. This is what the great national charter, bestowed in the Davidic covenant, had guaranteed.

Luke reports that Jesus dealt with the crisis by telling a parable. He compared Himself to a nobleman who was to depart to a far country to obtain his kingdom and return to reign (Luke 19:11-27) — a simple enough story and one which would quickly bring the churches together if they believed it. For it confirms in the most elementary terms that the promised reign of the Messiah, the Kingdom of God, was not to begin *in Jerusalem* until Jesus returned to the earth after an unspecified interval of absence. In the light of Jesus' subsequent departure after His resurrection, the disciples were quick to understand that they must transfer their Messianic hopes to a point of future time unknown — to His return in glory. To this great event the entire early Church, naturally enough, looked forward. Paul impressed on his converts the need for a forward-looking, Messianic outlook. Summarizing the essence of Christianity he reminded the faithful that they had "turned to God from idols to serve a living and true God, and to wait for His Son from the heavens, whom He raised from the dead, that is Jesus, who delivers us from the wrath to come" (I Thess. 1:10). The note of judgment is never lacking in Paul's preaching, and the goal is always the return of Jesus *from* heaven (I Cor. 15:47; Phil. 3:20), never the departure of the saints *to* heaven. Not for one moment did New Testament Christians suppose that the Messianic program had been permanently transferred to a locality away from the earth. It would have been an extraordinary innovation, requiring much explanation, to imagine that the throne of David had been permanently removed from Jerusalem to heaven.[5] Yet a widespread emphasis on the present "reign" of Jesus has distorted the Messianic picture of Him as ruler designate of a new world order destined to appear on earth.

The benefits of the divine program could be gained by the individual believers only on condition that they expressed their faith in the purposes which God was working out. It was clear that humanity had fallen under the curse of rebellion against its Creator.

---

[5] It is true that the New Testament occasionally associates the Kingdom with the ascended Christ, but never to the exclusion of the Messiah's future reign on earth.

An essential element in the divine program for rescue, therefore, was the sacrificial death of the Son of God, the Messiah, for the sins of the world. Prior to the crucifixion of Jesus as the sacrificial Lamb slain, in the divine purpose, before the foundation of the world (I Pet. 1:20), the disciples had found this part of the Plan impossible to grasp (Luke 18). They were unable to reconcile a dying Savior with the expected conquering, reigning Messiah. Yet contemporary believers have the opposite problem. Looking at the death of Christ as a historical event, they have little difficulty in seeing it at the center of their faith. Their conception of Him as destined to conquer the earth and rule the world from Jerusalem is far from clear to them. Yet the Bible is simply filled with assertions that the Christ is coming to rule the earth in power. We are constantly urged to be ready for the greatest event of human history, and in the Lord's prayer we are to pray for its coming.

Sometimes historians prove to be objective readers of the New Testament, but they may fail to commit themselves to belief in what they read. The strain of having to believe that God will carry out what He has promised seems to be too great. We cite one example to illustrate our point, with no intention of disparaging the excellent scholarship of a former learned professor of ecclesiastical history at the University of Edinburgh. Professor Mackinnon is typical of a school of theological thought, characteristic also of contemporary attitudes to the Bible, which begins by doubting the accounts of Jesus' birth:

> The Jewish-Christian sources [of the birth narratives] do not guarantee the historic reality of the miraculous conception. The narratives themselves contain features which tend to raise doubts on this point. In both writers [Matthew and Luke] the belief in it rests on angelic communications...The stories owe in fact much of their charm to this naive angelology.[6]

So much for the doctrine of the virginal conception of Jesus! It is apparently not something that modern thinkers can take seriously. But what of the promise that Jesus is to reign over the house of Jacob on David's throne?

> In the Lukan version the Messiah, whose birth the angel proclaims, is depicted in the form of a king who shall reoccupy and hold for

---

[6] *The Historic Jesus*, London, New York: Longmans, Green and Co., 1931, p. 4.

ever the throne of his father (ancestor) David. A restored Jewish Kingdom is predicted, and this prediction ultimately proved not only an illusion, but incompatible with the spiritual kingdom which Jesus proclaimed and sought to establish. Here again the angelic communication, under the influence of current belief, is based on a misconception of historic reality. It is, to say the least, rather disconcerting to find what purports to be a revelation from a heavenly source misinterpreting a prophecy and also predicting a restored Davidic kingdom which *failed to materialise.*[7]

It must be stated that we have in these remarks the whole problem of the modern rejection of Jesus and His Messianic Message. Apparently angels, if they exist at all, are unreliable as messengers. The authority of the Old Testament is ignored as the basis for the divine promise of the restoration of the Kingdom of David to Israel. In its place is substituted what commentators have chosen to call a "spiritual" kingdom, an attractive term designed to direct attention away from what is historical or geographical and promote the idea of an abstract, interior kingdom only. Finally, the angel Gabriel, and Luke who recorded his message as the foundation of Christian hope, was wrong. The sort of kingdom Gabriel announced for Jesus, on the strength of millennia of Messianic prophecy rooted in the seers of Israel, never appeared and so obviously never will! Luke's precious introduction to the faith is thus reduced to a calamitous mistake. It is based on what falsely claims to be a divine revelation and it turned out to be untrue. With this sort of exposition, the bottom falls out of Christianity and we are left to make the best of the wreckage.

It is little wonder that pulpits do not resound with excited proclamation of the most extraordinary political event ever to impact our earth — the appearance on earth of a new Davidic empire with Messiah Jesus as its appointed sovereign, exercising a benign government over all peoples and effecting an era of unparalleled peace and prosperity.

The prospect of such a government coming on earth is of course impossible without the historically witnessed return of Jesus from death by resurrection. Because the whole Jesus story is unacceptable

---

[7] *Ibid.*, pp. 5, 6, emphasis added.

to many, this event remains the target of skeptics, some amongst them claiming to be Christian teachers. That Jesus is now alive, having been brought to life again by a divine re-creation, has come in this century to be much less acceptable even to churchgoers.[8] Indeed there are many, including professional theologians, for whom the resurrection of Jesus as a fact of history is simply incredible. Their view of the world as a "closed continuum" forbids them to believe it. Yet they see no contradiction between this agnosticism over the resurrection of Jesus and a profession of the Christian faith. Business as usual may often continue within the walls of Christian churches with no sense of alarm that basic tenets of the biblical faith have been discarded.

In the interests of clarifying the faith of the New Testament, we must insist that the early Church would have regarded non-belief in the resurrection simply as unbelief. No candidate for baptism would have been acceptable apart from a firm conviction that Jesus had returned in bodily form from death, assumed immortality, and was coming again to rule and reign on the earth. This was the heart and core of the divine Message — the Gospel. Without it the hope for the salvation of the human race would be reduced to an empty dream. There would, in fact, be no Good News to tell. It is well known that Paul was ready to abandon his entire mission, if it could be shown that Christ had not been brought back to life by resurrection. As Paul put it to his converts at Corinth, "If Christ has not been raised from the dead, we have nothing to preach and you have nothing to believe" (I Cor. 15:14, GNB).

Satan was well aware that belief in the Savior and His Gospel Message of salvation opened for the believer the door to the blessings of immortality. He understood that the prerequisite for incorporation into the divine scheme for the rescue of mankind from death was an understanding and acceptance of the scheme itself. That understanding was gained by contact with the information contained in the Good News Message about the Kingdom — the Gospel which Jesus and the Apostles labored to proclaim, and for which they died as martyrs for the cause of Christ. The process of rescue could therefore be most effectively frustrated by tampering with the essential

---

[8] *Now* magazine of Dec. 1979 reported that 50% of those claiming to be churchgoing members of the Church of England did not believe in an afterlife at all.

information. A new set of facts calling itself the Gospel must be introduced in place of the real ones, and faith in these must be induced.[9] In this way a hope of salvation would be offered as before. But because of the subtle twist which had been introduced into the Message, the proposition put before the potential convert would no longer correspond to the terms laid down by the divine Architect. The essence of the Satanic plan would be to persuade the seeker for immortality that he had complied with the divine instructions, while these in fact would be hidden from him. He would be offered a distorted Good News which would impede his progress towards salvation. A brilliant analysis of the Devil's method was given by Jesus in His celebrated Parable of the Sower (Matt. 13:18-23; Mark 4:13-20; Luke 8:11-15). The Devil recognizes the Kingdom Message as the essential divine tool operating to bring about salvation. He must therefore find ways of obscuring it or obstructing its communication to the human mind: "When anyone hears the Message about the Kingdom, the Devil comes and snatches away the Message sown in his heart *so that he may not believe and be saved*" (Matt. 13:19 and Luke 8:12). These are verses which we ignore at our peril. Churches would be well-advised to ensure that whatever else they do the preaching of the saving Good News about the Kingdom is always at the forefront of their activity.

The central truth of the Good News about the Kingdom of God was that the promised Savior, the Messiah, was ultimately to assume the reins of world government and to introduce an endless theocracy. A share in that government, as a co-administrator with the Messiah, was offered as the gracious reward of all who chose to become involved with Jesus' mission. As long as language is read straightforwardly and words retain their dictionary definitions, these facts will be found stated in the plainest of terms and with complete unanimity by all the New Testament writers. Abraham was heir to the world (Rom. 4:13), the faithful were to inherit the earth (Matt. 5:5), to administer the world as rulers (Rev. 2:26; 3:21; 20:6; I Cor. 6:2), to reign with Christ, to become Kings with Him on the earth (Rev. 5:10). Language has no clearer way of conveying information about the

---

[9] Paul encountered this basic strategy amongst the Corinthians (see II Cor. 11:4).

future of the Church. It cannot say more distinctly than the Bible does that Christians are called to be the future rulers of the earth.

The Disintegration of the Messianic Vision

Division and loss of dynamic among the churches is traceable above all to the loss of that vital central Message, so relevant to our distracted planet. It is a loss of living faith and a loss of hope. It is also a defection from the Church's high calling to be the Messianic fellowship in training now, with the hope of fuller service to humanity in the age of the coming Kingdom. That is not to say that faith and hope have not been expressed, but they have been stunted by the introduction of a very different goal, one quite foreign to the early believers. What to Jesus and the Apostles would have appeared as a meaningless prospect, utterly incompatible with the Hebrew tradition, came to replace the hope offered by the divine Message. The work of the Serpent led to a wholesale shift away from the biblical hope embodied in the Good News, and it occurred soon after the death of the Apostles. The Message was dealt a lethal blow when strange notions about an afterlife as a disembodied spirit in heaven became confused with the Christian hope of resurrection to immortality in the Kingdom on earth, at the return of Jesus. The Serpent revived his original, favorite lie and worked hard to poison the Church with it. The success of his campaign may be witnessed everywhere in contemporary churches, especially at the preaching of funerals.

It was Satan, subtle master of the half-truth, who soon after the death of the Apostles began a massive propaganda campaign to divert attention away from the hope contained in the Good News of the Kingdom, as well as in the Abrahamic and Davidic covenants, to an objective which has gained almost universal acceptance as one of the first principles of the Christian faith. A powerful influx of Greek believers into the Church led to a radical shift in thinking amongst those desiring to attach themselves to the name of Christ. The result was a theological takeover on a massive scale. The name of Christ was appropriated to a system of belief hardly recognizable as Christian by New Testament standards. The world of Greek and Roman philosophy invaded the Church so successfully that the fundamentally different thought system on which the Hebrew, biblical theology was founded was forced out of the Church. While the pure

Message of the Kingdom and the Messiah — biblical Messianism — was eclipsed, the Church continued ostensibly as the legitimate successors to the Apostles. But was the Christ of this transformed ecclesiastical system really Jesus of Nazareth, herald of the Kingdom of God? If, as Archbishop Temple maintained, the Kingdom of God Message has figured very little in the history of the Church, one may be permitted to wonder how far the authentic voice of Jesus has been stifled. Perhaps more attention should be paid to those scholars who have tried to sound the alarm. From Cambridge comes the revealing observation of Don Cupitt that in the second century "a new religion was developed to replace the original faith."[10]

Professor Cupitt then notes that Jesus' and His early followers' emphasis on the future Kingdom poses "some very awkward questions to orthodox believers" which are "too often quietly ignored."[11] Often, also, theories have been espoused in order to "excuse" Jesus from what are thought to be His mistaken hopes for the Kingdom which never came. In every case we are witnessing a defection from belief in the Messianic promises guaranteed by the covenants with Abraham and David and confirmed by Jesus. It is impossible to believe, in a New Testament sense, if one does not subscribe with passionate conviction to the future reappearance of Jesus from heaven to inaugurate the era of Messianic peace on earth, for which purpose He is the appointed Messiah. Such an affirmation witnesses to faith in the God of the covenants made with Abraham and David — the God of Jesus.

If Messianism is no longer a concept acceptable to modern scholars and churchgoers, but belongs only on what one New Testament scholar calls "the sectarian fringe,"[12] and if "no one seriously looks for the Messiah who will be the single solution to all the world's problems, spiritually or politically,"[13] it is no fault of our New Testament documents. The problem lies elsewhere, namely in the Church's abandonment of the Hebrew vision of a restored Paradise on earth, consequent upon the return of Jesus to assume His royal office. The cause of the shift away from Jesus and His Messianic

---

[10] *The Debate about Christ*, p. 69.

[11] *Ibid.*

[12] J.A.T. Robinson, *The Human Face of God*, SCM Press, 1973, p. 9.

[13] *Ibid.*

Message is not hard to pinpoint. Canon Goudge's observation needs to be heard again: "When the Greek and Roman mind came to dominate the church, there occurred a disaster from which we have never recovered, neither in belief nor in practice."[14] In fact Dr. Robinson, who does not see Messianism as something to be believed in any more, describes the whole demise of New Testament views of the future. He speaks of:

> the remarkable transformation that overtook Christian eschatology almost as soon as the ink of the New Testament was dry. And it affects the center of interest or pivotal point of the entire subject...For in the New Testament, the point around which hope and interest revolve is not the moment of death at all, but the day of the Parousia, or appearance of Christ in the glory of His Kingdom...The center of interest and expectation continued, right through the New Testament period, to be focused upon the day of the Son of Man and the triumph of His Kingdom in a renovated earth. It was the reign of the Lord Jesus with all His saints that engaged the thoughts and prayers of Christians...The hope was social and it was historical. But as early as the second century AD there began a shift in the center of gravity which was to lead by the Middle Ages *to a very different doctrine*...In later thought it is the hour of death which becomes decisive.[15]

The Root of the Problem: Spiritual Versus Physical

That departure from the biblical blueprint is all too evident in today's fragmented Church and particularly in its various and mutually exclusive teachings about the future. To bring order out of chaos, the Kingdom of God must be defined again as Jesus understood it. The land promise (now conspicuous by its absence from books claiming to explain New Testament Christianity), which Jesus makes equivalent to the promise of the Kingdom, must be reinstated at the heart of the Gospel Message. The bringing together of land and Kingdom reunites the Hebrew Bible with Christianity after a long period of trying to divorce Jesus from His national, Jewish heritage. The Master has not abandoned the Old Testament revelation.

---

[14] H.L. Goudge, *Essays on Judaism and Christianity*, cited by H.J. Schonfield, *The Politics of God*, p. 98.

[15] *In the End God*, Fontana Books, pp. 42, 43, emphasis added.

His hope is firmly rooted in the promise of a renewal of Palestine. He can say, meaning the same thing, either: "Blessed are the poor in spirit, for the Kingdom of Heaven is theirs" (Matt. 5:3) or "Blessed are the meek; they shall have the earth [or land] as their inheritance" (Matt. 5:5). He quotes here from the thirty-seventh Psalm which five times assures the faithful of a place in the land forever: "He will exalt you to master the land" (Ps. 37:34, NEB). All Christian endeavor, according to Jesus, who echoes the Hebrew Bible, converges on the ancient land promise made to Abraham, who will be resurrected to enjoy what he had seen only with the eye of faith. The tribes will be regathered in the land,[16] as the Hebrew prophets had foreseen (Jer. 30:3, etc.), and Jesus and His followers will preside over a renewed society, establishing and maintaining a just order (Isa. 32:1). That commission is divinely authorized and represents the heart of the New Covenant. Just as Moses declared the words of the first covenant and then ratified them with the blood of animals (Exod. 19:5, 6; 24:7, 8), so Jesus, in His teaching ministry, proclaims the words of the New Covenant. Matthew reminds us of this by dividing his book into five sections (reminiscent of the five books of Moses) each ending with the words "When Jesus had finished all these sayings..." Jesus sums up the content of his Gospel with the magnificent promise given at the Last Supper: "Just as My Father covenanted with Me to give Me a Kingdom I covenant with you to give you royal office, and you will sit on twelve thrones to administer the twelve tribes of Israel" (Luke 22:28-30). The king then went to His death on behalf of the sins of the world, shedding His own blood to ratify the covenant — the covenant of kingship which constituted the disciples ministers of state in the coming Kingdom. The terms of the covenant are the words of Jesus which we must believe and obey. His blood brings the covenant into permanent effect.

Beasley-Murray says:

> The connection of thought between the eschatological covenant ratified in the giving of the body and blood of Jesus (Luke 22:19, 20) and the covenanting to give the Kingdom to the disciples in v. 29 is especially striking. While the term covenant does not appear

---

[16] Luke 22:28-30; Matt. 19:8. Cp. Ps. 122:5 which speaks of the "thrones of David set for judgment in Jerusalem."

in v. 29, the verb *diatithemai* [to dispose by covenant] is closely related to it.[17]

Jesus therefore said: "I appoint the Kingdom to you by covenant as my Father appointed it to me." The Kingdom of God of future hope is simply the land promised as an inheritance in perpetuity to Abraham, his seed and the faithful (Gal 3:29).

An alien, and obviously anti-Semitic, influence in theology has made the "Jewish" Messianic hope for the future of the earth seem strange to Gentile Christians, whose beliefs owe so much to the post-biblical influence of Greek ways of thinking. The hellenizing of the original faith creates an enormous problem for Bible readers. They are liable to make a considerable nonsense of what they read by starting with certain well-entrenched presuppositions about the nature of man and his destiny, the nature of God and the nature of faith. Theology must be done "from behind," that is to say by starting with the presuppositions held by Jesus and His early followers who knew nothing at all of later Greek creeds. If the churches are to unite it will be on the basis of agreeing to abandon a long-standing tradition of allowing denominational theology to dictate exposition of the Bible — an effective way of preventing the real Message of Scripture from being heard.

Specifically, the early believers knew nothing of the distinction which many draw between a "spiritual" kingdom and a political kingdom. When Jesus reappeared after His resurrection He was equipped with a spiritual body which was, however, palpable and material, though of a different substance from our present human flesh, which belongs to the first creation. Jesus was recognized as the same individual He had been prior to death. He was no phantom. He ate and drank and conversed (Acts 10:41). He is the example of a glorified human person, the model for those who expect to be resurrected to immortality as He was. The resurrected, however, will not disappear into the skies. Jesus' understanding of the future, like all His teaching, is Messianic and related to the earth: "Many will come from east and west and sit down with Abraham and Isaac and Jacob in the Kingdom of Heaven/God, but the children of the Kingdom will be thrown out into the darkness outside, where there will be weeping and

---

[17] *Jesus and the Kingdom of God,* p 276.

grinding of teeth" (Matt. 8:11, 12). The Kingdom of God is geographically situated. It will be located in Jerusalem which Jesus called "the city of the great king" (Matt. 5:35). It is not beyond space and time. It belongs to the coming age and the life of that coming age is the goal placed before the believer. It is a place to which the faithful come, and when it comes it will introduce "the global society of the future" (Heb. 2:5).

An ingrained, post-biblical, but false, spirituality has led to the bizarre tendency of expositors to castigate the followers of Jesus when they obviously subscribe to Jewish, Old Testament Messianic hopes. It does not seem to occur to these commentators that Jesus had taught the Apostles to revere the Hebrew Bible and had instilled in them the hope of the restoration of the throne of David. Thus after the crucifixion Jesus' disciples pathetically complain: "Our hope had been that He was the one to set Israel free," expressing their shattered conviction that Jesus was the Messiah (Luke 24:21). They demonstrate an impeccable understanding of Jesus' purpose. What they had yet to learn was that there would be a time for the development of the "present evil age" (Gal. 1:3), a ripening of evil prior to judgment associated with the advent of the Kingdom. They did not see how the Kingdom could come, now that the Messiah was no more. Not yet persuaded of the resurrection and the future return of Jesus to the earth, they imagine that the divine program has failed. Their dashed hopes are immediately revived when the risen Jesus makes Himself known. He then gives them six weeks of further instruction on the Kingdom of God, at the end of which it is most natural that they should ask: "Has the time now come for You to restore the Kingdom to Israel?" (Acts 1:6). Again the question is the right one and has the full approval of their teacher. They are cautioned only in regard to the time of the great event, which even He had said He did not know (Mark 13:32).

None of this is in any way difficult to understand once it is recognized that the Bible is a Messianic document and Jesus is the Messiah of Hebrew prophecy. That is the key to the riddle of the New Testament, which becomes a most obscure document when read with a Gentile, non-Messianic bias. Church tradition which presents Jesus as a "spiritual" Messiah only, who never actually rules the world from Jerusalem, erects an effective barrier between us and the Apostles.

Only when the scale of the disaster to which Canon Goudge pointed[18] is fully recognized will steps be taken to repair the damage. The first step towards recovery lies in the abandonment of a cherished notion that what is spiritual cannot be social, political or related to the earth. The fact is that the Kingdom of God of which Jesus spoke was spiritual and at the same time visible and material. It was both particular and Jewish *as well as* universal in its scope. The restored Kingdom of David meant a new political structure for the world, with its headquarters in Jerusalem and extending its influence across the globe. Jerusalem in the mind of Jesus was not a location for departed spirits but an international metropolis, capital of a renewed society on earth. Once the Kingdom idea is rooted again in the soil where it originated, it will become clear that "Kingdom" does not mean an abstract rule in the hearts of men and women. Nor does it mean an ethereal "heaven" for the dying — a place for disembodied souls. The Kingdom of God is to be a literal Kingdom with its divinely appointed sovereign sitting on a throne in a geographical location. According to the Hebrew mind it was "in the hands of the sons of David" (II Chron. 13:8), with an assured future when the Messiah ascended its throne. This is the whole point of Jesus and His mission as herald of the Kingdom. He came, in fact, recruiting followers who would believe God's Messianic Plan and in Himself as God's executive. Hence Jesus' opening salvo, as He inaugurated His ministry: "The Kingdom of God [promised, as you well know, to Israel forever] is coming. Believe it! Believe in this Gospel or Good News about the Kingdom. Align yourselves with the hope of Israel which, with the appearance of the Messiah, is sure to be realized. Be baptized for the remission of your sins." Such is the implication of Mark 1:14, 15 which provides a programmatic summary statement of Jesus' Christian agenda. He is the herald of the greatest Good News, which the nation, had they been spiritually attuned to God's voice through Jesus, would have accepted joyfully. When Israel failed to heed the Message, the same Gospel invitation to the Kingdom went out to all the nations. This does not mean that the Kingdom was postponed. It meant that a divinely planned extension of the present era allowed for the same Kingdom invitation to go on through many generations and to all nations. Its

---

[18] Cited by H.J. Schonfield, *The Politics of God*, p. 98.

call to repentance is the same today as always. It has never been superseded, despite various popular theological systems which have attempted to tell us otherwise.

Part of the offense of Jesus' Message was the delay of the coming of the Kingdom. The death of the one claiming to be Messiah placed too great a strain on the faith of many who heard Jesus preach. Their faith collapsed — and even Jesus' closest followers faltered — when He announced that He must first go to Jerusalem and die. What an absurd contradiction, when the Messiah was supposed to conquer the world! But God had His own time frame for the accomplishment of the promises. To counteract the crushing disappointment of a dying Messiah, a supernatural vision of the future Kingdom was given to the loyal few (Matt. 17:1-9; Mark 9:2-9; Luke 9:28-36). Jesus announced that some standing in His presence would see the Kingdom in their lifetime (Matt. 16:28). Six days later (Matt. 17:1) they were privileged to see into the future and to glimpse the Kingdom in advance of its manifestation. Jesus was seen with His face shining like the sun in the company of Moses and Elijah (Matt. 17:2). This was exactly the condition to be expected of those who "at the end of the age…will shine forth like the sun in the Kingdom of their Father" (Matt. 13:40, 43). When Peter recalls this "transfiguration" (II Pet. 1:16-18), he describes it as a preview of the future coming of Jesus to establish His Kingdom (the *Parousia*). What the disciples witnessed was a scene in which Moses and Elijah appeared in glorified, i.e., resurrected bodies talking to the glorified Jesus. The scene was set on the earth. It was no ghostly "heaven" — the dwelling of departed disembodied spirits. Such an idea, now so cherished and reinforced ceaselessly by funeral addresses and popular piety, was absolutely foreign to their understanding of the nature of man and of death.

The intense vision of the future Kingdom instilled into the early Christians by Jesus and the Apostles cannot be revived as long as we insist on comforting the bereaved with a promise that their relatives have survived as souls without bodies. To do so simply contradicts the biblical hope of resurrection. It directs attention away from the Messianic Kingdom to be introduced when Jesus arrives to raise the dead and occupy the restored throne of David. To this latter idea Bible readers should direct their attention. This will require shedding a considerable amount of traditional baggage, above all the false

distinction between a "spiritual" and political kingdom in the teaching
of Jesus. Our point was made tellingly by P.E. More, writing from
Princeton University in 1924. He was discussing Jesus' call to
repentance in view of the coming Kingdom:

> The straightforward understanding of Christ's eschatological
> [having to do with a Kingdom in the future] meaning has not been
> and still is not acceptable to a tender orthodoxy, for the sufficient
> reason that the promised event did not take place. And so our
> commentaries are full of attempts to explain away perfectly clear
> and concrete statements by allegorizing them into a prophecy of the
> Church which would gradually extend itself over the world...[19]

In plain terms the Church, embarrassed by the failure of the
Kingdom to arrive, decided to claim that the Church is in fact a
kingdom which will gradually conquer the world. This theory would
do away with the need for the return of Jesus and the restoration of the
Davidic theocracy. More goes on to say that this substitution of our
own theory for the Gospel of Christ "will not do. Anyone who has
read the apologetic literature must say that the methods of modern
criticism [analysis and exposition of the Bible] are often beyond his
comprehension."[20]
More then traces the idea of the Messianic Kingdom through an
unbroken line from the prophets to Jesus and Paul:

> From the beginning, when Amos uttered his warning: "Prepare to
> meet your God, O Israel," to the days when St. Paul comforted the
> Christians who grieved for those who had died before the expected
> appearance of the Lord, the note of immediacy is the same. Always
> the reckoning is at hand, yet always it is to come as a surprise: "The
> Day of the Lord comes as a thief in the night; for when they say,
> 'peace and safety,' then sudden destruction will come on them."
> *Paul was merely repeating the eschatology [expectation of the
> future Kingdom] of the prophets, and between him and them Christ
> uttered exactly the same warning*: The Kingdom was approaching
> with the stealth of a robber; it was by anticipation here and now, yet
> the actual day of Jehovah no one knew, neither the angels in heaven

---

[19] *The Christ of the New Testament,* Princeton University Press, 1924, pp. 67,
68.
[20] *Ibid.,* p. 68.

nor the Son himself — only the Father. The importance of that continuity cannot be too much emphasized.[21]

More insists that Jesus must be linked to His heritage: "Jesus' eschatology was simply that of his country and his age." But that link has been severed by the Church, and Jesus is made to float free from the vision of the prophets of Israel. This uprooting of Jesus from the soil of Israel has been achieved by writers who make much of a supposed

> opposition between the popular hope of a political kingdom and Christ's insistence on a spiritual reign of God in the hearts of men. There was no such opposition as theology loves to draw. The Kingdom which Jesus preached was at once political and spiritual; and that unquestionably was the form in which it came to him from the molding hands of prophecy.[22]

Professor More makes another fundamentally important observation. The Kingdom which Jesus announced was not only both spiritual and political; it was also national and universal. Such exactly was the Bible's vision. The Kingdom would be administered from Jerusalem and extend its godly influence to the ends of the earth. This is precisely what Isaiah and all the prophets meant by the Kingdom of God:

> It will happen in the final days that the mountain of Yahweh's house will rise higher than the mountains and tower above the heights. Then all the nations will stream to it, and many peoples will come to it and say, "Come, let us go up to the mountain of Yahweh, to the house of the God of Jacob so that He may teach us His ways so that we may walk in His paths." For the Law will issue from Zion and the word of God from Jerusalem. Then He will judge between the nations and arbitrate between many peoples. They will hammer their swords into ploughshares and their spears into sickles. Nation will not lift sword against nation, no longer will they learn how to make war (Isa. 2:1-5).

Here, truly, is Good News for the world. International disarmament, genuine and lasting, is possible only under the Kingdom of God, the rule of the returned Messiah assisted by the faithful of all

---

[21] *Ibid.*, emphasis added.

[22] *Ibid.*, pp. 69, 70.

ages. Such is the bright hope of Scripture and for that day Jesus urged His followers to pray always: "Thy Kingdom come...on earth." Read in this light the New Testament is a perfectly coherent document, logically structured and internally consistent. Its Message from start to finish is: "The Kingdom is coming. Prepare now. Christ at His return will confer immortality upon you, if you trust and obey Him, and give you authority to reorganize the world with Him along godly lines." The New Testament is a commentary on this underlying Messianic theme and an exhortation designed to bring believers to their goal.

For this picture of the Kingdom and the work of the Messiah we have not only the witness of a mass of scriptural texts. It is confirmed by distinguished experts on Judaism:

> The Jewish Messiah is a redeemer strong in physical power and in spirit, who in the final days will bring redemption, economic and spiritual, to the Jewish people — and along with this, eternal peace, material prosperity and ethical perfection to the whole human race...He redeems Israel from exile and servitude, and he redeems the whole world from oppression, suffering, war, and above all from heathenism and everything which it involves.[23]

Jesus' Gospel announcement is readily comprehensible in the light of the New Testament background. That Jesus issued in the Gospel a "last call" to the coming Kingdom is evident. It is evident too that by Kingdom he did not refer to an interior "kingdom of the heart":

> Central to Jesus' preaching and teaching was the imminent coming of the Kingdom of God. God Himself will establish His dominion at a time He ordains and will make an end of all the kingdoms of the world. God's Kingdom will come without man's assistance. It will not result from human effort and endeavor. It will come suddenly, "as the lightening which lightens out of one part under heaven, shines to the other part" (Luke 17:24). At the same time there will be signs that the Kingdom of God is near; these signs should be heeded. From them men are to recognize "that summer is near" (Mark 13:28ff.).[24]

---

[23] J. Klausner, *The Messianic Idea in Israel*, George Allen and Unwin, Ltd., 1956, p. 521.

[24] Johannes Schneider, "Jesus Christ: His Life and Ministry," in *Fundamentals of the Faith*, ed. C.F.H. Henry, Baker Book House, 1975, p. 101.

For the advent of that redeemer to take up His position as the first successful world governor, the New Testament longs on page after page. By a stroke of genius Luke, a Christian historian who knew how to teach with an economy of words, makes the Kingdom the subject of the disciples' eager inquiry as they bid farewell to the risen Jesus. Luke provides a confirmation of biblical Messianism in a verse which can correct centuries of misunderstanding. Until recently churches have not been willing to yield to its precious testimony. To that part of the story of God's Plan, and an account of its frustration by misguided Gentile commentary, we turn our attention.

9. Acts 1:6 and the Eclipse of the Biblical Kingdom

It is no complicated matter to detect the reason for the Church's uncertainty over Jesus' central Message. Our commentaries give evidence of hostility to the Christian Messianism of which Jesus was a superlative exponent. When the Church fell prey to the idea that Jesus had no political ambition, that He was interested only in a "spiritual" Kingdom, it put itself in conflict with the Hebrew Bible. Not only that, it had to confront the clear fact that Jesus' carefully trained Apostles were ardent advocates of political restoration even after the resurrection. They obviously had not abandoned the hope of Israel. With this fact many commentaries seem most unhappy. Instead of yielding to and being corrected by the "awkward" testimony of Scripture, they established a tradition which confronted the Bible and implied that the Apostles were wrong in their assessment of Jesus' intentions. Theology thus mounted its own theory in opposition to Jesus and the Apostles. It erected an effective roadblock against understanding the mind of the historical Jesus on the critical issue of the Kingdom.

Few passages of Scripture have suffered more at the hands of hostile expositors than Luke's brief and brilliant summary of Jesus' last conversation with His Apostles. It is in the nature of "famous last words" that they communicate something of supreme importance. The Apostles' inquiry related to Jesus' and Luke's favorite theme, the

Kingdom of God. They asked: "Lord, has the time now come for You to restore the kingdom to Israel?" (Acts 1:6).[1]

A common approach to this passage has been to treat the Apostles' question as utterly out of tune with their Lord's teaching. Their inquiry is supposed to reveal a tragically inadequate understanding of Christianity's central theme. How, it is asked, could these associates of Jesus still cling so stubbornly to the crude notion of a theocratic restoration of the Kingdom as the renewal of the Davidic empire on earth, typical of the allegedly false hopes of Judaism? Fortunately, the argument continues, the coming of the Spirit at Pentecost rescued the Apostles from their crudely literal understanding of the Kingdom of God and banished forever the Jewish national hope they were harboring.

Theology's treatment of Acts 1:6 exposes the failure of traditional Christianity to deal fairly with the issue of the Kingdom of God. It displays a serious lack of sympathy for the Jewish atmosphere in which the teaching of Jesus is set. William Barclay's response to the disciples' parting question in Acts 1:6 is typical. He despairs of the disciples' ability to grasp the meaning of Jesus' Message of the Kingdom, the heart of His Gospel:

> The trouble was that [Jesus] meant one thing by the Kingdom and those who listened to him quite another...The Apostles looked for a day when by divine intervention the world sovereignty they dreamed of would be theirs. They conceived of the Kingdom in political terms.[2]

Barclay then gives us what he considers to be the true definition of the Kingdom. It is "a society upon earth where God's will would be as perfectly done as it is in heaven,"[3] as shown by the parallel phrases of the Lord's prayer: "Thy Kingdom come" with "Thy will be done on earth." Such a Kingdom, he maintains, would never be founded on power.[4]

---

[1] The substance of this chapter was first published in *The Evangelical Quarterly* (3), 1994, and is used here with permission.
[2] *The Acts of the Apostles,* Edinburgh: The Saint Andrews Press, 1955, p. 3.
[3] *Ibid.,* p. 4.
[4] *Ibid.*

A number of deeply-rooted theological misconceptions underlie the disparaging attitude of commentators towards the disciples' question about the restoration of Israel. Disapproval of the Apostles in Acts 1:6 reveals more about the prejudices of expositors than the truth of Scripture and suppresses vitally important biblical information about the nature and the future of the Kingdom of God. An attack on the Apostles in Acts 1:6 implies an attack on Jesus who had taught them. Only recently have commentaries begun to be objective enough to see that nothing in the text suggests that Luke means us to view the Apostles as out of step with Jesus' intentions. Common sense would require that the disciples be given credit for asking not the wrong question but the right one. They had, after all, been in Jesus' company since the beginning. They had heard Jesus preach and teach the Good News about the Kingdom day after day. They themselves had been sent out in public to proclaim the same Gospel of the Kingdom (Luke 9:2, 6 etc.). They had been congratulated by Jesus for their special insight into the divine Plan associated with the Kingdom: "To you it has been given to know the mysteries of the Kingdom of Heaven..." (Matt. 13:11). Jesus had probed their understanding of the parables of the Kingdom to satisfy Himself that they had grasped their meaning: "'Have you understood all these things?' They said to Him, 'Yes'" (Matt. 13:51). To complete their training on the key issue of the Kingdom of God, the disciples had undergone an intensive forty-day "seminar" under the tutorship of the risen Jesus on earth (Acts 1:3) as He opened their minds to understand Scripture (Luke 24:32, 45). It is incredible, in view of this evidence, that after all this exposure to Jesus' instruction they had failed entirely to understand what was meant by the Kingdom! On those occasions when the disciples did not comprehend, the text says so plainly. When the crucifixion and resurrection of Jesus were first announced, Luke writes: "But they did not understand this statement, and it was concealed from them so that they might not perceive it" (Luke 9:45). On the issue of the Kingdom, however, the very opposite was true. They had been given the saving knowledge of the Kingdom and had preached the Gospel about the Kingdom.

The unsympathetic attitude of commentators to the notion of the Kingdom as a restoration of the sovereignty of Israel points to a serious flaw in what theology has traditionally thought Jesus meant by the Kingdom of God. Since Jesus' reply to the Apostles cautions them only in regard to the *time* of the expected restoration, it is amazing that commentators should feel justified in making the disciples the target of their indignation and adding to the text their own battery of arguments in favor of a superior view of the Kingdom of God. Their constant cry is that the Christian Kingdom is "spiritual" and not political.[5] The disciples were clinging to "crassly Jewish" notions about the future. A survey of a range of commentary will reveal the seriousness of the criticism leveled at the early followers of Jesus.

A Historical Survey

The commentary by Jamieson, Faussett and Brown is one of the few of its era[6] not to follow the usual pattern of condemnation:

> As their question certainly implies that they looked for some restoration of the Kingdom to Israel, so they are neither rebuked for this nor contradicted. To say, as many expositors do, that our Lord's reply was so intended, is not to listen simply to what he says, but to obtrude upon his words what men think they ought to mean.[7]

With far less sympathy, H.A.W. Meyer, writing in 1884, deplores the Apostles' lack of understanding: "By their 'to Israel' they betray that they have not yet ceased to be entangled in Jewish Messianic hopes, according to which the Messiah was destined for the people of Israel as such; cp. Luke 24:21."[8]

The Pulpit Commentary[9] reacted similarly:

---

[5] Cp. *Expositor's Bible Commentary*, ed. Frank Gaebelein, Zondervan, 1981, Vol. 9, p. 256: "The question the disciples asked reflects the embers of a once blazing hope for a political theocracy in which they would be leaders...But though [Jesus'] words about the Spirit's coming rekindled in the disciples their old nationalistic hope, Jesus had something else in mind." The commentary describes the question as "misguided."

[6] Philadelphia: Lippincott & Co., 1868.

[7] *Commentary on Acts*, pp. 2, 3.

[8] *Critical and Exegetical Handbook to the Acts of the Apostles,* Winona Lake: Alpha Publications, 1979, pp. 27-28.

[9] *Acts*, ed. Spence and Exell, exposition by A.C. Hervey, Chicago: Wilcox & Follett, 1880-1897. The same commentary on Luke 1:32, 33 (1889) recognizes that Jesus has not inherited the throne of David in the way predicted by Gabriel.

Even after the Master's crucifixion and resurrection they had asked, "Lord, wilt thou at this time restore the Kingdom to Israel?" It was not until after the effusion of the holy spirit at Pentecost that their imperfect view was corrected and they understood what Christ meant when he said, "My Kingdom is not of the world." The terrestrial proceedings of the Messiah were the subject of the keenest expectations and the ground of national aspirations.[10]

Later commentary on our passage is unrelentingly harsh. Writers on the book of Acts maintained a steady stream of negative reaction to the idea that the Kingdom could be in any way compatible with a national restoration of Israel. The trend had been set by Calvin, no sympathizer with Messianism, who dismissed Acts 1:6 as evidence of a complete misunderstanding on the part of Jesus' chosen agents:

There are more errors in the question [in Acts 1:6] than there are words...Their blindness is remarkable, that when they had been so fully and carefully instructed over a period of three years they betrayed no less ignorance than if they had never heard a word...[11]

Calvin's astonishing criticism implies eleven mistakes. He does not detail his objections other than to say that the Apostles confuse the Kingdom of Christ with a kingdom which belongs to Israel. Calvin is evidently angry that the Apostles had not given up their Jewishness and replaced it with an attitude more "Christian." Calvin's objection, however, exposes the whole problem of Gentile failure to explain central New Testament themes.

Commentary in the second half of the last century persisted with its attack on the alleged obtuseness of the Apostles. Albert Barnes, writing in 1863, took the opportunity to correct the Apostles and reflect on the dangers of prejudice:

The Apostles had entertained the common opinion of the Jews about the temporal dominion of the Messiah. They expected that he would reign as a prince and conqueror, and free them from the bondage of the Romans. Many instances of this expectation occur in the Gospels, notwithstanding all the efforts which the Lord Jesus made to explain to them the true nature of his Kingdom. This

---

[10] Republished Eerdmans, 1950, commentary on Matt. 19:27, p. 251.

[11] *Calvin's Commentaries, Acts of the Apostles,* ed. D.W. Torrance and T.F. Torrance, Grand Rapids: Eerdmans, 1965, p 25.

expectation was checked and almost destroyed by his death (Luke 24:21)...Yet though his death checked their expectations and appeared to thwart their plans, yet his return to life excited them again...and as they did not doubt now that he *would* restore the Kingdom to Israel, they asked whether he would do it *at this time.* They did not ask whether he would do it at all, or whether they had correct views of his Kingdom; but taking that for granted they asked him whether *that was the time* in which he would do it. The emphasis of the inquiry lies in the expression "at this time" and hence the answer of the Savior refers solely to this point of their inquiry and not to the correctness or incorrectness of their opinions. From these expectations of the Apostles we may learn: 1. That there is nothing so difficult to be removed from the mind as *prejudice in favor of erroneous opinions.* 2. That such prejudice will survive the plainest proof to the contrary. 3. That it will often manifest itself even after all proper means have been taken to subdue it. Erroneous opinions thus maintain a secret ascendancy in a man's mind, and are revived by the slightest circumstances even long after we supposed they were overcome; and even in the face of the plainest proofs of reason or of Scripture.[12]

In the present century the evident Jewishness of the disciples' question was noted and then dismissed, in the style of Harnack, as a useless husk within which we are to look for the true "spiritual" Kingdom. Early Christianity is couched in the language of Jewish Messianism, so the argument goes, but the essence of the faith lies elsewhere. *The Clarendon Commentary* explains Acts 1:6 as follows:

The question is put in the language of the old Jewish Messianic hope. The Restoration of the Kingdom to Israel was the regular phrase for that final establishment of the theocracy and spiritual renovation of mankind which had been the highest point of prophetic and apocalyptic expectation among the Jews. This hope was understood in a materialistic and nationalistic sense (as promising a time of material prosperity and Jewish world empire) by some, but not by all. Clearly the disciples felt that an epoch-making crisis of divine action was at hand, though clearly too they did not understand what its nature would be.[13]

---

[12] *Commentary on Acts,* London: Routledge, Warne and Routledge, 1863, p. 4.
[13] Oxford: Clarendon Press, 1923, p. 132.

In a note on the Messianic hope a typical attempt is made to distinguish between Christian preaching and its Jewish dress:

> So much of the Christian preaching in Acts is couched in the language of Jewish Messianism that an excursus on the Jewish Messianic hope is needed to grasp its significance...In time the rule of God would be established and this revived theocracy would mean the renovation of Israel, and through Israel of the nations as spiritual dependents of Mount Zion.[14]

The value of this comment lies in its concise description of the content of the hope revealed by the Apostles' question. They were expecting the reestablishment of the promised Davidic theocracy. Discussion of the Kingdom of God in Acts 1:3 provoked an eager response from the disciples. Mention of the Holy Spirit in the same context (Acts 1:5) naturally led to the supposition that the time had finally arrived for the manifestation of the Messianic Kingdom described by Old Testament prophecy. Our passage therefore, far from being an indication of apostolic ignorance, is of the highest significance as revealing the apostolic mind on eschatology (the doctrine of future events) and the nature of the Kingdom of God. Commentary seems, however, to have dismissed Luke's and the Apostles' testimony to early Christian views of the future.

John Bright's extensive study of the biblical theme of the Kingdom of God provides a further example of commentary expressing shock at the nationalism involved in the disciples' final remarks about the Kingdom:

> The Messianic hope of Israel was thus grimly tied to the line of David, to Jerusalem and the Temple...It meant that as long as the state lasted, each king in the popular mind was a potential Messiah. It helped to father the national delusion that, though Judah might be decimated, Jerusalem and the Davidic state could never be destroyed...It meant that when he who was the fulfillment of that longing should appear, men would demand of him things which were not in his nature to deliver: "Lord, will you at this time restore the Kingdom to Israel?" (Acts 1:6).[15]

---

[14] *Ibid.*, p. 156.

[15] *The Kingdom of God*, p. 93.

Later he adds: "Judaism's frenetic question would be: 'Lord, will you at this time restore the Kingdom to Israel?'"[16]

Surprisingly even George Ladd, whose sympathy with premillennialism (belief in a future reign of Christ and the saints on earth) is well known, was unable to break away from the tradition of exposition which took exception to what were perceived as Jewish and therefore by definition unchristian ideas of the Kingdom of God. Ladd pointed out that "the phrase 'to redeem Israel' [Luke 24:21]…does not refer to the redemption of men from their sins. In its present context the phrase means to deliver Israel from her bondage to foreign powers."[17]

He noted that:

> This same sentiment is expressed in Acts 1:6 where Luke summarizes the disciples' attitude by the question: "Lord, will you at this time restore the kingdom to Israel?" The disciples were still looking for a nationalistic and political savior for the people of Israel, a hope which we have found in the apocalyptic literature.[18]

He adds (though Luke does not say this): "Jesus rebuked them for failing to understand the prophetic scriptures."[19]

A Change of Attitude

In the same decade a distinct change of heart is to be observed in commentators' treatment of the problematic evidence of Acts 1:6. An objective examination of the text revealed that neither Luke nor Jesus whom he reports displayed the slightest discomfort or surprise about the prospect of the restoration of the Kingdom to Israel. No rebuke was issued to the disciples for their blindness. Everything in the context implies that they had asked a perfectly proper question. On other occasions Luke is not afraid to report the slowness of the Apostles to grasp truth, when this is appropriate. Earlier they were unable to accept that the Messiah had to die: "They understood none of these things" (Luke 18:34). In Acts 1:6, however, their question reflects an expectation which was simply the natural outcome of the

---

[16] *Ibid.*, p. 168.
[17] *I Believe in the Resurrection,* Hodder and Stoughton, 1975, p. 97.
[18] *Ibid.*
[19] *Ibid.*

detailed instruction about the Kingdom they had received from Jesus. The hope of a restored Davidic Kingdom was evidently part of the common view of the future held by Judaism and Jesus. Indeed, as Lukan eschatology and Kingdom theology have come under close scrutiny, its Jewishness has become more and more obvious. The results of this discovery have yet to filter down into the pulpit much less the pew. But they should set in motion a revolution in our understanding of Jesus and His Gospel.

Conzelmann observed that the hope for the restoration of the Kingdom to Israel met with not the slightest correction from Jesus: "Acts 1:6 speaks of the Kingdom being restored to Israel. It is not the hope of this which is rejected, but only the attempt to calculate when it will happen."[20]

Haenchen added his voice to those who saw the need to clear the disciples of the long-standing charge of spiritual blindness:

> Those gathered — Luke implies that not only the Apostles were present — ask whether Jesus will now restore the Kingdom to Israel. The question is not meant to show the disciples' ignorance, but provides an opportunity to clarify a problem of the highest significance. The earliest Christians regarded the outpouring of the spirit as a sign that the end of the world was at hand (*apokathistimi*, from Mal. 3:32, LXX onwards is a technical term in eschatology: the establishment of the right order by God at the end of time [sic][21] (cp. *Th Wb*, I, 386ff)).[22]

The Kingdom of God in Luke's Gospel

A number of important studies of Lukan theology have continued to clarify the meaning of key terms in Luke's account of Christianity.[23] Paramount among these is the Kingdom of God. Interest in the restoration of the Kingdom to Israel is not to be ascribed to a

---

[20] *The Theology of St. Luke*, New York: Harper and Row, 1960, p. 163.

[21] It is incorrect to speak of the "end of time." The Bible expects time to continue in the next age of the Kingdom which will be preceded by the "end-time."

[22] *The Acts of the Apostles*, Philadelphia: Westminster Press, 1971, p 143.

[23] For example, G.A. Krodel, *Acts, Augsburg Commentary on the New Testament,* Minneapolis: Augsburg Publishing House, 1986; Robert Tannehill, *The Narrative Unity of Luke-Acts, A Literary Interpretation,* Minneapolis: Fortress Press, 1990.

regrettable failure on the part of the disciples. *It is an essential element in what Jesus and Luke meant by the Kingdom of God.*

Taking Acts 1:6 as our cue we can see that Luke's hope for the future is fully in line with the Davidic Messianism presented by Hebrew prophecy. This is nowhere challenged in the New Testament and is confirmed elsewhere in Luke's writings. The *means* by which the desired restoration of Israel is to be achieved obviously received a new twist when Jesus announced His own death and resurrection and when the Israel of His generation failed to recognize their Messiah. Luke's major point, however, is that God's promise of redemption in Israel and Jerusalem would not occur until the Messiah had passed through death, resurrection and a period of exaltation to the right hand of the Father. Following this He will return to carry out the whole program of restoration foreseen by the prophets (Acts 3:21).

Jesus and the Messianic Program

The New Testament hope, epitomized by the disciples' question in Acts 1:6, is based on the fact that Jesus came to confirm the promises given to the fathers (Rom. 15:8). The first thing said about Jesus is that He is destined to succeed to the throne of His ancestor David and rule over the house of Jacob forever (Luke 1:32, 33). This statement is a precise summary of the Messianic hope which pervades the prophets and the Psalms. It was the prevailing expectation among Jesus' contemporaries.[24] Luke does not say that Jesus has already taken up a position on the throne of David. He closes the period of Messiah's ministry on earth by reverting to the Davidic theme announced by Gabriel before the conception of Jesus. He records Jesus' approval of the hope of Israel's restoration, noting that it lies in the future. By reporting the disciples' question about when the restoration will occur he allows us to know that Jesus *distinguishes between the immediate coming of the Spirit at Pentecost — "not many days hence"* (Acts 1:5) *— and the restoration of the Kingdom to Israel which is to occur at a time unknown* (Acts 1:7). In a sermon given by Peter shortly after Pentecost further light is thrown on the time for the expected fulfillment of Old Testament prophecy. In answer to the very reasonable objection that Jesus' disappearance to heaven does not seem to advance the Messianic program on earth, Peter explained that

---

[24] As shown, for example, by the Psalms of Solomon 17, 18.

"heaven must retain [the Messiah] until the times of the restoration of all things about which God spoke through the mouth of His holy prophets from ancient times" (Acts 3:21). The period which Israel is to look forward to is also a time of relief (*anapsuxsis,* Acts 3:19) to be introduced by the coming of the Messiah. We should not overlook the important connection between the *apokatastasis*[25] or restoration promised for the future Parousia and the related verb found in the earlier question of the disciples: "Is it at this time that You are going to restore (*apokathistaneis*) the Kingdom to Israel?" In the light of this verse it is highly unlikely that Luke intends to say that Jesus' session at the right hand of the Father marks the reestablishment of the throne of David. Luke has previously made a careful distinction between the coming of the Spirit (Acts 1:5), consequent upon the Messiah's ascension, and the *still future coming of the Davidic Kingdom* (Acts 1:6, 7).

Luke wants us to understand that the great Davidic themes announced earlier by the angel and prophesied by Mary, Zechariah and Simeon still await their fulfillment when Jesus returns (Luke 1:46-55, 68-79; 2:25-32). The promised restoration is the subject of the charismatic utterances which accompanied the birth of Jesus. The recipients of these prophetic visions were the faithful of the Messianic community. They were not Jews who did not understand the Christian hope. The same anticipation of the reestablishment of the throne of David remains a burning issue for the Apostles of Jesus just before His ascension. The biblical Christian expectation is for the renewal at the reappearance of the Messiah of the Davidic Kingdom so that Israel may serve the Lord "all their days" (Luke 1:74, 75) and be guided into the peace she has never experienced (Luke 1:79). The Magnificat and the Benedictus are of the highest significance as laying out Christian teaching about the future. That future is expressed in prophetic past tenses. It is clear that before Jesus' birth Israel had not yet been "saved from the hands of all who hate her" (Luke 1:74). Nor had the righteous been exalted to rule in place of the mighty who were to be deposed (Luke 1:52). The New Testament expects these Messianic events to be

---

[25] Philo uses this word to describe the liberation from Egypt (*Rer Div. Her* 293) and Josephus refers to the restoration of the temple following the Babylonian captivity (*Ant* 11:63).

fulfilled at the return of Christ (Matt. 19:28; Acts 3:21; Rev. 11:15-18).

Luke's Messianic Outlook

The songs of Mary and Zechariah are inspired utterances which do not deal with the immediate career of Jesus nor His death and resurrection but look ahead to the Second Coming which for Luke is the time for the redemption of Israel. For Mary and Zechariah the birth of Jesus guarantees the future long-awaited goal of all prophecy — the establishment of universal peace under the rule of the Messiah, the promised heir to the throne of David.

When a number of Luke's key terms are brought together we gain a coherent picture of a Messianic future which confirms the vision of Old Testament prophecy.[26] The righteous are eagerly anticipating (*prosdechomai*) the consolation (*paraklesis*) of Israel (Luke 2:25) which has *still not occurred* by the time of the crucifixion, since Joseph of Arimathea is still awaiting (*prosdechomai*) the Kingdom of God (Luke 23:51). The parallel language shows that Luke expects the coming of the Kingdom to involve the restoration of Israel. The righteous remnant, who enjoy the inspiration of "Holy Spirit," share this hope. Zechariah awaits the redemption (*lutrosis,* Luke 1:68) of Israel which for Anna the prophetess is the redemption (*lutrosis*) of Jerusalem (Luke 2:38). The hope is definitely territorial and tied to Jerusalem as the center of the expected Kingdom.

The hope expressed through Mary and Zechariah as mouthpieces of the Holy Spirit is not fulfilled at the crucifixion, for the disciples were still looking for Jesus to redeem (*lutrosthai*) Israel (Luke 24:21). Their desire for national deliverance is not rebuked by Jesus and it reappears in Acts 1:6 after the disciples have received further extensive teaching about the Kingdom from the risen Messiah. The ultimate restoration of Israel is certain, *as an event quite distinct from the coming of the Spirit at Pentecost.* It is the prerogative of the Father to determine when it will happen, since no man knows the day of the coming of the Son of Man in the power of His Kingdom. Jesus does not deny that He will bring about the restoration of Israel, but merely indicates that it is not for His disciples to know the time of the event

---

[26] Particularly the themes announced by Isa. 40-66.

(Acts 1:7) just as Jesus Himself did not know the day of His future coming (Mark 13:32).

Further information is provided by Luke in his version of Jesus' apocalyptic discourse. Jerusalem is to be trodden down until the times of the Gentiles are fulfilled (Luke 24:21). The implication is that Jerusalem, as capital of the Messiah's Kingdom, will not remain under Gentile control indefinitely. When the times of Gentile dominion, a period with links to Daniel's vision of heathen oppression of the holy land (Dan. 8:13), have run their course, the time for Jerusalem's redemption will have arrived. Luke describes the same scheme exactly when he postpones the manifestation of the Kingdom in Jerusalem to the time when the nobleman, who must first depart to a far country, returns to reign in the Kingdom which by then he has obtained (Luke 19:11-27).

The Old Testament basis for this whole eschatological outlook is clear. Isaiah 1:26 promises a restoration of Israel's administrators "as at the first," while in Isaiah 63:17, 18 God is urged to "return for the sake of Your servants the tribes of Your heritage.[27] Thy holy people possessed Your sanctuary a little while. Our adversaries have trodden it down."[28] Isaiah 65:9ff, along with a mass of other Hebrew prophecy, promises a grand restoration of the land of Israel with a new Jerusalem.

Jesus' and Luke's key eschatological terms are rooted in a number of other Old Testament passages. Isaiah 52:9-10 speaks of the consolation and redemption of Israel at the time when God reveals His holy arm and all the ends of the earth see the salvation of God. Isaiah 49:6 describes the recovery of the Diaspora of Israel. The important point is that Luke expects restoration to occur fully at the return of Jesus in power. The *apokatastasis* of Acts 3:21, which will bring

---

[27] Cp. Ps. 122:3-5. The theme of comfort in Jerusalem reflects the promises of Isa. 40:1; 49:13; 51:3; 52:9; 57:18; 66:11,13. The redemption of Jerusalem is foreseen by Isa. 43:1; 44:23; 51:11; 52:3; 63:4 (*lutrosis*, LXX). Restoration is expected in Isa. 1:26; 49:6, 8; 52:8; 58:12. Cp. Jer. 27:22; 3:17-19. The coming of the Kingdom is evidently the same event and is expected in Isaiah 52:7, "Your God reigns," where the Targum reads: "The Kingdom of God is revealed."

[28] Cp. Zech. 12:3 (LXX): "Everyone that tramples on Jerusalem shall utterly mock at it." The prophecy is repeated in Rev. 11:2: "They shall trample on the holy city for 42 months."

about restoration for Israel (Acts 1:6), will coincide with the coming of Jesus, when at the same time the disciples may "lift up their heads because their redemption (*apolutrosis*) draws near" (Luke 21:28), which is only another way of saying that "the Kingdom of God is about to come" (Luke 21:31). At that time, and not before, the Lord's prayer for the coming of the Kingdom will be fulfilled.

Luke's interchangeable phrases may be summarized as follows:

The arrival of the apocalyptic Kingdom (21:31) = the redemption of the disciples (21:28) = redemption in Jerusalem (2:35) = the redemption of Israel (24:21).

The expected future Kingdom (23:51) = the expected consolation of Israel (Luke 2:25).

The restoration of the Kingdom to Israel (Acts 1:6) = the times of the restoration of all that was promised through the mouth of the prophets (Acts 3:21) = the restoration of the house of David as promised through the mouth of the prophets (Luke 1:70) = the enthronement of Jesus on the throne of David to which He is heir (Luke 1:32, 33).

Contemporary Commentary on Acts 1:6

Recent commentary is happily no longer defensive in admitting the strongly political flavor of Luke's Christianity and allows for a recovery of a full understanding of the Gospel as it came from the lips of Jesus. R. Tannehill says: "John and Jesus are presented as the fulfillment of hopes for the redemption of Israel and Jerusalem. Jesus is the Davidic Messiah (Luke 1:32, 33, 68, 69) who will bring political freedom to the Jewish people (1:71, 74)."[29] He notes that "the narrator understands the Scriptures to promise a Messianic kingdom for Israel which will be a time of peace and freedom from oppressors. This promise is acknowledged as valid — if only Israel would accept its Messiah."[30] Tannehill explains that Luke's theme of redemption for Israel continues to appear as a future hope, even after the crucifixion. The biblical Christian teaching about the future has lost none of its Jewish, Old Testament orientation. It is still tied to the recovery of Israel and her resettlement in the land:

---

[29] *The Narrative Unity of Luke-Acts*, p. 19.

[30] *Ibid.*, p. 34.

"We were hoping that he was the one who was going to redeem Israel." Again it is a question of *Israel's* redemption. This hope is revived by Jesus' resurrection, which leads the disciples to ask, "Are you at this time restoring the Kingdom to Israel?" (Acts 1:6). Here the hope for Israel's messianic Kingdom, strongly expressed in the birth narratives, reappears. This question does not merely show the blindness of followers who have not yet received the Spirit. Jesus corrects their curiosity about times, but he does not reject the possibility of a restored Kingdom for Israel, and Peter, after receiving the Spirit, still holds out the hope of the "restoration of all the things which God spoke through the mouth of his holy prophets of old..." (Acts 3:21).[31]

Of particular interest is the fact that Luke 1:70 and Acts 3:21 both contain the all-encompassing phrase "which God spoke through the mouth of His holy prophets from of old." In a brief statement the whole sweep of Hebrew prophecy is brought before us. The promises of a royal Messiah succeeding to the throne of David and bringing about liberation for Israel and Jerusalem still await fulfillment at the Parousia. Jesus' words are to the same effect. The disciples are to expect their own redemption and the advent of the Kingdom at the return of the Messiah (Luke 21:28, 31). The great events marking the reestablishment of the Davidic Kingdom are not fulfilled when the Spirit is poured out and do not apply, therefore, to the Church this side of Christ's return. The Messiah's absence in heaven is temporary, extending to the end of the present age. Then will come the time for the realization of the hope which has run like a golden thread through the Hebrew Scriptures and onwards into the Gospels. Luke's reporting of the prophetic utterances of Mary, Zechariah and Simeon are a precious foundation for Christian hope as long as the Parousia is delayed. Gabriel's opening announcement about the restoration of the throne of David and the disciples' closing question about the restoration of Israel bracket the whole of Luke's account of the Christian faith.

Confirmation that this is Luke's and Jesus' consistent message is provided by Arthur Wainwright who observes that Luke demonstrates a considerable knowledge of Jewish tradition. The beloved physician, as a true believer,

---

[31] *Ibid.*, p. 35.

retained the influence of Judaism...Luke was deeply concerned about Israel's future...Luke appears to look forward to a time when Israel will be reinstated. His references to the restoration and redemption of Israel provide a clue to his theological presuppositions...This redemption will follow the return of the Son of Man.[32]

Modern readers of the Bible often find it impossible to share Luke's outlook and therefore miss the richness of the Messianic hope which is fundamental to biblical Christianity. The pressing question is whether the Church has not thrown away a central element of New Testament faith by calling the earlier chapters of Luke pre-Christian. Commentary's clamorous accusations that the Apostles were lamentably slow in growing out of their "Jewish" political views of the Kingdom may simply reveal how far we have departed from a New Testament understanding of the Kingdom of God. One of Luke's main purposes was to teach us Christian eschatology. We have rejected much of it and claimed a superior understanding which we label "spiritual," as distinct from Luke's Hebrew-based vision of the future which we find intolerably Jewish.

The record of exposition which finds fault with the Apostles on the crucial issue of the definition of the Kingdom should cause us to ponder what theologians have been up to. Gresham Machen, in his discussion of the early chapters of Luke, spoke of the "absence of specifically Christian ideas in the Magnificat and Benedictus, the absence of reference to facts in the life of Jesus."[33] He explained Luke's inclusion of these Messianic songs by saying that they point "to a time when the messianic Hope was still couched in the terms of Old Testament prophecy. [The songs of Mary and Zechariah] were produced at a time when Old Testament prophecy had not yet been explained by its fulfillment."[34]

But Luke thinks quite differently. Those early Christian songs declare future Messianic events which remain unfulfilled as long as Jesus is absent in heaven. To the eye of faith those great events appear fulfilled even before the beginning of the ministry of Jesus in

---

[32] "Luke and the Restoration of the Kingdom to Israel," *Expository Times* (89), 1977-78, pp. 76-79.

[33] *The Virgin Birth of Christ,* Harper and Row, 1930, p. 97.

[34] *Ibid.,* pp. 97-98.

Palestine, since they are certain in the divine Plan. A disastrous theory which equated the Kingdom with the time period immediately following the resurrection of Jesus, however, brought about a radical confusion over Jesus' and the New Testament's most fundamental concept — the Kingdom of God. Jesus still looked forward to the restoration and ultimate political liberation of Israel and the world at His return. He did not abandon a natural reading of the prophets. Many of His followers, however, have transmuted the prophets' obvious hope for the reinstatement of Israel in the land and applied it to the Church now. There is a need to rediscover the territorial element in salvation.[35]

Raymond Brown also finds that "there is nothing distinctively Christian in Gabriel's words in vss. 32-33 of Luke 1, except that the Davidic Messiah has been identified with Jesus."[36] On the contrary, Luke was documenting the Christian faith and presenting a view of the future which is in need of recovery if our claim to believe in the normative role of Scripture is to be genuine. Apostolic Christians maintained the Jewish Old Testament hope of peace on earth to be brought about by a new world empire centered in Jerusalem. Luke so understands the future of the Kingdom of God. He describes a faith which is universal in its embrace but, for all that, none the less focused on the hope of Israel, the destiny of Jerusalem, and the ultimate reestablishment of the throne of David.

The disciples' question in Acts 1:6 is the climax of a coherent series of sayings about the future Kingdom of God in Luke/Acts. From the beginning of the Gospel Luke presents the Kingdom of God as Messianic and Davidic. As both Mary and Zechariah exclaim, the root concept of the Kingdom is found in the covenant made with Abraham (Luke 1:55, 72, 73), of which the Davidic covenant is an extension. The restoration of the Kingdom to Israel at the Second Coming is the ultimate horizon of that Christian hope. If the spiritualizing and mystical influence of Origen, which is so deeply embedded in Christian tradition, is laid aside, and we consider the possibility that

---

[35] For excellent insights into New Testament eschatology in the light of its Hebrew background, see G.W. Buchanan, *The Consequences of the Covenant,* Leiden: Brill, 1970, and *Jesus, the King and His Kingdom,* Macon: Mercer University Press, 1984.

[36] *The Virgin Birth of the Messiah,* London: Geoffrey Chapman, 1977, p. 311.

the original faith should be read in terms of its own Hebrew Messianic presuppositions, it will not be difficult to see that Luke expects that Israel and the land are to be the arena of a restored Davidic theocracy (cp. Matt. 5:5; Rev. 5:10). This is just what we would expect from a community devoted to the Abrahamic and Davidic covenant, which were the backbone of Jewish piety, and to the Message of the prophets, for whom the Messiah and the Kingdom of God were intensely political, but not therefore unspiritual concepts.

When the Kingdom of God is redefined as "heaven" for departed souls, a synonym for the Church or a social program, or even Zionist hopes this side of the Second Coming, it is unlikely that the biblical Gospel of the Kingdom can be heard in terms which make sense of it in its own Jewish context.[37] The Christian Gospel presents salvation from sins for individuals, but salvation is linked to the future renewal of the earth and to a Kingdom centered in Jerusalem. The central Message of Jesus was the approach of the Kingdom of God for which men were to prepare with all urgency, and of which He was the appointed ruler. How faithfully has this Gospel been transmitted to us? A positive answer is hardly possible. A recent history of the doctrine of the Kingdom of God[38] suggests that the Kingdom has not received anything like the attention it enjoys in the New Testament as the heart of Jesus' Gospel of salvation. Moreover, it has suffered drastic reinterpretation when it has been forced to support various manmade agendas unrelated to the Messianic Kingdom or reduced to an interior Kingdom in the heart.

Speaking of the misuse of Luke 17:21 ("the Kingdom of God is among you") as a way of obscuring the much greater emphasis on the futurity of the Kingdom, B.T. Viviano says:

> Unfortunately this verse has been abused throughout history and led to an overly spiritual, depoliticized and then trivialized interpretation of the Kingdom. It is a mistake to make this verse the

---

[37] Liberation theology catches the spirit of Luke's vision of political freedom but tries to force into being now what the New Testament does not expect before the Parousia.

[38] B.T. Viviano, *The Kingdom of God in History.*

starting point of our understanding of the Kingdom in the proclamation of Jesus.[39]

The same might be said of the misuse of Jesus' statement that His Kingdom was "not of this world" (John 18:36). It has been assumed without careful reflection that the Kingdom will never be on earth. What Jesus meant, however, was that His Kingdom did not have its origin in the present evil systems dominated by Satan. When Jesus spoke of preparing places for the disciples "in My Father's house" (John 14:2), He was thinking of the future Kingdom of God on earth. He added immediately that He was going to *come back* to the earth (John 14:3) so that He and the disciples could be reunited in the places prepared by the Father, the Kingdom "prepared from the foundation of the world," which the disciples are to enter when Jesus returns (Matt. 25:34).

Eschatology and the Recovery of the Biblical Hope

Acts 1:6 is a valuable text as a starting point for the recovery of New Testament theology of the Kingdom. Until recently this verse has been dismissed out of hand because it did not seem to agree with what we thought the Kingdom of God should be. In 1924, A.F. Macinnes examined the Kingdom of God as described in the apostolic writings.[40] In a brief comment on Acts 1:6 he dismisses the Apostles as unreliable witnesses to the nature of the Kingdom:

> At the beginning of Acts we see that the Apostles still held to their erroneous conception of the Kingdom of God. They asked Jesus after the resurrection when He would restore the Kingdom to Israel (Acts 1:6); they were thinking of an earthly Kingdom.[41]

G.T. Stokes, reflecting a catastrophic misunderstanding of the Jewishness of Jesus, referred to the disciples' inquiry about the Kingdom as "the darkened utterance of carnal and uninspired minds groping after the truth." Such commentary marks the point at which the churches have "leapt the track" and departed into their own unbiblical version of the Kingdom. The question is, Whose minds are

---

[39] *Ibid.*, p. 27.
[40] *The Kingdom of God in the Apostolic Writings,* London: James Clark, 1924.
[41] *Ibid.*, p. 92.

in need of enlightenment, those of the makers of Christian tradition or those of Jesus' personally trained disciples?

Ramsay Michaels put his finger on the long-standing problem reflected in the antagonistic attitude of commentators and prepares for a reevaluation of what Harnack saw as the most critical of all questions: "Neither my theology nor yours matters; what matters is the right teaching of the Gospel." Michaels wrote:

> The tendency of much Christian scholarship has been to minimize the Jewishness or ethnicity of Jesus' vision of the Kingdom of God with the observation that he had no interest in a political kingdom, or one that could be established by military might or rebellion against Rome. The tacit assumption is that non-political means non-nationalistic, which in turn means non-ethnic and non-Jewish, but instead "spiritual" and "universal." Actually the Kingdom of God in Jewish expectation was both spiritual and national, both universal and ethnic...After the resurrection, according to the book of Acts, Jesus' disciples asked him (even after he had instructed them for forty days about the Kingdom of God!): "Lord, will you at this time restore the Kingdom to Israel?" (Acts 1:6). Jesus' reply gives no hint that this nationalistic expectation was in any way wrong or misguided, only that the time of the restoration was set in God's authority alone.[42]

We propose that commentators adopt the mind set of the Apostles for a moment and allow themselves the liberty of supposing that these disciples of Jesus in fact knew exactly what they were talking about. Such an experiment could revolutionize our understanding of the thrust of the whole New Testament. A kingdom which is "spiritual" need not mean a kingdom which cannot appear at the return of Christ localized in Jerusalem, with the new David as its sovereign in the company of the resurrected saints[43] and blessing the entire world with an era of unparalleled prosperity and security. Why should such a thing be thought incredible when prophets and Psalmists looked for the regathering of the tribes in the land and sang of the coming glorious reign of Messiah on earth? When the cloud of confusion over

---

[42] *The Kingdom of God in 20th-Century Interpretation*, ed. Wendell Willis, p. 114.

[43] Cp. Dan. 7:14, 18, 22, 27; Luke 22:28-30; 1 Cor. 6:2; 2 Tim. 2:12; Rev. 2:26; 3:21; 5:10; 20:1-6.

the Kingdom of God is lifted and when commentators believe what the New Testament says about the future, it will become clear that Acts 1:6 is a text which sits in judgment on our failure to believe the prophets and our reluctance to accept that the Apostles knew better than we do what Jesus meant by the Kingdom of God.

Bible readers are accustomed to hearing those parts of the text which fit with received ideas. It is possible that other elements of the Message are unconsciously rejected because they are unfamiliar. Christian concentration on individual salvation now and at death has seriously interfered with the massive New Testament emphasis on the Kingdom of God to be inaugurated when Jesus returns as conquering Messiah. In view of the delay of Christ's return, the Church seems to have lost its nerve when it comes to believing those elements of the Gospel which promise good things coming. Yet this should be the heart of her Message.

Faced with the obvious social and political implications of the Magnificat and Acts 1:6, expositors have resorted to various ways of bypassing the text. One technique is to offer a spiritualizing interpretation. A second is to read the text as authorizing political or social action this side of the Second Coming. A third solution is to maintain that earlier revolutionary attitudes are modified or even corrected by later developments in the teaching of Jesus. This third way round the difficulty founders on the evidence of Luke 21:24 and particularly Acts 1:6 and 3:21. While it is clear that the historical Jesus undertook no revolutionary action in the political arena, this does not mean that a political revolution is not envisaged for the future. The Day of the Lord is yet to come. It is to this event that Luke 24:21, Acts 1:6 and 3:21 point so clearly. It is fatal to a proper grasp of the Kingdom of God to rule the evidence of Acts 1:6 out of court on the grounds that the disciples did not share *our* perception of what the Kingdom should be. Once Acts 1:6 and other politically loaded verses are allowed to stand as testimony to the future Kingdom as a world government entrusted to the returning Jesus and the saints, a flood of light is thrown on the biblical Message.

It is important to note that a Kingdom involving the restoration of Israel to the land is neither worldly nor secular, because it is to be a Kingdom in the hands of the Messiah himself. The suggestion that Jesus' activity as a nonviolent preacher and healer is more "spiritual" than His implementation of a world government on the throne of David sets up a false dichotomy. Luke and the New Testament in general present us with a Jesus who is both the suffering Messiah and the conquering Messiah who brings in the Kingdom with power at His return. Our problem is that we have been reading the New Testament as though it is not a Messianic document in the sense indicated by Acts 1:6 (cp. Rev. 11:15-18; Luke 19:11-27). Tradition has taught us to believe (often very vaguely) in the future of the individual soul. Luke intends us to look forward to the restoration of the throne of David and of Israel to the land. A new orientation to Bible exposition is needed.

Jesus demonstrated the power of the future Kingdom in His ministry. The mighty, however, were not toppled from their thrones, the humble did not replace them and Jesus did not ascend the throne of David. Nor was the Kingdom of God reestablished in Israel. Luke is careful to tell us that the outpouring of the Spirit at the ascension, though it advances the Messianic program, is not the fulfillment of the promised restoration of Israel. Until that time the Spirit as the "Spirit of the promise" (Eph. 1:13) is given as a down payment of something much greater, namely our future inheritance of the Kingdom.

It is a misreading of the Gospel of Jesus to think that the content of His Message is confined to events which took place in Galilee. Nor is the Gospel complete in the death and resurrection of Jesus. The Gospel takes in the broad sweep of salvation history including the all-important Kingdom still to be established. Setting dates for that event is impossible. Making known that fact of the future is part of the task of relaying the Gospel faithfully. The presentation of the biblical view of the future, including the information supplied by Acts 1:6, clarifies the meaning of the hope which Paul sees as a solid basis for the development of faith and love (Col. 1:5; Eph. 1:18). Acts 1:6 does not represent a decline from the spirituality of Jesus but is part and parcel of the total spiritual expectation of the Kingdom to which Luke and the New Testament writings point. Acts 1:6 reflects the mature understanding of disciples who have been with Jesus.

There is value in reflecting anew on how Calvin and a whole tradition of exposition dealt with Acts 1:6.[44] Calvin's negative reaction

---

[44] Cp. the cavalier fashion in which the *Hastings Dictionary of the Bible* dismisses Acts 1:6 as valuable only as "an authentic little touch..., a veritable

to the Apostles gives point to the whole thesis of this book — that the Church has for too long presented its members with a demessianized Gospel and a demessianized Jesus. Since the whole point of the New Testament is to present Jesus as the Messiah, a hornet's nest of problems must arise when a self-contradictory, unmessianic Christ replaces the biblical Jesus. The lesson to be learned from Acts 1:6 is that apostolic testimony about the Kingdom is for our correction. For too long the Church has rejected a concept of the Kingdom which is foreign to our thinking but not to that of the Apostles, who saw more clearly than we what it means to believe in Jesus as the Messiah. The Jesus described in Luke's Gospel is heir to the throne of David in Jerusalem, restorer of the Kingdom to Israel and guarantor of worldwide peace on earth, a prospect foreshadowed in His spiritual activity in Palestine. That unity which at present eludes churches may be regained by rallying around the Jesus of Scripture, the Jesus who is the Messiah and King of the Jews, bearer of the saving Gospel of the Kingdom and destined to rule the world in Jerusalem.

---

reminiscence of what we may be sure was their real attitude at the moment, though it soon ceased to be. When they asked, 'Lord, dost thou at this time restore the kingdom to Israel?' their thoughts were still running in the groove of the old Jewish expectation. It is the last trace of them that we have in this naive form" (Vol. II, "Jesus Christ"). On the contrary, the same eschatology is confirmed in Acts 3:21.

10. The Faking of Christian Doctrine

No one who has spent time with the letters of Paul can fail to be impressed by the sense of earnest urgency which motivates him. He is evidently waging a campaign for a cause which he considers to be supremely important. He speaks of himself as having been put in charge of a service — the business of spreading far and wide the Gospel of salvation. It is a sacred duty which he must discharge at all costs (Acts 20:24). His life task is to propagate the Good News Message about the Kingdom of God (Acts 19:8; 20:25; 28:23, 31) — information which he sees as the only information having absolute value. Without it a man is perishing. With it he is on his way to achieving the purpose for which he was born — the attainment of immortality in the coming Kingdom, as co-administrator with Jesus, the Messiah. Paul made clear the nature of his commission in the first verses and at the conclusion of his letter to the Romans:

> Paul, a bondservant of Christ Jesus, called as an Apostle, set apart for the Gospel of God,[1] which He promised beforehand through His prophets in the holy Scriptures, concerning His Son who was born of a descendant of David, according to the flesh, who was declared the Son of God with power by the resurrection from the dead, according to the spirit of holiness, Jesus Christ our Lord, through whom we have received grace and apostleship to bring about the obedience of faith among all the Gentiles for His name's sake...Now to Him who is able to establish you according to my Gospel and *the preaching of Jesus Christ* according to the mystery

---

[1] The same term describes the same Gospel preached by Jesus (Mark 1:14) and by Peter (I Pet. 4:17). Paul uses the phrase often (Rom. 1:1; 15:16; II Cor. 11:7; I Thess. 2:2, 8, 9).

which has been kept secret for long ages past but now is manifested, and by the Scriptures of the prophets... (Rom. 1:1-5; 16:25, 26).

Anyone in search of the driving force behind the mission of Paul will find it clearly stated also in the book of Acts. In his parting speech to the Ephesian elders Paul provides us with a number of revealing summary statements about his evangelism. He had "solemnly testified to both Jews and Greeks of repentance towards God and faith in our Lord Jesus Christ" (Acts 20:21).[2] This had been the heart of his ministry. It could equally be called a solemn testifying to the "Gospel of the grace of God" (Acts 20:24). He then adds immediately a concise definition of the content of his preaching. It had been to "herald the Kingdom of God" (Acts 20:25), which was tantamount to "declaring the whole purpose of God" (Acts 20:27). After warning that the purity of his Message would be threatened after his departure by "savage wolves" interfering with the flock and "speaking perverse things" (Acts 20:29, 30), Paul again recommended the Gospel as "the Message of grace able to build you up and give you the inheritance amongst all those who are sanctified" (Acts 20:32). Inheritance implied, of course, inheritance of the Kingdom.

Paul's definition of evangelism provides a much-needed corrective to modern Gospel presentation. The strikingly simple fact is that his own Message is grounded in the same facts as the Message of the historical Jesus. While Jesus "heralds God's Gospel about the Kingdom of God" (Mark 1:14, 15), Paul "heralds the Kingdom of God" as the "whole counsel of God." The Apostle has not abandoned the Gospel as it fell from the lips of Jesus in favor of a Gospel only about the death and resurrection of Christ, as nearly all contemporary evangelism tells us. If Luke makes one thing clear it is that Jesus is the model of all true Gospel preachers. Just as Jesus, as was His custom, "welcomed them and began speaking about the Kingdom of God" (Luke 9:11), Paul is seen in Rome near the climax of his career "welcoming all who came to him, heralding the Kingdom of God and

---

[2] Luke's record of Jesus' expectation of the Church's ministry corresponds exactly with Paul's definition of his task: "Repentance for forgiveness of sins should be proclaimed in Jesus' name" (Luke 24:47). This entailed proclaiming the Kingdom (Acts 20:25).

teaching concerning the Lord Jesus Christ with all openness, unhindered" (Acts 28:30, 31).

The continuity between Jesus' and Paul's Gospel is unmistakably clear and may be traced throughout Luke's report of the early Church: Apostolic practice is uniformly to propagate the Message about the Kingdom.[3] Not only did Jesus immediately resume concentrated discussion of the Kingdom when He reappeared after His death, but Philip has the same evangelistic agenda. Luke provides what one might expect to be taken as a watchword for all subsequent evangelism. In a statement amounting to an early creed[4] he describes the work of Philip as "announcing the Gospel about the Kingdom and the name of Jesus Christ." It was only when the people "believed Philip who was preaching the Gospel about[5] the Kingdom" that they became candidates for baptism, "both men and women" (Acts 8:12). Intelligent reception of the Message about the Kingdom is the *sine qua non* for becoming a Christian, exactly as Jesus had declared "the Message about the Kingdom" (Matt. 13:19) to be the essential information which must pass from preacher to convert — the Message which Satan recognized as the one vital key to salvation needing to be suppressed by any and every means (Luke 8:12).

The Kingdom of God is evidently the goal of all Christian effort: "It is through much tribulation that we must enter the Kingdom" (Acts 14:22). The Kingdom of God is the principal topic of Paul's "speaking, reasoning and persuading" at Ephesus (Acts 19:8). The Kingdom of God is the one concept which best describes his whole ministry. "Explaining and solemnly testifying about the Kingdom of God and trying to persuade them about Jesus" (Acts 28:23, 31) again sums up Paul's missionary effort first to Jewish audiences and then,

---

[3] This is not to say that there is not a wide variety in the way in which the Message is conveyed. The substance, however, is unchanging.

[4] F.J. Badcock in *The History of the Creeds* (New York: Macmillan, 1938, p. 15) refers to Acts 8:12 as an early creed. How different modern Christianity would be if this precious, simple formula for baptism had been retained. Acts 8:12 shows what kind of profession of faith preceded initiation into the Church. A grasp of the Kingdom of God was evidently the basis of biblical Christianity.

[5] The "of" in the phrase "Gospel of the Kingdom" is objective and means "about." So Nigel Turner points out in *A Grammar of New Testament Greek,* ed. J.H. Moulton, Vol. 3, *Syntax,* T & T Clark, 1963, p. 211.

equipped with "this salvation" (Acts 28:28), i.e., the same Kingdom Message, to Gentiles who Paul expected would "listen." Luke leaves him in Rome "preaching the Kingdom of God and teaching concerning the Lord Jesus Christ with all confidence" (Acts 28:31). The evidence of Acts confirms what Paul stated to the Romans that his own Gospel was the proclamation of Jesus Christ (Rom. 16:25), meaning both the proclamation which Jesus had made as well as information about Jesus' death and resurrection. The Gospel for Paul was indeed "the Message of the Messiah,"[6] the stimulus of saving faith. Like Jesus, Paul regarded the Kingdom Message (including the message of the cross and the resurrection) as the essential tool of evangelism. It was nothing less than the divine creative Word (I Thess. 2:13) effecting, as it became the driving force in human hearts, the new creation of immortals.

The contemporary religious scene would appear nothing short of tragic to Paul. That the name of Christ could be appended to hundreds of different groups organized as separate fellowships would however confirm to him the remarkable accuracy of his own inspired predictions about the direction in which the Church would go after his death. He had persistently warned of "grievous wolves" (Acts 20:29, KJV) who, after his departure, would enter the Church and scatter the sheep, and of a wholesale apostasy from apostolic teachings. He anticipated that members of the Church would distort the Message and attract a following (Acts 20:30). This was a prospect which caused him the profoundest distress. He had admonished the church "with tears" (Acts 20:31) to be aware that apostolic faith would survive only with a struggle against opposing, perverted versions of the faith. There can be little doubt that Paul expected a suppression of the faith which he had struggled to preach.

Jude, the brother of Jesus, wrote a letter urging the Christians of his own day (towards the end of the first century) to contend earnestly for the faith which had been once and for all divinely communicated to the Christian believers (Jude 3). If earnest effort was required then to preserve the faith, how much more two thousand years later! John, the Apostle, wrote to a certain Diotrephes who refused to accept the admonitions contained in the letter, and was actually forcing real

---

[6] Rom. 10:17, which should be understood in harmony with Acts as the Message of the Kingdom which Jesus had also preached.

Christians out of the Church (III John 9, 10). A theological takeover was under way. A suppression of apostolic truth had begun even before the end of the first century. The malign spirit of Antichrist had already made its appearance (I John 2:18; 4:1; II Thess. 2:7).

It is not difficult to see that New Testament Christianity was under constant attack from false religion. There were ministers masquerading as agents of Christ (II Cor. 11: 3, 4, 13-15). Individuals were upsetting the faith of inexperienced believers by proposing radically new teachings calculated to obscure the genuine faith. In Paul's own time, the majority were already falsifying the Message (II Cor. 2:17),[7] principally to satisfy the demands of those who would not tolerate wholesome teaching, but chose to "wander off after manmade fictions" (II Tim. 4:4). Paul himself, like Jesus before him, was viewed as a religious deceiver by rival practitioners of religion. He was opposed by false brethren (II Cor. 11:26; II Tim. 4:14) and forsaken by close friends (II Tim. 4:10). He was "regarded as a phony" (II Cor. 6:8). His response was to declare that the virulent spirit of Antichrist was already active (II Thess. 2:7). Paul was convinced that the deception already under way was a prelude to a final and massive confusion which would spell doom for those who had not "received the love of the Truth" (II Thess. 2:8-10).

Jesus had been no less preoccupied with the dangers of false teaching. He expressed doubts as to whether genuine Christian belief would be found anywhere on earth by the time He returned (Luke 18:8). He envisaged a situation, at His return to establish the Kingdom, in which many would suffer bitter disappointment. There would be many who would protest that they had been fully committed members of what they thought was the Christian Church only to find that their work of preaching and even their performance of miracles and exorcism in the name of Christ had never been recognized by Jesus (Matt. 7:21-23; Luke 13:23-30). Surely these must be some of the most challenging warnings ever uttered by a religious teacher:

> Not everyone who says to me "Lord, Lord" will enter the Kingdom of Heaven, but he who does the will of My Father who is in heaven. Many will say to Me on that day, "Lord, Lord, did we not prophesy in Your name, and in Your name cast out demons, and in Your

---

[7] It was "the many who were corrupting the word of God."

name perform many miracles?" And then I will declare to them, "I never knew you; depart from Me, you who practice lawlessness" (Matt. 7:21-23).

This aspect of the teaching of Christ ought to be profoundly disturbing. It tells us in no uncertain terms that God means to be taken seriously. He will not accept intellectual or moral carelessness from those who profess to follow Him. He has declared the faith through His agents, the prophets and Apostles, and expects every professing Christian to pay close attention to what He has said. Evidently obedience to the words of Jesus is the criterion of success (Matt. 7:24-27). Founding one's life on the teaching of the Messiah is the only insurance policy against the storms of opposition Christians will encounter. Worship based upon human tradition has been pronounced invalid (Matt. 15:7-9). No one therefore should risk taking his faith on trust from the denomination in which he happens to be born, without careful inspection of its sources and teachings.

The New Testament warns constantly that traps are laid for the Christian on every side. The picture of a world peopled with preachers who are wolves in sheep's clothing (Matt. 7:17; Acts 20:29), and with Satan's agents in the guise of angels of light masquerading as ministers of righteousness (II Cor. 11:13-15), may seem fanciful in the twentieth century. But it cannot be denied that that is the environment in which the New Testament says a Christian must survive. Our failure to see the point of these biblical warnings may only be a measure of our blindness to the danger.

We should not neglect the obvious indications in the New Testament that the Apostles, and Jesus Himself, expected a large-scale departure from the original faith to occur in generations subsequent to their own.[8] They give no promise whatsoever that the faith would become comfortably settled. Rather, they envisage an apostasy continuing unabated. The apostolic view of the future is "telescoped," in the sense that it gives prominence to the principal events which are expected to occur, without clarifying the span of time (unknown to Jesus and the Apostles, Mark 13:32; Acts 1:7) needed for their fulfillment. The arrival of the Messiah to reign with the Church is, of

---

[8] I John 2:18, 19. John is writing at a time when Paul's prediction in Acts 20:29, 30 had come true.

course, the dominant expectation of the early Church (II Tim. 4:8; Luke 21:31, etc.), but comparable in significance is the expectation of a widespread departure from the truth of the divine Message and the appearance on the world scene of a human individual in whom all the characteristics of false religion are concentrated. He is pictured as a dreadful caricature of the Messiah Himself. He arrogates to himself divine titles, establishes himself in a temple and claims to be God. His sudden appearance as a Messianic pretender, in some dazzling way aping the Second Coming of Jesus, is accompanied by delusive miracles, supernatural feats calculated to fool those who have not come to understand that Satan is able to mimic the very power of God. The success of his mission to deceive will be a just judgment upon those who have not previously come to love the Truth or the divine Message. They will therefore be lured into believing a lie. It is the Garden of Eden tragedy all over again! (II Cor. 11:3). Paul could have given us no greater reason for grasping the truth while there is yet time. The Apostle's view of the dark future before the arrival of the Kingdom is given in II Thessalonians 2:1-14:

> And now, what about the coming again of our Lord Jesus Christ, and our being gathered together to meet Him? Please don't be upset and excited, dear brothers, by the rumor that this day of the Lord has already begun. If you hear of people having visions and special messages from God about this, or letters that are supposed to have come from me, don't believe them. Don't be carried away and deceived, regardless of what they say. For that day will not come until two things happen: first there will be a time of great rebellion against God, and then the man of rebellion will come — the son of destruction. He will defy every god there is, and tear down every other object of adoration and worship. He will go in and sit as God in the temple of God, claiming that he is God Himself. Don't you remember that I told you this when I was with you? And you know Who is keeping him from being here already; for he can come only when his time is ready. As for the work this man of rebellion and destruction will do when he comes, it is already going on, but he himself will not come until the One who is holding him back steps out of the way. And then this wicked one will appear, whom the Lord Jesus will burn up with the breath of His mouth and destroy by His presence when He returns. This man of sin will come as Satan's tool, full of Satanic power, and will trick everyone with strange sights, and will pretend to do great miracles. He will

completely fool those who are on their way to destruction because they have said "no" to the Truth; they have refused to believe it and love it and let it save them. So God will allow them to believe those lies with all their hearts, and all of them will be justly judged for believing falsehood, refusing the Truth and enjoying their sins. But we must forever give thanks for you, our brothers loved by the Lord, because God chose you from the very first to give you salvation, cleansing you by the work of the Holy Spirit and by your trusting in the Truth. Through us He told you the Good News. Through us He called you to share in the glory of our Lord Jesus Christ.[9]

The propagation of lies has been Satan's chief aim. The appearance in history of a major shift away from the teachings of the founder of Christianity provides evidence of the success of his campaign to mislead. We have referred to the disaster which overcame the Christian Church when Greek ideas were mixed with doctrinal tenets taught by the Apostles. That this occurred is admitted on all sides. The facts of church history are unmistakable. What is seldom noticed is the effect which the alien ideas have had on the preaching of the Good News Message. It is in this direction that we should look for the underlying causes of a divided Church.

One thing is certain from the writings of Paul. It is that the content of the Message of salvation is sacrosanct. Nothing must be permitted to interfere with it. Nothing must be added or taken away. The preaching of "another Gospel" or the preaching of "another Jesus" invites the divine curse upon any who would dare so to teach (II Cor. 11:4). Paul says so twice to the Galatians (Gal. 1:6-9), and the curse is clearly no empty imprecation. For Paul the perversion of the sacred Message is the ultimate horror. His concern over the Message proves beyond doubt that the Message had a very definite shape and content. All this fuss over doctrine seems odd to us in the twentieth century, but this may just be a measure of our own uncertainty and indifference.

Paul equates the failure to grasp truth with wickedness. Truth also has a strong intellectual content. One cannot dismiss its connection

---

[9] II Thess. 2:1-14, as translated in *The Living Letters: The Paraphrased Epistles*, K.N. Taylor, Tyndale House Pub., 1962. I have replaced the word "hell" with "destruction," as being closer to the original Greek.

with correct understanding. "Because *the love of the truth* they did not receive in order to be saved, God will send upon them a deluding influence so that they might believe the lie. All will be judged who did not *believe the truth* but took *pleasure in wickedness*" (II Thess. 2:10-12). Truth for Paul is to be believed, known and loved.[10] He can speak of his teaching as imparting faith and truth (I Tim. 2:7). Conviction is the result of insight and intelligence.[11] Truth is learned and it is found in the knowledge taught by Christ (Eph. 4:21). "Coming into the knowledge of the truth" is the Pauline way of describing conversion to the faith (I Tim. 2:4). The Gospel is something to be learned (Col. 1:7). This language, however, is strikingly absent from modern usage, suggesting that for contemporary Christians truth is not a high priority. After all, the argument goes, would not insistence on truth lead to doctrinal divisions? But what if loss of truth leads to the ruin of the faith, as Paul clearly believed?

The Christian Goal

The relevance of all this to our contemporary religious scene may be tested by inviting the average churchgoer to say what he understands as the goal of the Christian's life. The question will not be designed to catch him out, but simply as a test of contemporary understanding. It will be most unusual if his answer does not contain some reference to "going to heaven at death." Suppose now that he had given this answer in the middle of the second century, a little more than a hundred years after the death of Jesus. We have one very good piece of evidence of the reaction that it would have provoked in one who considered himself among the staunchest exponents of the Christian faith at that time. In a treatise on the faith, Justin Martyr wrote: "If you have fallen in with some who say they are Christians

---

[10] II Thess. 2:12, 13; I Tim. 2:4; 4:3; II Tim. 2:25; Titus 1:1; II Thess. 2:10; II Cor. 4:2; 13:8. In I Tim. 2:7 cp. David's words in Ps. 119:97, 142: "O how I love Your law [*torah*]…Your law is truth."

[11] So Nigel Turner renders Col. 2:2 (*A Grammar of New Testament Greek*, Vol. 3, p. 211). The biblical emphasis on intellect and understanding as a basis for sound faith has been largely lost in contemporary evangelicalism. According to John, who speaks much about truth, Jesus came to give us an "*understanding* in order to know God" (I John 5:20).

and who deny the resurrection, but who say that their souls when they die are taken to heaven, do not imagine that they are Christians."[12]

The statement may appear baffling, but it proves that early Christianity rejected as a heresy the notion that at death the soul of the believer departs to heaven. Yet this will be found as the common tenet of millions of adherents to Christianity in the twentieth century, and it has been so for many generations. These remarkable facts demand an investigation.

The radical shift in thinking about the destiny of the Christian which has obviously occurred can be traced to the fusion of Greek philosophy with the biblical faith. The process was a subtle one, and the design behind it was the promotion of the very same lie which Satan had foisted upon the unwary Eve. The Serpent had flatly contradicted the divine warning that disobedience would result in death (Gen. 3:4). Now he appears as a preacher of "Christianity" to announce that man is by nature immortal, that he cannot die! At death, according to this ingenious theory, a man is bound to survive in heaven or hell as a disembodied soul. It will not be difficult to see that this idea undermines the divine Message that man has fallen under the death penalty, and that there is absolutely no prospect of his gaining immortality apart from incorporation into the divine Plan through Christ. The introduction of the Greek idea of the "disembodied soul," as a part of every person which survives death, at once created an entirely new meaning for death. Death no longer meant the cessation of the whole conscious personality.[13] It now meant his survival as a disembodied soul in another realm. A man with an immortal soul "cannot surely die!"

The introduction of the "rogue" idea that man cannot really die effected a revolution in the Christian view of death. A leading British theologian noted that "the whole of our western tradition has contrived to give death an altogether inflated significance. There has been a vastly exaggerated focus on death and the moment of death."[14]

---

[12] Justin Martyr, *Dialogue with Trypho*, ch. 80, writing ca. 150 AD.

[13] Death in the Hebrew Bible means the cessation of consciousness (see Ecc. 9:5, 10; Pss. 6:5; 146:4; 115:17). The New Testament follows the Old in speaking of death as "sleep" (John 11:11; I Thess. 4:13-15; 5:10; I Cor. 15:6).

[14] J.A.T. Robinson, *On Being the Church in the World,* London: SCM Press, 1960, p. 129.

This remarkable change "began when the pages of the New Testament were hardly dry, and it is one of the most remarkable silent revolutions in the history of Christian thought."[15] Little does the churchgoing public realize that its cherished emphasis on "going to heaven" at death does not originate in the Christian Scriptures:

> The whole of our teaching and hymnology has assumed that you go to heaven — or, of course — hell when you die…This proposition is in clear contradiction with what the Bible says…The Bible nowhere says that we go to heaven when we die, nor does it ever describe death in terms of going to heaven. Wesley's words "bid Jordan's narrow stream divide, and bring us safe to heaven," have no biblical basis.[16]

Speaking in another context, but with equal emphasis on the dire consequences of allowing Greek thinking to dominate Christian theology, another scholar refers to the control exercised by "Neoplatonic philosophy and its claims to constitute an adequate vocabulary for the articulation of theological affirmations. It is not easy to say whether the whole tradition, over all the centuries, has been a distortion of the Gospel."[17] He urges that Protestants place "great emphasis on the Old Testament in catechesis and preaching."[18] A call to reform, which so far seems to have gone unheeded, was issued by Hugh Schonfield. Noting in the words of T.E. Laurence that Christianity (as it developed after the death of the Apostles) "is a hybrid faith compounded of the Semitic as to its origin, and the non-Semitic as to its development," he wrote:

> The point I am making is that Christianity is not the spiritual successor of Judaism, but a synthesis of Judaism and paganism. As such, it is a corruption of as much significance as the ancient Israelite defection in blending their religion with the cults of the Canaanites. Therefore, it is not for the Jews to embrace orthodox Christianity, but for the Christians, if they are to be Israelites indeed as the People of God, to review and purify their beliefs, and to

---

[15] *Ibid.*

[16] *Ibid.*, p. 130.

[17] Lamberto Schuurman, in *Faces of Jesus,* ed. J.M. Bonino, Orbis Books, 1977, p. 166.

[18] *Ibid.*, p. 176.

recapture what basically they have in common with the Jews, the Messianic vision.[19]

The Hebrews, to whom the divine Message was entrusted, had been taught to believe that man was an animated being sustained, like the animals, by the breath of life. When he died he returned to the grave and the dust from which he had been formed, and consciousness ceased at that moment (Gen. 3:19). The only hope of further life would be through a resurrection of the whole person from the state of death (Dan. 12:2; Isa. 26:19; Ps. 16:10). The divine Message had from the start made it clear that Abraham, David, the prophets, and all the faithful must in the future rise from their graves to share in the promised inheritance of land (Heb. 11:19; Matt. 8:11). Even if resurrection had not been spelled out in detail, it was logically necessary, since everyone knew that the patriarchs had died without having inherited their Kingdom (Heb. 11:13, 39).[20] They must therefore reappear by resurrection from death to join the company of all the faithful in the reign of Messiah. So Jesus clearly believed when He uttered these words:

> There will be weeping and gnashing of teeth there when you see Abraham and Isaac and Jacob and all the prophets in the Kingdom of God, but yourselves being cast out. And they will come from east and west and north and south, and will recline at the table in the Kingdom of God (Luke 13:28, 29; Matt. 8:11).

What Satan achieved in the early centuries was the suppression of the biblical doctrine of man as needing to attain immortality *through resurrection when the Messiah arrived to establish the Kingdom.* This would be a gift from his Maker. The biblical teaching was made to appear nonsensical, if, as the Greeks thought, man was *already* by nature immortal. The tragedy is that the Church was, and is, so slow

---

[19] *The Politics of God*, p. 99.

[20] Resurrection is known to the writers of the Old Testament, for example in I Sam. 2:6; Pss. 16:10; 17:15; 27:13; 49:15; 73:23ff; Job 19:25ff.; Isa. 26:19; Dan. 12:2. Hebrews implies that Abraham understood that he was going to be raised to life (Heb. 11:13, 19, 35, 39). Other passages show that the patriarchs were expecting to live again (Rom. 4:13; Gal. 3:29; Acts 7:5; 26:6ff; John 8:56). A useful article by Norman Logan summarizing the evidence appeared in *The Scottish Journal of Theology* (6), 1953, pp. 165-172.

to see that its trump card, the divine Message containing the promise of resurrection and entrance into the Kingdom, was being distorted. The new system of thought taught that the Christian goal was survival as a disembodied soul in heaven, rather than participation in the Messianic Kingdom on earth. The prospect of a harp-playing home in heaven is largely inconceivable, and it most effectively diverts attention away from the real biblical goal: the return of Jesus Christ to administer the world with justice in company with His followers.

The Greek doctrine of the survival of the soul separated from the body has so permeated the churches that its members are committed to believing and teaching the falsehood that the dead are really alive in heaven, an idea which is absolutely foreign to the Bible. Plain statements by leading New Testament theologians that "heaven in the Bible is nowhere the destination of the dying"[21] and that the doctrine of the immortality of the soul is diametrically opposed to Scripture seem to make no impact whatever on what is taught in Sunday schools and pulpits, and especially at funerals, throughout the land. The traditional mistake is simply too deeply entrenched and means to stay. Churches constantly comfort the bereaved with their cherished traditional teaching, never apparently having given serious thought to its origin. In so doing they fall prey to ideas which do not originate with the Apostles and deprive themselves of the blessing of the vision of a marvelous future for our earth. The promised Kingdom of the Bible has nothing whatsoever to do with life as a disembodied soul or spirit in a realm beyond the sky. "Our fathers aren't in heaven." They are sleeping the sleep of death (Ps. 13:3, etc.) until Jesus returns to awaken them to life.

A classic passage in the book of Daniel provided a proof text for early Christians as they looked forward to the gathering of the faithful of all ages in the coming Kingdom: "Many of those who are asleep in the dust of the ground will awake; some to the life of the coming age..." (Dan. 12:2). This information instructed the believers about the condition of the dead. They were in the ground and sleeping until resurrection day. That this is the authentic Christian understanding of death and the afterlife is shown by the fact that Jesus was an exponent of the "sleep of the dead." Hearing of the death of His friend Lazarus,

---

[21] J.A.T. Robinson, *In the End God*, p. 104.

He commented that he was "asleep" (John 11:11), which He then defined plainly as "dead" (John 11:14). The only solution was to "wake" Lazarus from the sleep of death: "I am going to arouse him from sleep" (John 11:11). *The International Critical Commentary* notes Jesus' use of exactly the same vocabulary of the sleep of death as found in Job,[22] proving again that Jesus derived His thinking about the crucial issues of human destiny from the Hebrew Bible.

By an act of power, testifying to the energy of God His Father at work in Him, Jesus then called Lazarus dramatically from his tomb to live again. Lazarus did not return from "heaven" (John 11:43, 44). According to Jesus, who has a right to have the final word in matters of Christian doctrine, "the time is coming in which all who are in the tombs will hear His voice and come forth" (John 5:28, 29). The view of death and resurrection presented by Daniel 12:2 underlies the whole of New Testament teaching about life after death. The state of the dead in Scripture is definitely not conscious existence in heaven or perpetual hellfire. The dead, as a standard Bible Dictionary states, are "unconscious, do no more work, take no account of anything, possess no knowledge nor wisdom, neither have any more portion in anything that is done under the sun."[23] This authority warns that

> we are influenced always more or less by the Greek, Platonic idea, that the body dies, yet the soul is immortal. Such an idea is utterly contrary to the Israelite consciousness, and is nowhere found in the Old Testament. The whole man dies, when in death the spirit or soul goes out of a man. Not only his body, but his soul also returns to a state of death and belongs to the nether-world; therefore the Old Testament can speak of a *death of one's soul* (Gen. 27:21).[24]

Christians surely ought to reject the influence of Greek, Platonic ideas.[25] They should be eager to know the mind of Christ. The New

---

[22] J.H. Bernard, T & T Clark, 1928, pp. 378, 379.

[23] *The International Standard Bible Encyclopedia*, ed. James Orr, Eerdmans, 1983, Vol. II, "Death," p. 812. For a recent excellent account of the biblical doctrine of the sleep of the dead and the annihilation of the wicked, see *Life, Death and Destiny*, by Baptist pastor and Bible professor Warren Prestidge, Auckland, New Zealand: Resurrection Publishing, 1998.

[24] *Ibid.,* emphasis added.

[25] Jesus' reference in Matt. 10:28 to the soul which man cannot kill does not mean that He believed in the immortality of the soul. He goes on to say that the soul

Testament has not abandoned the Hebrew understanding of the state of man in death. It makes no sense that the Apostles would depart from the belief of Jesus in John 11:11, 14 where He echoes Daniel 12:2, confirming the Scriptures in which He had been trained from childhood. What possible justification can there be for the Church continuing to embrace ideas from Plato in the name of Jesus?

It is a commonplace of the divine scheme that the dead must be resurrected from the grave to join the Messiah in His Kingdom which He will inaugurate at His return. It is only at the resurrection that the faithful will be made alive. They must therefore remain dead until then. The illusion that the dead are already alive with Christ reduces the future resurrection to an afterthought. "Tell me," wrote the great reformer William Tyndale, "what cause is there of the resurrection if the souls be in heaven?…In putting departed souls in heaven you [the Roman Catholics[26]] destroy the arguments by which Christ and Paul prove the resurrection."[27] By a strange paradox the work of Wycliffe and Tyndale (and a host of other distinguished scholars) is held in high esteem, while their teaching, which is in direct conflict with the popular tradition about the afterlife, remains quite unacceptable! Protestants continue to follow the Pope by talking of departed souls at present conscious in heaven or hellfire. The whole fiction of prayer to Mary is built on the same illusion. Such doctrines, which have played a massive role in the piety of sincere believers, could never have gained a foothold if the Hebrew Bible and the teaching of Jesus had been retained as the basis of Christian faith.

The Kingdom which Jesus is to establish has in popular thinking been removed from the earth. It is generally believed that He is now reigning *with the saints* in heaven. The traditional scheme has deprived the Messiah of His promised reign on the throne of David in the future, and the Christians of their hope of sharing that inheritance with Him. It has reduced the great future resurrection event to an appendage in our theological scheme. The resurrection receives only the briefest mention in the creed. A reference to the "life of the world

---

is destructible in Gehenna. What man cannot destroy is the life which God recreates in resurrection.

[26] The point is equally valid against most Protestants.

[27] *An Answer to Sir Thomas More's Dialogue*, book 4, ch. 2, pp. 180, 181.

to come"[28] is understood by many, in the absence of a clear explanation, as some sort of continued existence in heaven at the point of death. What the early Church looked forward to was the "life of the coming age" of the Kingdom of God *on earth*, following the return of the dead to life via resurrection at Jesus' return. The classic New Testament text is found in I Corinthians 15:23: "The Christians will be resurrected at Christ's coming." Resurrection would mean gaining their inheritance of the earth (Matt. 5:5). Until that future moment the Bible declares them to be dead (I Cor. 15:35, 52; I Thess. 4:16). Resurrection and the return of Christ are the object of the passionate longing of New Testament Christians, but the same cannot be said of many believers today. To that extent they are out of tune with the Bible they claim to be the source of their inspiration.

The straightforward scheme of death and a period of waiting in the grave followed by resurrection at Christ's return was not made clear to me despite many years of church attendance. The Greek notion of the natural immortality of the soul had swallowed up the powerful biblical emphasis on the future resurrection of the whole man to immortality. Clear teaching about the destiny of man and of our planet continues to be denied to church members as long as the bereaved are comforted by the idea that the dead are not really dead but actually alive in another realm. By introducing the theory that death is not actually death but survival in another place, the Church dabbled in a form of occultism. Job's question was not "If a man dies, will he continue to live on?" but "If a man dies, will he come back to life?" (Job 14:14), which is a very different thing. A Lutheran scholar, reflecting the view of Luther, who himself believed in the sleep of the dead,[29] calls our attention to the radical departure from Scripture represented by popular Christian teaching about death:

---

[28] The Nicene Creed.

[29] For further documentation of this and for a compendium of biblical and historical information on death as "sleep," see L.E. Froom, *The Conditionalist Faith of Our Fathers*, 2 vols., Review and Herald, 1965. An interesting indication of Luther's belief in the sleep of the dead is provided by Tyndale's quotation of his opponent Sir Thomas More: "What shall he care how long he live in sin, *that believeth Luther*, that he shall after this life feel neither good nor evil, in body nor soul, until the day of doom." The remark of More shows that he had a poor

The hope of the early church centered on the resurrection of the Last Day. It is this which first calls the dead into eternal life (I Cor. 15; Phil. 3:21). This resurrection happens to the man and not only to the body. Paul speaks of the resurrection not "of the body" but "of the dead." This understanding of the resurrection implicitly understands death as also affecting the whole man...*Thus the original Biblical concepts have been replaced by ideas from Hellenistic Gnostic dualism.* The New Testament idea of the resurrection which affects the whole man has had to give way to the immortality of the soul. The Last Day also loses its significance, for souls have received all that is decisively important long before this. Eschatological [forward-looking] tension is no longer strongly directed to the day of Jesus' Coming. *The difference between this and the Hope of the New Testament is very great.*[30]

A leading biblical scholar sums up the scriptural view of man's destiny:

The Bible writers, holding fast to the conviction that the created order owes its existence to the wisdom and love of God and is therefore essentially good, could not conceive of life after death as a disembodied existence ("we shall not be found naked" — II Cor. 5:3), but as a renewal under new conditions of the intimate unity of body and soul which was human life as they knew it. Hence death was thought of as *the death of the whole man,* and such phrases as "freedom from death," imperishability or immortality could only properly be used to describe what is meant by the phrase eternal or living God "who only has immortality" (I Tim. 6:16). Man does not possess within himself the quality of deathlessness, but must, if he is to overcome the destructive power of death, *receive* it as the gift of God "who raised Christ from the dead," and put death aside like a covering garment (I Cor. 15:53, 54). It is through the death and resurrection of Jesus Christ that this possibility for man (II Tim. 1:10) has been brought to light and the hope confirmed that the corruption (Rom. 11:7) which is a universal feature of human life shall be effectively overcome.[31]

---

understanding of the implications of "conditional immortality." The quotation proves that Luther's view of the state of the dead was biblical, not orthodox.

[30] Paul Althaus, *The Theology of Martin Luther*, Philadelphia: Fortress Press, 1966, pp. 413, 414, emphasis added.

[31] *A Theological Word Book of the Bible*, ed. Alan Richardson, pp. 111, 112.

While Bible writers "could not conceive of life after death as a disembodied spirit," Christian preachers persist with the dissemination of that very idea, with a consequent loss of vital information about the resurrection which will usher in the Kingdom of God. If, as our other expert maintains, original biblical concepts have been replaced by teachings from Hellenistic, Gnostic dualism, such stark facts must be squarely faced by the divided Church. Why is it that when biblical scholarship "rejects the idea of a purely spiritual 'immortality' of the soul in the afterlife, regarding it as an imposition upon the biblical view of personality,"[32] churches go on teaching that souls survive death? The divine Message has become hopelessly muddled by the mixing of two conflicting worlds of thought. The Hebrew view of the divine future cannot be reconciled with Platonic Greek philosophy.[33] The apostolic mind is clear on this question of alien philosophy. How different would have been the course of church history had Paul's words been heeded: "See to it that no one takes you captive through philosophy and empty deception" (Col. 2:8).

Learning the Biblical Language

If the message of the divided churches has become a feeble echo of the vibrant proclamation of the New Testament Christians, it is because tradition has interfered with the divine Message which the Church is commissioned to preach. The intrusion of Greek concepts which cannot be reconciled with the Hebrew thought world of the Bible has made it difficult for the reader of Scripture to understand the Apostles. A breakdown in communication has occurred. Even our translations of the Bible have played their part in the conspiracy (unconscious on the part of the translators) to conceal information. For though translation enables the early Christians to speak to us in our own English tongue, their words have been mediated to us by

---

[32] D. Willard, *The Spirit of the Disciplines,* San Francisco: Harper, 1988, p. 82. The author goes on to point out that leading scholars insist upon "resurrection as the true form of human existence beyond death" (*ibid.*). But churches have for centuries not made this at all clear to their congregations.

[33] This point was brilliantly made by Oscar Cullman in his *Immortality of the Soul or Resurrection of the Dead?* Epworth Press, 1958, reprinted in *A Journal from the Radical Reformation*, vol. 3, nos. 1, 2 (available from Atlanta Bible College, P.O. Box 100,000, Morrow, GA 30260, USA).

translators who were themselves steeped in the post-biblical Greek tradition.

Of all forms of commentary on the divine Word, a translation is the most subtle. The translator stands between us and the original Message of the Apostles. It is possible that he will fail to transmit the original faithfully. This can happen when a scholar does not appreciate the Jewish ways of thinking which are typical of New Testament writers. Fortunately modern commentators often provide background data about recurring phrases in the New Testament which illuminate original meanings. The greatest service has been done by those scholars who warn about the dangers of trying to read the Bible without being immersed in the Jewish environment in which the biblical documents were written. James Dunn's criticism of the way Paul's writings have been mishandled "for most of Christian history" deserves the widest hearing. What he says about reading Paul applies to our reading of the Bible as a whole:

> The first task of exegesis [explaining the Bible] is to penetrate as far as possible inside the historical context(s) of the author and of those for whom he wrote. So much of this involves the taken-for-granteds of both author and addressees. Where a modern reader is unaware of (or unsympathetic to) these shared assumptions and concerns it will be impossible to hear the text as the author intended it to be heard (and assumed it would be heard). In this case, a major part of that context is the self-understanding of Jews and Judaism in the first century and of Gentiles sympathetic to Judaism. *Since most of Christian history and scholarship, regrettably, has been unsympathetic to that self-understanding, if not downright hostile to it, a proper appreciation of Paul in his interaction with that self-understanding has been virtually impossible.*[34]

The Nature of Man

A primary question for Christians concerns our destiny as human beings. The basis of a good understanding is laid in the book of Genesis. What we have been learning in church, however, has tended to obstruct rather than promote the biblical facts. The trouble begins early on in the divine record. The Greek philosophical tradition which

---

[34] *Commentary on Romans, Word Biblical Commentary*, pp. xiv, xv, emphasis added.

218

early in the second century mixed itself with the original faith has done much to prevent us knowing who we are. We get off to a poor start unless we fully grasp the account of the creation of man. We are concerned first of all to track down the meaning of the word "soul." Without any kind of formal instruction we seem to imbibe the notion that "soul" must mean an immortal part of man which survives death. Such an idea misrepresents the biblical point of view. As a modern commentator points out:

> Immortal means death-proof. To believe in the immortality of the soul is to believe that though John Brown's body lies a-mouldering in the grave, his soul goes marching on simply because marching on is the nature of souls just the way producing apples is the nature of apple trees. Bodies die, but souls don't. True or false, *this is not the biblical view*, although many who ought to know better assume it is.[35]

Unfortunately our King James version of the Bible conceals the proper understanding of "soul" most effectively, and prevents us from seeing that "soul," far from being the possession of man alone, belongs in fact equally to all the animals. Here is what the biblical text really says:

> And God said, "Let the waters teem with swarming creatures, living *souls*..." And God created great whales and every living *soul* which moves, with which the waters teem...And God said, "Let the earth bring forth the living *soul* after its kind, cattle and creeping thing and living creature of the earth, after its kind." And the Lord God formed man from the dust of the earth and breathed into his nostrils the breath of life, and man became a living *soul*...And out of the ground the Lord God formed every living creature of the field and every foul of the air and brought them to Adam to see what he would call them, and whatever Adam called each living *soul*, that was its name (Gen. 1:20, 21, 24; 2:7; 1:30).[36]

---

[35] Frederick Buechner in *I Corinthians: Mastering the Basics*, Lyman Coleman and Richard Peace, Serendipity Foundation, 1986, p. 115, emphasis added.

[36] The Hebrew word *nephesh,* "soul," means living creature. Souls can be dead (Num. 6:6). "Soul" is also the equivalent of "person." Thus eight "souls" survived the Flood (I Pet. 3:20). A.R. Johnson points out that the Authorized and the Revised versions are "misleading if ['soul'] suggests any such dichotomy as that which finds early emphasis in Orphic myth and Platonic philosophy. The term *nephesh* is

Later the account of the Flood describes all living creatures as souls: "And God said, 'This is the sign of the covenant between Me and you and between every living soul which is with you. I will remember My covenant which is between Me and you and every living soul of all flesh'" (Gen. 9:12).

And in the Proverbs: "The righteous man cares for the soul of his beast" (Prov. 12:10). No wonder that the New Testament speaks of marine creatures as having souls (Rev. 8:9).

These simple facts establish at once that "soul" in the Bible is the common designation of man and animal. They are equally conscious beings, "souls." The Hebrews might also say that man and animal *have* conscious being, "soul." In neither case is there the slightest hint that soul has anything to do with innate immortality. The very opposite is true. At death the man who is formed from the dust of the ground returns to the dust (Gen. 3:19), and at the Flood "all in whose nostrils was the breath of life died" (Gen. 7:22), man and beast alike. The fundamentally important implication of our discovery is that immortality is not something we possess. It must be acquired; and it can be gained by no other means than through contact with the saving Message and resurrection. Once we establish this fact we shall begin to read the New Testament with a clear sense of its passionate longing for the return of Jesus to raise the faithful dead.

The consistent teaching of the Hebrew Bible is that at death man falls into unconscious "sleep." He joins his ancestors in the world of the dead which the Hebrews called *sheol*, with its Greek equivalent Hades.[37] This is not a place of punishment and rewards, meted out at death, but a place of complete inactivity. Ecclesiastes 9:5, 10 establish

---

obviously being used to indicate, not something conceived of as one (albeit the superior) part of man's being, but the complete personality as a unified manifestation of vital power; it represents what Pedersen has called 'the grasping of a totality'" (*The One and the Many in the Israelite Conception of God,* University of Wales Press, 1961, p. 2).

[37] Gen. 15:15; 25:8; Abraham joined his fathers in death. Gen. 47:30; Jacob lay down with his fathers. Gen. 31:16; Moses was told to "sleep with your fathers." Inactivity and sleeping in the dust describe death in Pss. 6:5; 30:9; 115:17; 146:3, 4; Job 14:12; Ecc. 9:5, 10; Isa. 26:19; Dan. 12:2. For the New Testament view see John 5:28, 29; 11:11, 14; Acts 2:34, 39. Delitzsch in his celebrated commentary on the Hebrew Bible says that the view of death as "sleep" pervades the Old Testament (*Commentary on the Old Testament,* Vol. VI, p. 361).

the proper notion of the condition of man after he dies: "The living know that they will die, but the dead do not know anything, nor do they any longer have a reward, for their memory is forgotten...There is no activity or planning or wisdom in *sheol* where you are going." These are the verses, along with many others with the same message, which ought to be heard at funeral services. This would allow for the stupendous prospect of resurrection in the future to be proclaimed as the only genuine hope for rescue from death. Attention would immediately be riveted on the future arrival of the Son of God in power. The biblical scheme would then cease to be neutralized by the very confusing idea that the dead have already achieved glory, even though Jesus has not yet returned to resurrect and reward them[38] by waking them from the sleep of death as Daniel 12:2 lays out. At present the incompatible Hebrew and Greek ideas struggle with each other to produce an uneasy confusion, a blurring of the Christian hope and a loss of the Good News of the coming Kingdom.

The Greek view of man's innate immortality must be banished once and for all before the Hebrew view of man's destiny, on which the teaching of Jesus is founded, can be grasped. When we see that the death of man is the death of his *whole person*, the cessation of his consciousness, not his survival as a disembodied spirit or soul in another realm, our minds will be turned towards our only hope — the hope for the resurrection of the faithful of all the ages.[39] The very unbiblical prospect of life as a disembodied spirit will be replaced by the glorious expectation of receiving a body empowered by divine Spirit, one which cannot die. The glorious future promised in Christ is the life of a resurrected individual functioning as an administrator with the Messiah in His Kingdom. That life can be conferred only by the Father "who alone has immortality,"[40] i.e., inherently. Christianity is therefore a religion whose goal is the acquisition of immortality. Christians are those who "by perseverance in doing good seek for glory and honor and immortality, life in the coming age" (Rom. 2:7). To say that a human being already has immortality, as a departed conscious spirit, makes a considerable nonsense of the Bible. It is,

---

[38] Jesus taught that rewards are given not at death but at the Second Coming (Matt. 16:27).

[39] I Cor. 15:23; I Thess. 4:13ff.; Rev. 11:15-18; Rev. 20:1-6.

[40] I Tim. 6:16. The reference is to the Father sending Jesus back to rule.

however, a biblical teaching that the living believers can taste, through the Spirit, something of the life of the future Kingdom (John 6:47; Eph. 1:14; II Cor. 1:21, 22).[41]

If the Bible to which Jesus appealed taught that all the dead were in the world of the dead, which was certainly not hellfire or heaven, how is it that the churches seem to have forgotten this fundamental Christian teaching? Why is it that the dead are now supposed to depart to heaven or hellfire the moment they die, quite apart from a resurrection? Something has evidently happened to change the way we think about death. The prophets of Israel expected to leave the world of the dead only by resurrection at the last day. Their hope as expressed by David was: "God will redeem my soul [i.e., me] from the power of *sheol*" (Ps. 49:15). The notion that man could live on as a disembodied soul or gain his promised inheritance *without first residing in the world of the dead* was unknown to them.

The Legend which Undermined the Resurrection

Unknown to most churchgoers, Protestants and Catholics have accepted, most uncritically, a fanciful legend claiming that Jesus altered the condition of the dead while He Himself was in the world of the dead. Protestants often chide Roman Catholics for subscribing to the doctrine of the bodily assumption of Mary to heaven as Queen of Heaven and mediatrix. No biblical support can be quoted for this revolutionary teaching. But Protestants as well as Roman Catholics hold to a tradition about the state of the dead which can be traced to an apocryphal story contained in the non-biblical *Gospel of Nicodemus*. This document, which relies on a tradition dating from the second century,[42] tells the story of Jesus descending to Hades in order to grant immortality to those who had died in previous ages. The same legend appears in several documents. The second-century *Odes of Solomon* also includes an account of Jesus' activity in Hades. To

---

[41] The reception of the Holy Spirit now does not, however, enable Christians to escape the first death, which is "appointed to all men" (Heb. 9:27).

[42] The tradition perhaps has an earlier origin. The *Ascension of Isaiah,* which may date from the end of the 1st century, teaches that "many of the righteous will ascend with Jesus on the third day" (ix. 16ff.).

the dead He says: "Come forth, you who have been afflicted and receive joy…and immortal life."[43]

As historians report, "Here we have the earliest appearance of the detailed doctrine of the Descent into Hell which is found in the *Gospel of Nicodemus* and was *afterwards universally prevalent in Christian circles*."[44] A Latin version of the *Gospel of Nicodemus* reports the words of two individuals who had been freed from death: "We rose with Christ from hell, and He Himself raised us from the dead. And from this you may know that the gates of death and darkness are destroyed, and the souls of the saints are set free and have ascended to heaven with Christ."[45]

The effect of this attractive but misleading story was to destroy at a blow the Hebrew Bible's teaching that deliverance from death and the gaining of immortality would come only by resurrection at the end of the age. Daniel 12:2, predicting that the dead would arise only when the Kingdom arrived (cp. I Cor. 15:23), was rendered obsolete by the new theory. The legend altered the whole meaning of death. For while Hades according to the Bible is a place of complete inactivity where "the dead do not praise God" (Ps. 115:17), and where they wait until the return of Christ, it was presented in this early folklore as a place where Christ was actively preaching to and delivering the dead.[46]

The new twist had a devastating effect on the Christian understanding of life after death. It meant that the dead could henceforth escape Hades and move immediately at death to Paradise (later tradition spoke of *heaven* as the immediate destination of righteous, disembodied souls). Although the legendary *Gospel of Nicodemus* seems to have taught an immediate *bodily* resurrection for the faithful Old Testament dead, consequent on Jesus' descent into

---

[43] Ode xxxi 1ff., cited in "Descent into Hades," *Dictionary of the Apostolic Church,* Vol. 1, p. 291.

[44] *Ibid.,* emphasis added.

[45] See the edition by Tischendorf.

[46] The account of a resurrection of certain "sleeping saints" in Matt. 27:52, 53 certainly does not hint that all the dead from Old Testament times were raised, nor that those who came back to life gained immortality or were removed to heaven. Such an idea is contradicted by Acts 2:34, 39 which state that David was still dead and buried after the resurrection.

Hades, later tradition recognized that this was a flat contradiction of the New Testament teaching that the dead will not be raised until the "Last Day." Eventually some kind of compromise was arrived at with the assistance of the Greek doctrine of the natural immortality of the soul. The souls of the righteous, it was said, went immediately to heaven (or according to another theory to Paradise as a compartment of Hades) since the time when Jesus had freed the patriarchs from death, but the soul would need to rejoin its body for a final resurrection at the end of the age. This has been the view of the great majority of Protestants since the 16th-century Reformation and before that of believers since the time of the church fathers. It was only the doctrine of an intermediate purgatory which Protestants discarded from the Roman Catholic system at the Reformation.

Saddled with a non-biblical tradition that Jesus delivered the patriarchs while He Himself was in "the heart of the earth" (Matt. 12:40), Protestants are left to search for biblical evidence for the departure of souls to heaven at death. There is no such evidence, despite the claim of one of the creeds that "Christ descended into Hades and abolished it for all believers."[47] Ephesians 4:8 speaks of Christ "leading captive a host of captives," in the context of giving certain gifts to the Church. It lends no support to the notion that Jesus freed the dead from Hades. As a leading Bible Dictionary says, "Ephesians 4:7-10 says nothing of any work of Christ, or any possibilities for the dead in Hades."[48] The same authority confirms our central thesis that New Testament teaching about the future "is in relation to the Hebrew faith and has its point of issue in the principles of the Old Testament."[49] The loss of the Hebrew view of death and the

---

[47] Formula of Concord. John Pearson, famous for his work on Christian creeds, did not himself accept the doctrine that Jesus freed the saints from Hades but admitted: "This is the opinion generally received in the schools, and delivered as the sense of the Church of God in all ages; but though it were not so general as the schoolmen would persuade us, yet it is certain that many of the fathers did so understand it." Eusebius, Cyril, Ambrose and Jerome are cited in favor of the idea that souls go immediately to heaven, while Justin Martyr, Irenaeus, Tertullian, Hilary, Gregory of Nyssa and others taught that the faithful do not go immediately to heaven but to Abraham's bosom, into "Paradise," where the Old Testament faithful remain also until the resurrection.

[48] "Eschatology," *Hastings Dictionary of the Bible*, Vol. I, p. 756.

[49] *Ibid.*

afterlife is therefore a major doctrinal disaster needing to be set right. Paul, indeed, recognizes that it is only at the sound of the seventh trumpet (I Cor. 15:52; Rev. 11:15), marking the resurrection at Christ's return to the earth, that Hades will be overcome and death swallowed up.[50]

If the Hebrew Bible had remained an authoritative source of divine teaching about the nature of man and the Plan for the recovery of his immortality, there would be no confusion over what happens when we die. But the example of Jesus, who upheld the Hebrew Bible always, was not followed, and Christians from the second century fell for various myths and legends (cp. II Tim. 4:4) which have ever since embedded themselves in Christian tradition. The removal of the patriarchs from the world of the dead at the time of Christ's resurrection was unknown to Peter, who spoke of David being still dead and buried after the ascension of Jesus (Acts 2:34, 39). The writer to the Hebrews knows nothing of the idea that Abraham, Isaac and Jacob had risen from the dead. They were to be brought back to life in company with all the faithful when Jesus came in the power of the Kingdom (Heb. 11:13, 39; 12:28).

The unfortunate antedating of the moment of Christian glory (a false teaching akin to the one which Paul identified as a potential cancer in the Church, I Thess. 2:18) began a process by which the biblical view of the future was dismantled. The mixing of competing ideas created a situation in which many are unable to distinguish tradition from biblical truth. Persistently rejecting the Old Testament view of the death of the whole man, they bend isolated New Testament verses in an attempt to force them into line with "received" tradition. It is common to hear churchgoers quote a portion of one verse of an extended discussion of the resurrection in II Corinthians 5. "Absent from the body and present with the Lord" (II Cor. 5:8) is thought to be proof that Paul was talking of immortal souls going to heaven at death. But this is not at all what he had in mind, as becomes clear if we read the whole context carefully.

Paul had already taught the Corinthians in I Corinthians 15 and I Thessalonians 4 that the dead sleep until the resurrection destined to

---

[50] In I Cor. 15:55 Paul cites Hos. 13:14, which speaks of the moment when Hades finally loses its sting, and applies the text to the *future* resurrection of all the faithful at the Parousia (cp. 1 Cor. 15:23).

happen at the coming of Christ. "Those who belong to Christ will be resurrected at His coming" (I Cor. 15:23).[51] In II Corinthians 5 he has not confused his readers by teaching a different idea — survival as a soul without a body. Such a concept was entirely alien to Paul's Hebrew way of thinking about death. His subject is still the resurrection: "He who raised the Lord Jesus will raise us also with Jesus and will present us with you" (II Cor. 4:14). What Paul was longing for was to be "clothed with a dwelling [a new body] *from heaven*" (II Cor. 5:2).[52] This would mean replacing our present bodies with immortal, spiritual ones. This great event was the resurrection. To be "Absent from the body and present with the Lord" (II Cor. 5:8) is the hope that we will meet Christ *when He comes to raise us from death.* Jesus is coming back to bring the dead to life. We are not going to Him at death. The Bible knows of only one way to escape death — that is by being resurrected at the return of Christ (those who are still alive when He comes will need only to be transformed by receiving their new body). To be "with the Lord" means to be with Jesus *through resurrection at Christ's return.* So Paul had explained to the Thessalonians when he elaborated on the divine arrangements by which the saints would be brought into the presence of the returning Lord. "*In this way* [i.e., by resurrection and transformation] we shall be always *with the Lord*" (I Thess. 4:17).

The Future of Immortalized Believers

One of the first tasks for the immortals thus created through the resurrection from the dead (not by never dying at all) will be to rid the world of the nightmare of nuclear war. Christians are to gain immortality for a purpose. They are going to administer the world and establish a just order (Isa. 32:1). Paul was surprised that some of his converts had lost sight of their goal: "Don't you realize that the saints are going to govern the world?" (I Cor. 6:2).[53] The Corinthians were actually taking each other to court before unbelievers. Paul was indignant. How nonsensical it was for Christians to get involved in

---

[51] Paul uses the phrase "wake up" as a synonym for resurrect (I Cor. 15:12, 14, 15, 16, 17, 20).

[52] Paul did not say he would be in heaven.

[53] Moffat catches the sense with "Don't you know that the saints are to manage the world? If the world is to come under your jurisdiction..."

litigation. After all, they were to be the arbiters of a new world order and, as the royal family in training, ought to be demonstrating a fitness for their future office.

It is reported that the world now spends every two weeks on weapons of mass destruction what it spends in a whole year on feeding, housing, clothing, and educating the population of the world. Facts like these can only mean that the world has come to the end of its tether. Nothing could be more lunatic than the squandering of such massive resources to threaten the lives of foreign men, women, and children (as well as those unborn) whom we have never met and whom we bear no personal grudge. A new system empowered to eradicate the insanity of international war will become a reality in the Kingdom of God.[54]

A crucial question facing the churches is their relationship to the war machine. They will sooner or later have to face the uncomfortable fact that participation in war must involve the destruction not only of their enemies but their fellow Christians (some of whom will have chosen to be non-combatants). In war the Church will inevitably, as so often in the past, be divided against itself, killing its own members. As long as Christians are committed to a policy, inescapable if they bear arms, of destroying their own brethren in enemy lands, they continue to demonstrate their belief in the priority of the national state over the Christian state. The international Christian nation — the Israel of God (Gal. 6:16) — is supposed to be the nucleus of the disciples of the Messiah preparing for service in the coming divine rule. The present participation of the Church in war is a denial of her role as an international world community, the microcosm of the divine Kingdom. The churches should consider very seriously the fact that there is no instance of a Christian bearing arms for the first 170 years of Christian history. Is it too much to ask that churches must require of their members at baptism that they renounce the right to take the lives of their fellow Christians? At present Christianity is often defined as a noble form of patriotism. Such an idea conflicts with the New Testament teaching that the kingdoms of this world are not the Kingdom of God and will not be until the return of the Messiah (Rev. 11:15-18).

---

[54] Isa. 2:4; Ps. 46:9; Zech. 9:10; Isa. 32:17.

The Life of the Age to Come

There are two familiar New Testament phrases which, as presently translated, stand in the way of a clear view of the Christian destiny, as Jesus and the Apostles understood it. The first of these is "everlasting" or "eternal life." That is not exactly what the early Christians had in mind when they described the ultimate purpose of the faith. The phrase "forever" in the Hebrew Old Testament was often understood to refer to a period of time in the remote future. With that period of time the promises contained in the divine Messages to Abraham and David were associated. When Daniel put on record his vision of the end of the current era of history, he described the resurrection of those who were asleep in the dust of the earth as "awakening to everlasting life" (Dan. 12:2). Our translators were thinking as Greeks, not as Hebrews, when they gave us that rendering. A Hebrew would have looked forward not to "everlasting life" but to "the life of the *coming age*." There was more history to come when God changed the course of events forever. The whole hope of the prophets was based on what would one day come to be on earth, an age of universal peace under the Messiah. Appropriately, the Old Testament writers had used a particular word to describe that future era. The word was *olam,* the remote, future age. It was customary for Jesus and His contemporaries (in common with the rabbis) to contrast the present age (*"ha'olam ha'zeh"* — this age) of human government with the future age (*"ha'olam ha'ba"* — the age to come) of the Messiah and His Kingdom. Thus when Daniel describes the resurrection of the faithful at the end of the current age, he sees the dead receiving "the life of the age to come" (Dan. 12:2). That is what every devout Hebrew desired. Daniel himself was invited to rest in death until the time came for him to take up his assigned position at the end of the age (Dan. 12:13).

It is well known that the New Testament takes this language over from the Old Testament and Judaism. Jesus spoke constantly of "the life of the coming [Messianic] age" and used the expression interchangeably with the Kingdom of God.[55] The translation "everlasting life" is not entirely inaccurate, for the life conferred in the

---

[55] For example Matt. 19:16 compared with v. 24 and many other texts. John uses the phrase "life of the coming age" rather than Kingdom of God (exceptions are John 3:3, 5; 18:36), but the meaning is the same.

coming age will indeed be life without end. Nevertheless, the Hebrew phrase is much clearer, since it conveys vital information about when and where that life will be attained and reminds us constantly that history is divided into two ages. The "life of the age to come" will be enjoyed in full in the Messianic age to come. It was to be in the age to come that men and women would "inherit the Kingdom." What a flood of light would be thrown on our Christian documents if when we read about "everlasting life" and "eternal life"[56] we would think with Jesus of "the life of the coming Kingdom" (tasted now in advance through the Spirit). As Nigel Turner observed: "It would be imprecise to translate *aionios* as 'eternal...' [but our translations continue to do so]. It means 'belonging to the future age or dispensation.'"[57] The same adjective *aionios* describes the fire which destroyed Sodom and Gomorrah thousands of years ago (Jude 7). That fire was not everlasting but similar to the supernatural punishment which God will inflict at the return of Christ. How very misleading also is the translation in Matthew 25:46 where the wicked are said to go into "everlasting punishment." Fortunately standard commentaries come to the rescue: "The adjective *aionios* [in Matt. 25:46] means belonging to a future age. It does not in itself mean 'unending.'"[58] What Jesus described was "the punishment which excludes one from the coming age." The popular promotion of "eternal torment" on the basis of this verse has no support in the original Greek language, which is strongly colored by the Hebrew mind of the New Testament writers.[59]

Knowing nothing of later Greek tradition, Jesus never spoke of "going to heaven." He offered His followers the inheritance of the earth (Matt. 5:5) as the fulfillment of the promises to Abraham and David. Abraham had once lived in the "land of the promise," but had never owned it. He had died without receiving it. It was obvious, then,

---

[56] Why did the King James version give us two expressions when the Greek for both is *zoe aionios*?

[57] *Christian Words*, T & T Clark, 1980, pp. 452, 455, 456.

[58] *The Cambridge Bible for Schools and Colleges, St. Matthew,* Cambridge University Press, 1889, p. 196.

[59] The prevailing expectation about the fate of the wicked is that they will be annihilated by being consumed in fire (Prov. 10:25; Obad. 16; Isa. 33:12; 41:11, 12; Ps. 118:12; Matt. 3:12; II Thess. 1:9).

that Abraham must one day rise from the dead in order to enter his inheritance with all the faithful. God had spoken, i.e. made promises, "to our fathers, to Abraham for the [coming] age" (Luke 1:55).[60] The inheritance was the Kingdom of God which, as James said, "God has promised to those who love Him" (James 2:5). Jesus also looked forward to the age of the Kingdom of God. His language is confined within the framework of the Hebrew outlook on the future. He does not speak of "heaven at death." He never says, "If you want to go to heaven…" or so and so is "in heaven." He and the Apostles speak of treasure being prepared now with God in heaven (Matt. 6:20; 19:21) — a reward "reserved in heaven"[61] as a "salvation ready to be revealed in the last time" (I Pet. 1:5), at Christ's return to the earth. Christians should follow Jesus and Paul and talk of "inheriting or entering the Kingdom."[62] This will enable us to think like the Master and not like a Greek philosopher. Popular preaching could learn much from the observation of the New Testament scholar who wrote: "The promise of future life is never described by Jesus in terms of being in heaven or going to heaven."[63] A revolutionary change of language is called for if we are to follow the example of Jesus. The use of Jesus' own words by Christians would have a remedial effect on the spiritual malaise created by the adoption of non-biblical language to describe life after death. With tremendous implications for the current confusion of denominationalism, Nigel Turner wrote:

> The language of the Church had better be the language of the New Testament. To proclaim the Gospel with new terminology is hazardous when much of the message and valuable overtones that are implicit in the New Testament might be lost for ever. "Most of the distortions and dissensions that have vexed the Church," observed the late Dean of York, "where these have touched theological understanding, have arisen through the insistence of

---

[60] *Eis ton aiona* means literally "for the age."

[61] I Pet. 1:4. Cp. Matt. 5:12, "Your reward is great in heaven," i.e., reserved in heaven in view of the future.

[62] Matt. 25:34; Gal. 5:21; I Cor. 6:9; Eph. 5:5.

[63] W. Strawson, *Jesus and the Future Life*, London: Epworth Press, 1959, p. 156.

sects or sections of the Christian community upon using words which are not found in the New Testament."[64]

The Two Ages

Our versions render us another disservice when they sometimes speak of the "world to come," instead of the "age to come." The "world to come" gives scope for the non-biblical idea that there is a heavenly realm to be entered at death. Such an idea is misleading: It draws a veil over the biblical goal — the hope of the divine Message — which is the arrival in history of a glorious Golden Age that will supersede the current age of human misrule. It is to that age that the Christian aspires. In "that age" he will receive "the life of the coming age" by being resurrected at the return of Christ. It will be most revealing for readers of the King James version, as well as other translations, to read "life of the coming *age*" or "life in the coming age" every time they encounter "eternal" or "everlasting life." In this way the atmosphere of the original faith may be recovered.

A similar loss of clarity has occurred where translations and commentaries speak of "the end of time." Salvation in the Bible is not beyond time and space. It will be granted fully at "the end of the age," when the New Age will begin. It is at the "end-time"[65] or "time of the end" that Christians can expect the coming of the Kingdom, not at "the end of time." Jesus' disciples questioned Him about the end of the age, not the end of the world.[66] The King James helped to obstruct clear understanding with its translation of Revelation 10:6: "there shall be time no longer." The mistake has been corrected in modern versions which tell us that "there will be no more delay."

By a strange irony the otherwise divided churches are united in their view of the Christian hope as a departure to heaven as a disembodied soul. There can be no more salutary shock than to awaken to the fact that such an idea is inconceivable to the Hebrew Christian writers of the Bible. So say also our best scholars, of whom

---

[64] *Christian Words*, p. viii. He warns equally against making the message "modern."

[65] Dan. 8:17, 19; 11:40; 12:4 (the last text is wrongly rendered in the NASV as "the end of time").

[66] Matt. 24:3; 28:20. The time referred to is the coming of the Kingdom. See also Matt. 13:39, 40, where the same event is called the harvest.

we quote just two examples: "Paul evidently could not contemplate immortality apart from resurrection; for him a body of some kind was essential to personality."[67] "The idea of a disembodied person is repugnant to the Hebrew mind."[68] F.F. Bruce, well-known to evangelicals, came to believe in the unconsciousness of the dead. Commenting on II Corinthians 5, Bruce refers to the instantaneous change-over from the old body to the new:

> Paul here envisages that there will be *no interval of conscious "nakedness" between the one and the other* [the old body and the resurrection body]. The tension created by the postulated interval between death and resurrection might be relieved today if it were suggested that *in the consciousness of the departed believer there is no interval* between dissolution and investiture [with the resurrection body], however long an interval might be measured by the calendar of earth-bound human history.[69]

It makes little sense that we should continue to comfort ourselves and our children with a hope for the dead so incompatible with the Bible — and all in the name of Christianity. The recognition that a large quantity of Greek philosophy has been imported into the faith and forced onto the New Testament records will be the first step to the recovery of apostolic Christianity. The words of a French scholar of the Bible deserve the widest publicity:

> Across the pages of the Old and New Testaments the clear waters of revealed truth flow like a majestic river. It is God, who only has immortality, offering to men and communicating to the believer His divine, imperishable life. But paralleling this stream flows the muddy river of pagan philosophy, which is that of human soul, of divine essence, eternal, preexisting the body and surviving it.

> After the death of the Apostles the two streams merged to make unity of the troubled waters. Little by little the speculation of human philosophy mixed with divine teaching. Now the task of evangelical theology is to disengage the two incompatible elements,

---

[67] F.F. Bruce, "Paul on Immortality," *Scottish Journal of Theology* (4), 1971, p. 469.
[68] Alan Richardson, *An Introduction to the Theology of the New Testament,* p. 196.
[69] *Paul, the Apostle of the Heart Set Free,* Eerdmans, p. 312, emphasis added.

to dissociate them, to eliminate the pagan element which has installed itself as a usurper in the center of traditional theology; to restore in value the Biblical element, which only is true, which alone conforms to the nature of God and of man, His creature.[70]

The path of wisdom would seem to lie in a personal reexamination of belief in the light of the biblical documents. The Bible recommends a diligent search for understanding. It commends those who daily meditate in the divine revelation. Jesus Himself was a devoted student of Scripture immersed, as were other rabbis, in the sacred writings of Israel. Throughout the New Testament the Apostles promised a resurrection to glory to those who have expressed their faith in Jesus by repentance, baptism as responsible adults, and belief and obedience to the divine Message of the Kingdom as presented by the Messiah and the Apostles. Salvation is offered on quite specific terms — belief in the Gospel as Jesus and the Apostles preached it. A clear definition of that Message should be an urgent priority for all truth-seeking believers.

---

[70] Alfred Vaucher, *Le Problème de L'immortalité*, 1957, p. 6, cited in Froom, *The Conditionalist Faith of Our Fathers*, Vol. II, p. 1028.

11. Arenas of Conflict

Sooner or later the churches must awaken to the fact that a radical paganization has occurred somewhere in the history of the faith. The denial of the Messianic Kingdom and the substitution of a reward in heaven at death point unmistakably to the influence of Greek philosophy in conflict with the Hebrew doctrine of the future. The situation will remain confused as long as the tensions created by competing thought worlds continue unresolved. At present "orthodoxy" battles hard to defend its traditional positions. Apparently the prospect of having to renounce some of its cherished dogmas is too unsettling. Yet while this attitude prevails restoration and unity are obstructed.

Admissions about the adverse effects of philosophy on the faith sometimes appear in footnotes of learned articles. They deserve to be made into headlines as a warning about the distortion which is bound to occur when an alien system is read into the Bible. Commenting on the popular use of Paul's phrase "absent from the body and present with the Lord" as proof that Paul thought that "souls" go to heaven at death to enjoy the "intermediate state," E.E. Ellis says: "In view of the influence of Greek philosophy from a very early period one would expect the exegesis to take this direction."[1] But why is it right that from the time of Clement of Alexandria and Tertullian until now Paul should have been misused to support popular, but unbiblical ideas about death and the afterlife?

---

[1] Cited by J.W. McCant, "Competing Pauline Eschatologies: An Exegetical Comparison of I Corinthians 15 and 2 Corinthians 5," *Wesleyan Theological Journal* (29), nos. 1 and 2, 1994, p. 46, fn. 84.

Standard authorities on the history of the development of Christianity leave us in no doubt about the break which has occurred with the original faith. They seem less enthusiastic about calling for a return to "the faith once delivered to the saints" (Jude 3), a phrase which hardly suggests that the Apostles would have been happy with a wholesale sellout or any accommodation to Greek or Roman theology. Protestantism claims that the Bible alone is the normative standard for its beliefs and practices and the Articles of the Church of England warn that Church Councils may have gone astray. If this is the case Protestants should be eager to show that their version of the faith really represents the authentic voice of Jesus. But have they reckoned with those changes that came over the faith soon after New Testament times?

The Harmful Influence of Philosophy

A learned professor of the history of Christianity writing towards the early part of this century described the switch of theological ideas which occurred when the Hebrew, biblical basis of Christianity was surrendered and replaced by a philosophically orientated system. Such telling expert opinion, encountered in the course of my reading, provides an eloquent answer to my initial question about why Christianity as taught in church seemed so different from the atmosphere created by the New Testament. I found the following statement immensely revealing:

> Like all concepts the meaning of religious terms is changed with a changing experience and a changing world view. Transplanted into the Greek world view, inevitably the Christian teaching was modified — indeed *transformed*. Questions which had never been asked came into the foreground and the Jewish pre-suppositions tended to disappear. Especially were *the Messianic hopes forgotten* or transferred to a transcendent sphere beyond death. When the empire became Christian in the fourth century, the notion of a Kingdom of Christ on earth to be introduced by a great struggle all but disappeared, remaining only as the faith of obscure groups. Immortality — the philosophical conception — took the place of the resurrection of the body. Nevertheless, the latter continues because of its presence in the primary sources, but it is no longer a determining factor, since its presupposition — *the Messianic Kingdom on earth* — has been obscured. As thus the background is

changed from Jewish to Greek, so are the fundamental religious conceptions...We have thus a peculiar combination — the religious doctrines of the Bible run through the forms of an *alien philosophy*.[2]

If this is so, it would be hard to imagine a more convincing indictment of our failure to guard the treasure of the faith as Paul commanded. How can "Messianic hopes be forgotten" when these were the pulsating heart of the Gospel of Jesus? How can the faith be "transformed" without a loss of original identity? Why is it in any way acceptable to mix Greek philosophy with divine revelation and still pretend that no damage has been done? How, indeed, can the Bible be claimed as the source book of Protestant faith when in fact we have departed from the Messianic framework in which its whole Message is set? It seems to us unacceptable that the Bible has been married to an alien philosophy. It would appear that the professor who delivered a lecture on "Christianity and Humanism" in 1938 uttered a much-needed warning when he said: "In its encounter with Greek philosophy Christianity became theology. That was the fall of Christianity."[3]

If we take our cue from Floyd Filson's observation about the incompatibility of the Hebrew mind set with alien cultures, we would expect a large-scale alarm at the intrusion of foreign ideas into the faith of Jesus:

> The primary kinship of the New Testament is not with the Gentile environment, but rather with the Jewish heritage and environment...We are often led by our traditional creeds and theology to think in terms of Gentile and especially Greek concepts. We know that *not later than the second century* there began the systematic effort of the Apologists to show that the Christian faith perfected the best in Greek philosophy...A careful study of the New Testament must block any trend to regard the New Testament as a group of documents expressive of the Gentile mind. This book's kinship is primarily and overwhelmingly with Judaism and the Old Testament...The New Testament speaks always of disapproval and

---

[2] G.W. Knox, "Christianity," *Encyclopedia Britannica*, 11th ed., Vol. 6, p. 284, emphasis added.

[3] Cited by Robert Friedmann in *The Theology of Anabaptism*, Herald Press, 1973, p. 50.

usually with blunt denunciation of Gentile cults and philosophies. It agrees essentially with the Jewish indictment of the pagan world.[4]

"Traditional creeds teach us to think in terms of Gentile and especially Greek terms," and "the New Testament speaks always of disapproval and usually with blunt denunciation of Gentile cults and philosophies." Traditional Christianity appears to be indicted by its own scholarly insights. A complete review of doctrine and a restoration of Jesus' own Hebrew faith would seem to be the only course available for a religion claiming to reverence and follow the Christ. The old question "Was Jesus a Christian?" appears to need a negative answer, if we are asking whether Jesus would have belonged to the "transformed" Christianity which took root in Greek soil in the second century and which orthodox churches have inherited. Jesus, however, is the model for Christians. Hence our need to follow Him and His teachings closely. It seems strange to speak of the "lordship of Jesus" and then to disregard His authoritative Kingdom Message, or any of His teachings, in favor of our own ideas and traditions. Christians seem to forget that Jesus is our Rabbi and prophet as well as our Savior. The Messiah came to "give us an understanding," so that we can know God (I John 5:20). But how can He teach us while we mix His teachings with "received" opinions on central Christian issues?

Quotations from the world of scholarly comment on the development of religion can be multiplied. Another professor of the history of early Christianity seems quite certain that the faith has not come down to us unscathed:

> Although the acute form of the secularization of Christianity in gnosticism was rejected, yet the Church...continued to lose more and more its primitive character and to be conformed to its environment in the Graeco-Roman culture. The process was advanced by the Apologists [spokesmen for the faith in the second century], seemed to suffer a check in the influence of Irenaeus, but was stimulated in the Alexandrian school of theology.... This development brought about *the definite transformation of the rule of faith* into the compendium of a Greek philosophical system...We cannot assume that the faith as delivered to the saints was

---

[4] F. Filson, *The New Testament Against Its Environment*, London: SCM Press, 1950, pp. 26, 27.

adequately and finally expressed in these Graeco-Roman intellectual forms...That the faith was expressed in ecclesiastical dogma always without obscuration or distortion cannot be maintained...That the Christian organism could not escape being affected by, in adapting itself to, its Graeco-Roman environment must be conceded; that this action and reaction were not only necessary but a condition of progress may be conjectured...This does not however exclude the frank recognition of the fact that there were characteristics of the Greek speculative genius and the practical Roman ethos not altogether harmonious with the distinctive character of the Gospel, so that there was *perversion amidst the progress* in the subsequent development — the salt in seasoning did lose some of its savour. Greek metaphysic and Law *misrepresented* as well as expressed the Gospel.[5]

The chief area of conflict is, as we have suggested, in eschatology, the doctrine of things to come. It is the Kingdom of God of the future which commentators so often seem to ignore. There is something unappealing about the idea that man on his own is not going to achieve peace on earth. It will take a divine intervention to restore harmony. Is there also a deep-seated anti-Semitic tendency in Christian commentary which works to reject the Jewish, biblical Messianism of Jesus?

A disturbance of the Bible's teaching about the future was not a minor ripple over matters of little consequence. Since the Gospel itself is about the Kingdom and the Kingdom lies in the future, the substance of Christian teaching was endangered.

De-Judaizing Jesus

While the writings of the Apostles concentrate on the development of the Church as the leaders-in-training of the coming Messianic era, there is no evidence that New Testament Christians had abandoned the "Jewish picture" of the Messiah as coming governor of a renewed world order. How could they when the Scriptures which Jesus endorsed had painted such a vivid picture of the Messiah's future intervention in world affairs? Based on the biblical hope, which Jesus never discounted, the Jews pray three times

---

[5] A.E. Garvie, "Christianity," *Encyclopedia of Religion and Ethics*, 1910, Vol. 3, pp. 587, 588, emphasis added.

daily that "speedily the world will be perfected under the Kingdom of the Almighty...Let all the inhabitants of the world perceive and know that to You every knee must bow, every tongue must swear...and let them all accept the yoke of Your Kingdom."[6]

On solemn occasions from the liturgy known as the Eighteen Prayers Jews ask God: "Give then glory, O Lord, to Your people..., joy to Your land [Palestine], gladness to Your city [Jerusalem], a flourishing horn to David, Your servant and a clear shining light to the Son of Jesse, Your Messiah."[7]

This is precisely the hope of both Testaments. The "clear shining light" is taken from the Messianic prophecy of II Samuel 23:4 and "the horn of David" reflects Psalms 89:17 and 132:17 which reappear in Luke 1:69 in a Christian setting. Matthew presents Jesus as "a ruler who will shepherd My people Israel" (Matt. 2:6). The Hebrew Bible had said precisely the same of King David: "You will shepherd My people Israel and you will be a ruler over Israel" (II Sam. 5:2). There could be no stronger evidence for the hope that Jesus must be installed as King of the regathered nation.

In a style characteristic also of Jesus, Jews do not minimize the negative aspect of the coming of the Kingdom: "May all wickedness be wholly consumed like smoke, when You make the dominion of arrogance pass away from the whole earth."[8]

The prayer which Jesus conferred on His followers for all time is woven from the same Messianic cloth as these prayers of Judaism. Jesus' hope is Jewish to the core. Among the prayers of the synagogues which Jesus attended, it is most likely that He would have heard the following petition for the coming Kingdom:

> Magnified and sanctified be His great Name in the world which He has created according to His will. May He establish His Kingdom during your life and during your days, and during the life of all the house of Israel, even speedily and at a near time: say Amen.[9]

Jesus' model prayer, "Sanctified be Your Name; may Your Kingdom come and Your will be done on earth" (Matt. 6:9, 10),

---

[6] *Alenu* prayer, cited by Klausner, *The Messianic Idea in Israel*, p. 521.
[7] Cited by Klausner, pp. 521, 522.
[8] Cited by Klausner, *The Messianic Idea in Israel,* p. 522.
[9] Ancient Kaddish prayer of the synagogue.

shows Him to be a true child of biblical Judaism at its best. With His own people Jesus longed for the establishment of justice on earth. Such had been the passionate expectation of the prophets of Israel:

> On that day the Lord will punish the host of heaven, in heaven, and the kings of the earth, on the earth. They will be gathered together as prisoners in a pit; they will be shut up in a prison, and after many days they will be punished. Then the moon will be confounded, and the sun ashamed; for the Lord of hosts will reign on Mount Zion and *in Jerusalem* and before His elders He will manifest His glory...Behold a king will reign righteously, and princes will rule justly...and the work of righteousness will be peace...My Servant...will bring forth justice to the nations...He will not be disheartened or crushed until He has established justice on earth...[Say to Zion], "your God reigns" (Isa. 24:21-23; 32:1, 17; 42:1, 4; 52:7).

Jewish commentary appropriately explained the hope of God reigning as the revelation of the Kingdom of God. Such is the hope of Judaism, as it is also of the biblical Christianity inspired by the master teacher Himself, whose Gospel was centered upon a single idea: the realization of the Kingdom of God upon the earth. The New Testament is a commentary on Jesus' master concept. The Christian Gospel is the Gospel about the Kingdom, a point of reference for all the blessings of faith in Jesus as the Christ. All this would be clear to the churchgoing public were it not for a counter-tradition which maintained the name of Jesus but persistently stripped His Message of its unwanted political and apocalyptic elements.

Controversy over the Future

A most sensitive battlefield is centered around those few passages of the New Testament which, taken alone and without reference to their wider context, stand the best chance of being forced into line with the Greek thinking which has buried the Message of the Hebrew prophets. Paul never comforted the bereaved, as we do, with the assurance that the dead were really alive with Christ in heaven. Our description of death as "passing on," or of the dead as having "gone home," betray the paganism which has entered the faith. The celebrated gospel hymn "We are *going*, we are *going* to a home beyond the skies, where the fields are robed in beauty and the sunlight never dies"[10] is not in harmony with the New Testament cry for the *coming* of Jesus to raise the dead. For Paul and the other Apostles, and for Jesus, the dead have gone to Hades to rest. They are simply dead awaiting the resurrection of the last day. The fact of a future resurrection is demanded by God's being the God of Abraham, Isaac and Jacob. The patriarchs are now dead. They must therefore rise in the resurrection in order to take their places in the coming Kingdom. In agreement with their predecessors of the Old Testament, the early Christians describe the dead as having joined their fathers in the sleep of death,[11] as sleeping in the dust until they awake in the resurrection.

Again, Paul insists that the dead have perished unless there is to be a resurrection (I Cor. 15:18). This is patently not true if in reality their souls have survived in another world. The whole matter is so very simple once the Greek dualism of body and separable conscious soul is erased from the mind. For while it is true that a man commits his spirit — himself as a vital thinking creature — to God at death, it is equally clear that the man himself falls into unconsciousness. Stephen in Acts 7 fell asleep in death after committing himself to God (Acts 7:60). Stephen in the next moment of consciousness will awake in the resurrection at the coming of Christ to earth. The notion of a surviving conscious spirit deprived of a body belongs in Scripture to the world of evil spirits, never to man.

In a handful of passages only, Scripture seems to speak of an immediate presence with Christ at death. When Paul contemplates the sleep of death for himself, he naturally envisages being immediately "at home with the Lord" (II Cor. 5:8) or "with the Lord" (Phil. 1:23; cp. I Thess. 4:17). This is because in sleep there is no awareness whatever of the passage of time. In that sense, to fall asleep in death is to wake up in the resurrection, even though millennia may elapse

---

[10] Words by Fanny Crosby.

[11] See Gen. 15:15; 25:8; 47:30; Deut. 31:16 in addition to 50 texts in I Kings-II Chronicles in which kings are said to "sleep with their fathers." See also Pss. 6:5; 30:9; 115:17; 146:3, 4; Job 14:12; Ecc. 9:5; Isa. 26:19; Dan. 12:2; John 5:28, 29; 11:11, 14, 43. Acts 2:34, 39 show that David was still dead and buried after the resurrection of Jesus. Like everyone else David "fell asleep and was laid among his fathers and underwent decay" (Acts 13:36). Jesus is coming back to raise (literally, "wake up") those who are asleep in death (I Thess. 4:15; 5:10; I Cor. 15:51).

before the dead are called forth from their graves. It is not that the dead have passed out of time. They are simply not conscious of it.

With little concern for the weight of scriptural evidence the reply of Jesus to the thief on the cross is cited as proof positive that death really means an immediate transfer to a conscious existence in heaven. Is that really what Luke intends us to understand? In other passages Luke records that Jesus taught His followers that they would be rewarded not at death but "at the resurrection of the just" (Luke 14:14) or "in the age to come" (Luke 18:30). Jesus spoke of "those who are accounted worthy of attaining to that [well-known] age and the resurrection of the dead" (Luke 20:35; see also Matt. 16:27; 25:19, 20). The hopes of the faithful are constantly directed towards the future Kingdom of God for which they are waiting even after Jesus' resurrection (Luke 23:51). It would be hard to imagine a more erratic departure from this simple scheme suddenly to teach that, after all, souls go to heaven the moment they die.

The Thief on the Cross

There is no need to read the words of Jesus to the thief in a way which makes Jesus contradict everything else the Bible says about life after death. The thief had asked to be remembered in the future when Jesus would return to inaugurate His Kingdom. Jesus more than satisfies his request. He assures him even on that day as they languish on the cross that the thief will indeed be with Jesus in the future paradise of the Kingdom. "Truly I tell you today, you will be with Me in paradise." Altering the punctuation (which is no part of the authoritative text[12]) clears up the difficulty. Leaving the punctuation as it is creates a considerable confusion for the following reasons:

1) Luke had already recorded Jesus as saying that He would not rise from death until the third day (Luke 18:33). How then could He be alive with the Father on the day of His death?

---

[12] E.E. Ellis notes that "a few reasonably early manuscripts place the comma after 'today' and thus continue the parousia reference of verse 42" (*New Century Bible, Commentary on Luke*, Eerdmans, 1964, p. 268). Ellis does not favor placing the comma after today, but in our opinion for insufficient reasons. Paradise is evidently parallel to the Kingdom of God in which the thief hopes to be at Jesus' return: "Remember me when You come in Your Kingdom."

2) Matthew 12:40 reports Jesus as saying that He would be "three days and three nights in the heart of the earth," not with the Father in Paradise.

3) Three days after Jesus' crucifixion — on the following Sunday — Jesus Himself stated that He had *not yet* ascended to the Father (John 20:17). It seems incoherent, therefore, that Jesus was alive and present with the Father the day He died.

4) The prophecy of Psalm 16:8-11, which Peter quoted in order to affirm the resurrection of Jesus (Acts 2:27-31), declared that God "would not abandon My soul to Hades, nor allow Thy Holy One to see corruption." Clearly Jesus was to be rescued from Hades by resurrection. This fits exactly with Matthew 28:5, 6, where the angel informs those who gathered at the sepulcher that "He is not here because He has risen." Jesus, on this evidence, left the tomb on the third day. He did not return from paradise in heaven. He had not been there. These considerations fully justify the change of punctuation we suggest. "Truly I say to you today..." gives solemn emphasis to the words of Christ. A parallel form of speech is found in Acts when Paul says: "I solemnly witness to you this very day..."[13]

A German translation of the Bible by Wilhelm Michaelis[14] renders the reply of Jesus to the thief as follows: "Truly I give you my assurance today: You will one day be with me in Paradise." The author adds in a note: "Jesus does not wait until the last day, but promises the thief even now ('today' should probably be attached to the first part of the sentence) that his request will be granted." *The Encyclopedia of Religion and Ethics* is also sensitive to the problem when it says: "Paradise, as used in Luke 23:43..., is evidently *not heaven* (John 20:17; Acts 2:31)."[15]

Paul himself shrank in horror from disembodiment, as any Hebrew would. Throughout the whole New Testament there is not a single reference to Christians surviving as spirits deprived of their bodies, much less of their having passed into the heavens.[16] For that reason that favorite text "absent from the body and present with the

---

[13] Acts 20:26. See also the same phrase in Deut. 30:16, 18, 19.

[14] Leipzig: Kroner Verlag, 1934.

[15] Vol. 5, p. 385.

[16] The New Testament speaks of Jesus only having gone to heaven (Acts 1:11; 10:16; 11:10; Heb. 9:24; I Pet. 3:22).

Lord" (II Cor. 5:8) ought no longer to be read through Greek spectacles as if Paul meant "at home" as a disembodied spirit. Throughout his writings he knows of only one homecoming. What he longed for was the new body and the life to be gained through resurrection and entrance into the Kingdom of God (I Cor. 15:50-55).

As for the parable of Lazarus and the rich man, it says nothing of a disembodied existence. Its characters obviously have bodies and Lazarus, whom the rich man encourages to go back to the living, does so as one who "*rises* from the dead."[17] The scene of the story, whose design is not to lay out precisely a program for the future, is set not in an intermediate realm of the dead but at the resurrection when (as so many Bible passages say) the good and the evil will be assigned their different destinies[18] and the patriarchs will sit down at the Messianic banquet (Luke 13:28, 29; Matt. 8:11). The plan for resurrection is clearly laid out in numerous passages from both Testaments, notably in Paul's letter to the Corinthian church (esp. I Cor. 15:23), as an essential part of the divine Message. Christians are to be granted immortality when Christ returns, not a moment earlier.

The Millennium

Another notorious battleground is the millennial vision of Revelation 20. Bible students prove themselves to be the fiercest opponents of the Old Testament prophets when they deny the reality of the coming Messianic Kingdom, which is the great theme of the biblical seers. Traditional teaching has so successfully put about the notion that Jesus came to remove the scene of the prophet's vision to another realm far from this earth, that many devoted students of Scripture are no longer persuaded that the hope for an earth filled with the knowledge of God and for Messiah enthroned as King are to be taken, as was intended, as a sublime prediction of the destiny of our world. The future rule of the Messiah and all His saints is beautifully portrayed in the Revelation in a passage immediately subsequent to the account describing the arrival of the King Messiah in power (Rev.

---

[17] Luke 16:31. Lazarus is the immediate subject of the discussion from vv. 27-31.

[18] The mention of Hades as a place of torment is exceptional in the Bible. In Jewish literature, however, Hades and Gehenna are sometimes used interchangeably, possibly with Ps. 9:17 as a basis: "The wicked will *return* to Sheol/Hades."

19:19-20:3). The period of the divine reign *follows* the arrest and incarceration of Satan "so that he can no longer deceive the nations" (Rev. 20:3). A more glorious release from the tyranny of Satanic deception cannot be imagined. This passage contains, surely, the grand climax to the entire biblical anticipation of the restoration of divine rule on earth. To refer it to the present chaotic state of our world is one of the bizarrest attempts to avoid biblical Messianism.

The efforts which have been made to obscure the future millennial Kingdom on earth are amongst the sorriest in the history of interpreting the Bible. The confusion of heaven with earth is so deeply ingrained that it has become almost impossible for Gentile-oriented churchgoers to read the words of John in sympathy with his thoroughly Messianic and apocalyptic perspective. The intensity of the struggle over the meaning of Revelation 20 is best illustrated by citing the words of the compiler of a well-known Bible commentary. He charges Augustine and his many followers in the Roman Catholic and Protestant evangelical world with "dishonest trifling, playing with terms"[19] when they suggest that the reign of Jesus and the saints, seen by John in vision in Revelation 20, has been in progress ever since the resurrection of Jesus. This would mean that Satan has already been bound "so that he can no longer deceive the nations" (Rev. 20:3). That men can be persuaded to believe that points only to the effectiveness of the Satanic deception! It should be clear that the period of time — the thousand-year reign of Christ and the saints — in which Satan's international deception ceases must lie in the future.

The millennial question is commonly believed to be only a peripheral matter in our understanding of the New Testament, a kind of "optional extra" for hairsplitting Bible enthusiasts to argue over. It is frequently shuffled off into the corner as a question unrelated to the Good News of salvation and of concern only to students of prophecy. This is very far from being the New Testament point of view. The very terms "millennium" and "millennial" hide the fact that the passage in Revelation 20 describing the thousand-year (i.e., millennial) reign of Christ and the saints contains essential information, by revelation from God through Jesus Christ (Rev. 1:1, 2), about the Kingdom of God; and the Kingdom of God is the heart

---

[19] *Peake's Commentary on the Bible,* Thomas Nelson and Sons, 1919, p. 941.

of the Christian Gospel Message, the burden of Jesus' whole mission (Luke 4:43).

The student of Scripture must solve a rather simple problem. When is this rule of Christ and the saints, described in Revelation, to take place? The millennial text reads as follows:

> And I saw thrones and they sat upon them, and judgment was given to them. And I saw the souls of *those who had been beheaded* because of the testimony of Jesus and because of the word of God, and those who had not worshipped the beast or his image and had not received the mark upon their forehead and upon their hand, and they *came to life and began to reign with Christ* for a thousand years. The rest of the dead did not come to life until the thousand years were completed. This is the first resurrection. Blessed and holy is he who takes part in the first resurrection. Over these the second death has no power, but they will be priests of God and Christ and will reign with Him for a thousand years (Rev. 20:4-6).

Two mutually exclusive views of this passage have been held. "Amillennialism" (originating in the theology of Augustine in the 5th century AD and supported later by the reformers, Luther and Calvin) denies that the millennial passage refers to a *future* reign of Christ and His saints. "Premillennialism" (which was the orthodox view of leading Christians of the second and third centuries) maintains that the reign described in our passage will begin at the Second Coming of Christ. The technical jargon must not be allowed to conceal the fact that this is a dispute about the Kingdom of God, and its place in the divine Plan. The difference of opinion should therefore be settled in order that the Gospel of the Kingdom of God can be presented clearly.

A fair way to resolve the question is by comparing it with the other biblical passages bearing on the resurrection and the joint reign of Christ and the saints and then examining the text of Revelation 20 in its own context in Revelation. Where does this reign fit into the biblical scheme?

An obvious parallel is found in Daniel 7, a biblical blueprint for the framework of New Testament teaching:

> The Son of Man [the supreme Human Being, who Jesus claimed to be] came to the Ancient of Days [the Father]...and there was given to Him dominion and glory and a *Kingdom* such that all people, nations and languages should serve Him. His dominion is an

everlasting dominion which shall not pass away and His Kingdom one which shall not be destroyed...The time came when the saints possessed the Kingdom [cp. "judgment was given to them" (Rev. 20:4)] (Dan. 7:13, 14, 22; see also vv. 18, 27).

What, then, is that "time when the saints take possession of their inheritance of the Kingdom?" The Kingdom of God is evidently a joint reign of the Son of Man and the saints. Does Scripture see this as a present fact or a hope for the future? Around this question a vast amount of discussion has centered.

Daniel 2:44 states that the Kingdom supersedes the kingdoms of the present age by destroying and replacing them:

In the days of these kings [i.e., rulers, represented by the great image] the God of heaven shall set up a Kingdom which shall never be destroyed, and the Kingdom shall not be left to other people, but it shall break in pieces and consume all these kingdoms, and it shall stand forever.

The same event is expanded in Daniel 7:27: "And the Kingdom and the dominion and the greatness of the Kingdom under the whole heaven shall be given to the people of the saints of the Most High, whose Kingdom is an everlasting Kingdom, and all dominions shall serve and obey them."

These are verses expressive of the Messianism with which Jesus was so well acquainted. His reliance on the book of Daniel is well known. Portrayed in these passages is a world revolution by which a new world government, presided over by the Son of Man and the saints, takes the place of present empires. It should not be difficult to understand that the nations and dominions of our present world are very far from being in subjection to Christ and the Church! This fact alone is proof that the Kingdom is dependent on the return of Jesus to establish it. "Thy Kingdom come!" is a petition for Jesus to come back to the earth and to set up His Kingdom. The petition does not read, as often thought, "Thy Kingdom spread."

The Kingdom envisaged by Daniel comes into power only after the defeat of the Antichrist whose rule proceeds for "a time, times, and half a time" (Dan. 7:25; Rev. 13:5). During that period the saints have been worn out and overcome by the tyrannical oppression of the antichristian system (Dan. 7:21, 25). It is only after the "beast is destroyed, his body given to the burning fire, and his dominion taken away and annihilated forever" (Dan. 7:11, 26) that rulership passes into the hands of the saints. Such exactly is the scheme laid out in Revelation 19 and 20. The beast is seized and thrown into the lake of fire (Rev. 19:20), whereupon the millennial reign begins. To propose that the thousand-year reign precedes the destruction of the beast in fire and the complete removal of Satan (which have obviously not happened) is a major disruption of the divine Plan.

The Joint Reign of Christ and the Church — Present or Future?

Our thesis must be carefully checked against the New Testament evidence. Where is the joint rule of Christ and the faithful placed? Matthew has recorded words of Jesus which provide an answer. The saints take up their royal office with Christ when He comes back: "When the Son of Man comes in His glory, *then* He will sit on the throne of His glory...In the New Age *when the Son of Man sits on the throne of His glory,* you also will sit on thrones administering the twelve tribes of Israel" (Matt. 25:31; 19:28).

The Kingdom is a gift to the disciples: "I appoint you to a Kingdom as My Father appointed Me to a Kingdom, so that you may eat and drink in My Kingdom and sit on thrones governing the twelve tribes of Israel" (Luke 22:28-30).

In the parable of the nobleman (Christ), the Kingdom is likewise placed at the return of the Messiah, when He destroys His enemies and puts His servants in charge of urban populations: "When he returned, having received the Kingdom..., he said, 'Bring hither my enemies who do not wish me to reign over them and slay them before me...' [To the disciples] he said, 'Have authority over ten cities'" (Luke 19:15, 17, 27).

Jesus clearly did not think the Kingdom had come nor that His disciples were in it: "I will no more drink of the fruit of the vine until the Kingdom *comes*...I shall never again eat [the bread of the Lord's Supper] until it is fulfilled in the Kingdom of God" (Luke 22:16, 18).

Jesus told the disciples to expect the Kingdom to arrive when He returned. Until then He (and they) would be "waiting until His enemies are put under His feet" (Heb. 10:13). Luke tells us decisively that the Kingdom will coincide with His spectacular return: "When you see all these [calamities preceding the Second Coming] happening, know that the *Kingdom of God* is near [*"about to come,"*

Good News Bible)]" (Luke 21:31). "Remember me [said the thief]
when You come to establish Your Kingdom..." To which Jesus
replied, "You will be with Me in Paradise" (Luke 23:43). The
Kingdom is equated with the coming Paradise.

The Tendency to Place the Messianic Kingdom in the Present

While maintaining that the saints had been transferred into the
Kingdom of the Son, in the sense that possession of the Spirit
guaranteed them a future inheritance,[20] Paul nevertheless corrected the
false notion, held by some of the Corinthians, that the saints are
already reigning. Writing first in a tone of irony and then expressing
his longing for the future joint rule of Christ and the saints, he said:
"You have become kings without us. Would to God that you were
reigning, so that we might be reigning with you!" (I Cor. 4:8).

He was indignant that the Corinthians had forgotten one of the
first principles of the faith — the believers' prospect of reigning with
Christ in the future: "Do you not know that the saints are to manage
the world? If the world is to *come under your jurisdiction*, are you
incompetent to adjudicate upon trifles?" (I Cor. 6:2, Moffat). By
contrast, "the unrighteous will not inherit the Kingdom of God" (I
Cor. 6:2, 9). The one statement interprets the other: Inheriting the
Kingdom is defined as "managing the world." We have here an
illuminating explanation of the significance of what Jesus and Paul
meant by "inheriting the Kingdom." It points to a time when *the world
comes under the jurisdiction of the saints.* Such a political notion may
well come as a shock, but it is precisely what we would expect from
everything we have read about the Kingdom in its Hebrew setting.
There was no question of the world being under Paul's jurisdiction
when he wrote to the Corinthians. He had specifically said that his job
in this present time was to administer only those inside the Church (I
Cor. 5:12) and that as an Apostle the world considered him to be "the
scum of the earth" (see I Cor. 4:9-13). The time was coming,
however, when, as a well-known Christian hymn in the apostolic
Church reminded believers: "If we suffer with Him [now], we shall
rule as kings with Him [then]" (II Tim. 2:12).

---

[20] Col. 1:13; 3:24. Since "flesh and blood cannot inherit the Kingdom" (I Cor.
15:50), the inheritance of the Kingdom must lie in the future at the resurrection.

The angelic chorus summed up the entire Plan of salvation with a song of praise to Jesus celebrating the fact that the Church of all nations "shall reign as kings on the earth" (Rev. 5:10). The New Jerusalem Bible makes the text more than clear: "You have made them [the believers] a line of priests and kings for God *to rule the world*." No wonder, then, that Jesus, as claimant to the throne of the royal house of David, was seen as a subversive in the Roman empire. Christianity is indeed a political threat to present world systems.

In the same book of Revelation, Jesus specifically promises the believer a place in the future Kingdom: "I will give him authority over the nations which I Myself have been given by My Father to rule" (Rev. 2:26, citing the Messianic Psalm 2). "I will grant him [the believer] to sit with Me in My throne, as I sat with My Father in His throne" (Rev. 3:21). The two thrones must be carefully distinguished. Christ is not now sitting on His own throne.[21] He will do so when He begins to reign on the earth at His Second Coming, as predicted by Psalm 2. The promises of rulership with Jesus are for those who "hold fast *until He comes*": "Hold fast *until I come*. To those who prove victorious and keep working for me until the end, I will give authority over the pagans" (Rev. 2:25, 26).

This text shows that rulership is not promised for the present, but for the time subsequent to the future coming of Jesus; and as a reward for faithful service in the present life.

It is at the last trumpet that "The kingdoms of this world have become the Kingdom of our Lord and of His Messiah and He shall reign forever" (Rev. 11:15).

At this *future* moment the heavenly elders say, "We give thanks, O Lord God, the Ruler of all, who are and was, because You have exerted Your power, Your great power, and have *become* King...The time for the dead to be judged [has come]" (Rev. 11:15-18).

When is that time? At the last trumpet. The last trumpet signals the resurrection of the faithful dead (I Cor. 15:23, 52).

---

[21] Acts 1:6, 7 carefully distinguish the coming of the restored Kingdom from the ascension of Jesus. It is confusing to read Acts 2:31-33 in a way which contradicts the scheme of Acts 1:6, 7. The resurrection and ascension of Jesus advance the Messianic program but do not complete it. Jesus' ascension guarantees His future enthronement in the Kingdom.

Exactly the same scheme appears in Revelation 19, where a future beginning of the reign of the Messiah is described: "Hallelujah! Because our God the Lord Omnipotent has *begun* His reign...For the marriage day of the Lamb has come" (Rev. 19:6, 7).

Jesus is the "man child destined to rule all nations with a rod of iron" (Rev. 12:5). "He will shepherd them with a staff of iron" (Rev. 19:15). These passages show that Psalm 2 has not been abandoned or "spiritualized." Until the great moment for the establishment of the Kingdom arrives, Jesus is to remain in heaven: "Heaven must retain Him until the time comes for the restoration of all things about which all the prophets spoke" (Acts 3:21). Jesus is therefore *"waiting from that time onwards until* His enemies are made a footstool for His feet" (Heb. 10:13). The point of time from which Jesus waits is stated a verse earlier. From the time of the ascension Jesus has been temporarily absent (Heb. 10:12), and that period of anticipation will come to an end when He returns to inaugurate the Kingdom worldwide.

With all this plain evidence before us we come finally to the disputed millennial passage in Revelation 20. Here we are told that the saints "came to life and reigned with Christ for a thousand years...This is the first resurrection. They shall reign with Christ for a thousand years" (Rev. 20:4-6). We have cited some twenty passages from the Old and New Testaments which describe the joint reign of Christ and the saints. In every case the reign is placed after the Second Coming. It begins with the return of Christ. In Revelation 20 we arrive at the long-awaited fulfillment of the expected Kingdom.

To set this passage at variance with the twenty other passages by claiming that it is a reign already in progress before the Second Coming is to break the first principle of sound interpretation. Our passage describes, as do its parallels throughout the Bible, a reign or Kingdom following the resurrection of martyred[22] (beheaded) Christians, and following the arrival of Jesus in power and glory. To speak in these texts of a present rule of God "in the heart" or the Church is to refuse simple information about the future Kingdom of God. All the texts in the New Testament, without exception, which speak of the Christians ruling as kings do so with verbs in the future

---

[22] The martyrs are singled out for special notice. This should not be taken to exclude believers, like John the Apostle and many others, who were not martyred.

tense.[23] No text makes the *inheritance* of the believers a present fact. Flesh and blood, indeed, cannot inherit the Kingdom of God (I Cor. 15:50).

Amillennialism — A Dislocation of the Biblical Scheme

There are a number of other reasons why the millennial reign of Christ and His saints in Revelation must lie in the future:

1) The reign of Christ and the saints in Revelation 20 *follows* the events of the return of Christ given in chapter 19. In Revelation 19:11 the words "and I saw" introduce a sequence of events, linked at verse 17 ("and I saw") and verse 19 ("and I saw") with the complete overthrow of the beast and the false prophet (v. 20) and the destruction of the remainder of those who oppose Christ (v. 21). In Revelation 20:1 "and I saw" continues the sequence and deals with the *complete removal* from the world scene of the ultimate enemy, Satan himself. Following that event comes the next stage of the drama: "And I saw thrones and they sat upon them..." (Rev. 20:4).

2) The reign of the saints with Christ *depends on a resurrection* (Rev. 20:5). The noun "resurrection" (*anastasis*) occurs some forty times in the New Testament. In every case (apart from a special use in Luke 2:24) it refers to a real resurrection of dead people to life, not a "resurrection" from the life of sin to life as a Christian (as amillennialism has to argue). It would be both unnatural and inconsistent to think of anything but the real resurrection of the dead in Revelation 20:4.

3) *John described a real resurrection and not a figurative one by saying that the occupants of the thrones "came to life" after being beheaded. The core of the millennial passage reads:* "I saw the souls of those who had been beheaded...and they came to life...This is the first resurrection." People are not beheaded at conversion, but they may die as martyrs. The "coming to life" of those "who had been beheaded" cannot by any stretch of the imagination describe

---

[23] Rev. 5:10 has a variant in the present tense, but even this may be a futuristic present: "They are to reign." Rom. 5:17 points also to a future Messianic reign for the saints, "life" being a synonym for the Kingdom of God (Matt. 19:17, 24). Paul used this coded language to avoid political offense. The vocabulary of Messianic salvation was well known to his converts in whom he invested much teaching.

conversion! Yet amillennialism has to deal with these words in this extraordinary way in order to avoid a literal resurrection.

4) In Revelation 20:3 Satan is bound "so that he can *no longer deceive the nations.*" Earlier in the same book John describes Satan as "the one [now] *deceiving the whole world*" (Rev. 12:9). Here in Revelation 20:3 he is bound and prevented from "deceiving the nations any longer." It is beyond question that Satan cannot *at the same time* be "deceiving the whole world" and "deceiving the nations no longer." Yet the whole "amillennial" school is committed to that contradiction.

Amillennialism teaches that the period of time in which Satan "no longer deceives the nations" (note: "the nations," not the Church) is the same as the period in which he is now "deceiving the whole" world. It would be hard to think of a more unsatisfactory method of reading the Bible! Amillennialists, we fear, are driven to these extremes by their dislike of the idea of a Messianic Kingdom of God, ruled by Christ and the saints.

5) In Revelation 12:12, 13 the Devil is thrown down from heaven into the earth. This, as all agree, is at a time *prior to* the Second Coming. However, in Revelation 20:1-2, Satan is banished entirely from the earth and sent to the abyss. This banishment into the abyss, which coincides with the beginning of the millennial reign, must lie in the future. Satan cannot be both confined to the earth and banished from the earth into the abyss at the same time.

6) Satan is represented as *extremely active* and powerful in the present evil age (Gal. 1:4). John describes Satan as now exercising power over the whole world: "The whole world lies in the power of the evil one" (I John 5:19). II Corinthians 4:4 sees Satan as "the god of this age." To grasp the New Testament view of the present activity of Satan the following passages should be examined: Luke 22:3; Acts 5:3; II Cor. 4:4; 11:14; Eph. 2:2; I Thess. 2:18; II Tim. 2:26; I Pet. 5:18: "Your enemy, the Devil, is prowling around like a roaring lion, seeking someone to devour."

Yet in our passage we have a description of the total cessation of the influence of Satan over the nations. He is removed from the scene, banished and sealed in the abyss. We urge our readers to abandon a view which makes Satan's present deceptive activity over the whole world (Rev. 12:9) compatible with a time when he is bound and unable any longer to deceive the nations (Rev. 20:3).

7) It is evident from Revelation 20:10 that Satan is finally cast into the lake of fire after the thousand years [millennium] (plus a "little season"). Thus a thousand years separates his binding and sealing in the abyss (Rev. 20:3) from his casting into the lake of fire. It is equally clear that the beast and false prophet are already in the lake of fire when Satan joins them a thousand years later (Rev. 20:10). In John's vision a thousand years separates the casting of the beast into the lake of fire and Satan's arrival there. If, as the amillennial school holds, the thousand years began at the crucifixion, or the conversion of the individual believer (opinions vary), what is the meaning of the casting of the beast and false prophet into the lake of fire *a thousand years earlier than that time*? What John obviously describes is the ruin of the beast and false prophet at the Second Coming, Satan's banishment to the abyss at the same time, and his casting into the lake of fire to join the beast and false prophet a thousand years later. The thousand-year reign thus follows the Second Coming — which is premillennialism, a recognition of the future Messianic Kingdom.

8) Amillennialists sometimes argue that the present freedom of Satan (assuming the premillennial scheme that he has not yet been bound) contradicts the effects of the crucifixion. They admit, however, that Satan must be let free for a little season (Rev. 20:3). This period of freedom would equally contradict the effects of the cross. The biblical facts are that Satan has already been defeated, but his sentence is put into effect when his authority as god of this age is finally removed by banishment, first into the abyss and subsequently by being cast into the lake of fire — a two-stage punishment.

9) Satan cannot possibly already be "deceiving the nations no longer" (as amillennialism has to say). In Revelation 19:15 Christ at His coming strikes the nations precisely because they have been so disastrously deceived by Satan into opposing the Messiah at His arrival.

10) Nearly all agree that the "rest of the dead" (those not included in the first resurrection) came to life *literally* at the close of the thousand years (Rev. 20:5, 12). Yet amillennialists deny that the "coming to life" of those in the first resurrection is a literal resurrection. The same Greek word describes the resurrection of both

groups, and the same words "came to life"[24] occur in two consecutive sentences. Henry Alford's celebrated protest against the inconsistency of this reading of the passage deserves to be heard again:

> I cannot consent to distort the words [of Revelation 20] from their plain sense and chronological place in the prophecy...Those who lived next to the Apostles, and the whole Church for three hundred years, understood them in the plain literal sense. As regards the text itself, no legitimate treatment of it will extort what is known as the spiritual [amillennial] interpretation now in fashion. If, in a passage where two resurrections are mentioned, where certain "souls" lived at the first, and the rest of the dead "lived" only at the end of a specified period after the first — if in such a passage the first resurrection may be understood to mean "spiritual" rising with Christ, while the second means literal rising from the grave — then there is an end of all significance in language, and Scripture is wiped out as a definite testimony to anything.[25]

The failure to see in Revelation 20:1-6 a future reign of Christ with His saints involves an extraordinary feat, by which the plain meaning of words and context are thrown aside in order to sustain a theory which did not appear in the Church until 300 years after the Apostles. As K.L Schmidt observed: "The man who refuses to find clear teaching about a future millennium in Revelation 20 approaches the text with preconceived ideas, and gains from it neither the exact sense nor the value."[26]

G. Ladd points to a whole tradition of anti-Messianic reading of the Bible when he writes: "The first anti-millenarians disparaged the natural interpretation of Revelation 20, *not for exegetical reasons*, because they thought the book did not teach a millennium, but *because they did not like millennial doctrine*."[27]

Opposition to the Jewishness of Jesus' Gospel about the Kingdom is explicit when commentators confront a straightforward (and in this

---

[24] Used also of literal resurrection life in Rev. 1:18 and 2:8.

[25] *Greek New Testament*, Vol. IV, pt. 2, p. 726.

[26] K.L. Schmidt, *Le Problème du Christianisme Primitif*, Paris: Leroux, 1938, pp. 84, 85.

[27] *Crucial Questions about the Kingdom of God*, Grand Rapids: Eerdmans, 1952, p. 149, emphasis added.

case a climactic) statement about the resolution of the world's ills when the Christ comes to reign.

Augustine and the Millennium of Revelation 20

The proclamation of the Gospel demands a decision about the Kingdom of God and its King, before the arrival of the "great and terrible day of the Lord." For those who respond to the challenge of the Kingdom, there is the hope of life in the New World. Meanwhile, "through much tribulation we must enter the Kingdom" (Acts 14:22).

The millennial Kingdom so concisely described in Revelation 20:1-6 is the first stage of the divine rule to be executed by the Messiah. This period of world history *follows* the Second Coming and is preceded by the first resurrection, which permits the faithful who have died to take part in the Kingdom. Disunity on this central element of the Plan is attributable again to the influx of an alien philosophy working to confuse the Hebrew, Messianic basis of the Gospel. The original intention of John's millennial vision is quite clear, but leading theologians deemed it unfit for inclusion in their system. The result was a decision to divert the meaning of the text, getting rid of its offensive Messianism:

> Christ is described as reigning with the martyrs for a thousand years. The interpretation of this statement has caused endless controversy...Since the age of Augustine, an effort has been made to allegorize the statements of Revelation and apply them to the history of the Church...[According to Augustine] the thousand years is not to be construed literally, but represents the whole history of the Church from the Incarnation to the final conflict. The reign of the saints is a prophecy of the domination of the world by the Church. The first resurrection is metaphorical, and simply refers to the spiritual resurrection of the believer in Christ. But exegesis of this kind is dishonest trifling...To put such an interpretation on the phrase "first resurrection" is simply playing with terms.[28]

Augustine's denial of the coming millennial reign of Christ and the saints on earth was adopted as official doctrine by the mainstream Church for twelve centuries. It dominated theological understanding until the 17th century. Augustine's amillennialism still grips the minds of many and distorts not only the book of Revelation but the

---

[28] *Peake's Commentary on the Bible*, p. 941.

Gospel of the Kingdom. Augustine promoted on a vast scale the notion that the faithful are now reigning in heaven — a concept which undermines the Bible and could have made no headway if the biblical view of death as sleep had been retained. The departure of the dead to heaven at death was the "thin edge of the wedge" which facilitated the dismantling of the divine drama leading to a restored earth. Augustine's immensely popular "reinterpretation" draws a veil over the Messianic hopes of the prophets. In view of these facts, the title of this book will, we trust, be considered fair criticism and a challenge to return to the biblical hope.

Unfortunately the critics who rightly understand that John had in mind a millennial Messianic Kingdom of the future come no nearer than many evangelicals to *believing* the prediction of the coming reign of Jesus and the saints. Scholarship dismisses the whole millennial vision as a piece of "Jewish speculation foisted upon Christianity." It is common practice for the critics to dismiss as Jewish any part of the Christian revelation found to be unpalatable to the minds of those unsympathetic to the spirit of Hebrew prophecy.[29] Traditional Christianity displays its anti-Messianic bias most obviously when it attempts to dismantle the plainest testimonies to the triumph of Messianic government over the world consequent upon the arrival of Jesus in power. The description of "souls[30] who had been beheaded" "coming to life and beginning to reign with the Messiah" (Rev. 20:4) can mean only one thing: Literally dead persons[31] (some had been decapitated) are seen being resurrected literally. To avoid this glorious vision of the future resurrection of the saints is to commit a considerable violence on Scripture. Commentators of the first rank have noted how terribly unfair are the attempts to avoid millennialism in the vision which claims Jesus as its author:

---

[29] A most extraordinary criterion for judging which parts of the recorded teaching of Jesus are genuinely His words has contributed to the dismissal of the Jewish Jesus. Some scholars have maintained that teaching which parallels Jewish ideas must not have originated with Jesus. But this is to set out with the intention of not finding a Jewish Jesus.

[30] Not "immortal souls" but simply "those persons who…"

[31] "Souls" of course are not disembodied. "Souls of…" means simply "those who…"

What Augustine was to stigmatize as the "ridiculous fancies" of Millenarianism, an initial selective resurrection inaugurating the 1000 years earthly rule of Christ and His saints, followed by a second general resurrection and judgment, gradually faded from the Christian imagination during the third, fourth and fifth centuries. Augustine exerted his immense authority against the Millenarianists, arguing not that the expectations expressed in the revelation to John were mistaken, *but that the passage in question does not mean what it says*...It is interesting to watch him at work reinterpreting scriptural passages, whose plain meaning he rejects. In this case he offers a Bultmann-like demythologization of the "first resurrection" consisting in the rising to faith of those souls who believe in Jesus and are baptized in His Name. The thousand years reign of the saints thus becomes the earthly life of the redeemed in the church during the present age...According to Augustine the second and general resurrection, unlike the first, was to be a literal bodily event.[32]

The influence of Augustine set in motion an entrenched anti-Messianic tendency in the Church which has persisted to our own times. There seems no good reason to reject plain language, unless, of course, faith in the promises of the Messiah's Kingdom has failed. The marks of a falling away from original truth are clear, and the Church has paid the penalty in division and loss of the central dynamic which the Gospel of the Kingdom, understood in its native Jewish environment, provides. The remark of Cranfield exposes the misunderstanding which plagues the Church. Defection from the teaching of Jesus at the heart of His Message surely must be cause for immediate concern: "It should be plain that the identification of the Kingdom of God with the Church made by Augustine, which has become deeply rooted in Christian thinking, is not true to the teaching of Jesus."[33]

---

[32] John Hick, *Death and Eternal Life*, New York: Harper and Row, 1976, p. 197.

[33] *The Gospel According to St. Mark*, Cambridge University Press, 1972, p. 67.

Belief in the Future Kingdom — The Heart of the Gospel of the Kingdom

We saw at the beginning of our study that the Kingdom or reign of God is the central Message of Christianity. The facts offered to converts in order to believe the Gospel include not only the death of Christ to atone for our sins, and His resurrection, but *also* the information about the Kingdom of God which Jesus proclaimed and demonstrated in advance of its worldwide inauguration at His Second Coming.

The present time is the time of preparation for the Kingdom which is to be the world rule of Messiah and His saints in the coming age. The words of Jesus in Luke 16:16 are quite clear: "From the time of John the Baptist the Gospel of the Kingdom is preached." Jesus did not say, "From the time of John the Kingdom has been here." Truly we may say that the Kingdom is present, in a different sense, wherever the Message is being proclaimed and the power of God is active. It is present when its powers are brought to bear on the demonic world (Matt. 12:28). It is not, however, present as the worldwide Messianic Kingdom predicted by the prophets, until Jesus returns to rule on earth. A great deal of argument about the presence and the future of the Kingdom could be laid to rest if protagonists would agree that the Kingdom cannot be both present and future *in the same sense.* As Caird said:

> The debate between those who hold that Jesus declared the Kingdom of God to have arrived and those who hold that He declared it to be imminent is reducible to its simplest terms when we recognize that the parties to the debate have differently identified the referent. If Jesus was referring to the final vindication of God's purposes in the reign of justice and peace, where the righteous are to banquet with Abraham, Isaac and Jacob (Matt. 8:11; Luke 13:28, 29), it is mere nonsense even to suggest that this was present on earth when Caiaphas was High Priest and Pilate Governor of Judaea. On the other hand, if Jesus was referring to the redemptive sovereignty of God let loose into the world for the destruction of Satan and all his works (Matt. 12:29; Luke 11:20), it

makes nonsense of the whole record of this ministry to argue that for Him this lay still in the future.[34]

The believer is invited by the Gospel to prepare, by a life of submission to the Lord, for servant-rulership with Christ in a restored earth in which a new civilization will be built. This hope gives Christianity its essential dynamic. The Messianic program will include the abolition of international warfare (Isa. 2:1-5). True worship of the One God through Jesus will be taught worldwide. The earth will be "filled with the knowledge of God" (Isa. 11:9). A system of perfect justice will operate for all mankind. "When Your judgments are in the earth the inhabitants will learn justice" (Isa. 26:9). The Kingdom of God for which we pray, "Thy Kingdom come!" is a restoration of the divine government in a perfected form.

That these are the facts of the biblical revelation is accepted by many scholars and commentators. They do not, however, treat them as more than a "Jewish dream." Historians have dismissed them as a fantasy. They are not persuaded that the dream will be realized. Yet the biblical Gospel is pledged to a promise of future peace on earth. The truth of divine revelation is at stake.

Commentators who treat the Bible as an inspired record avoid belief in the Gospel of the Kingdom by a different route. Their natural antipathy to the Hebrew thought world of the Bible has led to a development of a system of "interpretation" by which the plain meaning of words (for example in Revelation 20) can be sidestepped. In this way the entire import of Hebrew prophecy, which looks forward to the restoration of Israel and universal peace on earth under the reign of the coming Messiah and the Church, is negated. The reality of the Christian future, especially the millennial reign and even sometimes the whole idea of the Second Coming, is simply collapsed and hope has little definable meaning.

In proclaiming the Kingdom of God, the Church offers not only salvation and the promise of immortality to the individual, but the hope of a world at peace under the coming government of the Messiah, who has proved Himself fit to rule where Adam and mankind have failed. The cataclysmic events of the future will

---

[34] C.B. Caird, *The Language and Imagery of the Bible*, Philadelphia: Westminster Press, 1980, p. 12.

vindicate the divine Plan to restore to the earth what has been lost through the rebellion instigated by the Devil. A recovery of sane and sound government will bring God's intention for the human race to its logical conclusion. The earth and its inhabitants must learn the way to justice, and this cannot happen while Satan remains in office as "the prince of the power of the atmosphere," "the ruler who governs the air."[35] If Eden is not restored, it would appear that the Devil will have triumphed. But, as someone has said, the book of Revelation says that "we [the Christians] win," — and specifically by reigning with Jesus on the earth.

Judgment

There are other areas of misunderstanding in which traditional thinking must yield to the original intentions of the New Testament writers if the biblical teaching about Jesus as the Messiah is to be recaptured. One concerns the notion of judgment, the other the meaning of the term "Word of God."

Our creeds mislead us when they teach us to believe that Jesus is coming back only to "judge." Our Western concept of judgment as being primarily to do with sentence and punishment hides from us the Hebrew meaning of judgment. For the biblical writers judgment implies a much wider activity. It means administration, the exercise of every aspect of government. That is to be the function of the Messiah and His elect. The essence of the divine Message is that "God has appointed a day in which He will administer the world with justice" (Acts 17:31). This is the heart of biblical Messianism, which is only a synonym for Christianity. When Paul proclaimed a future "judgment" to the Athenians he was citing a Messianic Psalm in which the hope of God coming to "rule the world" was celebrated: "The trees of the forest will sing for joy before the Lord because He is coming to judge the earth. He will judge the world in righteousness and the peoples in His faithfulness."[36] The theme is repeated often in the Hebrew Bible and reinforces the vision of Messiah's benevolent rule: "May the King judge Your people with righteousness and Your afflicted with

---

[35] Eph. 2:2. The NIV has "the ruler of the Kingdom of the air."

[36] Ps. 96:12, 13. The Good News Bible catches the flavor of these verses: "When the Lord comes to rule the earth, He will rule the peoples of the world with justice and fairness."

justice...May He come down like rain upon the mown grass, like showers that water the earth. In His days may the righteous flourish...May He also rule from sea to sea" (Ps. 72:2-8). Such is the beautiful picture of the Messiah's administration to which the faithful are invited as assistants: "Don't you realize that the saints are going to administer the world?" (I Cor. 6:2). The "judges" of the book of Judges were administrators and governors, and "judging" is the function of a leader and king (Ps. 2:10, NASV margin).

"This Generation"

In the course of His elaborate discourse on events to be expected close to the end of the present age, as the prelude to the age to come of the Kingdom, Jesus made a startling statement that "this generation will not pass away until all these things take place" (Matt. 24:34; Mark 13:30). The "all things" in question included His Second Coming in glory described in the immediately preceding verses. In the western world "this generation" might suggest a period extending over the lifetime of one individual, although even then one could ask whether it is the "younger" or "older" generation that is meant. Jesus, however, cannot possibly have indicated a precise period of forty or seventy years. To have done so would be to contradict His own later statement that the disciples were not to know the "times and seasons" relative to the coming of the Kingdom (Acts 1:7).

"Generation" does not mean a fixed period of forty years, but a "block" of humanity characterized by its evil tendencies, something like "this evil brood" or "this perverse society organized in opposition to God." In Luke 16:8 Jesus observed that "the sons of this age [i.e., members of the present human society] are more shrewd in relation to their own 'generation' than the sons of light [the Christians as destined for the Kingdom]." "Generation" is here rendered "kind" (Luke 16:8, NASV), showing its meaning to be a "group with common characteristics." This meaning of the word goes back to the Hebrew Bible. In Deuteronomy 32:5 "generation" refers to the whole people of Israel during the entire period of their national opposition to God's direction. They are "a perverse and crooked generation."[37] Similarly in the Proverbs Scripture speaks of a "generation" who curses their fathers and a "generation" who are pure in their own eyes

---

[37] The same group are "children in whom is no faith" (Deut. 32:20).

(Prov. 30:11, 12). The word is appropriately rendered "kind of person" pointing to a group identified by a common characteristic. So also the Bible speaks positively of "the generation of the righteous" (Ps. 14:5) and of "the generation to come," equivalent to "a people who will be created" (Ps. 102:18). So also in the Psalms of Solomon reference is made to "the coming generation," "a good generation living in the fear of the Lord" (Pss. Sol. 18:6, 9). "Generation" means a social group united by common traits of character, good or bad.

Jesus, therefore, speaking in an eschatological context of "this generation," contrasted the present evil society with the coming society of the Kingdom. The same distinction is implied is Mark 8:38 where He contrasts "this adulterous and sinful generation" with the time when "the Son of Man comes in the glory of His Father." As a leading New Testament scholar says: "Probably 'generation' [in Mark 8:38] is best taken in the sense of 'age,' 'period of time,' which is the primary meaning of Hebrew *dor*"[38] — the word regularly rendered by "generation" in the Greek of the Septuagint. Thus "this generation" which will not pass until all the cataclysmic events described by Jesus have happened is "the present swiftly transient period of the world's history which is leading up to the day of judgment and the New Age."[39] Jesus made no chronological prediction about the time of His arrival to inaugurate the Kingdom (contrary to some of His followers who sometimes bring the faith into disrepute by asserting dogmatically that He will arrive on a certain date).[40]

Our point is confirmed in an excellent article by Neil Nelson who writes:

> "This generation" in Matt. 24:34 refers to a kind of people characterized by Matthew as unbelieving and headed toward eschatological judgment. In the context of the discourse it refers to that type of consummately evil and unbelieving people who deceive and persecute the disciples of Christ until the time of the *parousia*, when the true followers of Jesus are vindicated and "this generation" passes away in judgment...Any interpretation of *he genea haute* that implies that disciples in Jesus' (or the evangelist's)

---

[38] C.E.B. Cranfield, *The Gospel According to St. Mark*, p. 284.

[39] "Generation," *Dictionary of the Apostolic Church*, Vol. 1, p. 444.

[40] The current theory which maintains that Jesus actually returned to establish the Kingdom in AD 70 (ultra-preterism) undermines the entire New Testament hope.

time or at any future time can use the events of Matt. 24:4-28 to calculate and expect Jesus' return within a thirty- to forty-year period (allowing themselves time to prepare in the future for his coming) seems to run counter to the whole purpose and emphasis of the discourse.[41]

Justification by Faith

There is a vagueness in much contemporary religion, which all too easily borrows the name of Jesus without understanding the necessity of following His teaching. What a change might come over churches if the following New Testament texts were repeated often: "Unless your righteousness exceeds that of the scribes and the Pharisees you will not enter the Kingdom" (Matt. 5:20); and from Paul the preacher of grace (along with all New Testament Christians): "Not the hearers of the law are just before God but the doers of the law will be justified" (Rom. 2:13). Both Jesus and Paul make obedience a condition of salvation, and Paul taught his converts to think of salvation as past, present and future.[42] While much contemporary preaching implies that a Christian is secure once he believes in the death of Christ, the New Testament insists on a continuing life of righteousness in the power of the risen Christ. There is no genuine Christianity without ongoing discipleship and growth (II Pet. 1:5-11).

Justification for Paul is much more than simply forgiveness. It reinstates a person as a son of God and heir of the promise of a place in the land/Kingdom. The *Pulpit Commentary* notes:

> We must not restrict justification to deliverance from deserved penalty, but must attach it to the further idea of *inheritance*. As one writer has well remarked, "justification is applicable to something more than the discharge of an accused person without condemnation. As in our courts of law there are civil as well as criminal cases; so it was in old time; and a large number of the passages adduced seem to refer to trials of the latter description, in which some question of property, right or inheritance was under

---

[41] Neil D. Nelson, Jr., "'This Generation' in Matt 24:34: A Literary Critical Perspective," *Journal of the Evangelical Theological Society* 38:3 (Sept. 1996), pp. 369, 373.

[42] Salvation is past (Eph. 2:8), present (I Cor. 1:18), and future (Rom. 5:9, 10; 13:11).

discussion between the two parties. The judge, by justifying one of the parties, decided that the property in question was to be regarded as his. Applying this aspect of the matter to the justification of man in the sight of God we gather from Scripture that while through sin a man is to be regarded as having forfeited legal claim to any right of inheritance which God might have to bestow upon his creatures, so through justification he is restored to his high position and regarded as an heir of God.[43]

Justification restores men and women to their position before the fall. They are then candidates for royal office in the coming Kingdom and must dedicate themselves daily to making their calling and election (selection to kingship) sure (II Pet. 1:10).

Regeneration and the Reception of Seed

The loss of the Gospel of the Kingdom has affected evangelism at its core. "Regeneration" is seen throughout the New Testament as essential to salvation. In the words of Jesus to Nicodemus, "You must be born again" in order to enter the Kingdom (John 3:5-8). To grasp what the Bible says about spiritual birth it is necessary to encompass all the relevant data. A partial or selective approach will result in a defective understanding. The common tendency for evangelicals to rely on Paul, mostly in his letter to the Romans, makes it hard for many to see that Jesus is the original master teacher of regeneration. If Jesus is cited by evangelicals, it is from John's Gospel only, with disregard for the other three Gospels.

It is well known that Jesus makes rebirth the indispensable condition of salvation. How then does this rebirth come about?

In His classic conversation with Nicodemus Jesus teaches that the agent of rebirth is the Spirit of God. Closely connected with the Spirit is water (John 3:5-7) — perhaps a reference to baptism which is mandated in the Great Commission. The Apostles of Jesus include in their writing invaluable comments on the "born-again" process. James says that we are born again through the "word of Truth" (1:18). But just what is that "word of Truth"? Peter gives a fuller account. He connects rebirth with Hope: "God has caused our rebirth into a living Hope by the resurrection of Jesus Christ from the dead, to an

---

[43] *Pulpit Commentary*, Vol. XVIII, pp. 121, 122, citing Girdlestone, *Old Testament Synonyms*, pp. 259, 260, emphasis added.

incorruptible inheritance [of the coming Kingdom]" (I Pet. 1:3, 4). Christians are "born again, not from corruptible *seed*, but incorruptible *seed*, through the word of God which abides forever...This is the word which was preached to you as the Gospel" (I Pet. 1:23-25).

The essential ingredients of rebirth are clear. There is a word or Gospel. There is Spirit. Rebirth launches us into a living hope in view of a future inheritance of the Kingdom of God. And the whole process is traced to the action of "the incorruptible seed." Without the seed the process malfunctions.

Seed, of course, is responsible for the creation of life, human, animal and vegetable. This is no less true of the counterpart world of the Spirit and immortality. But what is that "word of Truth," "Gospel," "seed" with which the potential convert must make contact?

Seed causes the generation or creation of new life. So Paul writes: "If anyone is in Christ [a Christian] he is a new creation " (II Cor. 5:17). He describes the same regenerating process elsewhere as "the washing of rebirth and the renewing of the Holy Spirit" (Tit. 3:5).

John speaks often in his letters about Christians being "begotten" by the Father. In I John 3:9 he too refers to the essential *seed of God* which remains in the believer. He refers also to Jesus as one "born/begotten of God" (I John 5:18).

It is at this point that many attempted descriptions of rebirth break down. They omit to trace this essential Christian teaching to the master teacher Himself. Jesus gave by far the fullest account of how the seed of rebirth/regeneration/conversion operates. For this foundational teaching about rebirth, the teaching on which the brief remarks of Peter, Paul, John and James depend, is found in the Parable of the Sower, which we might also call "the Parable of the Seed" (Matt. 13; Mark 4; Luke 8). The parable provides an exact definition of the vitalizing seed referred to by John and Peter. Jesus said, "Whenever anyone hears *the word about the Kingdom* and fails to understand it, the wicked one [the Devil] snatches away what was *sown* in his heart" (Matt. 13:19). Others receive the seed and retain it for a while but fall away under the pressure of persecution. Still others receive the seed and retain it, but anxiety and other preoccupations choke the seed and it bears no fruit. The fourth category is successful.

The group represented by the good soil receive the seed "in an honest and good heart" (Luke 8:15) and bear fruit in varying degrees (see Matt. 13:18-23).

Mark and Luke report the same full account of how rebirth through the germ of the Gospel occurs. Luke reports Jesus as saying that "the seed is the word of God" (Luke 8:11) (cp. James' "*word* of Truth" and Peter's "*word* preached as Gospel"). The first gospel, Matthew, gives us the full definition of that word: It is the word/Gospel *about the Kingdom.* Satan, mounting his attack on the salvation process, deliberately tries to frustrate God's creative, sowing activity. The Devil "comes and takes away the word [of the Kingdom, Matt. 13:19] from their hearts [minds] so that they cannot believe it and be saved" (Luke 8:12).

This detailed instruction from the lips of Jesus is essential to our grasp of the doctrine of regeneration. Salvation according to Jesus begins when the creative Gospel/word of the Kingdom/Truth lodges in the mind of the listener and when the message is given an intelligent reception. That word must reside as the vital, energizing seed in the believer, and grow, until he is finally immortalized in the resurrection when Jesus comes back (I Cor 15:23, 50-52; Rev. 11:15-18, etc.).

Mark's account of Jesus' teaching on rebirth through seed emphasizes an important aspect of salvation. Jesus says:

> To you [who receive the Gospel with intelligence] the mystery of the Kingdom has been made known, but to those outside everything comes in parables, so that seeing they may see, yet not understand, and hearing they may hear and yet not understand what they hear. *If they did, they would be converted and their sins would be forgiven them* (Mark 4:11, 12).

It is remarkable that Jesus here makes intelligent reception of His Kingdom Message/Gospel/word the indispensable condition of conversion, repentance and forgiveness. Blindness to the Kingdom Gospel of Jesus obstructs repentance, conversion and rebirth.

Can the Gospel be successfully preached, then, if the Kingdom of God is not presented to the potential convert? Can Christ be accepted apart from Christ's own saving Gospel — the Gospel of the Kingdom? "He who *hears my word* and believes Him who sent me possesses the life of the age to come..." (John 5:24).

Once the Kingdom Message of Jesus comes to the listener, he makes a choice to receive it or not. Without understanding it he cannot receive it. Without receiving it he cannot be forgiven. Such are the steps required for rebirth into the family of God. "Faith indeed comes by hearing and hearing from Messiah's Message" (Rom. 10:17; cp. John 5:24).

It is important to observe that Jesus was not *at this stage* of His ministry speaking of the other great factor in salvation: Belief in His atoning death and His resurrection. These great teachings were later incorporated into the salvation program (Jesus first mentions His death only in Matt. 16:21, Mark 8:31 and Luke 9:22). The Kingdom/Seed/Gospel remains throughout the New Testament the most fundamental element for salvation. Jesus expects His Gospel of the Kingdom to be spread to all nations until His return at the end of the age (Matt. 28:19, 20; cp. 24:14). Paul consequently preached it everywhere (Acts 20:25; II Tim 4:1, 2).

To be "born again," "born of the Spirit," "born again through the word," "the word of Truth," "the Gospel," or to be a "new creation" means therefore to receive the saving seed of immortality sown by Jesus and the Apostles by means of *their Gospel about the Kingdom of God.* Paul was no stranger to the teaching of Jesus. He stated the same great truth about rebirth in other words:

> Abraham had two sons, the one [Ishmael] by a slave girl, the other [Isaac] by a free woman. The child of the slave girl was born according to the flesh [cp. Jesus: "he who is born of the flesh...." John 3:6] and the other, the son of the free woman, was born *from the promise*...Now we, brothers, like Isaac, are children born from the promise. But, as then, he who was born from the flesh persecuted the son who was *born of the Spirit,* so it is now (Gal. 4:22-29).

To be "born of the Spirit" is to be a child of the "free woman," the Jerusalem above, namely the Jerusalem destined to appear on earth when Jesus comes to establish the Kingdom in Jerusalem (see Ps. 87:5, LXX, cited by Paul in Gal. 4:26). Thus it is that all who are "born of the Spirit" are "children of the Kingdom."

The promise on which salvation is based is in fact the promise of the Kingdom. Christians are "heirs of the Kingdom which God has promised to those who love Him" (James 2:5). Abraham received as

Gospel (Gal. 3:8) the same promise of the Kingdom: "The promise to Abraham and his seed that he would be heir of the world..." (Rom. 4:13). So the Spirit is transmitted in the promise presented in the Gospel. Paul actually calls the Spirit the "Holy Spirit of the promise" (Eph. 1:13).[44]

Rebirth under the stimulus of the Gospel of the Kingdom is the key to God's creative activity (I Thess. 2:13), His New Creation through the *preaching* of Jesus, as the Messenger of the Covenant, as well as through His death and resurrection. Rebirth, being "born again," means hearing, understanding and receiving the Gospel preaching of Jesus Himself[45] as the Apostle of Christianity (Heb. 3:1) and model evangelist (Heb. 2:3). A "word" in the Bible is the instrument of God's creative energy and action. It was by a word that God said "let there be light." It is by the word of the Truth, the Gospel, that He illuminates our understanding, granting us light which we are then commanded to take to others (Mark 4:21-25). It is by the seed/Word of the Kingdom (Matt. 13:19) that God, through the Son, sets in motion the creation of immortal persons through the implanting of the divine nature and mind (II Pet. 1:3, 4; James 1:21). No wonder then that the Devil is enraged when that saving, creative word and Spirit are successfully conveyed to a willing, receptive mind. The Devil exerts every effort to snatch away the Gospel/Word of the Kingdom so that we cannot "receive it *and be saved*" (Luke 8:12). Luke has recorded for us a brilliant intelligence report from Jesus whose mind was steeped in the Spirit and insight of God, His Father.

Jesus was fully aware of the "mechanics" of regeneration. Parallel to Jesus' connection of rebirth with Spirit and water in John's Gospel are His famous statements about rebirth in the other Gospels: "Truly I tell you, unless you are converted and become like little children, you cannot enter the Kingdom of Heaven. Whoever will not receive the Kingdom of God as a little child will never enter it" (Matt. 18:3; Mark 10:15). "Unless a man is born again, he cannot enter or see the Kingdom of God" (see John 3:3, 5). A Christian is the product of the

---

[44] See KJV and Henry Alford's comment, *Greek New Testament*, Vol. III, p. 79.

[45] Note the NASV's correct translation of Rom. 10:14: "How shall they believe in him whom they have not heard [preaching]?" Salvation depends on hearing Jesus preach, not just hearing *about* Jesus (as NIV).

seed message of the Kingdom which makes him a "son of the Kingdom" (Matt. 13:38), or as Paul puts it "a child of the promise" (Gal. 4:28), one "born of the Spirit" (Gal. 4:29), destined to receive the inheritance of the Kingdom announced in the Gospel of grace (see Tit. 3:7). The Christian doctrine of regeneration is grounded in the Gospel as it came from the lips of Jesus Himself. It is a gospel of Hope for the future, not only the assurance of forgiveness in the present.

Tracts offering the way to salvation urgently need to be rewritten to include knowledge of the saving seed of the Kingdom Gospel announced by Jesus and the Apostles.

The Word of God

The concern of the early Christians to convey the essential information about man's personal and collective rescue is obscured as long as we continue to read the "word of God" as simply a synonym for the Bible as a whole. The scriptural term for the whole Bible is "the holy writings" (II Tim. 3:15) or the "writings" (Luke 24:27, 32).[46] The expression "word of God" should be understood to mean the Message of God, or more fully the "Message of the Good News of the Kingdom of God and the name of Jesus" (Acts 8:12). It is to that very specific corpus of information that each individual must respond in order to ensure his personal rescue from death. In Acts 8 "preaching the Message as Good News" (Acts 8:4) is equivalent to "preaching Christ" (Acts 8:5), and both phrases are shorthand expressions for the more comprehensive definition of the Gospel as centered on the Kingdom of God and the name of Jesus found in Acts 8:12.

Personal involvement in the Message of the Kingdom is never separate from a hope for the salvation of humanity at large and the establishment of peace on earth. The divine politics implied by the term Kingdom of God have everything to do with the future of our world. To maintain otherwise is to negate the message of the prophets of Israel.

---

[46] Jesus described the canon of the Hebrew Bible as "the Law of Moses, the prophets and the Psalms" (Luke 24:4). The order of the books was not the one known to us in the standard versions. The third division, the "Psalms" or "writings," consisted of Psalms, Proverbs, Job, Song of Solomon, Ruth, Lamentations, Ecclesiastes, Esther, Daniel, Ezra-Nehemiah and Chronicles.

"Word of God" in the New Testament is the counterpart to God's original word which brought into being the heavens and earth. Psalm 33 contains the classic passage describing the work of creation and the Plan for the world:

> By the word of the Lord the heavens were made, and by the breath of His mouth all their host...For He spoke, and it was done; He commanded and it stood fast. The Lord nullifies the counsel of the nations; He frustrates the plans of the peoples. The counsel of the Lord stands forever, the plans of His heart from generation to generation (Ps. 33:6-11).

The "Word" in the New Testament is the Gospel Message of the Kingdom taught by Jesus as the creative agent of God to effect the new creation of immortals, begun now and completed at the return of Christ. The "Word" or "Message" is also rooted in the covenants made with Abraham, Israel and David and celebrated in Psalm 105:

> God has remembered His *covenant* forever, the *word* which He commanded to a thousand generations, the covenant which He made with Abraham and His oath to Isaac. Then He confirmed it to Jacob for a statute, to Israel as an everlasting covenant, saying, "To you I will give the land of Canaan as the portion of your inheritance" (Ps. 105:8-11).

It was that "Word" which David loved (Ps. 119:97). On that bedrock foundation of God's faithfulness to the covenant New Testament Christianity takes its stand. Psalm 105 goes on to speak of the patriarchs as "messiahs" ("anointed ones"), i.e., kings (Ps. 105:15). The link between the patriarchs and the Christians is established when Paul describes his converts as "anointed" (II Cor. 1:21). From cover to cover the Bible reveals God to be a king-maker, selecting, by means of the invitation to kingship contained in His Message, the leaders of the "society to come" (Heb. 2:5). Christians, then, are those for whom the present life is a time of preparation, through trial and testing, for royal office. The Abrahamic covenant has been well named "the theological blueprint for the redemptive history of the world, a redemptive history which the call of Abraham sets in train."[47] On that blueprint, expanded and clarified in II Samuel

---

[47] W.J. Dumbrell, "The Covenant with Abraham," *Reformed Theological Review* (51), May- Aug. 1982, p. 46.

7 and Daniel 7, the structure of New Testament Christianity is built. The removal of its base in the Hebrew Bible, understood in a "concrete" fashion, must result in the collapse of the Message. To a widespread rejection of the vision of the prophets from Abraham to Malachi we attribute the present fragmentation of Christians.

12. Has the Kingdom Come?

A number of primary references to the Kingdom deserve to be advanced to the forefront of the discussion about Jesus' Message:

> There will be weeping and gnashing of teeth there when you see Abraham and Isaac and Jacob and all the prophets in the Kingdom of God, but yourselves being cast out. And they will come from the east and west, and from north and south, and will recline at the table in the Kingdom of God (Luke 13:28, 29).

> Truly I say to you, I shall never again drink of the fruit of the vine until that day when I drink it new in the Kingdom of God (Mark 14:25).

> For I say to you, I will not drink of the fruit of the vine from now on until the Kingdom of God comes (Luke 22:18).

> When you see these [cataclysmic events of the end of the age] recognize that the Kingdom of God is near (Luke 21:31).

> Thy Kingdom come! (Matt. 6:10).

> Joseph of Arimathea was waiting for the Kingdom of God (Mark 15:43; Luke 23:50).

The Kingdom sayings listed above provide simple evidence that Jesus was looking forward to the advent of the Kingdom. This fact bears directly on the content of the Gospel. It is easy to demonstrate from Scripture that Jesus built His whole mission and ministry around the Kingdom idea. It is, therefore, disconcerting, to say the least, that modern evangelism has little to say about the Kingdom. It appears that the Gospel itself is in jeopardy when the Kingdom is absent from the Message. The honest seeker for truth will find this startling difference between what Jesus and the Apostles taught as the Good News and what is now presented as the Gospel, a stimulus to dig further in the quest for the authentic voice of Jesus in Scripture.

It is commonly agreed by commentators on the New Testament that the Kingdom of God has a present and future reference in the teaching of Jesus. Attempts to define the Kingdom more precisely are plagued by a tendency to focus almost exclusively on the present aspect of the Kingdom. The future Kingdom is usually dismissed with a vague reference to its "consummation."

It is impossible to grasp the meaning of Jesus' favorite term "Kingdom of God" unless we pay full attention to the overwhelming volume of references to the Kingdom as an event of the future. It appears to be a dislike of this essential New Testament fact which causes Bible readers to fix upon Luke 17:20, 21 as their favorite Kingdom text:

> Now having been questioned by the Pharisees as to when the Kingdom of God was coming, He answered them and said, "The Kingdom of God is not coming with signs to be observed; nor will they say, 'Look, here it is,' or 'There it is!' For behold the Kingdom of God is in your midst."

Reading this text to the exclusion of scores of verses which describe the Kingdom as a future fact associated with the Second Coming, one might conclude that the Kingdom was first and foremost present in its King, Jesus, or, following the King James version of Luke 17:21, that it is "within you," i.e., in your heart.

If the immediately following context of Luke 17:20, 21 is taken into account, it becomes clear that the coming of the Son of Man (which Luke elsewhere says is the coming of the Kingdom of God, Luke 21:31) will be

> just like lightning, when it flashes out of one part of the sky, and shines to the other part of the sky...On the day that Lot went out from Sodom it rained fire and brimstone from heaven and destroyed them all. It will be just the same on the day that the Son of Man is revealed (Luke 17:24, 29, 30).

In a later chapter Luke reports Jesus as saying:

And there will be signs in the sun and moon and stars, and upon the earth dismay among nations, in perplexity at the roaring of the sea and the waves, men fainting from fear and the expectation of the things which are coming upon the world; for the powers of the heavens will be shaken. And then they will see the Son of Man coming in a cloud with power and great glory...When you see these things happening, recognize that the Kingdom of God is near (Luke 21:25-31).

With this evidence before us, it is impossible to confine the Kingdom of God to the presence of the Messiah in Palestine in the first century, much less to a religious ideal established in the heart or a post-mortem place for souls. The Kingdom of God for Luke and the other New Testament writers is primarily the rule of God to be imposed upon a wicked world by the powerful intervention of Jesus at the end of the age. If we do not reckon with this fundamental Old and New Testament fact, we strip the teaching of Jesus of its motivating dynamic — the need for us all to prepare now for "the great and terrible day" (Joel 2:31). We must all face the Messiah, and give an account of our deeds (II Cor. 5:10), either through resurrection or survival until His coming.

Has the Kingdom Come?

It is important that we examine the massive evidence for the Kingdom of God as a new stage of world history to be introduced at Jesus' return. To speak of this, as so many textbooks do, as the "consummation" of the Kingdom conveys very little meaning. The New Testament says that the present evil age is going to be "consummated" (i.e., come to its end, Matt. 24:3) when Jesus returns. The Kingdom of God will at that time be manifested publicly. It will then be inaugurated as the governing body of the New Age. Since the Kingdom comes into power only when Jesus comes back, it is confusing to say that it has already come. Its coming lies in the future.

We are to pray continuously "Thy Kingdom come!" We must guard against watering down the significance of this petition by making it mean something like "may Thy Kingdom grow," "may Thy Kingdom spread" or "may Thy Kingdom be perfected." For Jesus and the disciples the Kingdom has not yet come. Christians are to long for its coming and pray for it to be established so that God's "will may be done on earth." The petition contains the perfect definition of the

Kingdom. It is a state of affairs on earth when God's ways will be followed. That state of affairs, however, cannot possibly be realized worldwide until the banishment of Satan from his present position as "god of this age" (II Cor. 4:4). The deposing of Satan must, in the divine Plan, await the return of the Messiah. Such is the "philosophy of history" which permeates the whole New Testament.

The attempts of professing Christians to bring in the Kingdom before the predetermined time must end in failure. Jesus operated always within the consciousness of what "must be" in God's purposes. Christendom, as a whole, has ignored the divine program and has even attempted (since the time of Constantine) to establish itself as the Kingdom of God ruling now, sometimes in partnership with the secular state. Such a thing is impossible within the world view of the New Testament. Satan is the "ruler of this world system." Linking arms with him in an effort to turn his kingdoms into the kingdoms of God is fraught with disaster, the very same temptation which the Lord rejected when the Devil invited Him into partnership. The danger of taking this path is simply that we become "friends of the world" and in consequence "enemies of God" (James 4:4). "What have I to do with judging (i.e., administering) outsiders?" says Paul (I Cor. 5:12). Christian administration is confined to the body of believers: "Do you not administer those who are within the Church?" (I Cor. 5:12). Some believers seem intent on trying to force the world into subjection to Christ, not realizing that their only tool is the Gospel of the Kingdom, not the power of legislation. The kingdoms of this world are not yet the Kingdom of God and will not be this side of the return of Christ. Paul nevertheless expected the day to come when the world would "come under the jurisdiction of the saints" (I Cor. 6:2, Moffat). Paul's infectious excitement over the coming Kingdom deserves to be heard often:

> The sufferings which we have to undergo in this phase of our career I count not worth a thought in view of that dazzling splendor which will one day break through the clouds and dawn upon us. For the sons of God will stand forth revealed in the glories of their bright inheritance. And for that consummation not they alone but the whole irrational Creation, both animate and inanimate, waits with eager longing; like spectators straining forward over the ropes to catch the first glimpse of some triumphal pageant. The future and not the present must satisfy its aspirations. For ages ago Creation

was condemned to have its energies marred and frustrated. And that by no act of its own: it was God who fixed this doom upon it, but with the hope that as it had been enthralled to death and decay by the Fall of Man so too the Creation shall share in the free and glorious existence of God's emancipated children. It is like the pangs of a woman in childbirth. This universal frame feels up to this moment the throes of travail, feels them in every part and cries out in its pain. But where there is travail, there must needs also be a birth (Rom. 8:18-22).[1]

The Coming of the Kingdom

Certainly in the New Testament the Kingdom has not yet "come." Speaking shortly before His death, the Lord Messiah did not expect to drink again of the wine of the Passover cup until the Kingdom had come (Luke 22:18). Moreover, Joseph of Arimathea, who was a disciple of Jesus (Matt. 27:57), was "waiting for the Kingdom of God to come," after the crucifixion (Mark 15:45; Luke 23:50). Cleopas speaks for the disciples when, after the resurrection of Jesus, he expresses their hope, now apparently frustrated, that "it was Jesus who was going to redeem Israel" (Luke 24:21). The redemption of Israel was linked in their minds with the coming of the Kingdom in power. That event still lay in the future. Confirmation of Luke's understanding that the Kingdom had not come with the ministry of Jesus is found in Luke 21:31. The dramatic events which will lead up to the return of the Son of Man in power and glory herald the coming of the Kingdom of God: "When you see all these things happening, know that the Kingdom of God is about to come" (Luke 21:31, GNB).

The nobleman in the parable of Luke 19 is to depart to a far country (i.e., heaven) to receive his authority to rule and then to return as king to initiate the Kingdom. This information is given by Jesus to correct the misunderstanding that the Kingdom was to be "manifested immediately" (Luke 19:11). According to Jesus, there is no question that the Kingdom will appear, but not in the immediate future. It is instructive to note that it was Jesus' proximity to Jerusalem at the time which prompted the excitement that the Kingdom would come into power then. In its historical setting, this is exactly the kind of

---

[1] As rendered by W. Sanday and A.C. Headlam in the *International Critical Commentary: Romans.*

Kingdom we should expect. Its capital would be Jerusalem, the seat of Messianic government, "city of the great King," just as all the prophets had envisaged it. Jesus says nothing, then or at any time, to suggest that their conception of the Kingdom was fundamentally wrong (or "crude" — the disparaging term sometimes used by commentators). It is only the time of the arrival of the Kingdom which needs to be clarified. No precise chronological data are offered here or anywhere in the Bible to allow setting of dates. Much harm has been done to the New Testament doctrine of the Second Coming by those who succumb to the illusion that the date of the great event may be known in advance.

The parable of Luke 19 makes two important points about the Kingdom of God. Firstly, the Kingdom has not yet arrived, late in the ministry of Christ. Secondly, it will appear in power when Christ returns from the "far country" at the end of an unspecified period of absence. When the Messiah returns He will reward His faithful followers by putting them in charge of urban populations (Luke 19:17) and executing those of His enemies who "did not want Me to reign over them" (Luke 19:27). The Kingdom thus described is certainly not confined to a reign of Jesus "in the hearts of men." It has authority to confer power on those who followed the Messiah and the right to banish the incorrigibly wicked.

In every case where *the coming* of the Kingdom is described, an event of the future is meant.

"In the Kingdom"

The phrase "in the Kingdom" is first found in Matthew 8:11, where Jesus says that many will come and recline with Abraham, Isaac and Jacob "in the Kingdom," while others will be refused entry into the Messianic banquet. The event is, of course, the celebration promised by Isaiah 25:6-8. There will be a "feast prepared in this mountain [Jerusalem]" at which the faithful will rejoice with Jesus. Further reference is made to this great occasion when Jesus announces, at the Last Supper, that He will no more drink of the wine of the Passover until He drinks it new "in the Kingdom of God" (Matt. 26:29; Luke 22:18). Jesus obviously expects to celebrate with the disciples "in the Kingdom" when the "Kingdom comes" (Luke 22:18).

The Kingdom is certainly future when James and John request from Jesus prominent positions with Him "in Your Kingdom" (Matt. 20:20, 21). This is a request for recognition in the future reign. Although the petition cannot be granted, Christ confirms the reality of the future Kingdom, and its nature as a real government, by stating that the highest offices in it will be assigned to those whom God chooses (Matt. 20:23). Similarly, Matthew 19:28 places the inauguration of the Kingdom in the New Age or New World (Moffat and NIV). It is then that Christ "sits on His throne of glory," that is, "when the Son of Man comes in His glory" (Matt. 25:31), and His authority to govern is shared with His Apostles. At the same time the righteous "shine forth in the Kingdom of their Father" (Matt. 13:43, citing Dan. 12:3). This event occurs at the "end of the age" (Matt. 13:40), a time when the wicked will be cast into the lake of fire (Matt. 13:42).

A composite version of Matthew's and Luke's description of the Kingdom leaves no room for doubt that the Kingdom of God is a world government associated with the return of Jesus:

> "I tell you positively," Jesus replied, "in the reborn world, when the Son of Man takes His seat on the throne of state, you too shall be seated on twelve thrones, governing the twelve tribes of Israel. You are those who have stayed with Me through all My trials, and just as My Father has promised Me His Kingdom, so do I now promise you that you shall eat and drink at My table in My Kingdom and you shall sit on thrones governing the twelve tribes of Israel" (Matt. 19:28; Luke 22:28-30).[2]

Matthew tells us quite precisely when it is that Jesus is to sit on His throne of glory: "When the Son of Man shall come in His glory and all the holy angels with Him, then shall He sit upon the throne of His glory...Then shall the King say...inherit the Kingdom" (Matt. 25:31, 34).

Entering and Inheriting the Kingdom

When the center of systematic theology is founded on the recorded words of Jesus, the Kingdom of God will be seen as the sum total of biblical Christianity. Unless we strip the Kingdom of its historical

---

[2] *Authentic New Testament*, translation by Hugh Schonfield.

significance and invent new meanings for it, we will have little difficulty grasping its essential character as a real world government to be prepared for now, and awaiting manifestation at the Second Coming. Within this Messianic framework, the New Testament tells a coherent story. Without it, the New Testament can be (and has been) bent to suit almost any ideology.

The concept of entry into the Kingdom or inheriting the Kingdom of God appears throughout the New Testament. When is this to occur? We find an unequivocal answer in Matthew 25, where the blessed are invited to "inherit the Kingdom prepared for you from the foundation of the world" (Matt. 25:34). This will happen "when the Son of Man comes in His glory and sits on His glorious throne" (Matt. 25:31). Evidently the inheritance is to be acquired in the future at the return of Jesus. Elsewhere in Matthew, Mark, and Luke entry into the Kingdom is equated with entry into "Life" or "the life of the New Age" (or as we might say, "New Age Life," which has nothing whatsoever to do with popular movements under that title!).

Mark places entry into "Life" at a time when the wicked living at the coming of Christ will "go into Gehenna, into the unquenchable fire" (Mark 9:43). Entrance into "Life" or "the Life of the coming age" (in our versions inaccurately translated "everlasting" or "eternal life") is exactly the same as entrance into the Kingdom of God:

> Teacher, what good thing shall I do to obtain eternal life?...If you wish to enter life, keep the commandments...Truly I say to you, it is hard for a rich man to enter the Kingdom of Heaven...It is easier for a camel to go through the eye of a needle than for a rich man to enter the Kingdom of God [Kingdom of Heaven = Kingdom of God]...Who then can be saved? [entering the Kingdom = being saved]...In the New World, you will sit on thrones to govern the twelve tribes of Israel [being saved = ruling with Christ in the Kingdom]. Everyone who has left houses...for My sake shall inherit eternal life [i.e., life in the coming age of the Kingdom — the concept is based on the prediction in Dan. 12:2] (Matt. 19:16-29).

This basic "vocabulary" controls the New Testament. The Christian inheritance is always placed in the future. In one verse only Paul speaks of the transfer of Christians into the Kingdom of God as already a fact (Col. 1:13). This is not untypical of Paul's thinking, since all the realities of the future may be tasted in the present. The Kingdom exists now in heaven where Jesus is preparing to establish it on earth. A single verse should not, however, be used to contradict the predominant evidence of Matthew, Mark, and Luke, nor the clear statements of Paul elsewhere in which he places Christian inheritance of and entry into the Kingdom in the future.

The phrase "Kingdom of God is used normally in St. Paul of that Messianic Kingdom which is to be the reward and goal of the Christian life...Hence it comes to mean the principles or ideas on which that Kingdom is founded, which are already exhibited in this world."[3] Here Paul speaks of the Kingdom being "righteousness, peace, and joy in the Holy Spirit." This should not be taken to contradict his sayings elsewhere which place the inheritance of the Kingdom at the Second Coming. Though Christians have already been transferred out of the kingdom of darkness (Col. 1:13), only a few verses later Paul says, "You *shall* receive the reward of the inheritance [of the Kingdom]" (Col. 3:24).

The Kingdom Is Mainly Future as a New World Order

It is important that we emphasize that the arrival of the Kingdom of God in the New Testament is predominantly a future event, leading to a new world order on earth. The following plain statements from leading authorities provide a necessary corrective to the widely-held view that the Kingdom is mainly in the present:

> In the New Testament the Kingdom of God is conceived, first of all, as something in the future (Mark 9:1, 47; 14:25; Mat. 13:41-43; 20:21; Luke 22:16,18; I Cor. 15:50, et al.) which comes from God (Mark 9:1; Mat. 6:10; Luke 17:20; 19:11). Therefore it is something man can only wait for (Mark 15:43), seek (Mat. 6:33, cf. Luke 12:32), and inherit (I Cor. 6:9ff.; Gal. 5:21; James 2:5), but he is not able to create it by himself.[4]

---

[3] *International Critical Commentary on Romans* 14:17.

[4] Eduard Schweizer, *The Good News According to Mark*, Atlanta: John Knox Press, 1970, p. 45.

The objective analysis of the Kingdom of God in Matthew, provided by the *Dictionary of Christ and the Gospels*,[5] ought to serve as a much-needed guide to all our thinking about the Kingdom:

> The Kingdom — the central subject of Christ's doctrine. With this He began His ministry (4:17) and wherever He went He taught it as Good News (4:23). The Kingdom He taught was coming, but not in His lifetime. After His ascension He would come as Son of Man on the clouds of heaven (16:17, 19:28, 24:30) and would sit on the throne of His glory...Then the twelve Apostles should sit on twelve thrones judging the twelve tribes of Israel. In the meantime He Himself must suffer and die and be raised from the dead. How else could He come on the clouds of heaven? And the disciples were to preach the Good News of the coming Kingdom (10:7, 24:14) among all nations making disciples by baptism (28:18). The body of disciples thus gained would naturally form a society bound by common aims. Hence the disciples of the Kingdom would form a new spiritual Israel (21:43).

The same authority goes on to say:

> In view of the needs of this new Israel of Christ's disciples, who were to await His coming on the clouds of heaven, it is natural that a large part of the teaching recorded in the Gospel should concern the qualifications required in those who hoped to enter the Kingdom when it came...Thus the parables convey some lesson about the nature of the Kingdom and the period of preparation for it. It should be sufficiently obvious that if we ask what meaning the parables had for the editor of the first Gospel, the answer must be that he chose them because...they taught lessons about the Kingdom of God *in the sense in which that phrase is used everywhere in the Gospel of the Kingdom which was to come, when the Son of Man came upon the clouds of heaven.*

Thus the Parable of the Sower illustrates the varying reception met with by the Good News of the Kingdom as it is preached amongst men. That of the tares also deals not with the Kingdom itself, but with the period of preparation for it. At the end of the age, the Son of Man will come to inaugurate His Kingdom...There is nothing here nor elsewhere in this Gospel to suggest that the scene of the

---

[5] Vol. II, p. 145.

Kingdom is other than the present world renewed, restored and purified.[6]

The last sentence of our quotation makes the excellent point that Matthew does not expect believers to "go to heaven" but that Jesus will come back to rule with them in a renewed earth. The perceptive reader of the New Testament will note the striking difference between the biblical view of the Kingdom and what in post-biblical times was substituted for it: a departure of the faithful at death to a realm removed from the earth.

"The Kingdom He taught was coming, but not in His lifetime." "In the New Testament the Kingdom of God is conceived, first of all, as something in the future" (cited above). So say leading analysts of the Gospel records. We may add a further statement from a recognized authority on Luke:

> It cannot really be disputed that Luke means by the Kingdom a future entity. The spiritualizing interpretation according to which the Kingdom is present in the Spirit and in the Church is completely misleading...It is the message of the Kingdom that is present, which in Luke is distinguished from the Kingdom itself. He knows nothing of an immanent [i.e., already present] development on the basis of the preaching of the Kingdom.[7]

The Kingdom as in some sense present in the ministry of the Church has been vastly exaggerated in proportion to the Kingdom as future. Certainly the Message of the Kingdom is to be proclaimed now, and certainly the conduct fitting candidates for the Kingdom must be demonstrated by Christians now (I Thess. 2:12), but the Kingdom, properly speaking, is the Kingdom to be established when Jesus returns.

In confirmation of this central key to reading the New Testament with understanding, we add the statements of two further well-recognized authorities:

> There is nothing in Matthew, Mark, and Luke antagonistic to the eschatological [i.e., future] view of the Kingdom. The Kingdom is

---

[6] *Ibid.,* emphasis added. The same view of the Kingdom is expressed by the author of this article on Matthew in his commentary on Matthew (W.C. Allen, *The International Critical Commentary, St. Matthew,* T & T Clark, 1907, pp. lxvii-lxxi).

[7] Hans Conzelmann, *The Theology of St. Luke,* p. 122.

not present in any sense not reconcilable with the fact that it is also and mainly future...The references to the Kingdom are prevailingly of futuristic implication...Jesus did not dissociate Himself from the traditional view that the end would come in the form of a catastrophic transformation, culminating in the Advent of Messiah Himself, who would come from heaven...He seems everywhere to set His seal to this view...He steadfastly contemplated a final wonder of destruction and reconstruction which would be the perfect establishment of the Kingdom of God on earth.[8]

The Grimm-Thayer Lexicon discusses the word "Kingdom" in the New Testament and makes the following important point:

By far more frequently [than the use of the Kingdom as present] the Kingdom of Heaven [or God] is spoken of as a *future blessing*, since its consummate establishment is to be looked for on Christ's solemn return from the skies, the dead being called to life again and the ills and wrongs which burden the present state of things being done away...[9]

The Kingdom in the Rest of the New Testament

If we examine the evidence outside Matthew, Mark, and Luke, we find that the writers consistently use the term "Kingdom of God" to denote the future reward and objective of the present Christian life. *The Theological Word Book of the Bible*, among many other authorities, confirms this fact quite simply:

God's Reign is still to be established...It is generally in this [future] sense that the expression Kingdom of God is used in the New Testament outside the Gospels...The Kingdom of God is the dominant theme of the recorded teaching of Jesus...The Christian inheritance is identified with the Kingdom of God, the earth, eternal life, salvation, the grace of life, glory (cp. Mark 10:37, "glory" = Mat. 20:21, "Kingdom"), a place (i.e., Canaan), the world...Kingdom of God is the most characteristic description of the inheritance...For Christians the inheritance is future...The

---

[8] "Eschatology," *Dictionary of Christ and the Gospels,* Vol. 2, pp. 530, 531.

[9] "Basileia" [Kingdom], *Thayer's Lexicon,* p. 97.

inheritance is the object of hope...Christians are heirs presumptive; their entering into their inheritance is still to come.[10]

Clear references to the future Kingdom are found in the following texts:

It is through much tribulation that we must enter the Kingdom of God (Acts 14:22).

Do you not understand that the wicked will not inherit the Kingdom of God? (I Cor. 6:9).

People who indulge in such practices will never inherit the Kingdom of God (Gal. 5:21).

Be sure of this, no one guilty of sexual vice, or impurity or lust (which is as bad as idolatry) has any inheritance in the Kingdom of Christ and God (Eph. 5:5).

Listen, my brothers, has not God chosen the poor of this world to be rich in faith and to inherit the Kingdom which He has promised to those who love Him? (James 2:5).

By developing Christian qualities of character now, "there shall be supplied to you entrance into the eternal Kingdom of our Lord and Savior, Jesus Christ" (II Pet. 1:11).

Once again I will make heaven and earth quake...Therefore let us give thanks that we receive an unshakable Kingdom (Heb. 12:26, 28).

Flesh and blood [i.e., human beings in their present constitution] cannot inherit the Kingdom of God (I Cor. 15:50); i.e., a transformation of our present bodies into a spiritual body is required for inheritance of the Kingdom. This will happen at the Second Coming (I Cor. 15:50-52).

The kingdoms of this world have become the Kingdom of our God and of His Messiah [at the Second Coming] (Rev. 11:15).

---

[10] *A Theological Word Book of the Bible*, ed. Alan Richardson, pp. 113, 121.

The conclusion that the Kingdom is essentially the object of all Christian aspiration may be reached by anyone conducting his own careful Bible study. Confirmation appears also in standard works by biblical scholars: "The preaching of the Kingdom in Acts obviously refers to the Kingdom of God which will begin with the Parousia [Second Coming of Christ]."[11]

"Nothing obviously distinguishes the term 'Kingdom of God' in Acts from such apocalyptic [i.e., future and dramatic] use it has in the gospels; for example one enters it through much tribulation (Acts 14:22)."[12]

"Luke's understanding of the Kingdom is that it is still in the future and it will mean the restoration of Israel."[13]

"In Acts the term 'Kingdom of God' is used only of a future event."[14] "Luke's theology anticipated a restored Israel" (i.e., a real, external Kingdom on the earth (Acts 1:6) in the future).

A final quotation correctly summarizes the New Testament evidence for the Good News about a future Kingdom of God on earth. What Luke describes as apostolic belief and teaching is remarkably different from what is presented as the Gospel in our day:

> Acts includes many familiar elements in the New Testament preaching. The preachers preach the Kingdom of God or the things about it (Acts 1:3, 8:12, 20:25, 28:23, 28, 31). The term "Kingdom of God" appears from almost the first verse to the last verse in the book. "Kingdom of God" constitutes a formula apparently parallel to the writer's more characteristic single verb "evangelize."[15]

The Presence of the Kingdom
While the Kingdom is explicitly a future event in the New Testament, there are a few verses presenting, in another sense, the

---

[11] E. Haenchen, *The Acts of the Apostles*, p. 141, fn. 2.

[12] H.J. Cadbury, "Acts and Eschatology," *The Background of the New Testament and Its Eschatology*, ed. W.D. Davies and D. Daube, Cambridge University Press, 1956, p. 311.

[13] Kevin Giles, "Present-Future Eschatology in the Book of Acts," *Reformed Theological Review* (40), Sept-Dec. 1981, p. 66.

[14] E.E. Ellis, *New Century Bible, Commentary on Luke*, p. 13.

[15] H.J. Cadbury, "Acts and Eschatology," *The Background of the New Testament and Its Eschatology*, p. 311.

Kingdom as active in the ministry of Jesus. A serious distortion of the teaching of Jesus has occurred when the minority texts are used, to the exclusion of the majority, to make Jesus the teacher of a present Kingdom "in the heart."

From start to finish Mark's account of Jesus ministry makes the Kingdom an event which is "at hand" (Mark 1:14, 15) but not yet present. At the end of Mark's Gospel, the disciple Joseph of Arimathea was still "waiting for the Kingdom of God" (Mark 15:43). Matthew and Luke, however, while presenting exactly the same picture of a Kingdom yet to come, occasionally view the Kingdom in a different light. Matthew and Luke record Jesus as saying: "If I cast out demons by the Spirit of God, then the Kingdom of God has come upon you" (Matt. 12:28; Luke 11:20).[16] Obviously the arrival of worldwide restoration of the Davidic Kingdom in Jerusalem cannot be the meaning of "Kingdom" in these verses. Nevertheless, since the Hebrew mind "grasps the totality of an idea,"[17] "Kingdom of God" can sometimes be extended to refer to the power of the future Kingdom unleashed in the present. That power of the Spirit, or power of the Kingdom, was manifested as a sign of Jesus' Messiahship, and the same power is offered to Christians as a down payment or guarantee of their *future* inheritance of the Kingdom (II Cor. 1:22; 5:5; Eph. 1:14).

There is another possible explanation for the unusual expression translated "has come upon" you. The same verb recurs in I Thessalonians 2:16 in connection with the wrath of God which "has come upon" the Jews. Paul actually believed that God's judgment was still in the future as "the wrath to come" (I Thess. 1:10). What Paul may have meant is that the Jews were destined for the (future) wrath of God. In the same way Jesus may have implied that those from whom demons are cast out are "destined for the Kingdom."[18]

---

[16] The work of C.H. Dodd, who has been called a Christian Platonist, relied heavily on these texts for a definition of the Kingdom.

[17] A.R. Johnson, *The One and the Many in the Israelite Conception of God*, p. 2, citing J. Pedersen, *Israel: Its Life and Culture*.

[18] See the excellent comments on this question in "Kingdom of God/Kingdom of Heaven," *The Dictionary of Jesus and the Gospels*, eds. Greene, McKnight, Marshall, Intervarsity Press, 1992, pp. 422, 423. The same article points out that "during Jesus' ministry the Kingdom of God is spoken of always as a future event. It

There is another sense in which the Kingdom may be said to be present. The Kingdom of God was from the first associated with the personnel who would form the ruling elite (the elect) in the Kingdom. Israel was God's Son and firstborn (Exod. 4:22), and as such constituted a royal family: "You shall be to Me a Kingdom of priests" (Exod. 19:5, 6), an appointment which formed the basis of the covenant. The New Testament teaches that this honor of potential kingship is now offered to the Church. Jesus "has made us to be a Kingdom, priests to His God and Father" (Rev. 1:6).[19] Thus it may well be that when Matthew records Jesus as saying "From the days of John the Baptist until now the Kingdom of Heaven suffers violence and violent men seize it by force" (Matt. 11:12),[20] the meaning is that the royal family is being mistreated by hostile rulers of the present evil systems.[21] A similar reference to the presence of the Kingdom in its royal personnel is found in Luke 17:20, 21 where Jesus diverts the attention of the Pharisees away from the future Kingdom in an effort to get them to see that the Kingdom of God, in the person of its monarch, is standing right in their presence — "in your midst" (Luke 17:21).[22]

Summary

A world of information is involved in the Christian Gospel of the Kingdom. The genius of Christianity is concentrated in the word "Kingdom," which takes in the whole range of God's Plan to restore sound government to the earth. This essential saving information is

---

is expected, hoped for and prayed for. But it is never said explicitly to have arrived, not even at the Last Supper. What is present is the agent of the Kingdom of God, Jesus." Because of this, the Kingdom may be said to be potentially present.

[19] Cp. I Pet. 2:9; Rev. 5:10; 20:1-6.

[20] John was in prison at the time of this remark. See Matt. 11:2.

[21] Cp. Dan. 7:21, 25, where the power of Antichrist wears down and overcomes the Messianic community.

[22] The King James "within you," which has been corrected by modern versions, gave rise to a complete misunderstanding of the Kingdom of God as an interior kingdom of the mind and heart, which Jesus would hardly have seen as in the hearts of the Pharisees. Another possible meaning of Jesus' statement is "the Kingdom of God is within your grasp." Yet another possibility, supported by a number of commentators, is that "the Kingdom of God will be [is to be] in your midst all of a sudden like lightning"(see Luke 17:24).

often withheld from the public, though they are deluged with appeals to accept the "Gospel," or "receive Christ," in the absence of any clear description of Jesus' Message. Centuries of tradition have contrived to convince Bible readers and churchgoers that the Kingdom of God is mainly an abstract rule of God in the heart of the believer or "heaven" at death. This is in flat contradiction to the New Testament. Though the Christian documents recognize that the power of the future Kingdom has already intruded into the present evil world system (the Kingdom has "come upon" individuals when they are freed from demon oppression, Matt. 12:28; Luke 11:20), the Kingdom of God is firstly and predominantly the new world order which cannot and will not arise on earth until Christ returns to inaugurate it. This fact is revolutionary in its implications for the understanding and practice of the Christian faith.

It means that the whole concept of the Christian future as a departure of the believer at death "to heaven" is a misrepresentation of the biblical teaching. The Bible views the future in terms of hope for rulership with Christ on earth at the Second Coming. Attempts to move the millennial Kingdom of Christ and the saints into the present ("amillennialism") are symptomatic of the dislocation of the biblical scheme which has occurred through a fundamental misunderstanding about the Kingdom. This affects the Gospel and every facet of New Testament teaching. Our whole traditional structure is colored by Augustinian Platonism, which continues to receive uncritical acceptance by whole denominations claiming to base their faith solely on the Bible.

Underlying the rejection of the biblical view of the future is an anti-Jewish and anti-Messianic tendency. Churches have fallen under the spell of the notion that what is "spiritual" cannot be related to a New Political Order on earth. Theology therefore constantly suppresses or ignores the obvious Messianic themes of both Testaments or tries to "reinterpret" them and make them fit its own Platonized version of the faith. This continuing "soft-pedaling" of the plain teaching of the Apostles about the future prevents whole sections of the Bible from having their intended impact as a stimulus to hope and persistence in view of the glorious future of our world. A whole dimension of the New Testament — indeed its Hebrew framework — is, in varying degrees, missing from contemporary theology and preaching. In biblical Christianity the future is so much more sharply defined, making a correspondingly greater impact on life now. Recovery of the New Testament dynamic will go hand in hand with a clarification of the Good News about the Kingdom of God. The recognition that Jesus was a Jewish apocalyptic restorationist preacher of the Kingdom and thoroughly versed in the Hebrew Bible enables Bible readers to approach His teaching intelligently. Jesus ought to be accepted for what He obviously claimed to be: the Jewish Messiah commissioned to announce and further the divine program for the rescue of mankind. Desmond Ford was right when he observed that:

> Old Testament prophecy teaches that the Kingdom of God will be ushered in by a divine intervention rather than through the natural processes of history, and it is this view point which is indispensable to apocalyptic eschatology. *Jesus shared this outlook...*[23]

An amazing revolution would take place in churches if converts understood that simple concept. A major clarification of the Kingdom would occur, too, if the seventh chapter of Daniel were understood with New Testament Christians as the framework in which they worked out their hope for themselves and the world. Only after the defeat of the final "antichristian" power does the Kingdom of God become the possession of the Son of Man and the saints (Dan. 7:21-27).

---

[23] *The Abomination of Desolation in Biblical Prophecy,* Washington, DC: University Press of America, 1979, p. 14, emphasis added.

13. Opposition to the Messianic Kingdom

Distinguished voices in the churches sometimes confess to their discomfort about some aspects of Jesus' teaching. J.B. Phillips speaks of the "apocalyptic passages in Luke which frankly I find a bit of an embarrassment."[1] Georgia Harkness, writing about the Kingdom of God, is certain that Jesus cannot have spoken the words attributed to Him in Luke 19:27: "Bring My enemies here and slay them in My presence."[2] The apocalyptic Jesus has for a long time been unwelcome in the Church bearing His name. Harkness speaks of "the difficulty encountered by even His closest disciples to grasp His message…When they came together they asked Him, 'Lord, will you at this time restore the Kingdom to Israel?' The Davidic Messiah was still their dream!" At work in such commentary is a deep-rooted prejudice against the Messiah of the New Testament. Harkness goes on to say: "Jesus apparently thought that it was useless to argue with them, for He told them that it was not for them to know the times or the seasons fixed by the Father's authority."[3] But these surmisings do not appear in the text at all. Jesus positively did not correct their Davidic Messianism, which they had learned in His company.

Theology has a tragic history of trying to get rid of the teaching of Jesus which it does not like. Its animosity to Jesus stems from the fact that it has inherited a non-apocalyptic tradition dating from the time when the essentially Jewish framework of all that Jesus said was

---

[1] *Plain Christianity*, Wyvern Books, 1954, p. 51.

[2] *Understanding the Kingdom of God,* Abingdon Press, 1974, p. 24.

[3] *Ibid.,* p. 88.

discarded by uncomprehending Gentiles. Paul would not have allowed this departure from Messiah's Gospel to have happened without the strongest protest. He painstakingly instructs the Gentiles at Rome and in Galatia in the detail of the Abrahamic basis of the Christian Gospel. He did not excuse the Gentiles from the task of gaining a thorough understanding of the Hebrew roots of the Gospel. He never departed during the whole of his career from the apocalyptic future-Kingdom Message which he preached everywhere. The same certainly cannot be said of historic Christianity, in which the Kingdom conceived of as a revolutionary Message about God's intention to restore sovereignty to the earth at the return of Jesus has been conspicuous by its absence. There are clear indications in the theological literature of a desire to keep the historical Jesus and His apocalyptic Message at arm's length. When this happens the Gospel is jeopardized. The goal of Christianity is transformed into a vague hope of "heaven," instead of a passionate longing for peace and prosperity in the Messianic Kingdom on earth. A shrewd observer of the damage which has occurred to biblical faith observed that:

> The shift from apocalyptic to other forms of thought does indeed constitute something like a "fall of Christendom"...It was a fall from the apocalyptic world of early Christianity to Platonic categories of thought...The surrender of apocalyptic thought forms produced an alienation of Christianity from its original Jewish matrix, with the result that the Messianic expectations of Judaism — evoked by God's promises to Israel — were diverted into non-apocalyptic Christology.[4]

A Systematic Avoidance of the Gospel of the Kingdom

Close inspection of the writings of modern theologians uncovers a deep-seated desire on their part to be rid of the uncomfortable Gospel as Jesus proclaimed it. The Jewishness of Jesus' and the Apostles' Message is the obvious cause of offense. Modern man, says one immensely powerful school of thinking, will not tolerate teaching about a divine intervention to change the course of human history. That part of the teaching of the Bible is unfit for audiences in the

---

[4] J.C. Beker, *Paul's Apocalyptic Gospel, The Coming Triumph of God,* Philadelphia: Fortress Press, 1982, pp. 107-108.

scientific age. Yet there is much that is good in the Gospel, so the argument runs. We need to present the Message stripped of its regrettable Jewish clothing. To use the technical term, we must "demythologize" it — remove it from its Hebrew framework and place it in the vastly superior atmosphere of contemporary philosophy. In this way it will be palatable.

What needs to be pointed out is that the "it" of the Gospel, after it has been put through the wringer of modern theological theory, is scarcely the Message as Jesus gave it. Nor is Jesus any longer the messenger. He has been superseded though His name remains on the expurgated package thought suitable for contemporary audiences.

The process by which Jesus' Gospel of the Kingdom was transformed worked liked this: Theologians have argued that the Jewish apocalyptic and national-political elements of Jesus' preaching were merely the Jewish "husk" containing the valuable kernel of abiding truth. Once the husk was removed there remained a timeless Message which can appeal to every generation. In this way the embarrassment of believing in a Messianic Kingdom which never arrived can be smoothed over by turning the Kingdom into the Church and its unobjectionable religious message. For centuries the illusion was maintained. Typical of this point of view are the words of a theologian writing in 1913:

> The apocalyptic ideas and beliefs in which the great word of Jesus was embodied are, after all, of transitory significance. Not inaptly it is said of Messianism that it was "the nationalistic and contemporaneous encasement of the life work of Jesus which has been long since riddled and overturned in the process of historical development": Who today regards it as the characteristic mark of Jesus that He claimed to be the Messiah of the Jews?[5]

This immensely influential school of thought succeeded in "dumping" the unwanted Jewishness of Jesus, dismissing His Messianic Gospel as transitory and obsolete.

---

[5] H.L. Jackson, *The Eschatology of Jesus*, Macmillan and Co. Ltd., 1913, pp. 343, 344.

A Theological Bombshell

It was in the 19th century that theology awoke to the recognition that Jesus was a Jew with a Jewish Message for all mankind ("salvation is of the Jews," John 4:22). A book of only 67 pages by a German theologian[6] proved to be a theological bombshell when it pointed to unarguable evidence for Jesus' belief in an objective apocalyptic Messianic Kingdom of the future. Such an idea was revolutionary, since it had been traditional to think of the Kingdom as a religious experience or a moral force working to improve society. The new and shocking understanding that Jesus was in the best Jewish prophetic and apocalyptic tradition forced scholars of the Bible to deal with a difficult situation, not least the possibility of having to admit that the Church had been misreading its own documents and misinterpreting its own founder.

Paradoxically those who saw that Jesus had been the bearer of the news of the coming apocalyptic Kingdom did not suggest that such a Gospel was appropriate for the Church now. Albert Schweitzer, whose independent investigation led him to see that Jesus was not a "liberal" theologian, but a preacher of a future apocalyptic Kingdom, was unable to embrace such a Gospel as the object of faith. Both Weiss and Schweitzer were scholars, as someone has said, who did not belong to their own school of thought. Quite astonishingly, they deemed it "better to cling to the modernized ethical construction of Jesus' Message — although it rests on a misunderstanding — than try to retain Jesus' antiquated eschatological ideas."[7] Avoidance of the awkward Jewishness of Jesus' Gospel was achieved by variations of the same "husk and kernel" theory. Jesus must be stripped of His local Jewish garb and made respectable for modern man. Bultmann's theory of "demythologizing" arrives at the same goal by a similar method. What counts for Bultmann is the permanent call to decision in Jesus' Message. The Jewish framework can be dispensed with as the relic of a primitive world view which we have outgrown.

---

[6] Johannes Weiss, *Jesus' Proclamation of the Kingdom of God,* ed. and trans. Hiers and Holland, Philadelphia: Fortress Press, 1971.

[7] *Christian Dogmatics,* ed. Carl Braaten and Robert Jenson, Philadelphia: Fortress Press, 1984, Vol. I, p. 484.

In England the famous C.H. Dodd proposed the extraordinary theory that Jesus spoke only of the presence of the Kingdom and not of any future cataclysmic manifestation by which a new age would be introduced. Dodd was confident, with his theory of "realized eschatology," that the early Church must be blamed for reverting to the old Jewish concept of a future Kingdom and of Jesus as the Messiah destined to "come in the clouds with power and great glory."

It must be said that all attempts to separate Jesus from His Jewish apocalyptic background and teaching are doomed to fail. It would be much more honest if the Church were to say plainly, "We reject Jesus," rather than affirming that we accept Him, but only on condition that He gives up His unfortunate Messianic insistence that the Kingdom is going to enter history in the future as a world event for which the Church of every generation is to prepare with solemn urgency. Christianity divorced from its prophetic-apocalyptic framework is a pale reflection of the faith of the Bible, and it seems that the Protestant claim to be following Scripture is an empty boast as long as theology feels free to interpret away whatever is deemed unwanted and unsuitable. As one observer of the Church's method of dealing with the Kingdom of God observes:

> Analysis of the precise character of the eschatological beliefs of Jesus and the early communities has been complicated by a high degree of semantic confusion, if not obfuscation…There can be no doubt that Jesus and the evangelists looked for the future actualization of the decisive "last" events: the coming or manifestation of the Son of Man, the judgment of the living and the coming of the Kingdom or the coming age. That *this certainty has played but little part in contemporary exegesis and theology* can be attributed primarily to the dogmatic or philosophical interests (or aversions) of the "doers" of exegesis and theology. It is only quite recently that these "futuristic" beliefs are coming to be recognized as something other than a primitive Jewish and early Christian absurdity to be disposed of quickly and, if possible quietly.[8]

Little does the average churchgoer know of what has been happening behind the scenes in the halls of theology, in which his leader most probably has received his official training.

---

[8] Richard Hiers, *The Kingdom of God in the Synoptic Tradition*, Gainesville: University of Florida Press, 1970, pp. 94, 96, emphasis added.

Dispensationalism

For schools of theology committed to believing the authoritative word of Scripture, there are other ways of circumventing the Gospel of the Kingdom. One popular Gospel tradition has erected a scheme by which the Gospel of the Kingdom is specifically *not* the Gospel of salvation now to be offered to potential believers. It is a system known as "dispensationalism." All students of the Bible recognize that God appointed different "dispensations" or arrangements for different periods of history. The Mosaic dispensation, for example, made demands on the faithful different from those required under the New Testament Gospel. But "dispensationalism" goes much further. It maintains that the Gospel of the Kingdom was preached by Jesus to Jews only, until they refused the offer of the Kingdom; whereupon a different Gospel, the Gospel of grace, was introduced by Paul. The theory then holds that the Gospel of the Kingdom will be reinstated seven years before the return of Christ, a time when, according also to dispensationalism, the Church will have been removed from the earth by the so-called "pretribulation rapture."[9]

The dispensationalist system has been forced upon the text of Scripture in the interests of a theory alien to the Bible. As we have pointed out, Luke went to great lengths to show that Paul's Gospel was not different from that of Jesus. Both men preached the Gospel about the Kingdom.[10] Paul, contrary to dispensationalism, knew nothing about a difference between "the Gospel of grace" (Acts 20:24) and "preaching the Kingdom" (Acts 20:25). He deliberately equates them. As F.F. Bruce says: "It is evident from a comparison of Acts 20:24 with the next verse that the preaching of the Gospel of

---

[9] Jesus spoke about gathering the elect Christians *after* (i.e., post) the tribulation (Matt. 24:29-31; the elect, of course, are the Christians: see Matt. 22:14, where "chosen" represents the same Greek word "elect"). He also urged His followers to expect their redemption *after* the cataclysmic events leading to the end of the age (Luke 21:28). Since Jesus instructed His followers to "flee to the hills" at the onset of the tribulation, it should be obvious that He had no departure to heaven in mind! Paul expected Christians to have to survive until the public manifestation of Jesus in power and glory (II Thess. 1:7-9). He expressly warned against any system which taught that Christians would be gathered together before the appearance of the Antichrist (II Thess. 2:1-4).

[10] Luke 4:43, etc.; Acts 19:8; 20:25; 28:23, 31.

grace is identical with the proclamation of the Kingdom"[11] This incontrovertible evidence is flatly contradicted by contemporary dispensationalism. Dr. Erwin Lutzer, of Moody Church Radio Ministries, states: "I believe that the gospel of the kingdom is different from the gospel of the grace of God...The gospel of the grace of God has nothing to do with the Kingdom per se."[12] But this confusing of the one saving Gospel was learned from tradition unexamined, not from the Bible. By positing "two forms of the Gospel," dispensationalists have invented a most unfortunate distinction which does not exist in the scriptural text.

Dispensationalism formally cancels the Gospel as Jesus preached it. Could the Church have suffered a greater disaster than this systematic curtailing of Jesus' own Gospel preaching? A.C. Gaebelein was a leading exponent of the "divided Gospel" theory. Referring to Jesus' words in Matthew 24:14, "This Gospel of the Kingdom will be preached in the whole world to all the nations," he wrote:

> The preaching which is mentioned is that of the Gospel of the Kingdom, but that Gospel is not now preached, for we preach the Gospel of Grace...With the stoning of Stephen the preaching of the Gospel of the Kingdom ceased. Another Gospel was preached. The Lord gave it to the great Apostle. And Paul calls this Gospel "my Gospel." It is the Gospel of God's free Grace to all who believe, the gospel of the Glory of God...Now during the time that the Kingdom was preached to be at hand the Gospel of Grace was not heard, and during the time the gospel of Grace is *preached the Gospel of the Kingdom is not preached.*[13]

By this extraordinary exegetical blunder, Jesus' Christian Gospel of the Kingdom was ruled out of court — dismissed as suspended, and decreed impermissible for the present time. The situation would seem to call for a profound repentance and the reinstatement of Jesus' full Gospel at the heart of evangelism. Can there be such a thing as evangelism which does not hold in highest honor and emphasis the very Gospel heralded by Jesus and mandated by the Great Commission until the end of the age? If Paul had in fact preached, as

---

[11] *Commentary on Acts*, London: Tyndale, 1952, *ad loc. cit.*

[12] From correspondence, Oct., 1996.

[13] *The Olivet Discourse*, Baker Book House, 1969, pp. 9, 39, 40, emphasis added.

Gaebelein says, "another Gospel," he would have put himself under his own curse (Gal. 1:8, 9). He would have been in violation of Jesus' instructions that *His* teachings were to go to the entire world.

The article on "Gospel" in *Unger's Dictionary of the Bible* represents the same common dispensationalist tendency to bypass the Gospel as Jesus preached it. This kind of thinking about the Gospel and salvation has had an immense influence particularly in America, but its effects are felt throughout the evangelical world:

> Forms of the Gospel to be differentiated. Many Bible teachers make a distinction in the following:
>
> (1) *The Gospel of the Kingdom.* The Good News that God's purpose is to establish an earthly mediatorial kingdom in fulfillment of the Davidic Covenant (II Sam. 7:16). Two proclamations of the gospel of the kingdom are mentioned, one, past, beginning with the ministry of John the Baptist, carried on by our Lord and His disciples and *ending with the Jewish rejection of the Messiah.* The other preaching is yet future (Matt. 24:14) during the great tribulation, and heralding the Second Advent of the King.
>
> (2) *The Gospel of God's Grace.* The Good News of the death, burial and resurrection of Christ as provided by our Lord and preached by His disciples (I Cor. 15:1-4).[14]

The tragic suppression of the Gospel of the Kingdom is evident in the New Scofield Reference Bible at Revelation 14:6. The system of Gospel definition described in this note has affected the entirety of evangelical presentation of salvation, even where Scofield is not specifically recognized. Scofield begins by defining the saving Gospel as the Gospel of the grace of God which, he maintains, is confined to facts about the death and resurrection of Jesus. Scofield then goes on to speak of "another aspect of the good news," the "gospel of the Kingdom." We are informed that Christ preached this Gospel of the Kingdom at His first coming, and "it will be proclaimed during the great tribulation." Scofield thus banishes the Gospel of the Kingdom from the present message of salvation by stating that the Christian Gospel *now is only about Jesus' atoning death and His resurrection.*

---

[14] M.F. Unger, *Unger's Dictionary of the Bible,* Moody Press, 1969, p. 420, emphasis added.

In this way Jesus is cut off from His own Gospel preaching. We may well observe that Satan's master trick is to separate Jesus from His teaching. One may proclaim "Jesus" with all earnestness, but is the real Jesus made known apart from His complete Gospel and teaching? Jesus well knew the danger of preaching "faith in Jesus" without actually telling the public about the "words of Jesus." Only those whose faith is founded on the rock foundation of the teachings/Gospel of Jesus are on solid ground (Matt. 7:24-27; Mark 8:35-38; and see the whole Gospel of John with its constant insistence on the word/words/teaching of Jesus).

Uncertainty about the Christian Gospel is not surprising when such evident misreading of the Bible is built into a system with a massive influence in pulpits and Christian literature. Surely the words of Paul in Acts 20:24, 25 should banish the artificial distinction proposed by the Bible Dictionary and the Scofield Bible. Paul looked back on his career and noted that he had "finished his course, the ministry which I received from the Lord Jesus to testify solemnly of the *Gospel of the grace of God*...to all of you among whom I went about *preaching the Kingdom.*" *Clearly there is no difference between the Gospel of grace and the Gospel of the Kingdom.* It is true, of course, that Jesus did not initially preach His resurrection as part of the Gospel. The death and resurrection of Jesus were later critical elements in the proclamation of Paul. They did not, however, replace the preaching of the Kingdom, which remained as much the heart of Paul's Gospel as it had been the center of Jesus' own Message.

When Jesus embarked on His intensive evangelistic campaign in Galilee in about 27 AD, He summoned His audience to a radical change of heart based on the national belief that God was going to usher in the worldwide Kingdom promised by Daniel and all the prophets. Intelligent belief in the promise of the Kingdom is to be the disciple's first step, coupled with a major U-turn in lifestyle. In this way men and women can align themselves with God's great purpose for the earth.

The nature of Jesus' activity was that of a herald making a public announcement on behalf of the one God of Israel. The thrust of the Message was that each individual should undertake a radical redirection of his life in face of the certainty of the coming Kingdom of God. This was, and still is, the essence of the Christian Gospel.

How can it be otherwise, when it is the Gospel Message which comes from the lips of Christ Himself?

It is a matter of common sense to recognize that by using the term "Kingdom of God" Jesus would have evoked in the minds of His audience, steeped as they were in the national hope of Israel, a divine worldwide government on earth, with its capital at Jerusalem. This is what the Kingdom of God would certainly have meant to His contemporaries. The writings of the prophets, which Jesus as a Jew recognized as the divinely authorized Word of God, had unanimously promised the arrival of a new era of peace and prosperity. The ideal Kingdom would rule forever. God's people would be victorious in a renewed earth. Peace would extend across the globe.

Thus to announce the coming of the Kingdom involved both a threat and a promise. To those who responded to the Message by believing it and reordering their lives accordingly, there was a promise of a place in the glories of the future divine rule. To the rest the Kingdom would threaten destruction, as God executed judgment upon any not found worthy of entering the Kingdom when it came. This theme governs the whole New Testament. In the light of this primary concept the teaching of Jesus becomes comprehensible. It is an exhortation to win immortality in the future Kingdom and to escape destruction and exclusion from the Kingdom.

Traditional systems of Gospel preaching are saddled with the unbiblical destiny of the believer described as "heaven." The Abrahamic covenant which underlies the Christian Gospel of the Kingdom is then applied to Jews only! But it is the *Christians* who according to Jesus are destined to "inherit the earth" (Matt. 5:5) and the Kingdom.

Further Opposition to the Messianic Jesus

The association of the Kingdom of God with a spectacular divine intervention leading to the establishment of a new world order has proven to be an embarrassment to much of the theology of the past 1600 years. Various techniques have been employed to eliminate from Jesus' teaching this central notion of the Kingdom of God as a real government to be imposed upon our world. However, the vision of the prophets which Jesus came to confirm (Rom. 15:28) is unmistakably clear. And there is ample evidence in the New Testament to show that

Jesus shared with His contemporaries the hope for an actual "exterior" Kingdom in which He and His followers would enjoy positions of authority. What, for example, could be more explicit than the Savior's promise to the faithful Christians:

> To those who prove victorious, and keep working for Me until the end, I will give the authority over the pagans which I Myself have been given by My Father, to rule them with an iron scepter and shatter them like earthenware...Those who prove victorious I will allow to share My throne, just as I was victorious myself and took My place with My Father on His throne (Rev. 2:26; 3:21, Jerusalem Bible).

These assurances were given to the Church as the "Message of the Son of God, the faithful and true witness" (Rev. 2:18; 3:14). They proceed directly from Jesus to His Church. As is well known, they reflect accurately the Jewish (and New Testament Christian) hope for world dominion under the promised Messiah and His faithful people, just as Daniel had predicted. In the same book we find an angelic chorus singing of the wonders of God's Plan. Their hymn is in praise of the Messiah, the executive of the divine Plan:

> You are worthy to take the scroll and break the seals of it, because You were sacrificed, and with Your blood You bought men for God of every race, language, people and nation and made them a line of *kings and priests to serve our God and rule the world* (Rev. 5:9, 10, Jerusalem Bible).

The tendency to want to collapse these plain statements and render them less "offensive" is apparent in contemporary Christian literature, but it must be consciously overcome. In order to make Jesus more "religious" and less political, many have tried to think only of a present "reign" of the Church or a "reign" of Christ "in the heart," but this is evidently not what these Kingdom texts say. The rulership promised to the believer will be granted only after he has become victorious through the trials of the present life. He will share the Kingdom with Jesus at the (future) resurrection, just as Jesus gained His position of authority on the Father's throne only at His resurrection.

Commentators on these passages frequently attempt to keep such promises at arm's length. They seem to want to distance themselves from anything so "Jewish," even sometimes labeling these biblical texts "unchristian." Referring to Psalm 2 which speaks of the conquest of the world by the Messiah, one commentator wrote:

> Psalm 2 cannot be strictly regarded as referring to Jesus, partly because the establishment of the King upon the holy hill of Zion would have no relevance in His case; partly because the conception of His function as dashing His enemies in pieces is unchristian.[15]

The problem with this sort of reasoning is that it contradicts the teaching of the New Testament. Psalm 2 reappears in the book of Revelation describing the future coming of Christ to rule in the Kingdom. Paul also warned of a day of divine wrath on which

> the Lord Jesus will be revealed in flaming fire dealing out retribution to those who do not obey the Gospel of our Lord Jesus, and these will pay the penalty of destruction which excludes them from the Age to Come, away from the presence of the Lord and the glory of His power, when He comes to be glorified in all His saints on that Day (II Thess. 1:7-10).

Paul merely reiterates the message of Isaiah about the Day of the Lord at which men will "enter the rock and hide in the dust from the terror of the Lord and the splendor of His majesty...when He arises to make the earth tremble" (Isa. 2:10, 19). The shattering of unrepentant enemies of the Messiah is as much a New Testament doctrine as an Old Testament one. John the Baptist who preached exactly the same Message of the Kingdom of God warned the Pharisees to "flee from the wrath to come" (Luke 3:7). The burden of John's Gospel preaching was that the Messiah would one day "gather the wheat into His barn, but burn up the chaff with unquenchable fire" (Luke 3:17). Luke comments that with these tough words John "was preaching the Gospel to the people" (Luke 3:18). Matthew reports that both Jesus and John proclaimed the same Kingdom Message: "Repent for the Kingdom of Heaven [or God] is at hand" (Matt. 3:2; 4:17).

Another way of avoiding this uncomfortable material is to categorize it as belonging to a genre of literature known as "apocalyptic," as though classifying it might make it less offensive. The teaching of Jesus, set as it is within the framework of the book of

---

[15] *Dictionary of Christ and the Gospels*, Vol. II, p. 452.

Daniel, is indeed Christian apocalyptic. It includes, along with all its assurances of the grace and mercy of God, a description of a catastrophic divine intervention, introducing a new era and a new government on earth. The book of Revelation comes to us as the revelation granted to Christ by God (Rev. 1:1, 2). It is no less a reflection of the mind of Jesus than any other of His sayings recorded in the New Testament. If to some the promise to the followers of Jesus of "power over the nations" seems too political, it may be because the nature of the Kingdom of God has not been grasped. What is political is not therefore necessarily unspiritual. Deeply ingrained habits of thought have long caused us to think that things "spiritual" are divorced from real political structures functioning on earth. The Hebrew outlook which Jesus shared does not, however, operate in those dualistic terms. Nor, therefore, must we, if we wish to be in tune with the historical and risen Jesus.

Jesus had earlier spoken at the Last Supper of His intention to share rulership with His disciples in the Kingdom. He assured them of a place of honor as ministers of state in a new government. This, in fact, was the essential point of the New Covenant, reflecting a theme found also in the covenant mediated by Moses which was also centered on kingship in the Kingdom (Exod. 19:5, 6):

> You are the ones who have stood by Me in My trials; and just as My Father has *covenanted* a Kingdom to Me, I *covenant* with you the right to eat and drink with Me in My Kingdom, and you will sit on thrones, governing the twelve tribes of Israel (Luke 22:28-30).[16]

Precisely the same political reward had been promised to the Apostles on an earlier occasion, with a special note of the time when the Messianic government would come into power: "And Jesus said to them, 'Truly I say to you, that you who have followed Me, in the New World when the Son of Man will sit on His glorious throne, you also shall sit upon twelve thrones governing the twelve tribes of Israel'" (Matt. 19:28).[17]

---

[16] Michael Wilcock in *The Savior of the World, The Message of Luke's Gospel*, Intervarsity Press, 1979, p. 192 renders "appoint" as "covenant to give you." The noun "covenant" occurs in the immediate context (Luke 22:20).

[17] Job 14:14 (LXX) links the regeneration (*paligennesia*) with the resurrection of the dead. Job expects to "wait until he 'comes to be again'" (*palin genomai)*. This

Formidable barriers have been erected over the centuries against our grasping the fundamental concept presented to us by Jesus in His "Good News about the Kingdom of God." By removing the Kingdom from its biblical context, it has been possible to "reinterpret" it (a sophisticated way of abandoning the original meaning!) and replace it with our own more acceptable "kingdom in the hearts of men." Thus a new version of the Gospel of Jesus has replaced His original Message. Jesus' name has been added to our "good causes," while the Good News about the Kingdom, understood as Jesus meant it, has largely been discarded.

Opposition to the Messiah's Kingdom and the Book of Revelation

A major underlying cause of the traditional attempts to tone down "uncomfortable" aspects of Jesus' teaching is found in the attitude of some Christian commentary on the book of Revelation. It has been the habit of some to display a dislike of Jesus, the Christ, when they are confronted with the Savior's Messianic outlook. We can most easily illustrate this antipathy to the Messianic Kingdom (and thus to the Gospel of the Kingdom) by citing a school of thought which denies that the book of Revelation derives its inspiration from Jesus Christ. To scholars of this persuasion, the Revelation was written by one who:

> lives on the learned results of past ages. He has studied books and digested books. He has drawn his great eschatological [relating to the future] system from them...This very human wisdom he produces *as if it were God's word*, and he tries to conceal from himself his insight into the real origin of the book by making as loud assertions of its divine origin as possible...Thereby his work becomes a memorial of the decay of prophecy...The final act of the drama is described by him in two stages...First of all, after the battle of the Messiah, there is the thousand years' reign of Christ and the martyrs...This is indeed the official Jewish eschatology...We have here the most entire reversion conceivable to the old familiar national Jewish language. The Christian people takes the place of the Jewish, and takes over its contempt for the Gentiles...For such Christians the whole transformation which

---

is his response to his own question: "If a man dies, will he come to life again?" (Job 14:14.)

Jesus effected of the conception of the Kingdom of God has been in vain.[18]

So much for the Jesus of the book of Revelation! He is just an ignorant Jew. Unfortunately those who belong to this school, which represents an influential theological tradition, begin by misunderstanding Jesus and His Message of the Kingdom. They then accuse Jesus (in the Revelation) of contradicting their misconception! It appears that unbelief carries with it an inevitable penalty: "If you will not believe, neither shall you understand" (Isa. 7:9, LXX).

We cite further evidence of the fact that Jesus' Message in the book of Revelation, and thus His whole Messianic outlook, has been dismissed as unfit for modern believers:

> One book requires notice by reason of its peculiar character and of its influence on Christian eschatology [teaching about the future], namely the Revelation of John...Most of the visions contain *so little that is specifically Christian* [although given by Jesus Christ!] that it has been seriously questioned whether they were not appropriated entire from Jewish sources with only a superficial adaptation to Christian use. Whatever degree of literary originality may be allowed the author, the matter is Jewish throughout. The resurrection of the saints to enjoy the thousand-year reign of the Messiah; the war of Gog and Magog at the end of the millennium, and their destruction; the general resurrection and the last judgment; the new Jerusalem descending from heaven in all its glitter of gold, even to the river of life and the trees bearing monthly crops of new fruit and medicinal leaves, are the trite ideas and imagery of Jewish eschatology...with its corporeal resurrection and its millennial reign. [These were] brought over into the church, and found acceptance...*among ignorant Christians.* In the second century millenarian eschatology [belief that the saints will rule with Christ for a thousand years] was orthodoxy in Asia Minor and the wide regions which took their theology from that source; it is the faith of Irenaeus. It has survived through all the vicissitudes of theology, and over and over again, has broken out in epidemics of enthusiasm.[19]

---

[18] Paul Wernle, *The Beginnings of Christianity*, London: Williams and Norgate, 1903, Vol. I, pp. 364, 372-374, emphasis added.

[19] G.F. Moore, *History of Religions*, pp. 144, 145, emphasis added.

We may applaud this excellent summary of what the book of Revelation expects in the future, while marveling at the cavalier fashion in which the great truths of the New Testament are banished as non-Christian and Jesus' vision dismissed as "trite."

A little-known fact about the "founding fathers" of large sections of Protestant Christianity will help to explain why large sections of the Christian world have rejected the Messianic Gospel of Jesus:

> Luther at first (Preface to his Translation of the New Testament, 1522) expressed a strong aversion to the book [of Revelation], declaring that to him it had every mark of being neither prophetic nor apostolic...He cannot see that it was the work of the Holy Spirit. Moreover, he does not like the commands and threats which the writer makes about his book (22:18,19), and the promise of blessedness to those who keep what is written in it (1:3, 22:7), *when no one knows what that is*, to say nothing of keeping it, and there are many nobler books to be kept. Moreover, many Fathers rejected the book..."Finally everyone thinks of it whatever his spirit imparts. My spirit cannot adapt itself to this book, and a sufficient reason why I do not esteem it highly is that *Christ is neither taught nor recognized in it*, which is what an Apostle ought before all things to do."

> Later (1534) Luther finds a possibility of Christian usefulness in the book...but he still thought it a hidden, dumb prophecy unless interpreted, and upon the interpretation no certainty had been reached after many efforts...He remained doubtful about its apostolicity, and (in 1545) printed it with Hebrews, James and Jude as an appendix to his New Testament, not numbered in the index...Zwingli [a leading Reformer] regarded Revelation as "not a Biblical book," and even Calvin, with his high view of inspiration, does not comment on II and III John and Revelation.[20]

Readers should reflect on the remarkable fact that churches have continued to place considerable faith in the spiritual leadership of Calvin and Luther, despite the former's hesitancy about the Apocalypse (Calvin wrote no commentary on Revelation) and the

---

[20] *Hastings Dictionary of the Bible*, "Revelation," Vol. IV, p. 241, emphasis added.

latter's apparent failure to heed the warnings of Jesus given in the Revelation:

> I testify to everyone who hears the words of the prophecy of this book, if any one adds to these things, God will add to him the plagues written in the book; and if any one takes away from the words of the prophecy, God will take away his part out of the book of life, and out of the holy city, and from the things which are written in this book (Rev. 22:18, 19).

> Blessed is he who keeps the sayings of the prophecy of this book. Blessed is he who reads and they who hear the words of this prophecy and keep the things which are written in it: for the time is at hand (Rev. 1:3).

This hardly sounds as if the book could be safely relegated to an appendix!

The book of Revelation, as is well recognized, draws together the strands of Old Testament prophecy (it contains hundreds of allusions to and quotations from the Hebrew Bible) and describes the establishment of the Kingdom of God on earth at the Second Coming of Jesus. It is the fitting climax to the expectations of both Old and New Testament, depicting the triumph of the Kingdom of God over a hostile world.

The Kingdom of God announced by Jesus will finally come to power on earth when the seventh angel sounds. Paul had spoken of the same last trumpet signaling the resurrection of the dead (I Cor. 15:50-52).

> The kingdoms of this world have become the Kingdom of our Lord and of His Messiah; and He shall reign forever and ever...We give You thanks, O Lord God Almighty, who is, and was and is to come; because You have assumed power and have begun to reign. [Cp. Ps. 97:1 and 99:1, "The Lord has begun to reign."] And the nations were angry and Your wrath has come, and the time of the dead that they should be judged, and that You should give reward to Your servants the prophets, and to the saints, and to those who fear Your name, small and great; and should destroy those who destroy the earth (Rev. 11:15-18).

This is the Kingdom of God announced in the Gospel Message, and the Kingdom for which Christians are to pray, "Thy Kingdom come!" It is not widely recognized that in so praying, Christians anticipate the overthrow of human governments, in order that peace and harmony may prevail across the globe. One fact is unmistakably clear in the New Testament: the Kingdom of God will come only as a result of a divine intervention bringing to an end the "present evil age."

An Anti-Messianic Tendency

The rejection of the book of Revelation points to a deeply-rooted, anti-Messianic tendency in much traditional theology. When commentators assess the Revelation as unchristian, attempt to remove it from the canon of Scripture, or "reinterpret" it to avoid its "Jewish" millennial prophecy (the future thousand-year reign of Christ and the faithful), they display their distaste for the Jesus whose all-consuming concern was to bring peace to the earth and justice for all through His Kingdom.

The real Jesus never abandoned the prophets' hope for Messianic government on earth. Jesus knew, however, that the worldwide triumph of the Kingdom must await His Second Coming in glory. His miraculous activity in Palestine was indeed a demonstration of the power of the Kingdom in advance of its coming Thus in the New Testament the Day of the Lord is expected to arrive when Jesus returns "in flaming fire taking vengeance on those who do not know God" (II Thess. 1:8). Then the Kingdom would come; then the hopes of all the ages would reach fulfillment; then only could the agonized cry, "How long, O Lord?" find its answer. It is to this Messianic future that the New Testament strains in verse after verse. (Someone has calculated that the Second Coming is mentioned over 300 times in the New Testament. The number is much higher when synonyms for the return of Jesus are taken into account.) Once, however, the tension line between the believer and the bright future in the Kingdom is slackened, the vitality and excitement of the faith can be lost, and the point of discipleship destroyed. At present, churchgoers often lack that essential drive to reach the promised Kingdom. They have not been told what that Kingdom is. So many of their mentors seem to have an unclear view of the Christian future. There is a blank in their conception of what the future holds for the believer, needing to be filled with all the riches of the biblical hope for the reign of Christ on earth.

It is impossible to exaggerate the importance of the prophetic vision of the future. One writer on the message of the prophets gathered the material relating to the coming Kingdom in a book which he entitled *The Hebrew Utopia*, which he described as follows:

> No words can describe the glory and the beauty, the grand perfection and the sweet comfort, of that marvelous age of which prophet after prophet came forward to utter some fresh prediction. Plato's model Republic and Sir Thomas More's Utopia are cheerless and uninviting beside this ravishing dream of the future...portrayed often as hovering just beyond their horizon, but always as certain to be enjoyed in this weary world at the fitting time.[21]

A Future with No Substance

The prospect of the coming reign of Christ and the faithful on earth is part and parcel of the Gospel Message, inextricably linked with the sacrificial death of Jesus and His resurrection (Acts 8:12; 19:8; 28:23, 31). Tragically some have disparaged the hope of the coming Kingdom by treating it as disposable, a relic of a primitive mentality which we, with our vastly superior scientific outlook, are unable to embrace. This places the Christian doctrine of the Kingdom under a fog. The Christian future is reduced to a meaningless non-event, rather than a stupendous climax in history for which all are commanded to prepare. The fact that not everyone will survive until the coming of Jesus in power is no excuse for neglecting the teaching about the Messiah's return. The date of that return is known to no one. Those believers who have died before the end of the age will take part in the glory of the Kingdom through resurrection (I Thess. 4:13; I Cor. 15:23; Rev. 11:15-18).

The following inquiry was addressed to a representative of the clergy in a Presbyterian magazine. The response illustrates the unwillingness of some to take seriously the reality of Jesus' warnings about the future:

---

[21] W.F. Adeney, *The Hebrew Utopia*, London: Hodder and Stoughton, 1879, p. 328.

Q. Why are there so few sermons in our churches on the Second Coming? Is this part of our belief or not?

A. Not all Christians think alike on matters of theology, but it would be hard for someone to feel at home in our tradition, who did not understand God as the One who has come, who is present (Christ is risen) and who is yet to come in whatever form the future winds up taking. To literalize the Second Coming is to ruin both its beauty and its significance. To ignore it is to avoid what may be the most important part of the Gospel we know about since the past and the present, relatively speaking, are brief, while tomorrow borders on the forever.

An appropriate reaction to this answer appeared in a later issue of the magazine:

I compliment the Rev._____ for his illusive non-answer to what I am sure was a serious question concerning the Second Coming of Jesus Christ. If I understand his answer, he said, in effect, "We don't all agree. But if you want to be comfortable in our fellowship, you will need to agree that Jesus is coming again, but not really — for if you actually believe in the Second Coming you will ruin both its beauty and its significance. Yet you can't ignore it because it is in the future." Why not a simple answer? Why not admit that those who cannot receive the Bible literally must spiritualize the Second Coming because it is too large a segment of the New Testament to be ignored?[22]

This approach to the New Testament doctrine about the future is not untypical of much of what has gone under the name of Christian teaching over many centuries. It has been hard for many to detect the trick being played with words, when an outright rejection of the biblical doctrine of the Kingdom is veiled by impressive "theological" language. What much traditional theology has done to the Second Coming should not be graced with the term "spiritualize." It has neutralized and evaporated the return of Christ. The whole vision of the prophets and the whole Gospel of the Kingdom is in jeopardy if its dominant future element is removed. Even the Gospel proposed by

---

[22] Cited from *The United Presbyterian AD* (Oct. and Dec. 1981) in J.C. Beker, *Paul's Apocalyptic Gospel*, pp. 12, 13.

many evangelicals suffers from the same absence of any future reference in the Message.

Definitions of the Gospel

A definition of the Gospel was offered by the Lausanne Conference on Evangelism in 1974. It speaks of the forgiveness of sins through the death of Jesus, of His resurrection and of His present reign in heaven. It says nothing, however, about the Kingdom of God as the goal of the Christian believer. The future dimension of salvation, so prominent in the New Testament, is absent. This absence of the Kingdom appears to cut the Gospel Message in half, stripping it of its strong emphasis on God's Plan to send His Son back to the earth to reign with His followers in the Messianic government promised by the prophets:

> To evangelize is to spread the good news that Jesus Christ died for our sins, and was raised from the dead according to the Scriptures, and that as reigning Lord he now offers the forgiveness of sins and the liberating gift of the spirit to all who repent and believe.[23]

This definition lacks the central future "Kingdom component" characteristic of the Bible. We propose that the statement might be amended as follows:

> To evangelize is to spread the Good News that God has planned as the goal of history and for the reassertion of His sovereignty on earth to establish the Kingdom of God when Jesus returns; that Jesus now offers forgiveness and new life through His death and resurrection to all those who repent and believe the Message (Mark 1:14, 15), the promise of the Spirit to those who obey Him (Acts 5:32), and an invitation to all who respond to the Good News of the Kingdom and the name of Jesus Christ (Acts 8:12) to prepare for positions of responsibility with Jesus in the coming Kingdom.

A Suppression of Information

There is a marked absence of the phrase "Kingdom of God" in places where we would most expect it to be found. A prominent

---

[23] *The Lausanne Covenant*, International Congress on World Evangelization, Lausanne, Switzerland, July, 1974.

leader of the ecumenical movement, who served as Associate General Secretary of the World Council of Churches, observes that

> the Kingdom of God was the central theme of the preaching of Jesus as we find it in the New Testament...And yet *it cannot be said that it has been the central theme in the great classical traditions of Christendom.* It is not mentioned in the Apostles' Creed. The Nicene Creed says of Christ that "His kingdom shall have no end," but does not use the phrase Kingdom of God. The main traditions stemming from the Reformation have spoken of "preaching the gospel," or "preaching Christ," but *seldom of "preaching the Kingdom."*[24]

A recent tract issued by the Billy Graham Evangelistic Association bears the title, "What is the Gospel?" The writer makes no reference to the "Gospel of the Kingdom," but tells us that the Gospel is "the Gospel of God," "the Gospel of Christ," "the Gospel of our Salvation," and "the Gospel of Peace." Mention is made also of the phrase "Gospel of the grace of God" (Acts 20:24) but, amazingly, the illuminating, explanatory phrase which occurs in the very next verse is entirely omitted. Paul here defines the "Gospel of the grace of God" as "the proclamation of the Kingdom" (Acts 20:25).

A pattern of presenting "the Gospel" with texts only from Romans and John (with the addition of some other references to Paul's letters) can be seen in scores of tracts offering "salvation." The widely-used "Four Spiritual Laws" counsels its readers to "begin with John,"[25] and makes no reference to the Gospel about the Kingdom.

The *International Standard Bible Dictionary* discusses the term "Gospel," and explains that it refers to the Message which Christ and His Apostles announced. The Gospel is the instrument through which the Holy Spirit works. It then points out that

> in some places it is called "the gospel of God" (Mark 1:14; Rom. 1:1; I Thess. 2:2, 9; I Tim. 1:11). In others it is called "the gospel of

---

[24] Leslie Newbigin, *Sign of the Kingdom*, Grand Rapids: Eerdmans, 1981, p. vii, emphasis added.

[25] *Have You Heard of the Four Spiritual Laws?* Campus Crusade for Christ, 1965, p. 14. More than 1,000,000,000 copies are in print. R.A. Torrey's *How to Witness to Anyone* (Whitaker House, 1986) contains no references to the Kingdom of God.

Christ" (Mark 1:1; Rom 1:16; 15:19; I Cor. 9:12,18; Gal. 1:7). In another it is called "the gospel of the grace of God" (Acts 20:24); in another "the gospel of peace" (Eph. 6:15); "the gospel of your salvation" (Eph. 1:13); and yet another "the glorious gospel" (II Cor. 4:4, AV).[26]

Despite the fact that the Gospel is directly connected to the term Kingdom, as "the Good News of the Kingdom of God," in some twenty places in Matthew, Mark and Luke, as well as by implication in scores of verses throughout the New Testament where the word "Gospel" or "Message" ("Word") appears, the dictionary omits entirely to tell us of the phrase "Gospel of the Kingdom." This extraordinary silence about the Kingdom of God is characteristic of so much that is known as Christian evangelism.

It is reasonable to ask why the Kingdom of God features so little in modern evangelism. The answer is to be found in a long-standing de-emphasis on the Gospels of Matthew, Mark and Luke, dating from Calvin and Luther. An unconscious offense at the Messianic Jewish Jesus caused these two Protestant leaders to express a curious preference for the Gospel of John over the other three Gospels. Luther, writing the preface to his translation of the New Testament (1522), stated: "John's Gospel is the only Gospel which is delicately sensitive to what is the essence of the Gospel, and is to be widely preferred to the other three and placed on a higher level."[27] He was followed by Calvin in this opinion. Calvin even ventured to suggest a different order for Matthew, Mark, Luke and John, making John the ideal introduction to his three fellow reporters of the life of Jesus:

> The doctrine which points out to us the power and the benefit of the coming Christ, is far more clearly exhibited by John than by the [synoptists]. The three former [synoptic Gospels] exhibit [Christ's] body...but John exhibits his soul. On this account I am accustomed to say that this Gospel is a key to open the door for understanding the rest...In reading [the four Gospels] a different order would be advantageous, which is, that when we wish to read in Matthew and

---

[26] *The International Standard Bible Encyclopedia*, Eerdmans, 1939, reprinted 1983, p. 1281.

[27] Cited by D. Fuller, *Gospel and Law: Contrast or Continuum*, Grand Rapids: Eerdmans, 1980, p. 160.

others that Christ was given to us by the Father, we should first learn from John the purpose for which he was manifested.[28]

Christians should awake to the fact that their various traditional systems, claiming to be based on Scripture, have not served them well. Scripture nowhere says that John's Gospel is to be preferred over Matthew, Mark and Luke. Nor does it teach that Jesus preached a Jewish Message up to the cross; whereupon Paul then took a Message of grace to the Gentiles. The New Scofield Bible, read by millions, says that a "strong legal and Jewish coloring is to be expected up to the cross."[29]

We are at the crux of the problem which this book seeks to address. A false distinction and division is being created by the so-called "dispensationalist" school. The teachings of Jesus do not remain at the center of the scheme of salvation proposed by dispensationalists. John Walvoord says that the Sermon on the Mount:

> treats not of salvation, but of the character and conduct of those who belong to Christ...That it is suitable to point an unbeliever to salvation in Christ is plainly not the intention of this message...The Sermon on the Mount, as a whole, is not church truth precisely...It is not intended to delineate justification by faith or the gospel of salvation.[30]

Rather ambiguously he adds that it should not be relegated to "unimportant truth."[31]

The words of Jesus in the Sermon on the Mount could hardly express more clearly that obedience to His teachings are in fact the basis of salvation: "Unless your righteousness exceeds the righteousness of the scribes and Pharisees you will not enter the Kingdom of Heaven [i.e., be saved]" (Matt. 5:20). "Not everyone who says to Me, 'Lord, Lord,' will enter the Kingdom of Heaven but he who does the will of My Father..." (Matt. 7:21). Jesus goes on to say that those who fail to gain salvation are those who fail to obey His

---

[28] Foreword to Calvin's commentary on John.

[29] *New Scofield Bible*, p. 987. The fact is that the whole New Testament faith is Jewish in character and consistently makes strong demands for obedience.

[30] *Matthew: Thy Kingdom Come*, Moody Press, 1984, pp. 44, 45.

[31] *Ibid.*, p. 45.

words (Matt. 7:24-27).[32] And this is, in the words of Walvoord, "not church truth precisely"?

Until churches renounce the disparagement of the teaching of Jesus implied in their various systems, we cannot hope for unity. We must rally around the great central theme of the Gospel of the Kingdom, which expresses the genius of the Christian faith and brings us close to the heart of Jesus. L.S. Chafer's distinction drawn between what some label the "legal" teachings of Jesus and the grace Message of Paul seems to us to be entirely mistaken:

> Under the conditions laid down in the kingdom teachings, life is entered into by a personal faithfulness (Matt. 5:28-29; 18:8)...[Luke 13:24] opens with the words, "Strive to enter in at the narrow gate." The word *strive* is a translation of *agonidzomai*, which means "agonize." It suggests the uttermost expenditure of the athlete's strength in the contest. Such is the human condition that characterizes all the kingdom passages which offer entrance into life. [But] an abrupt change is met after turning to the Gospel of John, which was written to announce the new message of grace, which is, that eternal life may be had through believing. No two words of Scripture more vividly express the great characterizing relationship in law and grace than agonize and believe. Grace is the unfolding of the fact that One has agonized in our stead, and life is "through His Name," not by any degree of human faithfulness and merit.[33]

While dispensationalism upholds the authority and integrity of Scripture it proceeds to divide the Apostles against each other, making John and Paul rivals of Jesus. It makes the Kingdom Gospel of Jesus, by which salvation is to be sought,[34] of historical interest only, since the Message was changed, according to the theory, at the cross. It is simply not true that believing is a new idea in the Gospel of John and in Paul. Believing the Gospel of the Kingdom of God is the platform of Jesus' presentation of the saving Message in Matthew, Mark, Luke and John (John refers constantly to the "Word" and "words" of Jesus), and Paul likewise traces all sound faith to belief in the "Message of Messiah" (Rom. 10:17).

---

[32] Cp. John 3:36; 8:51; 12:44-50.

[33] *Systematic Theology*, Dallas Seminary Press, 1947-48, Vol. IV, p. 224.

[34] Mark 1:14, 15; Matt. 13:19; Luke 8:12; Acts 8:12; 19:8; 28:23, 31.

Christ and the Land

We have suggested that Jesus was in the best Jewish tradition when He promised the meek that they would have the land as their inheritance. Matthew 5:5 is one of many indications that Jesus has not abandoned the Hebrew Bible. There is no good reason for attaching to the term "land" a meaning other than Palestine renewed and refreshed under the Messiah's government.[35] Jesus has not ceased to expect a divine empire in a renovated earth, as Psalm 37:11 and the whole of Israel's prophetic tradition had hoped for. As W.C. Allen wrote:

> It seems best to suppose that this clause ["the meek shall inherit the earth"] should be understood literally...The earth purified from sin and purged of the ungodly, who now oppress the "poor" and meek godly people, will then be extensive with the Kingdom.[36]

Thus the Kingdom is correctly defined as the future earth renewed under the Messiah's government. Clayton Sullivan, in a perceptive study of the Kingdom and the confusion over its meaning because of theologians' persistent attempts to make it a timeless idea, writes:

> That Jesus conceived of the Kingdom as a realm — compatible to a territory or to a city — becomes obvious when attention is given to *all* synoptic data (not just to selected, slanted data from Mark and Q). This insight is significant; it is contrary to Professor Dodd's conception of the Kingdom (*basileia*) as a curative power operative in Jesus' exorcisms.[37]

Sullivan shows that the Kingdom of God is "a realm or place," "a place of eating and drinking," "a place with stations of honor," "a place with different ranks," "a place to be entered bodily and seen with the eye."[38] John's Gospel confirms the expectation that Jesus is

---

[35] Was it a dislike of the Jewishness of Matt. 5:5 which unconsciously prompted the translators of the Good News Bible to substitute for "land," "what God has promised" — surely a classic case of preferring vagueness over clear-cut definition.

[36] *The International Critical Commentary, Matthew*, Edinburgh: T&T Clark, 1907, p. 42.

[37] Clayton Sullivan, *Rethinking Realized Eschatology*, Mercer University Press, 1988, p. 37. Sullivan charges Dodd with using "slippery language," defining the Kingdom in about 28 different ways (pp. 45, 46) and approaching the texts of the New Testament with a Platonic frame of reference (pp. 43, 44).

[38] *Ibid.,* pp. 48-54.

heir of Palestine renewed. "He came to His own country, and His own people did not receive Him" (John 1:11).[39]

At present many commentators seem most unwilling to yield to the plain testimony of Jesus' expectation for the land. It is clear to all that Jesus did not during His historical ministry take any steps to assume governorship over any territory whatever. Nevertheless He claimed to be the Messiah, a word with the strongest possible political implications. It is to be expected, then, that He will yet carry out the program of world rescue for which the Second Adam is destined, by returning to reign on earth.

No one should mistake the point of view of this book for the prevalent idea among some Bible students that the Jewish people of today have rights to the land as non-believers in the Messiah Jesus. The promises made to Abraham are reserved for believers in Jesus as the Christ.[40] Evangelical writers are right to point out that

> The [present] nation of Israel is a nation among nations, and...it must be judged as any other political state. But to identify modern Israel, the state or the Jewish people, with the "Israel of God" is to miss the teaching of the New Testament at one of its most vital points.[41]

The biblical point of view is that no one has a right to the blessings of Abraham outside the covenant in Christ. This is a central conviction of the New Testament writers. There is no evidence in the New Testament, however, that the promise of the land and the world has been scrapped in favor of "heaven." Jesus' contemporaries knew what the prophets had said and reflected this conviction, for example, in the Psalms of Solomon written only a half century before the birth of Jesus: "And He shall gather a holy people...and He shall divide

---

[39] "Canaan is the Holy Land and Jehovah's own inheritance; and the Messiah...'came to His own country, and His own people received Him not'" ("Inheritance," *Hastings Dictionary of the Bible*, single vol., T & T Clark, 1958, p. 383). The NASV has "domain" in the margin.

[40] Matt. 16:16-18; John 20:31; I John 2:22; I John 5:1, etc.

[41] Frank Stagg, "The Israel of God in the New Testament," in *Christians, Zionism and Palestine*, Beirut: Institute for Palestine Studies, 1970, pp. 65-66, cited by G.M. Burge in *Who Are God's People in the Middle East?* Zondervan, 1993, p. 127.

them according to their tribes *upon the land* and neither sojourner nor alien shall sojourn with them any more" (Ps. Sol. 17:26, 28).

In the same vein the "Eighteen Benedictions" looked forward to the time when God would

> be merciful...towards Israel Thy people, and towards Jerusalem Thy city, and towards Zion, the abiding place of Thy glory, and towards Thy temple and habitation, and towards the Kingdom of the house of David, Thy righteous anointed one. Blessed art Thou, O Lord God of David, the builder of Jerusalem (Benediction 14).

Nothing in the teaching of Jesus, nor the destruction of Jerusalem in AD 70, renders these hopes obsolete. The New Testament expects their fulfillment at the return of the Messiah. As we have seen the territorial expectation is alive in the believers known to Luke, who rejoiced in salvation for Jerusalem (Luke 2:25, 38; 24:21; Acts 1:6). The land is the object of Jesus' future reward in Matthew 5:5. He speaks with His Jewish compatriots of a regathering of the tribes, of assigning the Apostles rulership over them and of people of all nations coming "from the east and west" to participate in the banquet marking the inauguration of the Kingdom (Matt. 8:11). Future salvation focuses on the earth. That is the whole point of Jesus coming back.

Jesus' promise that the meek will inherit the land is an explicit statement that the land promise is alive and well in Messiah's thinking. In fact He equates the Kingdom with the land.[42] In His beatitudes He can equally well say: "Blessed are the poor in spirit for theirs is the Kingdom of Heaven" (Matt. 5:3) or "Blessed are the gentle for they will inherit the land/earth" (Matt. 5:5). Christians, therefore, should think of the renewal of the land every time they encounter the word Kingdom. For a reorganized society under Messiah's government the Lord urges us to pray, "Thy Kingdom come."

I am puzzled by the assertion of G.M. Burge in his interesting book, *Who Are God's People in the Middle East?* that "the New Testament never refers to the land promises of Abraham directly" and that "Jesus fails to mention the land in any significant way. The land

---

[42] W.D. Davies speaks of "Matthew's collocation [i.e., placing together as equivalents] of entering the Kingdom and inheriting the land" (*The Gospel and the Land*, p. 361).

and the city of Jerusalem are not featured in His teachings."[43] Burge does not discuss Matthew 5:5 in his chapter on "The New Testament and the Land."

Since Jesus upheld the Hebrew Bible, it is clear that He cannot have come to abolish the promise made to Abraham and the faithful. New Testament writers mean all the promises made to Abraham, including the land, when they refer to the "promise," "covenant," or "inheritance." These terms are shorthand expressions not needing to be given in full, in the same way that Americans understand what is meant by "the States," as an abbreviation for "the United States of America." "The Message" in the New Testament is itself a compressed label for "the Message of the Kingdom and the name of Jesus" (Luke 4:43; 5:1; Acts 8:4, 5, 12). Paul speaks of the promises made to Abraham, specifying the promise that "he would inherit the world" (Rom. 4:13). Jesus taught parables about the vineyard, a term which His audience would recognize as another word for the land. The book of Hebrews describes the Christian future as gaining "the coming inhabited earth" (Heb. 2:5).[44] The promise of the risen Christ dwelling in believers does not make inheritance of the world/land/earth redundant.

Again, I cannot follow Gary Burge's contention that Hebrews 11 redefines the land to mean something other than a place on this planet.[45] We are not arguing, of course, that the land *in its present condition* as the home of unbelievers is the promised land of the future. Nevertheless Hebrews 11:9 expressly says that Abraham resided as a foreigner in the promised land. Canaan is not a metaphor for a place removed from the earth. Abraham must yet return to the land guaranteed to him, in which he lived but which he never inherited. The "heavenly land" (Heb. 11:16) is not a land *in* heaven any more than the Kingdom of God is a kingdom *in* heaven. Attention needs to be paid to the danger of reading traditional notions about the afterlife into the text of Scripture: "The circumlocution [Kingdom of Heaven] is unfortunate because it misleads people into thinking that

---

[43] *Who Are God's People in the Middle East?* pp. 128, 130.

[44] Paul was looking forward to the divine Kingdom on earth when he spoke of the "heavenly" Kingdom and the crown which he would receive "on that [future] day" (II Tim. 4:8, 18).

[45] *Who Are God's People in the Middle East?* p. 136.

the Kingdom is only in heaven and not to be on the earth (Matt. 6:10)."[46]

Since the word "land" means also "earth," "heaven" as the goal of the believer is a term most likely to confuse the biblical hope. But Jesus never promised "heaven" to His disciples. So says an expert who devoted a book to investigating *Jesus and the Future Life,*[47] and the point may be examined by Christians using a concordance:

> In few, if any, instances of the use of the word "heaven" in the synoptic gospels is there any parallel with modern usage. The gospel records of our Lord's life and teaching do not speak of "going to heaven," as a modern believer so naturally does. Rather is the emphasis on that which is "heavenly" coming down to man, when any movement is thought of. Again, our modern way of speaking of life with God as being life "in heaven," is not the way the gospels speak of the matter. Especially is there *no suggestion that Jesus is offering to His disciples the certainty of "heaven" after this life.* This is not to say that there is no such assurance in the teaching of Jesus...But *certainly the term "heaven" is not used of that assurance.*[48]

It seems most strange, then, that "heaven" is today the normal Christian expression for the afterlife, although Jesus had nothing to say about "heaven" as the Christian objective. The difference illustrated by the loss of biblical language in a matter as central as the Christian hope points to a deep-seated problem needing to be addressed by those seeking to follow Jesus and His teaching.

W.D. Davies and the Land

If "heaven" has been substituted by the Church for "Kingdom of God," a loss of the land promise, and thus of a major element in the covenant made with the fathers, has been almost inevitable. When W.D. Davies produced his magnificent study of *The Gospel and the Land,*[49] he was unable to explain Jesus' obvious commitment to the

---

[46] *The New Jerome Biblical Commentary*, Prentice Hall, 1990, p. 639.

[47] William Strawson.

[48] *Jesus and the Future Life*, p. 38, emphasis added.

[49] University of California Press, 1974.

Hebrew promise of Psalm 37:11.[50] He seems most uneasy with the idea that Jesus could have shared the "concrete" view of the future of the world held by fellow Jews. He discusses the possibility that Matthew "created the interpretative beatitude we now have in 5:5. If Spiecq be followed, there can...be no question of 5:5 going back to Jesus...It is at least dubious whether Jesus uttered 5:5...It is difficult not to disengage the verse, in its Matthean context, from the territorial promise of the Old Testament and Judaism."[51] But the argument is circular, and falls into the trap of dividing the local and territorial from the universal and spiritual. Davies says: "It has become widely customary...to spiritualize the possession of the land, so that 'to inherit the land' becomes a symbol for inheriting conditions under the Rule of God in a spiritual sense."[52] He feels himself bound to "divorce Matthew 5:5 from its meaning in Psalm 37:11. Certainly the 'inheritance' of Christians in other parts of the New Testament is supra-terrestrial."[53] But why should we think of separating Jesus from the Hebrew texts in which He was steeped? We are bound to think that "theology" is dictating exegesis and in such a way as to dejudaize and demessianize the Savior and lift Him out of His Jewish matrix. This is the Church's ongoing tragedy. The failure to see Matthew 5:5 as the confirmation of the prophecy of Psalm 37:11, understood as the Psalm intended, symbolizes the Church's persistent tendency to uproot Jesus from His Hebrew environment.

The Awkward Evidence of Acts 1:6

G.M. Burge follows the tradition which is unwilling to believe that the Apostles might have been well-instructed Christians when they ask about the restoration of the Kingdom to Israel.[54] It seems to us unsatisfactory in the extreme to set Jesus in opposition to the thinking of the Apostles, on the eve of their world mission, when He had personally discipled them so extensively, especially on the critical issue of the Kingdom. Burge says, "The disciples' minds were on

---

[50] *The Theological Dictionary of the New Testament* states that Ps. 37:11 promises the meek "Palestine perfected in the Messianic glory" (Vol. 1, p. 677).

[51] *The Gospel and the Land*, p. 361.

[52] *Ibid.*

[53] *Ibid.*, p. 362.

[54] *Who Are God's People in the Middle East?* p. 131.

political restoration [in Acts 1:6], but for Jesus, God's Kingdom was fundamentally God's reign over the lives of men and women — not an empire."[55] But what if the Messianic Kingdom begins by capturing the hearts and minds of the believers, becoming a living power in their lives, and ends with the establishment of a restored Davidic theocracy on earth in the hands of the Son of Man and the saints? Such an ideal would prompt the highest ethical effort in preparation for worldwide service with the Messiah at His return. The hoped-for Kingdom is *both* an ideal in the heart *and* also a real government in Jerusalem dependent upon the return of the Christ. There is nothing unspiritual about Messiah ruling the world with the saints in Jerusalem.

The Church seems to have abandoned hope for the restoration of the earth and the land. In an article entitled "Christianity: Judaism Internationalized,"[56] John McRay observes:

> Paul argues in Galatians 3:16 that the use of the singular shows that Christ, not the Israelites in general, was the object of the promise. This argument is indeed strange from both the Christian and Jewish perspectives, *since neither Abraham nor Christ inherited the land.*[57]

The same loss of confidence in the divine promise is expressed by the writer of the article on Christianity in the *Encyclopedia of Religion and Ethics:*[58] "The apocalyptic hope has not found a literal fulfillment and there is no likelihood that it ever will."

It is our conviction that the Gospel is the answer to that very enigma. The Bible is pledged to the faithfulness of God to His promises to Abraham in Christ. The resurrection has as its primary purpose, not only the conferring of immortality, but the granting of the long-awaited land and Kingdom to the people of God. The territorial promise in its fullest extent awaits fulfillment at the return of Christ to rule. That is the Bible's story and the point of glory to which it strains from cover to cover. The paradox is that neither Jew nor orthodox Christian sees how the story ends. The Jew still hopes to gain the land, apart from Christ (hence the ongoing struggle in the Middle East). That cannot be, because in God's Plan the holy land must be peopled

---

[55] *Ibid.*

[56] *Restoration Quarterly* (32), 1990, No. 1, p. 6.

[57] Emphasis added.

[58] Edinburgh: T & T Clark, 1910, Vol. 3, p. 585.

by holy inhabitants, and this is possible only in Christ. The Christian hopes to avoid the land by going to heaven. Neither position is apostolic. Both point to a defection from the Christian Messianism of the New Testament.

Restoring the Gospel Terminology of the Early Church

A valuable step towards clearing up confusion over the Kingdom of God would be taken if Christians adopted the Bible's primary Gospel language. In Acts 8 Luke uses several parallel phrases to describe the evangelistic activity of the Church. They were "preaching the Message as Good News" (literally, "evangelizing the Word," Acts 8:4). Philip "proclaimed the Christ to them" (Acts 8:5). Samaria thus "received the Message of God" (Acts 8:14). After "they had testified and spoken the Message of the Lord, they returned to Jerusalem, preaching the Gospel to many villages of the Samaritans" (Acts 8:25). At the center of this account, however, Luke provides the most comprehensive description of the content of the saving Message. With a carefully worded formula, he lets us know exactly what "proclaiming the Christ" or "proclaiming the Message" or "preaching the Gospel" mean. It is "preaching the Gospel of [i.e., about — Gr. *peri*] the Kingdom of God and the name of Jesus Christ" (Acts 8:12). This is Luke's fullest summary of the Gospel. He repeats it at two other critically important points in his narrative.[59] It defines his other "shorthand" statements, appearing in his Gospel as well as in Acts, and ought to serve as a rallying point for all proclamations of the Gospel. Quite extraordinarily, these texts receive almost no mention in literature defining the Gospel. If they were taken seriously, current "gospels" would be exposed as lacking a primary biblical element. The all-important fact would emerge that the Apostles were no less insistent upon the Kingdom of God as the center of their Message than Jesus had been. They were following their Master faithfully. But can the same be said of evangelism in the twentieth century? "The Gospel of Christ" is an ambiguous phrase in the 20th century, though not in its New Testament context where it is assumed to be a synonym for the Gospel of the Kingdom. Contemporary evangelism chooses the

---

[59] Acts 28:23, 31, linking it directly to Jesus' proclamation in Luke 4:43.

ambiguous label for the Gospel and dispenses with its clear title as the Message about the Kingdom.

A very misleading idea has become ingrained in much contemporary evangelism. The idea has been widely accepted that the Kingdom of God was not the main emphasis of Paul's preaching, though it was the leading topic in Jesus' evangelism. One has only to read Acts 20:25 to learn what Luke constantly tells us about Paul's Gospel: that it was a "proclamation of the Kingdom of God." It is puzzling that such an obvious clue to the mind of Paul should have been so neglected. Not only does the centrality of the Kingdom in Paul's Message appear frequently in Luke's accounts of Paul's evangelism, it is found indirectly throughout his own writings. He reminded the Thessalonians that they had received "the Word" (Luke's synonym for the Gospel of the Kingdom, Luke 4:43; 5:1) and in so doing were expressing their faith in God as they "waited for His Son from heaven whom He raised from heaven, that is Jesus who delivers us from the wrath to come" (I Thess. 1:10). (The theme of the return of Christ and the wrath associated with the coming of the future Kingdom are exactly John the Baptist's and Jesus' Gospel themes.) Paul then refers to his proclamation as the Gospel of God (I Thess. 2:2, 8, 9), which is precisely the phrase used by Mark to denote Jesus' preaching of the Gospel about the Kingdom (Mark 1:14, 15). Almost in the same breath Paul exhorts his converts to "walk worthy of the God who is inviting you into *His own Kingdom and glory*." It is clear that the Gospel of the Kingdom is at the center of Paul's thought, exactly as Luke reports that the Kingdom was always the heart of Paul's Gospel (Acts 19:8; 20:25; 28:23, 31). Moreover he goes on to tell the Thessalonians that this "Word," or "Word of God," both synonyms for the Gospel of the Kingdom, was "performing its work" in the believers. The concept is exactly that of Jesus who spoke of the essential saving "Message of the Kingdom" taking root in the heart of the believer as the life-giving seed able to produce fruit (Matt. 13:19, 23).

Another evidence of the Gospel of the Kingdom throughout the New Testament is provided by the term "glory" which is closely related to Kingdom. Matthew recalls that the mother of James and John requested for her sons close association with the Messiah in the administration of the coming Kingdom (Matt. 20:20, 21). Mark reports the same event but substitutes the word glory for Kingdom: "Grant that we may sit in Your *glory*, one on the right and the other on the left" (Mark 10:37). Thus when Mark speaks of the Son of Man coming in the glory of His Father (Mark 8:38) there is an immediate reference to the Kingdom of God (Mark 9:1). The whole discussion is closely related to Jesus' words about losing one's life for the sake of Jesus and *the Gospel* (Mark 8:35). When Paul speaks of future glory he always has the Kingdom in mind. In Romans 8 he recognizes that Christians are "heirs with Christ" and goes on to say that "the sufferings of this present time are not to be compared with the *glory* that is to be revealed for us" (Rom. 8:17, 18).[60] Just as Joseph of Arimathea, a Christian disciple, was waiting for the Kingdom of God, so Paul sees the creation as "waiting for the revealing of the Sons of God," a Messianic title (Rom. 8:19). He takes up exactly the same theme when he summarizes the faith: "If we suffer with Him we shall also be kings [i.e., in the Kingdom] with Him" (II Tim. 2:12). "Salvation," "inheritance of the Kingdom of God," inheritance of "life" or "life in the coming age," "ruling with the Messiah as kings" and "glory" are all interchangeable ways of describing the same goal of the Kingdom. Paul may sometimes have chosen politically less explosive words like "glory" and "salvation," rather than Kingdom. Such "code words" were clear to his readers. Provided Paul's synonyms for Kingdom are detected, there is every reason to find in his epistles complete confirmation of his claim to have been a preacher of the Kingdom of God, faithfully speaking for the risen Christ whose Message of the Kingdom was continued in the Apostles' ministries.

Without an understanding of the phrase "Gospel of the Kingdom," it is hard to see how there can be intelligent response to Jesus' first command. We are asked to "repent and *believe the Good News about the Kingdom of God*" (Mark 1:14, 15). That is the essence of faith. All subsequent preaching in the New Testament should be referred to this basic thesis statement about the Gospel of salvation. Cut loose from Jesus' appeal for belief in the Gospel of the Kingdom, preaching exposes itself to the menace of a distorted and thus "another gospel." That such a distortion has occurred will not be hard to see. One has

---

[60] Christians are rejoicing in the hope of glory, i.e. the Kingdom (Rom. 5:2).

only to listen to preachers of "the Gospel" to recognize that whatever else they may preach, there is precious little mention of the Kingdom of God. This can only mean that the principal element of Jesus' proclamation has been silenced. Such a "muzzling" of the Savior, in the name of the Savior, remains the baffling and disturbing feature of contemporary preaching and of the history of the Church from the earliest centuries.

The Kingdom of God in Relation to the Death and Resurrection of Jesus

The urgent demand by Jesus to "repent and believe the Good News of the Kingdom" (surely an excellent place for Gospel preaching to begin) implies an understanding of the term "Kingdom of God." While Jesus' leading phrase remains unclear, the Gospel itself is obscured. Perhaps it is this uncertainty over the meaning of Jesus' proclamation about the Kingdom that has caused evangelicals to drop all reference to the Kingdom of God in their definition of the Gospel, and to rely on what they think is a full account of the saving Message: the death, burial and resurrection of Jesus. It is customary to appeal to Paul's words in I Corinthians 15:1-11:

> Now I make known to you, brethren, the Gospel which I preached to you, which also you received, in which also you stand, by which also you are being saved, if you hold fast the message which I preached to you, unless you believed in vain. For I delivered to you as of first importance [literally "among the first," NASV margin] what I also received, that Christ died for our sins, according to the Scriptures, and that He was buried, and that He was raised on the third day according to the Scriptures, and that He appeared to Cephas and then to the twelve...Whether then it was I or they, so we preached and so you believed.

An important key to understanding Paul's fine statement about his own Gospel Message is found in the little phrase *"en protois,"* "amongst things of primary importance" (I Cor. 15:3). The point at issue in the Corinthian letter was the resurrection of Jesus which some of the Corinthians were beginning to doubt — "How do some among you say there is no resurrection of the dead?" (I Cor. 15:12). In response to this particular crisis of belief, Paul reminds his audience that the death and resurrection of Jesus are of absolutely fundamental significance in the Christian Gospel. Without the death of Jesus to gain forgiveness for all of us, and without His return from death to life through resurrection, there can be no hope of salvation in the coming Kingdom. The Gospel of the Kingdom is nullified if in fact Jesus has not been raised from the dead.

It is a mistake, however, to argue from this text that the facts about Jesus' death and resurrection formed *the whole Message of the Gospel*. Paul is careful to say that these central facts were preached "amongst things of primary importance." This, however, was not his entire Gospel. There were other things also, of equal importance in the Gospel, namely the announcement about the Kingdom of God.[61] We recall that Jesus had proclaimed the Kingdom of God as the Gospel *long before He spoke of His death and resurrection,* a fact which proves that the Kingdom of God is not a synonym for the death and resurrection of Christ (Luke 4:43; cp. Luke 18:31-34). As a leading authority notes:

> Neither Romans 1:1-3 nor I Cor. 15:1-4 is meant to be a full statement of what Paul understood by the Gospel. We can see this from the fact that the death of Jesus is not mentioned in Romans 1:1ff...The Gospel of Paul is identical with that which Jesus Himself preached during His earthly life. Christ Himself speaks in the Gospel of Paul. Paul is not referring [in Romans 16:25] to his Gospel added to the preaching of the risen Lord. He is emphasizing the agreement of his preaching with that of the earthly Jesus. Hence the "proclamation of Jesus Christ" can only mean the message which Jesus Christ proclaimed.[62]

It is evident that Paul was not in I Corinthians 15 directly addressing the subject of the Kingdom of God as a future event coinciding with the return of Jesus. The Corinthians had already accepted that belief as part of the Gospel of salvation. Thus Paul is able to elaborate on the already understood doctrine of the Kingdom only a few verses later. Having just mentioned the future coming of Jesus (I Cor. 15:23), he speaks of the Kingdom over which Jesus will preside at His coming (I Cor. 15:25-27). That Kingdom, it should be

---

[61] Acts 8:12; 19:8; 20:25; 28:23, 31, in addition to frequent use of synonyms like "mystery," "Gospel," "Word," which cover the same ground.

[62] *Theological Dictionary of the New Testament*, "kerygma," pp. 730, 716.

carefully noted, is the Kingdom which "flesh and blood" cannot inherit, for "the perishable cannot inherit the imperishable" (I Cor. 15:50). In order to *enter the Kingdom of God*, Christians must be summoned from death at the last trumpet and be changed, in the twinkling of an eye, into immortal persons (I Cor. 15:51, 52). These verses confirm, once again, the fact that the Kingdom of God comes into power at the Second Coming. Following Jesus, Paul speaks of entering or inheriting the Kingdom in the future.

The Kingdom has a principal place in the New Testament Gospel Message in addition, of course, to the equally essential preaching of the death and resurrection of the Savior. It is a serious mishandling of the Bible to place I Corinthians 15:1-4 in conflict with the massive evidence for the central importance of the Kingdom of God in the pre- and post resurrection proclamation.[63] Once again we must emphasize the importance of Acts 8:12 (echoed in Acts 19:8; 28:23, 31) as Luke's comprehensive summary statement about the Gospel Message: "When they believed Philip as he preached the Good News about the Kingdom of God and the name of Jesus Christ, they were being baptized, both men and women" (see also Matt. 13:19; Luke 8:12). "Kingdom of God" "frames" the entire writing of Luke. For him and for the New Testament Church it was the term par excellence to denote the restoration of the land under the reign of the Messiah, as well as the urgent present necessity for converts to prepare for the high honor of ruling with the Messiah.

The substitution of the word "heaven" for Kingdom of God is a major contributing factor in a loss of clarity about the Gospel of Jesus. When the language of Jesus is abandoned the damage in terms of the loss of the mind of Jesus is untold. Such a loss, tragically, has been characteristic of the history of the development of the central Christian idea — "the Gospel of the Kingdom and the things concerning Jesus." Out of deference for Jesus, as God's Messiah, and in obedience to His original challenge to belief in the Good News of the Kingdom, we must insist on defining the Kingdom according to its biblical setting and restoring it to a central position in all exposition of the Gospel. Can intelligent response to the Gospel mean anything less?

---

[63] Luke 4:43; Mark 1:14, 15; Matt. 4:17; Acts 8:12; 19:8; 20:25; 28:23, 31, etc.

Kingship as the Christian Goal

The nation of Israel had long been convinced of its high destiny in the purposes of God. As part of the covenant between the nation and its God, Israel was to enjoy a position of special privilege: "If you obey My voice and hold fast to My covenant, you of all the nations shall be My very own, for all the earth is Mine. I will count you a kingdom of priests, a consecrated nation. These are the words you are to speak to the sons of Israel" (Exod. 19:5, 6).

Israel as a whole had repeatedly failed to live up to her high calling. Nevertheless, the promise of world supremacy was reserved for a faithful remnant destined to inherit the future Kingdom of God. The invitation to kingship was repeated through the prophet Isaiah:

> Pay attention, come to Me; listen and your soul will live. With you I will make an everlasting covenant out of the favors promised to David. See, I have made of you a witness to the peoples, a leader and a master of the nations. See, you will summon a nation you never knew, those unknown will come hurrying to you, for the sake of Yahweh, your God, of the Holy One of Israel who will glorify you (Isa. 55:3-5, Jerusalem Bible).

In the New Testament the prospect of royal position in the Kingdom is offered to the New Israel of the Church (Gal. 6:16) gathered from both Jews and Gentiles. We have already referred to Jesus' own assurance to the faithful Church: "Those who prove victorious, I will allow to share My throne, just as I was victorious Myself and took My place with My Father on His throne...To those who prove victorious, and keep working for Me until the end, I will give the authority over the pagans which I Myself have been given by My Father, to rule them with an iron scepter and shatter them like earthenware." This prospect gave rise to the Christian "slogan" found in II Timothy 2:12: "If we suffer with Him, we shall also reign as kings with Him."

In Revelation 2:26 Jesus quotes the celebrated Messianic Psalm 2, one of many which describe the glories of the future Kingdom of God. It will be initiated by a decisive intervention by God, sending His Messiah to crush political rebellion and establish a new government in Jerusalem. The fact that appeal is made to this Psalm in the book of Revelation shows that the traditional Messianic hope was taken over into Christianity, with full approval of Jesus Himself:

Why this uproar among the nations? Why this impotent muttering of pagans — kings on earth rising in revolt, princes plotting against Yahweh and His Anointed [Messiah]. "Now let us break their fetters! Now let us throw off their yoke!"

The One whose throne is in heaven sits laughing, Yahweh derides them. Then angrily He addresses them, in a rage He strikes them with panic, "This is My King installed by Me on Zion, My holy mountain."

"Let me proclaim Yahweh's decree; He has told Me, 'You are My son, today I have become Your Father. Ask and I will give the nations for Your heritage, the ends of the earth for Your domain. With an iron scepter You will break them, shatter them like potter's ware.'"

So, now, you kings, learn wisdom, earthly rulers, be warned: Serve Yahweh, fear Him, tremble and kiss His feet, or He will be angry and you will perish, for His anger is very quick to blaze. Happy are all who take shelter in Him (Psalm 2, Jerusalem Bible).

The promise of "the ends of the earth for Your domain" is reflected in Jesus' own claim to the "authority which I Myself have been given by My Father" (Rev. 2:26). The same theme is taken up by the angelic chorus when they sing of the faithful who "shall rule as kings on the earth" (Rev. 5:10) and in the famous millennial passage which foresees the saints ruling with the Messiah for a thousand years (Rev. 20:4-6).

Recentering on Jesus as the Messiah

Any plan for the uniting of churches misses the point unless it concerns itself with the recovery of the divine Message in its apostolic form. A Catholic writer senses the weakness of schemes aimed at revitalizing the churches, apart from a clarification of the Good News: "The main thrust of renewal in the Church has proceeded on the basis of presupposing that the basic Christian Message has been effectively appropriated by the Christian people...The saving Message, the *kerygma*, has not been effectively understood or appropriated by the

330 It has been too hastily assumed that the Gospel

Church as a whole."[64] It has been too hastily assumed that the Gospel has been understood. The possibility of "another Gospel, another Jesus, and another spirit" being presented in Christianity has not been given enough attention. As long as the subject matter of the New Testament Good News is in question, all other considerations are peripheral. Parallel to the definition of the Gospel is the question of the biblical identity of Jesus. Another Catholic writer goes to the heart of the problem when he states:

> The Christian attitude in relation to Messianism is rather strange. Christians believe in a personal Messiah. Notwithstanding this belief, they are far less Messianically-minded than the Jews...Christians have largely lost the sense of Jesus' Messiahship. And they have, largely also, lost the Messianic vision. The Greek name "Christos" means "the anointed" and is the literal translation of the Hebrew "Mashiach" — Messiah...Now the idea of the Anointed is a specifically Jewish idea. It fell decidedly into the background when Christianity left its Palestinian home and became a Gentile religion...Christians who think or speak of Christ almost forget the Semitic word and the ideas which the name translates; in fact they forget that Jesus is primarily the Messiah. The very idea of Jesus' Messiahship has passed from their minds. Having lost the original sense of the word "Christ," many Christians have also lost the Messianic vision, i.e., the expectation of the divine future, the orientation towards "what is coming" on earth as the dénouement of the present era of history.[65]

This perceptive commentator might have added that the Christian Gospel is intimately bound up with the Messianic vision. The loss of the latter means the loss of the Gospel.

Of all Satan's attempts to corrupt the Christian faith, none could be as insidious as the plan to replace the Jesus of the Good News with another Jesus. History records that this very method was tried on the church at Corinth. It was effectively thwarted when Paul unmasked its exponents as ministers of Satan masquerading as ministers of

---

[64] Ralph Martin, *Unless the Lord Build the House,* Ave Maria Press, 1971, pp. 10, 11.

[65] Lev Gillet, *Communion in the Messiah, Studies in the Relationship Between Judaism and Christianity,* London: Lutterworth Press, 1942, cited by Hugh Schonfield, *The Politics of God,* pp. 50, 51.

Christian Truth. Serious thought ought to be given to the possibility that popular preaching may have succumbed to some of the tendencies against which Paul warned.

If we ask a man to believe in John Baker, we give very little idea of what that belief entails. If, however, we urge faith in John, the baker, we have given a much clearer definition of the object of belief. Similarly, it will be quite ineffective to invite belief in Jesus Christ unless a full account is given of the term "Christ." Otherwise we shall not know whom we are being asked to believe in. Preaching can so easily become lost in a dust-cloud of vagueness and generality.

The confirmation of the genuineness of Peter's discipleship depended upon this very question of the true identity of Jesus. A correct "Christology" became the foundational principle of the Church. "This rock" [i.e., the recognition of Jesus as Messiah or Son of God] was the essential basis of the faith as Jesus expounded it. Peter's reply was to a test question: "Whom do you say that I am?" And the answer which proved the soundness of his understanding was: "You are the Messiah, the Son of the Living God" (Matt. 16:16-18). In Peter's mind the name Messiah was invested with a rich complex of associated ideas drawn from the Hebrew Scriptures. The Messiah was to be the last in a long line of divinely appointed priests, prophets, and kings. In him alone the ideal of Kingship would be fully realized. The claim of Jesus to be the Messiah was based on His identity with the Messiah promised in the divine revelation provided by the Hebrew Bible. This is shown repeatedly in the New Testament by Jesus' constant reference to the fulfillment of the sacred writings in Himself. It is therefore utterly impossible, without destroying His own credibility, that He could have made a valid claim to Messiahship on any other basis than the one outlined by the Hebrew Scriptures. A claim to be a Messiah different from the one upon whom the whole divine Plan was built would have been evidently false.

If, as our quotation suggests, "Christians have forgotten that Jesus is primarily Messiah; the very idea of Messiahship has passed from their minds," we must ask whether they can truly be called Messianists, followers of Jesus in the New Testament sense. The question is of first importance, since all are agreed that salvation is possible only by belief in Jesus, the Messiah. If Jesus has been replaced by another Jesus, the real Savior will not be preached and the whole process of salvation will have been rendered ineffective.

The claim to Messiahship was revolutionary in the extreme. The Messiah was to supervise a world government and rule in power and justice from Jerusalem renewed and restored. It is this fact which makes the New Testament (and indeed the whole Bible) a thoroughly political document. It was for His claim to Messiahship that Jesus was put to death. The threat of political upheaval was too great. The point is that the Christianity of Jesus promised a divine intervention to put a stop to injustice on earth. A new world order was the great driving force behind the Good News of the Kingdom.

In the minds of many in our time the prospect of the return of Jesus in glory sounds like a piece of science fiction; and this we rate with popular light entertainment, having little to do with the real world. Much of contemporary theology, seeing the difficulty, proposes that whatever in the Bible does not make sense to modern man can be disregarded as belonging to the superstitions of a former age. Following the dictates of the "modern scientific view" Jesus' personal battle against the unseen but for Him very real forces of Satan and his demons must not detract from our acceptance of His central message of love and tolerance. As for His promise to return as King and Judge, that can be satisfactorily explained away as the invention of his over-excited followers. The idea cannot have originated with Him. All we need to do is to reinterpret what we call the primitive beliefs of the first-century disciples in the light of our vastly superior understanding of the twentieth century.

The notion that we are reinterpreting the New Testament when we discard the teaching about the Second Coming disguises the real fact that we are abandoning faith in Jesus Christ altogether. We are losing sight of the central proclamation of the New Testament that Jesus is the Messiah, the promised King, in whom alone the chaos of the present world system can find its solution. The preaching of Jesus as Savior, without reference to His appointment to the office of king over a renewed earth, runs the risk of being a preaching of another Jesus. Messiahship, with all that that means in its New Testament context, is the one indispensable ingredient of the faith which must not be abandoned. The point is made repeatedly in the New Testament.

If the churches are to unite, it can only be on the basis of a recovery of the Messianic vision, the expectation of the divine future. The Church has been placed in the world to offer to struggling humanity the prospect of better things to come, the guaranteed triumph of good over evil. But a solution to be realized in some far-off realm removed from the earth is no solution at all. Apart from the Messianic Kingdom, the Kingdom of God on earth, there is no hope for the world.

From a study of the New Testament documents, it will not be difficult to ascertain that Jesus is the promised Messiah of the Old Testament. He is the expression of the eternal divine Plan for the creation of the New Race of Immortals, and a harmonious universe. Having been uniquely conceived under the influence of the divine Spirit, yet taking the role of the servant of mankind, He gathered around Him a group of followers, believers in His Messiahship. In His Message of the Kingdom of God the promises and covenants of the Old Testament were confirmed and the divine future was declared. He suffered the death penalty at the hands of His unbelieving compatriots whose traditional religious systems had blinded them to the Truth of their own Scriptures and His teaching. The Roman authorities were also glad to be rid of one claiming to be king.

The resurrection was proof of His appointment as God's Messiah, and creation now awaits His manifestation in power to assume the royal office for which He has been destined. Associated with Him in His royal administration will be those who have believed in His claim to Messiahship and followed Him at all costs. Those who survive until the moment of His coming will be immortalized without dying. Those who have died as believers will awake from the sleep of death and share immortality with the whole company of believers. The challenge to every man is to believe that in Jesus the One God of Israel has spoken; to believe in the divine Plan for the rescue of the human race, and in Jesus as Messiah; to repent and be baptized, trusting in the sacrificial death of Jesus for the forgiveness of sins; and, within the power of divine Spirit operating as a ministry of the risen Christ, to live worthily of the high calling to the Kingdom of God.

If such were taken to be the faith of the early Church and the faith of all ages, disputes over premillennialism versus amillennialism would not need to continue. The prospect of the reign of Jesus and all the saints described in Revelation 20 must lie in the future (as the early Church believed) for the simple reason that the saints who have died cannot possibly now be active in the Messianic reign. They must therefore come to life in the resurrection, to take their place with all the saints in the divine Kingdom of the coming age. This is exactly what Revelation 20 describes, and it is one of the astonishing phenomena of contemporary evangelical theology that there could be any doubt on the question. Theories about the validity of prayer to the saints or to Mary would be seen as empty illusions, once it is grasped that no New Testament Christian held that the dead were really alive. The gullible would also be protected from the cults of spiritism, which early Christians would have viewed simply as demonism. All such errors connected with the "departed soul" would have been avoided, as long as the biblical Hebrew view of the nature of man was maintained. The introduction of the notion of the separable conscious soul, unable to die, must be seen for what it is: The disaster from which the churches have yet to recover, and a fatal distortion of her prophetic Message. The banishment of Greek philosophical speculation from the creeds will quickly put the resurrection and the Second Coming back into the central position they enjoy in New Testament writings. Along these lines the way back to the divine Message will be found and the way forward for the united Church will be made plain. In this way, also, the Jews who do not believe in Jesus (deterred often by the unscriptural teachings of the Church) may be persuaded to accept their Messiah, Son of the One God of Jewish monotheism, and the Christians whose ideas about the Messiah are often quite unmessianic may be united with them.

An extraordinary harmony and beauty emerges when the Bible is read as a Messianic document celebrating the arrival past and future of Jesus as the central Messianic figure. Kingship was lost in Eden, but it will be regained in the Eden of the land and the earth restored. Even the oceans of theological words written to avoid the Messianic drama of the Bible cannot erase the simple truth that once Scripture's Kingdom key is applied to the text — with "Kingdom" understood firstly within its Jewish, Hebrew environment — the Bible's treasures are unlocked.

14. Conclusion

The Good News about the Kingdom, the Christian Gospel, has its roots in the prophecies of the Old Testament. These announced the coming of a golden age on earth, following a decisive, catastrophic intervention by God. God's intention is to establish a just government throughout the world under the supervision of His chosen agent, the Messiah (Christ). The climactic last part of the Gospel drama is missing from the religious education of many who attend church. A depleted version of the Gospel can claim support in Scripture only if:

1) The Old Testament roots of the Gospel about the Kingdom, especially in Daniel 2, 7-12, are ignored and the "concrete" Hebrew concept of the Kingdom is rejected.

2) "Kingdom of Heaven" is not given its biblical meaning as the Kingdom *from* Heaven (Dan. 2:44; 7:27) and not a Kingdom *in* heaven.

3) The unambiguous testimony of Matthew, Mark and Luke to what Jesus preached as the Gospel is disregarded.

4) The plain statements in Acts about the Church's continued proclamation of the Kingdom of God as the heart of the Gospel are bypassed.[1]

5) Jesus' official title as Messiah is reduced to a kind of proper name.

6) The Gospel is defined by texts drawn from the epistles only, ignoring the "master texts," in particular the phrase "Gospel about the

---

[1] Acts 8:12; 19:8; 20:25; 28:23, 31. The same emphasis on the future Kingdom of God is found in the earliest post-biblical writers. See Everett Ferguson, "The Kingdom of God in Early Patristic Literature," *The Kingdom of God in 20th-Century Interpretation,* pp. 191-208.

Kingdom," provided by Matthew, Mark, Luke and Acts,[2] which report the "first-level" activity of Jesus and the Apostles.[3]

The Christian documents demonstrate, beyond any argument, that Jesus preached the Gospel of the Kingdom of God. Not only this, He did not initially say anything about His own death and resurrection (Luke 18:31-34). This must prove conclusively that the Message about the Kingdom contains information other than about the death and resurrection of the Savior.

This point is so crucial to our whole argument that we must emphasize it further. Jesus proclaimed the Gospel of the Kingdom in the company of the twelve Apostles: "Now after this He made His way through towns and villages preaching and proclaiming the Good News of the Kingdom of God. With Him went the twelve" (Luke 8:1). Later, "He called the twelve together and gave them power and authority over all demons and to cure diseases, and He sent them out to proclaim the Kingdom of God and to heal" (Luke 9:1-2).

At this stage the disciples had no knowledge of the death and resurrection of Jesus. This is proved by their subsequent reaction to Jesus' announcement of His impending arrest and crucifixion:

> Then taking the twelve aside He said to them, "Now we are going up to Jerusalem, and everything which is written by the prophets about the Son of Man is to come true. For He will be handed over to the pagans and will be mocked, maltreated and spat on, and when they have scourged Him, they will put Him to death; and on the third day He will rise again." But they could make nothing of this; what He had said was quite obscure to them, they had no idea what it meant (Luke 18:31-34).

Now if, as is often said, the Gospel consists of information about the death and resurrection of Jesus only, how is it that both Jesus and the twelve proclaimed the Gospel without reference to the Savior's

---

[2] Matt. 3:1 (John the Baptist); Matt. 4:23 (Jesus); 10:7 (the Apostles); 11:1 (Jesus); 24:14 (the Church); 26:13 (the Church); Mark 1:14, 15 (Jesus); 14:9 (the Church); Luke 4:43 (Jesus); 8:1 (Jesus and the Apostles); 9:2 (the Apostles); 9:11 (Jesus); Acts 1:3 (Jesus); 8:12 (Philip); 19:8 (Paul) 20:25 (Paul); 28:23, 31 (Paul). The same Gospel is implied in scores of other passages.

[3] I am puzzled by the remark of C.S. Lewis that "the Gospels are not 'the Gospel,' the statement of Christian belief" (Introduction to J.B. Phillips' *Letters to Young Churches*, Fontana Books, 1956, p. 9).

death and resurrection? The answer is clear. The Gospel of the Kingdom was announced before Jesus died and, as the book of Acts informs us, after the resurrection.[4] In Acts, however, we find added to the Gospel about the Kingdom, the new facts about the death and resurrection of Jesus, which had now become history. The result is a Gospel Message about the Kingdom of God and the name of Jesus Christ (Acts 8:12). The Kingdom Message remains as the primary component of the Gospel; Jesus' death and resurrection are additional, indispensable subjects for belief. Christianity, then, urges belief not only in the work of Jesus, but in His saving words.

In this connection the words of F.C. Grant deserve a wide hearing: "The theological basis of the Reformation was Paulinism, chiefly as understood by Luther and Calvin, not the teaching of the Gospels, which were demonstrably Jewish in tone and outlook as well as in language and presuppositions."[5] He complains that "theologians begin with Paul and the 'gospel' means for them the seventh chapter of Romans."[6] The result is that what we call the Gospel "is not the teaching of Jesus, but the interpretation of Jesus, chiefly his death and resurrection, as set forth by Paul...The consequences of this misinterpretation are far-reaching, not only for Jews but for Christians."[7] There was a "shift in the whole center of gravity in the gospel; it placed in the forefront of consideration, as the real subject of the gospel, the person of Jesus rather than the Kingdom of God...and the hope of the Kingdom receded and became eventually only another name for 'heaven,' the state of bliss beyond death."[8] There could be no more astute analysis of the defection of the Church from the Gospel of Jesus.

The Loss of the Messianic Element in the Gospel

The attempts of commentators to avoid the New Testament's Messianic material are a monument to theology's effort to construct its own "demessianized" versions of Christianity. The crux of the problem is that man does not want God to impose His rule on the

---

[4] Acts 8:12; 19:8; 20:25; 28:23, 31 and implied by the synonym "Word."

[5] *Ancient Judaism and the New Testament*, p. 15.

[6] *Ibid*, p. xv.

[7] *Ibid.*, p. 15.

[8] F.C. Grant, *The Earliest Gospel*, Abingdon Press, 1943, pp. 256, 258.

earth. Much less does he like to think of Jesus shattering the nations and ruling them with a rod of iron. The original Messianic version of Christianity, preached and taught by Jesus and the Apostles, has therefore been dismantled. Its Messianic framework has been removed. What remains as "Christianity" has tenuous links with the faith of the New Testament. The name of Jesus has been attached to a system of religion markedly different from His own belief system. A classic example of the avoidance of Jesus and His Message is Thomas Aquinas who "does not devote any significant portion of his principal theological enterprise to the Kingdom of God, the central theme of the preaching of Jesus."[9]

The New Testament has as its supreme goal the establishment, by divine intervention, of world peace under the government of the coming Messiah. The "revised" version of the faith promises a salvation for the individual in a realm far removed from the earth. Jesus, however, offered His followers positions of responsibility in a future new world order — the Kingdom of God. Belief in that new world order was, and is, the first step in intelligent faith in the Gospel: "The Kingdom of God is at hand; repent and believe in the Good News" (Mark 1:14, 15). To grasp the concept of the Kingdom is to become involved with the divine Plan for the rescue of the human race, a project which spans the whole Bible.

The loss of Christianity's central point may be likened to a team hoping to go to the moon. They decide that they need a launching pad and a spaceship in order to realize their dream. After they have acquired the necessary equipment for the journey, they forget what it was they needed the equipment for. Their interest in the pad and the spacecraft remains, but the trip to the moon is forgotten.

In New Testament Christianity the prospect of a place in the future Kingdom of God provides the stimulus to the whole Christian venture. The death and resurrection of Jesus make possible the believer's hope for a share in that Kingdom. Grasping the nature of that hope is the first step to be taken by the disciple. Belief in Jesus provides the way to the goal and guarantees its ultimate realization.

In contemporary presentations of the "Gospel" people are being asked to "believe in Jesus," in the absence of a clear idea of what

---

[9] B.T. Viviano, *The Kingdom of God in History,* p. 61.

Jesus stands for. They are not exposed to Jesus' Message about the Kingdom, which He preached long before He spoke of His death and resurrection. The situation is comparable to a political campaign in which a candidate appeals for support before the voters know what his manifesto is. It is difficult to express intelligent faith in Jesus unless one understands what Jesus meant by His "News about the Kingdom" — the Gospel as Jesus proclaimed it.

Discussion about the Kingdom of God has been tortuous. Scholarly writing is characterized by the desire to get rid of the future Kingdom in the interests of a modern world view. Happily many of the greatest commentators correctly describe what they find in the text of Scripture, but they do not challenge the Church to adopt the scriptural scheme. While evangelists constantly substitute "heaven" for the Christian goal of inheriting the earth/Kingdom, standard commentaries often support a historically accurate understanding of the words of Jesus: The meaning of the Kingdom of Heaven is provided by Jesus when He promises the meek an inheritance of the earth. Jesus confirms the prophetic hope of the Psalms.

At the root of the inconsistency of churches is the loss of the Hebrew background to the teaching of Jesus and the Apostles and the substitution of a non-Messianic philosophical mold into which the ethical teachings of the New Testament have been poured. The result is a hybrid religion, an amalgam of the Greek spirit with the Hebrew prophetic vision. Churchgoers are not told about the mixture of two incompatible worlds of thought. When they are instructed to read the Bible they unconsciously read the mixed version of the faith back into the Christian documents, isolating and bending various verses to fit their preconceived idea. At the same time the Protestant Church claims that it "goes by the Bible." Some Protestants spend inordinate amounts of time defending the "inerrancy" of the text while continuing to extract from Scripture an unmessianic system of beliefs.

The principal casualty in this loss of Jesus' Messianic teaching is the doctrine of the Kingdom of God, which commentators say either cannot be defined, or was wrongly attributed to Jesus by the early Church, or is no longer relevant to the modern world. A variety of techniques enable scholars to circumvent the plain meaning of the Kingdom, often because they believe that since it has not arrived in a

Messianic sense it never will. This attitude represents the failure of
faith in the ongoing Plan for rescue.

Throughout Christian history writers of the first eminence have
complained about the problematic state of the Church's theology. A
warning note was sounded by Jacques Ellul when he isolated the root
problem of the Church's troubles:

> A familiar example of the mutation to which revelation was
> subjected is its contamination by the Greek idea of the immortality
> of the soul. I will briefly recall it. In Jewish thought death is total.
> There is no immortal soul, no division of body and soul. Paul's
> thinking is Jewish in this regard. The soul belongs to the
> "psychical" realm and is part of the flesh. The body is the whole
> being. In death, there is no separation of body and soul. The soul is
> as mortal as the body. But there is a resurrection. Out of the
> nothingness that human life becomes, God creates anew the being
> that was dead. This is a creation by grace; there is no immortal soul
> intrinsic to us. Greek philosophy, however, introduces among
> theologians the idea of the immortal soul. The belief was
> widespread in popular religion and it was integrated into
> Christianity, but it is a total perversion...All Christian thinking is
> led astray by this initial mutation that comes through Greek
> philosophy and Near Eastern cults...Belief in the soul's celestial
> immortality arose in the second half of the fifth century BC on the
> basis of astronomy. Pythagorean astronomy radically transformed
> the idea of the destiny of the soul held by Mediterranean peoples....
> It substitutes the notion of a soul of celestial substance exiled in this
> world. This idea completely contaminates biblical thinking,
> gradually replaces the affirmation of the resurrection, and
> transforms the kingdom of the dead into the kingdom of God.[10]

Such insight illuminates the damage which apostolic faith has
sustained. There is obviously an urgent need for repair. A catena of
complementary statements[11] from various biblical experts point in the
same direction: Our system of biblical interpretation has been diverted
into channels alien to the biblical founding fathers, though compatible
with the post-biblical Greek "church Fathers":

---

[10] Jacques Ellul, *The Subversion of Christianity,* Eerdmans, 1986, p. 25.
[11] Emphasis mine in each case.

For most of Christian history Paul has been misunderstood:

The first task of exegesis [explaining the Bible] is to penetrate as far as possible inside the historical context(s) of the author and of those for whom he wrote. So much of this involves the taken-for-granteds of both author and addressees. Where a modern reader is unaware of (or unsympathetic to) these shared assumptions and concerns it will be impossible to hear the text as the author intended it to be heard (and assumed it would be heard). In this case, a major part of that context is the self-understanding of Jews and Judaism in the first century and of Gentiles sympathetic to Judaism. *Since most of Christian history and scholarship, regrettably, has been unsympathetic to that self-understanding, if not downright hostile to it, a proper appreciation of Paul in his interaction with that self-understanding has been virtually impossible.*[12]

Modern English Christians misunderstand the Bible:

The modern English Christian gives a meaning to the words of the New Testament different from that which was in the minds of the Jewish writers. Greek was the language they used to convey the universal Christian message, but their mode of thinking was to a large extent Hebraic. For a full understanding it is necessary for the modern Christian not only to study the Greek text, but to sense the Hebraic idea which the Jewish writers sought to convey in Greek words. I cannot claim to have become very skilled in this, but made enough progress to discover how greatly I had misinterpreted the Bible in the past. Like all ordained Christian ministers I had spoken dogmatically, authoritatively from a pulpit which no one may occupy without licence from a Bishop; and much of what I had said had been misleading.[13]

In regard to scriptural teaching about the destiny of man, original biblical concepts have been substituted with ideas from Hellenism and Gnosticism:

---

[12] James Dunn, *Commentary on Romans, Word Biblical Commentary,* pp. xiv, xv.

[13] David Watson, *Christian Myth and Spiritual Reality,* Victor Gallancz, 1967, pp. 28, 29.

The hope of the early church centered on the resurrection of the Last Day. It is this which first calls the dead into eternal life (I Cor. 15; Phil. 3:21). This resurrection happens to the man and not only to the body. Paul speaks of the resurrection not "of the body" but "of the dead." This understanding of the resurrection implicitly understands death as also affecting the whole man...*Thus* [in traditional Christian teaching] *the original Biblical concepts have been replaced by ideas from Hellenistic Gnostic dualism.* The New Testament idea of the resurrection which affects the whole man has had to give way to the immortality of the soul. The Last Day also loses its significance, for souls have received all that is decisively important long before this. Eschatological [forward-looking] tension is no longer strongly directed to the day of Jesus' Coming. *The difference between this and the Hope of the New Testament is very great.*[14]

Christian teaching was transformed. Messianic hopes were forgotten. The notion of the Kingdom of God on earth disappeared. Immortality at death took the place of the resurrection into the Kingdom on earth:

Like all concepts the meaning of religious terms is changed with a changing experience and a changing world view. Transplanted into the Greek world view, inevitably *the Christian teaching was modified — indeed transformed.* Questions which had never been asked came into the foreground and the Jewish pre-suppositions tended to disappear. Especially were *the Messianic hopes forgotten* or *transferred to a transcendent sphere beyond death.* When the empire became Christian in the fourth century, *the notion of a Kingdom of Christ on earth* to be introduced by a great struggle all but disappeared, remaining only as the faith of obscure groups. Immortality — the philosophical conception — took the place of the resurrection of the body. Nevertheless, the latter continues because of its presence in the primary sources, but it is no longer a determining factor, since its presupposition — *the Messianic Kingdom on earth — has been obscured.* As thus the background is changed from Jewish to Greek, so are the fundamental religious conceptions...We have thus a peculiar combination — *the religious*

---

[14] Paul Althaus, *The Theology of Martin Luther*, pp. 413, 414.

doctrines of the Bible run through the forms of an alien philosophy.[15]

Our creeds teach us to think in Gentile terms contrary to the New Testament:

> The primary kinship of the New Testament is not with the Gentile environment, but rather with the Jewish heritage and environment...*We are often led by our traditional creeds and theology to think in terms of Gentile and especially Greek concepts.* We know that *not later than the second century* there began the systematic effort of the Apologists to show that the Christian faith perfected the best in Greek philosophy...A careful study of the New Testament must block any trend to regard the New Testament as a group of documents expressive of the Gentile mind. This book's kinship is primarily and overwhelmingly with Judaism and the Old Testament...*The New Testament speaks always of disapproval and usually with blunt denunciation of Gentile cults and philosophies.* It agrees essentially with the Jewish indictment of the pagan world...The modern Church often misunderstands its relation to the Old Testament and Israel, and often inclines to prefer the Greek attitude to the New Testament view.[16]

> The New Testament remains basically Jewish, not Greek — though Greek in language...and it can be understood only from the historical vantage point of the modified Judaism which provided the early church with its terminology and its whole frame of thought.[17]

Original Christianity was submerged under Graeco-Roman culture resulting in a perversion of the original faith:

> Although the acute form of the secularization of Christianity in gnosticism was rejected, yet *the Church...continued to lose more and more its primitive character and to be conformed to its environment in the Graeco-Roman culture.* The process was advanced by the Apologists [spokesmen for the faith in the second century], seemed to suffer a check in the influence of Irenaeus, but

---

[15] G.W. Knox, D.D., LL.D, professor of philosophy and the history of religion, Union Theological Seminary, New York, *Encyclopedia Britannica*, 11th ed., Vol. 6, p. 284.

[16] F.V. Filson, *The New Testament Against Its Environment,* pp. 26, 27, 43.

[17] F.C. Grant, *Ancient Judaism and the New Testament*, p. 133.

was stimulated in the Alexandrian school of theology...This development brought about the definite transformation of the rule of faith into the compendium of a Greek philosophical system...*We cannot assume that the faith as delivered to the saints was adequately and finally expressed in these Graeco-Roman intellectual forms*...That the faith was expressed in ecclesiastical dogma always without obscuration or distortion cannot be maintained...That the Christian organism could not escape being affected by, in adapting itself to, its Graeco-Roman environment must be conceded; that this action and reaction were not only necessary but a condition of progress may be conjectured...This does not however exclude the frank recognition of the fact that there were characteristics of the Greek speculative genius and the practical Roman ethos not altogether harmonious with the distinctive character of the Gospel, so that *there was perversion amidst the progress in the subsequent development* — the salt in seasoning did lose some of its savour. Greek metaphysic and Law *misrepresented* as well as expressed the Gospel.[18]

The influence of Greek philosophy upon the early Christian theology is too obvious to be questioned.[19]

Christians do not understand the meaning of "Messiah" nor the vision of His Kingdom:

Christians have largely lost the sense of Jesus' Messiahship. *And they have largely lost the Messianic vision.* The Greek name "Christos" means "the anointed one" and is the literal translation of the Hebrew "Mashiach" — Messiah...Christians who think or speak of Christ almost forget the Semitic word and the ideas which the name translates; in fact they forget that Jesus is primarily the Messiah. The very idea of Jesus' Messiahship has passed from their minds. Having lost the original sense of the word "Christ," many Christians have also lost the Messianic vision, i.e., the expectation of the divine future, the orientation towards *what is coming on earth* as the denouement of the present era of history.[20]

---

[18] A.E. Garvie, "Christianity," *Encyclopedia of Religion and Ethics*, 1910, Vol. 3, p. 588.

[19] G.P. Fisher, *History of Christian Doctrine*, T&T Clark, 1908, p. 32.

[20] Lev Gillet, cited by Hugh Schonfield in *The Politics of God*, pp. 50, 51.

"Heaven" is not what Jesus promised His followers, though Christians today constantly say it is:

William Strawson, a tutor in systematic theology and the philosophy of religion, made a detailed study of *Jesus and the Future Life* and dedicated 23 pages to an examination of the word "heaven" in Matthew, Mark and Luke. He concluded:

> In few, if any, instances of the use of the word "heaven" is there any parallel with modern usage. The gospel records of our Lord's life and teaching *do not speak of going to heaven*, as a modern believer so naturally does. Rather the emphasis is on that which is "heavenly" coming down to man...Our modern way of speaking of life with God as being life "in heaven" is not the way the gospels speak of the matter. *Especially is there no suggestion that Jesus is offering to his disciples the certainty of "heaven" after this life.*[21]

> Heaven as the future abode of the believers is [a conception] conspicuous by its absence from St. Paul's thought. The second coming is always from heaven alike in the earliest (I Thess. 1:10) and the latest (Phil. 3:20) of Paul's letters...Possibly he so takes it for granted that believers will have their place in a Messianic earthly Kingdom that he does not think it necessary to mention it.[22]

> Jesus was not thinking of a colorless and purely heavenly beyond, but pictured it to Himself as a state of things existing upon this earth — though of course a transfigured earth — and in His own land.[23]

A disaster occurred when, after the death of the Apostles, the Jewish element in original Christianity was ousted in favor of a new Gentile religion:

> The creation of the Christian religion necessarily involved a retreat from the teaching of Moses, the Prophets and Jesus, which more and more became a rout...As one Protestant Christian wrote: "The great people of God's choice [the Jews] were soon the least adequately represented in the Catholic Church. That was a disaster to the Church itself. It meant that the Church as a whole failed to

---

[21] p. 38.

[22] "Heaven," *Dictionary of Christ and the Apostles*, Vol. I, p. 531.

[23] W. Bousset, *Jesus*, London: Williams and Norgate, 1906, p. 82.

understand the Old Testament and that *the Greek mind and the Roman mind in turn, instead of the Hebrew mind, came to dominate its outlook: from that disaster the Church has never recovered either in doctrine or in practice...*If today another great age of evangelization is to dawn we need the Jews again...Christianity is a synthesis of Judaism and paganism. As such, it is a corruption of as much significance as the ancient Israelite defection in blending their religion with the cults of the Canaanites. Therefore, it is not for the Jews to embrace orthodox Christianity, but for the Christians, if they are to be Israelites indeed as the People of God, to review and purify their beliefs, and to recapture what basically they have in common with the Jews, the Messianic vision.[24]

On what basis should we deny that Jesus shared Jewish beliefs?

Many of us like to think that Jesus denied Jewish beliefs about supernatural revelation and exclusive privilege, because our minds are so profoundly influenced by the philosophical way of looking at things. But have we any right to assume that He knew the falsity of the Jewish belief? Was it false? Have we a right to assume that, because a non-Jewish universalism based on philosophical modes of thought appeals to us of the twentieth century, it must therefore be the absolute truth and the divine will? Surely we must seek for some evidence. But there is no evidence in the Gospels..., and His disciples believed as firmly in the exclusive value of the Jewish religion after His resurrection as before.[25]

The entire Christian system, both Catholic and Protestant, is flawed by the mixing of the Bible with alien Greek ideas:

Our position is that the reinterpretation of Biblical theology in terms of the Greek philosophers has been both widespread throughout the centuries and everywhere destructive to the essence of the Christian faith...There have always been Jews who sought to make terms with the Gentile world, and it has in time meant the death of Judaism for all such. There have been Christians from the beginning who have sought to do this...*Neither Catholic nor*

---

[24] H.J. Schonfield, *The Politics of God*, pp. 98, 99, citing Canon Goudge, *Essays on Judaism and Christianity*.

[25] H.D. Hamilton, *The People of God*, Vol. I, p. 260.

Protestant theology is based on Biblical theology. In each case we have a domination of Christian theology by Greek thought.[26]

The Church as it developed after Bible times was poisoned by elements of Gnosticism:

Who can maintain that the Church ever overcame the Gnostic doctrine of the two natures or the Valentinian Docetism? Even the later councils of the Church which discussed the Christological problems in complicated, nowadays hardly intelligible definitions, did not manage to do this; *the unity of the Church foundered precisely on this.*[27]

While Protestants claim that the Bible is their authority, they have in fact accepted a Greek-influenced version of Christianity which abandons the Bible:

The difference is obvious between the mental patterns of the New Testament and most of our accustomed Christian thinking…The explanation of this contrast lies in the fact that *historic Christian thought in this regard, as in others, has been Greek rather than Hebrew.* Claiming to be founded on the Scripture, it has, as a matter of fact, *completely surrendered many scriptural frameworks of thinking* and has accepted the Greek counterparts instead.[28]

The Church says one thing and does another:

The Church has not usually in practice (whatever it may have claimed to be doing in theory) based its Christology [understanding of who Jesus is] exclusively on the witness of the New Testament.[29]

From the second century a new form of Christianity was beginning to replace the faith of the Bible:

Developed Gentile Christianity of the sort which was beginning to take shape towards the end of the first century has very little to do

---

[26] N.H. Snaith, *The Distinctive Ideas of the Old Testament*, London: Epworth Press, 1955, pp. 187, 188.

[27] Kurt Rudolph, *Gnosis: The Nature and History of Gnosticism*, Harper and Row, 1983, p. 372.

[28] H.E. Fosdick, *A Guide to Understanding the Bible,* Harper Bros., 1938, p. 93.

[29] Maurice Wiles, *The Remaking of Christian Doctrine*, London: SCM Press, 1974, pp. 54, 55.

with Jesus or the faith of the first generation. *It is a new religion developed to replace the original faith.*[30]

The essentially political term Kingdom of God, Jesus' central theme, has been distorted in both the Church and academic circles:

> For the Kingdom of God to have resulted in the crucifixion of Jesus, it must have carried political connotations that the governing authorities in Jerusalem considered dangerous. Astounding as it may seem, however, neither in the church nor in academic circles has the Kingdom of God been assigned the political significance its derivation and consequences demand. *Scholarly debate has largely ignored any overt political dimensions of the kingdom.*[31]

Symptoms of the malaise of Christian theology are seen clearly when some contemporary evangelists declare with confidence that the teachings of Jesus are not really the essential heart of the faith:

> Many people today think that the essence of Christianity is Jesus' teachings, but that is not so. If you read the Apostle Paul's letters, which make up most of the New Testament, you will see that there is almost nothing said about the teachings of Jesus. Throughout the rest of the New Testament, there's little reference to the teachings of Jesus, and in the Apostles' Creed, the most universally-held Christian creed, there's no reference to Jesus' teachings. There is also no reference to the example of Jesus. Only two days in the life of Jesus are mentioned — the day of His birth and the day of His death. Christianity centers not in the teachings of Jesus, but in the Person of Jesus as Incarnate God who came into the world to take upon Himself our guilt and die in our place.[32]

Such statements appear to us to be a calamitous misreading of the New Testament. Luke provides as much of the New Testament as Paul (more if Hebrews is taken to be non-Pauline). Though the creeds unfortunately pay no attention to the teachings of Jesus, Paul preaches the same Gospel as Jesus: "The word of God for Paul is not primarily

[30] Don Cupitt, *The Debate About Christ*, p. 69.
[31] R.D. Kaylor, *Jesus the Prophet, His Vision of the Kingdom on Earth,* Westminster/John Knox Press, 1994, p. 70.
[32] D.J. Kennedy, "How I Know Jesus Is God," *Truths that Transform*, Nov. 1989.

a story about Jesus Christ, but a saving summons from Jesus Christ through the mouths of His heralds."[33] Paul points us to an imitation of Jesus as he imitates Jesus and warns against any departure from the words of Jesus (I Cor. 11:1; I Tim. 6:3). The teaching of Jesus emphasizes repeatedly the need to believe and obey His teachings, which are made the basis of salvation (Matt. 7:24-27; Mark 8:38; John 12:44-50). John the Apostle cautioned the Church against anyone who "goes too far and does not abide in the teaching of Christ," identifying such a tendency as the spirit of Antichrist (II John 7-9). Commentators describe the erroneous teaching which John condemned so emphatically. What those first-century champions of false teaching attempted to do was *"disunite the saving word of life from the historic Jesus*, and to seek another path to fellowship with God."[34] The word and words of Jesus must be maintained against any and every theory which moves them away from the center of faith. Apparently in some forms of contemporary evangelism, Paul is twisted and Jesus rejected. Hence the need for a return to the Gospel as Jesus preached it.

A widely-circulated tract entitled "What is the Gospel?"[35] which contains no reference to the Kingdom of God, declares that Jesus "came to do three days work" and that "He came not primarily to preach the Gospel…, but He came rather that there might be a Gospel to preach." It is difficult to reconcile these statements with Jesus' declaration that He was commissioned for the very purpose of proclaiming the Gospel of the Kingdom (Luke 4:43; Mark 1:38).

It cannot be too strongly emphasized that Christianity which is not rooted and anchored in the historical Jesus may turn out to be just another faith. If people are asked to "accept Christ" without being told about the Message of the historical Christ, how can we be sure that "Christ" is not just an abstract symbol? The real question then is, in the words of Jon Sobrino,

> whether this Spirit is the Spirit of Jesus or some vague, abstract Spirit that is nothing more than the sublimated embodiment of the natural "religious" person's desires and yearnings. If it is the latter,

---

[33] J.F. Kay, "Theological Table-Talk: Myth or Narrative?" *Theology Today* (48), 1991, p. 330.

[34] H.R. Mackintosh, *The Doctrine of the Person of Jesus Christ*, T & T Clark, 1912, p. 121, emphasis added.

[35] Published by The Billy Graham Evangelistic Association, 1980.

then it is not only different from, but actually contrary to the Spirit of Jesus.[36]

The history of Christianity ought to give churchgoers cause for alarm. Because of an anti-intellectual approach to faith, many choose to remain in ignorance of the great issues affecting their relationship with God. When theologians ponder the condition of the Church over the centuries, they often expose an extraordinary departure from the historical Jesus. R.D. Kaylor writes:

> *Christian faith has not centered on the historical Jesus.* The Apostles' Creed demonstrates the truth of this statement, for it moves from "born of the Virgin Mary" to "crucified under Pontius Pilate." The Creed's omission suggests that the intervening years and activities of Jesus were of no real consequence to faith…Theologically and ethically, it is not enough to say that a death and resurrection have occurred. Who Jesus was whom the Romans executed and God raised from the dead matters not only for the historian but for the theologian and believer. The historical character of Jesus, and not merely a spiritual Christ, provides Christian faith with its reason for being and its power to bring about change in personal social life.[37]

If the Jesus claimed as Savior is not anchored in the historical figure recorded in the New Testament, who knows what kind of Jesus may be embraced? It seems to me clear that Satan could well play on the weakness of the religious spirit of man by presenting a Jesus who is only superficially the Jesus of the Bible. The counterfeit could, however, be most subtle. Satanic strategy would work hard to separate Jesus from His own teachings (laid out in their clearest form in Matthew, Mark and Luke). "Jesus" might then be only a religious symbol offered as a spiritual panacea for the world's and individuals' ills. The Jewish, apocalyptic Jesus, preacher of a coming just society on earth, might then fall into disrepute and obscurity. His reappearance in preaching would probably appear strange and unwanted even to churchgoers who have been fed a diet missing the New Testament Hebrew ingredients.

---

[36] *Christology at the Crossroads*, p. 384.

[37] R.D. Kaylor, *Jesus the Prophet, His Vision of the Kingdom on Earth.*

The safest policy against deception would be to reinstate the Gospel about the Kingdom at the heart of all preaching. This would ensure against the tendency to make Jesus up out of our own minds.[38] It would also safeguard believers against the extravagant assertion of a leading theologian who remarked: "What can be said about the historical Jesus belongs to the realm of the 'Christ according to the flesh.' That Christ, however, does not concern us. What went on within Jesus' heart I do not know, and I do not want to know."[39] This tendency, less blatantly expressed, plagues a number of theological schools of thought, not least the school which relegates the teaching of Jesus to a ministry to Jews only and applies His ethical instructions to the future millennium.

Confessing Jesus as Messiah, Son of God

It is with good reason that Christology, the study of the identity of Jesus, has always engaged the attention of theologians. When Jesus inquired of Peter: "Who do you say that I am?" (Matt. 16:15), Peter's truthful response that He was the Messiah was greeted with the highest praise. The correct answer to the question, so Jesus said, can only be supplied by divine revelation. To recognize Jesus as the Messiah is to grasp the secret of Christianity and open the way to possession of the Kingdom (Matt. 16:19). To acknowledge Jesus as something other than the Messiah, Son of God, is to miss the point of the Christian faith. John echoes his Master when he says: "There is no

---

[38] Unitarian Universalist theology seems to have fallen into the very trap against which the Bible warns (II John 7-9). A tract on Unitarian Universalist views of Jesus says: "It is not possible to describe the historical Jesus, yet many descriptions of Him exist...Each of us may imagine the historical Jesus as we wish...The important aspect of personal reality with which we must come to terms is not the historical Jesus, but the idea of Jesus as it exists in our contemporary culture...I find it exhilarating to believe that the perfection we have poured into the figure of Jesus has come from the minds of human beings, from human imagination and ethical aspiration...I'm for a better and better Jesus, born from the aspiring heart of humanity" (J.G. Mackinnon).

[39] R. Bultmann, "Zur Frage der Christologie," in *Glauben und Verstehen*, cited by G.R. Beasley-Murray in "The Kingdom of God and Christology in the Gospels," in *Jesus of Nazareth: Lord and Christ*, ed. J.B. Green and M. Turner, Grand Rapids: Eerdmans, 1994, p. 23.

falsehood so great as the denial of the Messiahship of Jesus" (I John 2:22).[40]

It is proper then that churches seek to enshrine the great Truth about who Jesus is in creedal statements. What, however, if those statements misrepresented the apostolic records? What if Canon Goudge was right in his assertion that when "the Greek and Roman rather than the Hebrew mind came to dominate the church," there occurred "a disaster in doctrine and practice from which the church has never recovered"?[41] We may have to admit the possibility that "orthodoxy" has been mistaken in its definition of Jesus as "God the Son." Today powerful voices are urging us to reconsider the biblical doctrine of God. Is a Godhead of "three persons in One" conceivable within the Hebrew framework which all recognize to be unrelentingly monotheistic? Many are beginning to see the gravity of the problem. Hans Küng speaks of the Trinitarian formulation as "the unbiblical, very abstractly constructed speculation of the School tractates," of "the Hellenization of the primordial Christian Message by Greek philosophy," and of "the genuine concern of many Christians and the justified frustration of Jews and Muslims in trying to find in such formulas the pure faith in One God."[42] Has the Church the courage to look again at the biblical doctrine of God?

Scripture does, of course, teach that Jesus is the very reflection of His Father; that in Jesus, God speaks; that Jesus declares the Father to us. But it teaches with equal clarity (and this is so often overlooked) that the Father alone is "the only true God," "the one who alone is God" (John 5:44; 17:3). It is impossible, therefore, that Jesus can be the only true God in exactly the same sense. Jesus' Father alone is the one God of biblical monotheism. A disaster occurred, indeed, when the post-biblical theologians began to tamper with the fundamental monotheism in which Jesus was reared and which He supported at every point.[43]

---

[40] As rendered by J.W.C. Wand, *The New Testament Letters, Prefaced and Paraphrased,* Oxford University Press, 1946.

[41] Cited by H.J. Schonfield, *The Politics of God,* p. 98.

[42] *Jewish Monotheism and Christian Trinitarian Doctrine,* Philadelphia: Fortress Press, 1981, p. 40.

[43] For example in Mark 12:28ff. Jesus subscribes to the Jewish monotheism of His fellow Jews.

In describing Jesus as God, the Son, the so-called "Church Fathers" of post-biblical times imposed non-biblical, non-messianic terminology on the leading figure in the drama of salvation. They created a non-biblical problem by positing a Godhead of two (and later three), and spent centuries attempting to find a non-biblical solution. The "solution" was then forced upon the Church on pain of excommunication. Dissenters to the official dogma at the time of the Reformation were dealt with by imprisonment or death.

The assertion that Jesus is God detracts from the apostolic teaching that He is the Son of God, the Messiah. If He is the Messiah, He must fit the description of Messiah given in advance by the prophets. Of an eternal being, distinct from the One God the Father, who becomes man while remaining God, the Old Testament says nothing. Of a second Moses arising by supernatural conception from a descendant of David, it speaks plainly (Deut. 18:15, 18; Acts 3:22; 7:37). Of a man reflecting the divine majesty, functioning in perfect harmony with God, His Father (John 10:30), showing forth the Spirit of the One God, His Father, the Bible's pages are filled. That promised Man was the Messiah, God's Son, the lamb of God, the High Priest of the faithful and the King of the coming age.

The Jesus of history will be rediscovered when it is understood that He is God's chosen King, the hope of Israel and a light to the Gentiles. That Jesus will not submit to titles which belong to abstract Greek metaphysics. It is both unnecessary and misleading to describe Jesus in terminology unknown to Himself and the Apostles.

The "genesis" of Jesus is described by Matthew (Matt. 1:18). The Messiah's origin as Son of God is likewise traced by Luke to a supernatural conception (Luke 1:35). Luke knows nothing of Sonship in the eternal past. Furthermore an angel appears as divine witness to the fact that Jesus is to be a King who shall reoccupy and hold forever the throne of His ancestor David. A restored Kingdom is predicted, as everywhere in Scripture. When these divine communications about the Messiah and His Kingdom are taken seriously and believed, the return to New Testament Christianity will be under way.

A "demessianized" Christianity is both pallid and self-contradictory. In contrast, the New Testament's outlook on the future, with its irrepressible hope for the return of the Christ to rule on earth, can revive and encourage. It will put us in touch with the mind of

Jesus. When this happens the churches will repossess the great unifying cause which belongs to the Church. The Gospel about the Kingdom of God will be heard once more.

15. Epilogue: In Praise of the Messiah

The signs are that theology is beginning to detect the flaw in the non-Messianic Gospel of the divided Church as well as in its un-Jewish Jesus. A writer from Australia complains that the term Gospel has been "too narrowly construed, too personalized, too subjectively applied." He points out that the subject matter of the early Christian Gospel included "the Lord's universal victory over the world and His consequent kingly rule, with a new era beginning this way. With the Old Testament eschatology from which it derives its force behind it, the Gospel settles for no less than the restitution of all things."[1] A number of scholars, happily, now concede with Johannes Weiss that

> the Kingdom of God as Jesus thought of it is never something subjective, inward, or spiritual, but is always the objective Messianic Kingdom, which usually is pictured as a territory into which one enters, or a land in which one has a share, or as a treasure which comes down from heaven.[2]

The gulf that has been fixed between the Hebrew Messianism of both Testaments and traditional views of the afterlife "on far-off shores" can be bridged only when Christians become attuned to the biblical exultation over the future coming of the Messiah.

---

[1] W.J. Dumbrell, "The Content of the Gospel and the Implications of that Content for the Christian Community," *The Reformed Theological Review* (40), 1981, pp. 33, 35, 39.
[2] Johannes Weiss, *Jesus' Proclamation of the Kingdom of God*, p. 133.

The divine Plan for the future has become dislocated and obscured through the intrusion of an anti-Hebraic philosophy; yet a common sense rereading of the biblical literature, backed by the refined tools of contemporary scholarship, will be sufficient to bring about a restatement of the genuine Christian view of the future. The fullest emphasis must be placed upon the biblical fact that the Messiah has never yet begun to reign in His Kingdom. Exalted Lord at the right hand of the Father He certainly is. Enthroned in His own Kingdom He certainly is not. His Kingship in glory is associated by the early Christians with His reappearance on earth, in the power of His Kingdom. Tragically the millennial passage, torn from its context, and unrelated to the central Christian hope, has so often been used to contradict the biblical scheme. Once it is understood that the dead are dead until the resurrection, the belief that Christ is already reigning as Messiah with His saints will be seen as the mirage on which a false eschatology has been built.

To recapture the authentic Christian hope, we can do no better than to join the heavenly host in their new song in praise of the Christ. Their words are a summary of the divine Message embodied in the Christian revelation: "Worthy art Thou to take the book, and to open its seals; for Thou wast slain, and didst purchase to God with Thy blood of every tribe, tongue, people, and nation, and made them unto our God kings and priests, and they shall reign on the earth" (Rev. 5:9, 10).

The heavenly court thrills again at the completion of the divine Plan and prospect of the Messianic triumph: "We give thanks, O Lord God, the Almighty, who art and who wast, because Thou hast taken Thy great power and hast begun to reign" (Rev. 11:17). And again: "Hallelujah! The Lord God Almighty has begun to reign!" (Rev. 19:6). The promised reign of the Messiah is destined to begin at the climax of history, and that crisis is everywhere in the biblical literature placed at the return of the Christ. Apart from that event the whole divine Message is reduced to a fairy tale.

The aging Apostle Paul gave his last word to the world in a solemn declaration of the Christian Message: "Before God and the Lord Jesus Christ who will judge the living and the dead, I attest both to His coming and His Kingdom" (II Tim. 4:1). He then instructed Timothy to:

proclaim the Message. Never lose your sense of urgency, whether the opportunity seems favorable or unfavorable. Convince, correct, warn and encourage. Be unflagging in your patience. For the time is coming when people will not tolerate sound instruction, but with ears itching for something gratifying, they will gather to themselves one teacher after another, chosen to satisfy their own liking and to foster the errors they hold. They will turn away from hearing the Truth and wander off into myths and manmade fictions (II Tim. 4:2-4).

Each of us is called to make clear his own response to the risen Jesus and the coming divine event. The summons to repentance and baptism is a call to respond to the King and His coming Kingdom. His divine appointment to rule has been decreed by the Architect of the divine Plan for our rescue. We should welcome the Message as mankind's last and only hope. Our acceptance of the Good News means reconciliation with our Maker and an end to our involvement in the universal deception. If individually we stand perplexed and helpless in our guilt, the Lamb has been provided in sacrifice for our sins. The ransom has been paid. The death penalty can be lifted, and we may go free.

The cry of the Apostles rings out as clearly and urgently to our generation as to theirs: "God commands all men everywhere to repent; for He has appointed a day in which He intends to administer the world in justice in the person of a man whom He has destined for this work, and He has given assurance of this by raising Him from the dead." Paul addressed the Greeks in terms of the purest Jewish-Christian Messianism. His quotation is from the jubilant Psalm 96 which celebrates the future arrival of the Kingdom of God, in the person of God's agent the Messiah Jesus, to bring sane government to the world. In those same terms Jesus had announced the Kingdom, a task which He assigns to His Church until the dawn of the great day. In the conviction that the Message of Jesus is still the Gospel let Christians everywhere unite.

APPENDIX: The Various New Testament Titles of the Gospel about the Kingdom

The following list of expressions provides first the "master definition" of the Gospel and then gives the equivalent Gospel titles found throughout the New Testament. All evangelism in the Bible is evangelism about the Kingdom of God as Jesus preached it. All invitations to salvation are invitations not "to go to heaven," but *to inherit the Kingdom of God.* Following Jesus involves using His terminology, not our own. To speak like Jesus (allowing, of course, for translation into our mother tongues!) means to think as He did and does.

If one combines references to "the Gospel of the Kingdom," "the Gospel" and "preaching" or "proclaiming," there are some 325 references to the Gospel of the Kingdom. "Believing" in the New Testament means believing in "the Gospel about the Kingdom and in the name of Jesus Christ" (Acts 8:12). The next verse (Acts 8:13) says that Simon "believed," i.e., believed in the Gospel of the Kingdom and the Name of Jesus. That is the meaning of Christian faith (in Simon's case belief did not last).

In Acts 28:24 some were persuaded by the Gospel of the Kingdom (v. 23) and some did not believe. To believe, therefore, in the New Testament is to be persuaded about the Kingdom of God and Jesus.

The Kingdom of God is the key which unlocks the secret to the teaching of Jesus and gives us knowledge of God's Plan for ourselves, the whole of the human race and the future of this earth.

The "parent definition" of the Gospel comes from Jesus Himself, as the model exponent of the Gospel (Heb. 2:3). Jesus was the original herald of the Message of the Kingdom (introduced briefly by John the Baptist, Matt. 3:2). The Gospel comes with a specific definition. Its primary and fundamental title appears eighteen times:

THE GOSPEL ABOUT THE KINGDOM OF GOD (Matt. 3:2; 4:17, 23; 24:14; 9:35; Luke 4:43; 8:1; 9:2, 6, 11, 60; 10:9; 16:16; Acts 8:12; 19:8; 20:25; 28:23, 31)

A variety of interchangeable phrases describe the same Gospel about the Kingdom:

=THE *WORD* ABOUT THE KINGDOM (Matt. 13:19; see 2 Tim. 4:1, 2; Rev. 1:9)
=*THE GOSPEL OF GOD* (Mark 1:14 (= "believe in the Kingdom," v. 15); Rom. 1:1; 15:16; 2 Cor. 11:7; 1 Thess. 2:2, 8, 9)
=*THE GOSPEL* (Matt. 11:5; Mark 13:10; 14:9; 16:15; Luke 3:18; 4:18; 7:22; 9:6; + 80 times)
=*THIS GOSPEL ABOUT THE KINGDOM* (Matt. 24:14)
=*THIS GOSPEL* (Matt. 26:13)
=*THE GOSPEL OF THE GRACE OF GOD* (Acts 20:24)
=*PROCLAIMING THE GOSPEL OF THE KINGDOM* (Acts 20:25)
=DECLARING THE WHOLE COUNSEL OF GOD (Acts 20:27)
=THE GOSPEL OF SALVATION (Eph. 1:13; Rom. 1:16)
=*THE GOSPEL OF JESUS CHRIST* (Mark 1:1)
=THE GOSPEL OF CHRIST (2 Cor. 9:13)
=THE GOSPEL OF THE GLORY OF CHRIST (2 Cor. 4:4)
=THE GOSPEL OF THE BLESSED GOD (1 Tim. 1:11)
=THE MYSTERY OF THE GOSPEL (Eph. 6:19; Rom. 16:25)
=YOUR (GOD'S) WORD(S) (John 17:6; *17:8,* — *"receive* WORD")
=*THE WORD OF GOD (37 times) = HIS WORD (Tit. 1:3; 1 John 2:5)*
=*THE WORD* (46 times)

=THE WORD OF TRUTH (2 Cor. 6:7; Eph. 1:13 Col. 1:5; 2 Tim.
2:15; James 1:18)
=THE KNOWLEDGE OF THE TRUTH (1 Tim. 2:4; 2 Tim. 2:25;
3:7; Tit. 1:1; Heb. 10:26)
=THE TRUTH (50 times)
=REPENTANCE AND FORGIVENESS OF SINS IN JESUS'
NAME (Luke 24:47)
=THE WORD OF THE LORD (Acts 8:25; 12:24; 13:48, 49;
15:35, 36; 16:32; 19:10; 19:20; 1 Thess. 1:8; 4:15; 2 Thess. 3:1; I Pet.
1:25)
=THE WORD OF THE GOSPEL (Acts 15:7)
=OUR GOSPEL (1 Thess. 1:5; 2 Thess. 2:14; 2 Cor. 4:3)
=THE GOSPEL OF OUR LORD JESUS (2 Thess. 1:8)
=THE WORD OF HIS GRACE (Acts 14:3; 20:32)
=GRACE AND TRUTH (John 1:14)
=THE WORD OF THE CROSS (1 Cor. 1:18)
=THE WORDS OF GOD (John 3:34; 8:47; Rev. 17:17; 19:9)
=THE WORDS OF THE LIFE OF THE COMING AGE (John
6:68)
=MY (JESUS') WORD (John 5:24; 8:31, 37, 43, 51, 52; 14:23,
24; 15:20; Rev. 3:8)
=MY (JESUS') WORDS (Matt. 24:35; Mark 8:38; 13:31; Luke
6:47; 9:26; 21:33; John 5:47; 14:10, 24; 15:7)
=MY TEACHING (John 7:16; II Tim. 3:10)
=THESE WORDS OF MINE (Matt. 7:24, 26)
=MY SAYINGS (John 12:47, 48)
=MY (PAUL'S) GOSPEL (Rom. 16:25)
=MY (PAUL'S) WORDS (Acts 26:25)
=MY (PAUL'S) MESSAGE (1 Cor. 2:4)
=MY (PAUL'S) PREACHING (1 Cor. 2:4)
=*THE MYSTERY OF THE KINGDOM OF GOD (Matt. 13:11;
Mark 4:11; Luke 8:10)*
=THE PREACHING OF JESUS CHRIST (Rom. 16:25)
=THE MYSTERY OF CHRIST (Col. 4:3; Eph. 3:4; Col. 1:27)
=THE MYSTERY (Rom. 16:25; Eph. 1:9)
=THE MYSTERY OF THE GOSPEL (Eph. 6:19)
=THE MYSTERY OF THE FAITH (1 Tim. 3:9)
=THE MYSTERY OF GODLINESS (1 Tim. 3:16)

=THE WORD OF LIFE (Phil. 2:16)
=THE MYSTERY OF GOD (Rev. 10:7)
=THE WORD OF FAITH (Rom. 10:8)
=THE WORD OF GOD'S MESSAGE (1 Thess. 2:13)
=THE WORD OF CHRIST (Acts 10:36; Rom. 10:17; Col. 3:16)
=THE ABIDING WORD OF GOD (1 Pet. 1:23)
=THE IMPLANTED WORD OF GOD (Jam. 1:21)
=OUR REPORT ("the word of hearing") (John 12:38; Rom. 10:16)
=THE FAITH (32 times)
=THE WORD OF THIS SALVATION (Acts 13:26)
=THIS SALVATION (1 Pet. 1:10)
=THIS SALVATION OF GOD (Acts 28:28)
=OUR COMMON SALVATION (Jude 1:3)
=THE FAITH ONCE AND FOR ALL DELIVERED TO THE SAINTS (Jude 3)
=THE MANIFESTATION OF TRUTH (2 Cor. 4:2)
=THE WORD OF RECONCILIATION (2 Cor. 5:19)
=THE SWORD OF THE SPIRIT (Eph. 6:17)
=THE WORD OF RIGHTEOUSNESS (Heb. 5:13)
=THE WORD OF MY PERSEVERANCE (Rev. 3:10)
=THE WORD OF THEIR TESTIMONY (Rev. 12:11)
=THE TESTIMONY OF JESUS (Rev. 1:2, 9; 12:17; 19:10; 20:4)
=THE GOSPEL ABOUT THE COMING AGE (Rev. 14:6)[1]

For evidence of the Gospel deprived of the Kingdom see the New Scofield Reference Bible on Revelation 14:6 and the article "Gospel" in *Unger's Bible Dictionary.*

---

[1] "Eternal Gospel" is a mistranslation. The Gospel is not eternal; it is Good News of the Coming Age of the Kingdom. "*Aionios*" in Greek means "to do with the coming age." "The *aionios* Gospel is not in Christian language the 'everlasting Gospel,' but 'the Gospel concerning the Kingdom-age'" (Nigel Turner, Ph.D., *Christian Words*). "Eternal" ("everlasting") is thus in many passages equivalent to "millennial" or "having to do with the age to come of the Kingdom."

Bibliography

Achtemeier, Elizabeth. *Preaching as Theology and Art*. Nashville: Abingdon Press, 1984.

Adeney, W.F. *The Hebrew Utopia*. London: Hodder and Stoughton, 1879.

Alford, Henry. *The Greek New Testament*. London: Rivingtons and Deighton, Bell and Co., 1861.

Allen, W.C. *The International Critical Commentary, Matthew*. Edinburgh: T&T Clark, 1907.

Althaus, Paul. *The Theology of Martin Luther*. Philadelphia: Fortress Press, 1966.

Badcock, F.J. *The History of the Creeds*. New York: Macmillan, 1938.

Baigent, Michael et al. *The Messianic Legacy*. Jonathan Cape, 1986.

Barclay, William. *The Acts of the Apostles*. Edinburgh: The Saint Andrews Press, 1955.

Barnes, Albert. *Commentary on Acts*. London: Routledge, Warne and Routledge, 1863.

Beasley-Murray, G.R. *Jesus and the Kingdom of God*. Grand Rapids: Eerdmans, 1986.

Beker, J.C. *Paul's Apocalyptic Gospel, The Coming Triumph of God*. Philadelphia: Fortress Press, 1982.

Bonino, J.M. ed. *Faces of Jesus*. Orbis Books, 1983.

Bousset, W. *Jesus*. London: Williams and Norgate, 1906.

Braaten, Carl and Robert Jenson, eds. *Christian Dogmatics*. Philadelphia: Fortress Press, 1984.

Bright, John. *The Kingdom of God*. New York: Abingdon Press, 1953.

Brown, Raymond. *The Virgin Birth of the Messiah*. London: Geoffrey Chapman, 1977.

Bruce, F.F. *Commentary on Acts*. London: Tyndale, 1952.

Bruce, F.F. *Paul, the Apostle of the Heart Set Free*. Grand Rapids: Eerdmans, 1977.

Buber, M. *Israel and Palestine*. London: East and West Library, 1952.

Buchanan, G.W. *Anchor Bible, To the Hebrews*. Doubleday and Co., 1972.

Buchanan, G.W. *The Consequences of the Covenant*. Leiden: Brill, 1970.

Buchanan, G.W. *Jesus, the King and His Kingdom*. Macon: Mercer University Press, 1984.

Burge, G.M. *Who Are God's People in the Middle East?* Zondervan, 1993.

Burton, Henry. *Expositor's Bible, St. Luke*. A.C. Armstrong, 1896.

Buzzard, Anthony and Charles Hunting. *The Doctrine of the Trinity*. San Francisco: International Scholars Publications, 1998.

Cadoux, C.J. *The Historic Mission of Jesus*. Lutterworth Press, 1941.

Caird, C.B. *The Language and Imagery of the Bible*. Philadelphia: Westminster Press, 1980.

Chafer, L.S. *Systematic Theology*. Dallas: Dallas Seminary Press, 1947-48.

Conzelmann, Hans. *The Theology of St. Luke*. New York: Harper and Row, 1960.

Cranfield, C.E.B. *The Gospel According to St. Mark*. Cambridge University Press, 1972.

Cullman, Oscar. *Immortality of the Soul or Resurrection of the Dead?* Epworth Press, 1958, reprinted in *A Journal from the Radical Reformation*, Vol. 3, Nos. 1, 2 (available from Atlanta Bible College, P.O. Box 100,000, Morrow, GA 30260, USA).

Cupitt, Don. *The Debate about Christ*. London: SCM Press, 1979.

Daube and Davies, eds. *The Background of the New Testament and Its Eschatology*. Cambridge University Press, 1956.

Davies, W.D. *The Gospel and the Land.* Berkeley: University of California Press, 1974.

Dunn, James. *Romans, Word Biblical Commentary.* Dallas: Word Books, 1988.

Ellis, E.E. *New Century Bible, Commentary on Luke.* Eerdmans, 1964.

Ellul, Jacques. *The Subversion of Christianity.* Grand Rapids: Eerdmans, 1986.

Evans, Tony. *What a Way to Live!* Nashville: Word, 1997.

Filson, F.V. *The New Testament Against Its Environment.* London: SCM Press, 1950.

Fisher, G.P. *History of Christian Doctrine.* T&T Clark, 1908.

Ford, Desmond. *The Abomination of Desolation in Biblical Eschatology.* Washington, D.C.: University Press of America, 1979.

Fosdick, H.E. *A Guide to Understanding the Bible.* Harper Bros., 1938.

Friedmann, Robert. *The Theology of Anabaptism.* Herald Press, 1973.

Froom, L.E. *The Conditionalist Faith of Our Fathers.* 2 vols., Review and Herald, 1965.

Fuller, D. *Gospel and Law: Contrast or Continuum.* Grand Rapids: Eerdmans, 1980.

Gaebelein, A.C. *The Olivet Discourse.* Baker Book House, 1969.

Gillet, Lev. *Communion in the Messiah: Studies in the Relationship Between Judaism and Christianity.* London: Lutterworth Press, 1942.

Goppelt, L. *Theology of the New Testament.* Grand Rapids: Eerdmans, 1981.

Goudge, H.L. "The Calling of the Jews," in the collected essays on *Judaism and Christianity.* Shears and Sons, 1939.

Grant, F.C. *Ancient Judaism and the New Testament.* New York: Macmillan, 1959.

Grant, F.C. *The Earliest Gospel.* New York: Abingdon Press, 1943.

Green and Turner, eds. *Jesus of Nazareth: Lord and Christ.* Grand Rapids: Eerdmans, 1994.

Groome, Thomas. *Christian Religious Education.* San Francisco: Harper and Row, 1980.

Haenchen. *The Acts of the Apostles*. Philadelphia: Westminster Press, 1971.

Hamilton, H.D. *The People of God*. Oxford University Press, 1912.

Harkness, Georgia. *Understanding the Kingdom of God*. Abingdon Press, 1974.

Hartman, Lars. *Prophecy Interpreted*. Coniectania Biblica, NT Series 1, Sweden: Gleerup Lund.

Henry, C.F.H, ed. *Fundamentals of the Faith*. Baker Book House, 1975.

Hick, John. *Death and Eternal Life*. New York: Harper and Row, 1976.

Hiers, Richard. *Jesus and the Future*. Atlanta: John Knox Press, 1981.

Hiers, Richard. *The Kingdom of God in the Synoptic Tradition*. Gainesville: University of Florida Press, 1970.

Hoskyns, E.C. *The Fourth Gospel*. London: Faber and Faber, 1947.

Hughes, H.P. *Essential Christianity*. Isbister and Co., 1894.

Jackson, H.L. *The Eschatology of Jesus*. Macmillan and Co. Ltd., 1913.

Jamieson, Faussett, Brown. *A Commentary, Critical and Explanatory, on the Old and New Testaments*. Philadelphia: Lippincott & Co., 1868.

Johnson, A.R. *The One and the Many in the Israelite Conception of God*. University of Wales Press, 1961.

Kaylor, R.D. *Jesus the Prophet: His Vision of the Kingdom on Earth*. Westminster/John Knox Press, 1994.

Keil and Delitzsch. *Commentary on the Old Testament*. Hendrickson, 1989.

Klausner, J. *The Messianic Idea in Israel*. George Allen and Unwin, Ltd., 1956.

Krodel, G.A. *Acts, Augsburg Commentary on the New Testament*. Minneapolis: Augsburg Publishing House, 1986.

Küng, Hans. *On Being a Christian*. New York: Doubleday, 1976.

Ladd, George. *Crucial Questions about the Kingdom of God*. Grand Rapids: Eerdmans, 1952.

Ladd, George. *I Believe in the Resurrection.* Hodder and Stoughton, 1975.

Ladd, George. *A Theology of the New Testament.* Grand Rapids: Eerdmans, 1974.

Lapide, Pinchas and Jurgen Moltmann. *Jewish Monotheism and Christian Trinitarian Doctrine*: *A Dialogue.* Philadelphia: Fortress Press, 1981.

Lloyd-Jones, Martin. *Commentary on Romans.* Grand Rapids: Zondervan, 1976.

Machen, Gresham. *The Virgin Birth of Christ.* Harper and Row, 1930.

Macinnes, A.F. *The Kingdom of God in the Apostolic Writings.* London: James Clark, 1924.

MacKinnon, James. *The Historic Jesus.* London, New York: Longmans, Green and Co., 1931.

Mackintosh, H.R. *The Doctrine of the Person of Jesus Christ.* T & T Clark, 1912.

Martin, Ralph. *Unless the Lord Build the House.* Ave Maria Press, 1971.

McClain, A.J. *The Greatness of the Kingdom.* Chicago: Moody Press, 1968.

Meyer, H.A.W. *Commentary on John.* Funk and Wagnalls, 1884.

Meyer, H.A.W. *Critical and Exegetical Handbook to the Acts of the Apostles.* Winona Lake: Alpha Publications, 1979.

Moore, G.F. *History of Religions.* New York: Charles Scribner's Sons, 1926.

More, P.E. *The Christ of the New Testament.* Princeton University Press, 1924.

Moulton, J.H., ed. *A Grammar of New Testament Greek.* T & T Clark, 1963.

Newbigin, Leslie. *Sign of the Kingdom.* Grand Rapids: Eerdmans, 1981.

Perrin, Norman. *The Kingdom of God in the Teaching of Jesus.* SCM Press, 1963.

Perrin, Norman. *Language of the Kingdom.* Philadelphia: Fortress Press, 1976.

Peters, G.N.H. *The Theocratic Kingdom.* Grand Rapids, reprinted by Kregel, 1952.

Phillips, J.B. *Letters to Young Churches*. Fontana Books, 1956.

Phillips, J.B. *Plain Christianity*. Wyvern Books, 1954.

Phillips, J.B. *The Ring of Truth*. Hodder and Stoughton, 1967.

Phillips, J.B. *The Young Church in Action*. London: Geoffrey Bles, 1955.

Prestidge, Warren. *Life, Death and Destiny*. Auckland, New Zealand: Resurrection Publishing, 1998.

Reumann, John. *Jesus in the Church's Gospels*. Fortress Press, 1968.

Richardson, Alan. *An Introduction to the Theology of the New Testament*. London: SCM Press, 1958.

Richardson, Alan. *A Theological Word Book of the Bible*. London: SCM Press, 1957.

Robertson, Archibald. *Regnum Dei*. New York: The Macmillan Co., 1901.

Robinson, J.A.T. *The Human Face of God*. London: SCM Press, 1973.

Robinson, J.A.T. *In the End God*. Fontana Books, 1968.

Robinson, J.A.T. *On Being the Church in the World*. London: SCM Press, 1960.

Rudolph, Kurt. *Gnosis: The Nature and History of Gnosticism*. Harper and Row, 1983.

Russell, D.S. *Apocalyptic, Ancient and Modern*. Philadelphia: Fortress Press, 1988.

Schmidt, K.L. *Le Problème du Christianisme Primitif*. Paris: Leroux, 1938.

Schonfield, H.J. *The Politics of God*. Hutchinson, 1970.

Schotroff, ed. *Essays on the Love Commandment*. Philadelphia: Fortress Press, 1978.

Schweizer, Eduard. *The Good News According to Mark*. Atlanta: John Knox Press, 1970.

Seiss, J.A. *The Last Times and the Great Commission*. Philadelphia: Smith, English and Co., 1863.

Sine, Tom. *The Mustard Seed Conspiracy*. Waco: Word Books, 1981.

Skinner, J. *Prophecy and Religion*. Cambridge University Press, 1922.

Snaith, N.H. *The Distinctive Ideas of the Old Testament*. London: Epworth Press, 1955.

Sobrino, Jon. *Christology at the Crossroads*. Maryknoll, NY: Orbis Books, 1978.

Strawson, William. *Jesus and the Future Life*. London: Epworth Press, 1959.

Sullivan, Clayton. *Rethinking Realized Eschatology*. Mercer University Press, 1988.

Tannehill, Robert. *The Narrative Unity of Luke-Acts: A Literary Interpretation*. Minneapolis: Fortress Press, 1990.

Temple, William. *Personal Religion and the Life of Fellowship*. Longmans, Green and Co. Ltd., 1926.

Thomas, John. *Elpis Israel*. First pub. 1848.

Torrey, R.A. *How to Witness to Anyone*. Whitaker House, 1986.

Turner, Nigel. *Christian Words*. T & T Clark, 1980.

Viviano, B.T. *The Kingdom of God in History*. Wilmington: Michael Glazier, 1988.

Von Rad, Gerhard. *The Problem of the Hexateuch and Other Essays*. New York: McGraw-Hill, 1966.

Wagner, Peter. *Church Growth and the Whole Gospel*. San Francisco: Harper and Row, 1981.

Walvoord, John. *Matthew: Thy Kingdom Come*. Moody Press, 1984.

Watson, David. *Christian Myth and Spiritual Reality*. Victor Gallancz, 1967.

Weiss, Johannes. *Jesus' Proclamation of the Kingdom of God*, ed. and trans. Hiers and Holland. Philadelphia: Fortress Press, 1971.

Wernle, Paul. *The Beginnings of Christianity*. London: Williams and Norgate, 1903.

Westermann, C., ed. *Essays on Old Testament Hermeneutics*. Atlanta: John Knox, 1979.

Wilcock, Michael. *The Savior of the World: The Message of Luke's Gospel*. Intervarsity Press, 1979.

Wiles, Maurice. *The Remaking of Christian Doctrine*. London: SCM Press, 1974.

Willard, Dallas. *The Spirit of the Disciplines*. San Francisco: Harper, 1988.

Willis, Wendell, ed. *The Kingdom of God in 20th-Century Interpretation*. Peabody, MA: Hendrickson, 1987.

Zeitlin, Irving. *Ancient Judaism*. Cambridge: Polity Press, 1988.

Scripture Index

Author Index

Achtemeier, Elizabeth, 138
Adeney, W.F., 308
Albrecht, Ludwig, 149n
Alford, Henry, 74, 78, 254, 268n
Allen, W.C., 281-82, 315
Althaus, Paul, 215, 342
Aquinas, Thomas, 338
Augustine, 244-45, 255-57

Badcock, F.J., 201n
Baigent, Michael, 106
Barclay, William, 177
Barnes, Albert, 180-81
Beasley-Murray, G.R., 146, 167-68
Beker, J.C., 291, 309n
Bernard, J.H., 212
Bousset, W., 345
Braaten, Carl, 293
Bright, John, 131, 182
Brown, Raymond, 192
Bruce, F.F., 33, 231, 295-96
Buber, M., 57
Buchanan, G.W., 66, 192n
Buechner, Frederick, 218
Bultmann, Rudolf K., 257, 293, 351
Burge, G.M., 317-18, 320-21

Burton, Henry, 92

Cadbury, H.J., 285
Caird, C.B., 258-59
Calvin, John, 180, 197-98, 245, 305,
312-13, 337
Chafer, L.S., 314
Cole, R.A., 136
Conzelmann, Hans, 184, 282
Cranfield,C.E.B., 257, 262
Cullman, Oscar, 216n
Cupitt, Don, 11,127,165,347-48

Davies, W.D.,57,59-60,317n,319,320
Dodd, C.H., 286n, 294, 315
Dumbrell, W.J., 26, 116, 270, 355
Dunn, James, 62, 68-70, 217, 341

Ellis, E.E., 233, 241n, 285
Ellul, Jacques, 340
Evans, Tony, 147

Filson, F.V., 235-36, 343
Fisher, G.P., 344
Ford, Desmond, 289
Fosdick, H.E., 347

Subject Index